SYNGE AND THE IRISH LANGUAGE

SYNGE AND THE IRISH LANGUAGE

Declan Kiberd
M.A. (Dublin), D.Phil. (Oxon.)

© Declan Kiberd 1979

First published 1979 by
THE MACMILLAN PRESS LTD
London and Basingstoke
Associated companies in Delhi
Dublin Hong Kong Johannesburg Lagos
Melbourne New York Singapore Tokyo

Typeset by Santype International Ltd., Salisbury, Wilts

Printed in Great Britain by
Redwood Burn Ltd
Trowbridge and Esher

British Library Cataloguing in Publication Data

Kiberd, Declan
  Synge and the Irish language
  1. Synge, John Millington—Criticism and
  interpretation
  I. Title
  822'.9'12   PR5534

  ISBN 0-333-26229-8

FOR MY FATHER AND MOTHER

Contents

Contents

Preface

I wish to thank Professor Sir Idris Foster for unfailing advice and encouragement at all stages of this work. Professor Richard Ellmann offered thoughtful criticisms of a number of earlier drafts; and Professor Seán Ó Tuama gave me great encouragement by his incisive and detailed critique of my Oxford dissertation. But for the generous support and constructive suggestions of Professor A. Norman Jeffares this book would never have been possible. All four scholars may yet find much to question in the following study, but they will also see just how closely I have attended to their advice.

My thanks are also due to Dr Nicholas Grene, Professor Brendan Kennelly and Rev. Terence McCaughey for helpful suggestions; and to Miss Marguerite Kiberd for immense assistance with the technicalities of translation. To Dr Roy Park, Mr Hossein Farzin and Mrs Rosalind Brain in Oxford I send sincere thanks for their kindness and support. I am grateful also to Mrs Stephens and the Trustees of the Estate of J. M. Synge for kind permission to quote from the manuscripts held in the Library of Trinity College, Dublin; to the Oxford University Press for permission to use quotations from their four-volume *Collected Works* of J. M. Synge; and to Katherine B. Kavanagh and Martin Brian and O'Keeffe Ltd for allowing me to quote three stanzas of a poem by Patrick Kavanagh. I am indebted to the staff of a great number of libraries including the Bodleian Library, Oxford; the English Faculty Library, Oxford; the British Library; the Colindale Library of Newspapers and Journals; the National Library of Ireland; the Library of Trinity

College, Dublin; and the Government Publications Office in Dublin. Parts of this book have appeared in slightly different form in a number of journals: *The Review of English Studies, Scríobh 4, Hermathena, The Crane Bag, Long Room, The Maynooth Review, Studies, Éire-Ireland, Comhar* and *Folklore* (Oxford). The author thanks the various editors for kind permission to re-work and re-publish this material.

By way of conclusion, I should like to clarify certain terms which are employed in this study. The term 'Anglo-Irish' has been used for decades to describe the particular brand of English spoken in rural Ireland, under the historic influence of the Irish language. The strict linguistic term for this idiom is, of course, 'Hiberno-English', since the basic language in question is English, conditioned by the Irish *substratum*. In fact, 'Anglo-Irish' as a technical term would more appropriately be applied to that brand of Irish, known as 'Béarlachas', which has been greatly contaminated by English usage. However, the term 'Anglo-Irish' has been used in its loose traditional sense in this book, because Synge himself and subsequent scholars of his work have used it in this way. In paragraphs where the writings of previous scholars are enmeshed with the present author's commentary, it might have been irritating and even confusing to have oscillated endlessly between the two terms. It seemed wiser to follow the practice of Synge. In a similar fashion, the terms 'Irish' and 'Gaelic' are used indiscriminately in this work to describe the Irish language—although some purists would prefer the single term 'Irish', Synge, like most Anglo-Irish writers, more often employed the word 'Gaelic'.

Declan Kiberd

Dublin
August 1978

Abbreviations

In referring to the four-volume edition of Synge's works (Oxford University Press, 1962–8), I have employed a system of abbreviations in parentheses in the course of my text—for example, (*Prose*, p. 10), (*Poems*, p. 11), (*Plays 1*, p. 12) and so on. Full bibliographical details of this definitive edition of Synge's writings are given in the Bibliography.

1 Introduction

In August 1970 at a symposium at Trinity College, Dublin, a professor remarked, to the outrage of many colleagues, that he 'would take no student of Anglo-Irish literature seriously unless that student were bilingual'.[1] In a subsequent essay on Anglo-Irish poetry, another critic confirmed this judgement when he argued that 'a total understanding of Anglo-Irish literature certainly depends on an accurate and sensitive knowledge of that Gaelic Irish literature which has increasingly affected and conditioned it'.[2] It remains true, nevertheless, that the major commentators on the great Anglo-Irish writers are, without exception, untrained in the literature and language of Irish. This lack of knowledge is of little consequence when the critic is dealing with writers such as W. B. Yeats and James Joyce, whose command of Irish was limited to a few words. However, in dealing with a writer such as John Millington Synge, whose debt to written and oral Irish is as subtle as it is immense, that ignorance can be a real barrier to understanding. The foremost living critic of Synge's work, David H. Greene, concluded the definitive biography with the assertion that this artist's work 'more than that of any of his contemporaries comes closest to achieving the assimilation of the Gaelic past which the Irish Renaissance stood for'.[3] Yet Greene lacked the expertise in Irish which might have helped him to substantiate a mere assertion. Ten years later, in an essay entitled 'J. M. Synge—A Centenary Appraisal' (1971), he candidly admitted the deficiencies in his knowledge and called for a radical change in the approach of scholars to the dramatist. He said: 'Nobody with the linguistic training necessary has yet to my knowledge made a definitive study of the language of Synge's plays . . . We will want to know first what relationship Synge's idiom bears to Irish'.[4]

The major reason for this gap in our knowledge lies in the fact that none of the recognised experts on Synge—David H. Greene, Ann Saddlemyer and Robin Skelton—is Irish. Ever since the *Playboy* riots in 1907, the reaction of Irish critics to the work of Synge has been uneasy and even sometimes volatile. Some clear-headed essays have been written by native scholars such as Denis Donoghue and T. R. Henn, while Nicholas Grene has recently published a sensitive study of the plays. However, the only full-length assessment of all Synge's work, written from an avowedly Gaelic viewpoint, was published over forty-five years ago. This was *Synge and Anglo-Irish Literature* by Daniel Corkery and, in the judgement of Alan Price, it was biased: '. . . it is distorted by Corkery's fervent nationalism and his habit of praising Singe where he fitted in with Corkery's idea of a Catholic-Irish peasant and of condemning him when (as happened more frequently) he did not fit in. It is unfortunate that Corkery's has been the book on Synge most widely studied in Ireland and it has contributed to the gross underrating of Synge in his native land.'[5] Nobody can quarrel with this, nor with the assertion that 'the best literary criticism of our modern writers in English has been written mainly by writers outside Ireland'.[6] It remains true, however, that no foreign critic of Synge has acquired a training in both Irish and English literature and it is unlikely that such a scholar ever will appear. Synge's literary and linguistic debts to his native language will have to be evaluated by his fellow-countrymen. The following study, by one who has studied Irish and English at Synge's own university, represents an initial foray into this uncharted land.

If the international army of experts on Synge lacked the means of assessing his debt to his native language, it must also be said that scholars of the Irish language offered very little encouragement in this enterprise. After the *Playboy* riots, Synge was regarded with suspicion and even hatred by most members of the Gaelic League. Those scholars of Irish who might have done most to explain his debt to the language found themselves cast in the role of spokesmen for a movement which had officially rejected his plays as travesties of life in rural Ireland. In challenging the authenticity of his portrayal of this life, it became fashionable also to deny his competence in the Irish language. As late as 1962, in a study of the Aran Islands, P. A. Ó Síocháin asserted that Synge had only 'an imperfect knowledge of the Irish language'. Even more sweepingly, he alleged that 'Synge never did succeed in becoming one with the islanders. Nor did he become one with the Gaelic speech and the Gaelic way of life.'[7] Curiously, this statement, in both its parts, is directly at odds with what the dramatist wrote in a notebook at the end of his second visit to Aran in 1899. In this private diary, where there was no one to deceive but himself, he remarked with some satisfaction that 'this year I have learned little but Gaelic and nearer understanding of the people'.[8]

Even those members of the Gaelic movement who admired Synge as a man had deep misgivings about his dramatic works. Seán Mac Giollarnáth, a kindly but rather rigid editor of the Gaelic League's weekly paper, tried to explain his disquiet about the plays by pointing to what he considered to be Synge's incomplete assimilation of Irish: 'If Synge had come down from the little room into the bar, or walked with the jolly girls on the road to Kilronan until his mind became saturated with the Irish word and phrase, as his soul did with the rain and the cold, he would surely have left us something more lasting, if less fanciful, than his plays, fine as they are'.[9] It will be unnecessary to point out, even to the cursory reader of *The Aran Islands*, that the playwright not only walked and bantered with the girls, but fell half in love with one of their number before he left. Mac Giollarnáth here is not really questioning Synge's knowledge of Irish, which earlier in the same paragraph he admits to have included such evanescent qualities as its 'edge and flexibility'. Rather, he is seeking to come to terms with his own unease about the plays, which he mistakenly assumed were intended as realistic portrayals of life in the west. Like many nationalists of his day, he could not question their authenticity without also being lured into a ritual denial of Synge's competence in Irish.

It is not altogether surprising that such statements by native experts on the Irish language should have been taken up and syndicated throughout the world by critics of high standing. Nevertheless, given the notorious distrust of Synge in nationalist circles, it is surprising that these comments were not treated with some degree of caution. The eagerness with which some scholars accepted these assertions may have been heightened by the recognition that such findings absolved them of further study in a new and difficult field. As long as it was accepted that the dramatist's knowledge of

Irish was slender and had, therefore, little effect on his work, then the expert who knew no Irish retained the status of an accredited specialist in the eyes of the world. For six decades no Irish scholar bothered to investigate this matter because the oracles of the Gaelic movement had firmly stated that there was no material worthy of investigation. Now and again a more open-minded professor of Irish might write a short article suggesting, in appropriately tentative terms, that Synge was really in harmony with the Gaelic literary tradition;[10] but no self-respecting Irish scholar would risk his reputation by making a systematic study of so contentious a thesis. It was easier to go off and write a pedantic, neutral article on the prefix 'ro', for, as Austin Clarke observed in 1941, the revival of Irish had fallen into the hands of grammarians. What suited the Gaelic scholars at home was also acceptable to the major critics abroad. The prejudices of the Gaelic League were unchallenged and the status of the foreign experts was secure. So, T. R. Henn could write in all good faith by 1950 that Synge had but 'a little Gaelic'[11] and David H. Greene could remark, with facile defeatism, eleven years later that 'it would be impossible to estimate the fluency he ultimately developed in the language'.[12] These assumptions were shared by a great number of other scholars who, lacking any training in Irish, imputed a similar ignorance to Synge. Elizabeth Coxhead, in the course of her excellent portrait of Lady Gregory, concedes Synge's competence in academic Irish but goes on to assert that 'he had no facility in the spoken language'.[13] Nicholas Newlin, in a study of the language of the playwright, admits that 'doubtless he understood the fundamental grammar of modern Irish quite well', but foolishly assumes that he 'never remained long enough where Irish was current to become a fluent speaker'.[14] The only reason which Newlin gives for this assumption is that 'Synge was not infected with that fanatical and almost mystical enthusiasm for the language that was characteristic of so many of his countrymen in his time'. It will be shown that, in general, the more mystical the commitment, the less actual Irish such an enthusiast was likely to know in the turbulent decades before the Easter Rebellion. Synge's refusal to acquiesce in the public fanaticism about the language was matched only by a thoroughgoing private devotion to its study. This study bore fruit in the artist's plays, poems and prose—so much so that we might argue that he was inspired by the life and literature of the Irish language, although he set down his works in English.

When Patrick Pearse wrote in 1899 that the concept of a national literature in the English language was untenable,[15] he cannot have reckoned with the emergence of a writer such as Synge. Pearse's doctrinaire statement became a major policy of the Gaelic League and this led to an artificial division between writing in Irish and English on the island. Such a division persists in Irish schoolrooms to this very day, where Anglo-Irish literature is studied in one class and literature in the Irish language is considered in another. The short stories of Liam O'Flaherty are examined in courses on the Anglo-Irish tradition, with no reference to the fact that many of them were originally written in the native language. Similarly, the Irish-language versions of such stories are studied in a separate class, with no attempt to appraise the author's own recreation of these works in English. It was Synge's particular achievement to ignore this foolish division and to take both literatures out of quarantine. In an article introducing Irish literature to a French audience in March 1902, he criticised his fellow-writers for their neglect of Irish and pointed out how much more inspiration was to be found in Old Irish literature than in the less vibrant Anglo-Irish tradition of the nineteenth century.[16] This did not imply a repudiation of his heritage as an Anglo-Irishman, but rather an attempt to synthesise the two traditions. In the wake of the Parnell split, Yeats had called upon all Irishmen to resign themselves to the cursed versatility of the Celt. Synge also believed in a fusion of the two Irelands, Gaelic and Anglo-Irish, so that neither should shed its pride—a challenge which confronts Irishmen more urgently than ever today. While Pearse argued against the logic of history that the Irish language alone could save the soul of the nation, writers like Yeats and Synge had set their course with greater realism. There were now two traditions to be confronted and the more exciting challenge was to forge a literature which would bring into alignment the world of Berkeley, Swift and Burke with that of O'Hussey, Keating and Raftery. At home Synge was always keen to emphasise his Anglo-Irish heritage, but he invariably presented himself in foreign countries as a Gael. In his strictures to the narrow nationalists of the Gaelic League, he celebrated the Anglo-Irish tradition as a vital component of 'the nation that has begotten Grattan and Parnell'[17]; but, in a programme note for a German audience, he was also at pains to insist that the Synges 'have been in Ireland for nearly three centuries, so that there is a good deal of Celtic, or more exactly, Gaelic blood in the family'.[18] In his art, he succeeded in his search for a bilingual style through which he could translate the elements of Gaelic culture into English, a language ostensibly alien to that culture. Of course, he ignored the division between those rival traditions at his peril and, in the Ireland of his time, he paid the inevitable price. Those who might have admired him for his commitment to the native culture denounced him for his belief in the higher claims of art. Those who admired his art could never fully appreciate the extent of his commitment to the native culture.

It is one of the most cruel ironies of literary history that the attempt to restore the Irish language coincided with the emergence of some of the greatest writers of English whom Ireland has ever produced. It is certainly true that many of these writers drew their initial inspiration from the revival of interest in the native culture; and it is even possible that one or two of them might never have emerged without that inspiration. Nevertheless, as Yeats, Joyce, Synge, Moore and, later, O'Casey, proceeded to win the admiration of readers of English throughout the world, the quality of writing in Irish continued on its drastic decline, as art was renounced in favour of nationalist propaganda. In time, however, the leaders of the Gaelic movement succeeded in convincing their readers and writers that a vibrant literature could not be founded on the pro-pagandist play and the patriotic lyric. They prayed for the emergence of a writer of European stature who might deliver the language from its bondage; but the self-imposed quarantine in which writers of Irish had placed themselves, from the time of Pearse, retarded such a development. As Synge had predicted, these writers failed to become European lest the huckster across the road might call them English. When a genius of international stature finally did emerge in the Irish language, it was too late. By the time Máirtín Ó Cadhain's *Cré na Cille* was published in 1949, there were few readers left who could understand the rich idiom of that book, much less the magnitude of its intellectual achievement.

The artificial division between writing in English and Irish still holds sway. Synge was its first and most spectacular victim. He bravely broke the quarantine decreed by Pearse only to find it sedulously observed by the nation's theatre-goers and readers. His work, so deeply rooted in the Gaelic tradition, was rejected by the strident professional Gaels of his own time because it was written in the English language. If Joyce and Beckett had to endure the hard-ships of exile in order to write their masterpieces, then the kind of inner exile endured by Synge in his own country can have been scarcely less severe. He was, of course, a victim of such intolerance only in Ireland; in the eyes of the world he was seen, even in his own lifetime, as a master. The ultimate victim of the introversion of the Gaelic movement was its greatest modern writer, Máirtín Ó Cadhain. He had steeped himself in the literature of modern Europe and expressed his sophisticated mind in his native and mother tongue, only to find that his readers had no sense of the significance of his achievement. Unlike Synge, he wrote in Irish and could not appeal over the heads of his detractors to the more enlightened tribunals of Europe.[19]

Seventy years after the death of Synge, a literary partition between writing in Irish and English divides the classrooms of Ireland as surely as a political partition divides the land. This division begins on the child's first day in primary school and is maintained even at post-graduate level in the universities. This is the major reason why no scholar has ever been able to write a systematic study of Synge's creative confrontation with the Irish language. Such work is not encouraged by a system which ignores the fact that writers of Irish and English live on the same small island and share the same experiences. The absurdity of this division becomes acutely apparent in any attempt to study the work of such writers as Patrick Pearse, Brendan Behan, Flann O'Brien or Liam O'Flaherty, all of whom wrote with facility and fame in both languages. It is ironic that Pearse, whose critical pronouncements were the major cause of this partition, should, as a creative writer, have become one of its foremost victims. In the case of O'Flaherty, so enmeshed are both traditions in his work that there is a protracted critical dispute as to whether certain of his stories were originally written in English or Irish, following his own wicked admission that he cannot remember himself. It is greatly to the credit of most modern writers that they have not succumbed to the partitionist mentality in their art. Synge was one of the first writers of twentieth-century Ireland to incorporate his experience of Gaelic literature into his art, but he has had many followers since—Thomas MacDonagh, Austin Clarke, F. R. Higgins, Frank O'Connor, Brendan Behan, Flann O'Brien. That list reads like a roll-call of modern Irish writers, for the problem which Synge confronted is as acute as ever today. A contemporary poet and translator, Thomas Kinsella, has expressed the dilemma well:

A modern English poet can reasonably feel at home in the long tradition of English poetry . . . An Irish poet has access to the English poetic heritage through his use of the English language, but he is unlikely to feel at home in it. Or so I find in my own case. If he looks back over his own heritage the line must begin, again, with Yeats. But then, for more than a hundred years, there is almost total poetic silence. I believe that silence, on the whole, is the real condition of Irish literature in the nineteenth century—certainly of poetry; there is nothing that approaches the ordinary literary achievement of an age. Beyond the nineteenth century there is a great cultural blur: I must exchange one language for another, my native English for eighteenth-century Irish. Yet to come on eighteenth-century Irish poetry after the dullness of the nineteenth century is to find a world suddenly full of life and voices, the voices of poets who expect to be heard and understood and memorised. Beyond them is . . . the course of Irish poetry stretching back for more than a thousand years, full of riches and variety. In all of this I recognise a great inheritance and, simultaneously, a great loss. The inheritance is certainly mine but only at two enormous removes—across a century's silence and through an exchange of worlds. The greatness of the loss is measured not only by the substance of Irish literature itself, but also by the intensity with which we know it was shared; it has an air of continuity and shared history which is precisely what is missing from Irish literature, in English or Irish, in the nineteenth century and today. I recognise that I stand on one side of a great rift, and can feel the discontinuity in myself. It is a matter of people and places as well as writing—of coming from a broken and uprooted family, of being drawn to those who share my origins and finding that we cannot share our lives.[20]

The problem is succinctly summarised by the title of Kinsella's essay, 'The Divided Mind'. The division is symbolised by the virtual absence of good writers in both languages through the whole nineteenth century, when the people were painfully shedding one language and slowly acquiring another. Synge, who began to write in the closing years of that century, stood on the very edge of that great rift. He saw that he could never hope to return to the other side—that an attempt to re-impose Irish would lead only to another barren century for literature—but he resolved to fill the rift by uniting the divided traditions. Those writers who knew no Irish, such as Yeats and George Russell, relied on translations and popularisations of the ancient Irish literature for the same purpose. To Standish James O'Grady's *History of Ireland: Heroic Period* Russell said he owed the re-awakening of his racial memory. It was doubtless for the same reason that Yeats remarked that to O'Grady every Irish writer owed a portion of his soul. Like Kinsella, each writer since the Irish Revival has recognised that he stands on one side of a great rift and has tried, as best he can, to heal the sense of discontinuity in himself. That sense of severance from one's own heritage has been poignantly expressed by John Montague in his poem, *A Lost Tradition*, which deals with his homeland in County Tyrone. The map of his native county is studded with placenames derived from the Irish language, which has been dead in that area for generations. In an ancient Gaelic manuscript, which no contemporary reader can understand, he finds an image of his own geography of disinheritance:

> All around, shards of a lost tradition . . .
> The whole countryside a manuscript
> We had lost the skill to read,
> A part of our past disinherited,
> But fumbled, like a blind man,
> Along the fingertips of instinct.[21]

Once again, in *A Lost Tradition*, a contemporary poet has described that very rift which his poem seeks to fill, by drawing on both traditions of the island.

Many other writers in English have sought to bridge the rift by producing occasional translations from Irish poetry and prose. This exercise had real validity in the early decades of the century, when writers such as Yeats and Russell yearned for a glimpse of the poetry hidden in a language which they could never hope to learn. Nowadays, however, when most Irish writers have a reading knowledge of Irish, these translations are less immediately useful. They appear, more and more, as conscience-stricken gestures by men who feel a sense of guilt for producing their major creative work in an Anglo-Irish or even an English literary tradition. Synge was one of the earliest of these twentieth-century translators, but he did not see such work as an end in itself, nor even as a public expiation for the sin of writing in English. Rather, his translations were a deeply private exercise, written not for public approval but as a practice which helped him to forge his own literary dialect and to recreate

the Gaelic modes in English. To this day, there are in Ireland a
number of writers who produce translations from Irish for public
consumption on the one hand, while continuing to compose
straightforward modern English poems on the other. They place
their works in the same kind of quarantine as that in which the
study of Irish and English is placed in their schools. Synge did not
believe that an artist could so divide his own creations, neatly slotting
each work into one or other tradition. Each of his plays and poems
represents a fusion, *in a single work,* of both traditions and an attempt
by the power of his imagination to make them one. He saw that
those who neatly produce translations from Irish on the one hand
and modern English poems on the other are doomed only to per-
petuate the very rift which they profess to deplore. It was for this
reason, perhaps, that he never published in full any of his own
translations from Irish poetry and prose. This reticence was costly,
for it gave further credence to the allegation that he knew little Irish.
Nevertheless, it was necessary if he was to achieve his aim of filling
rather than deepening the rift in his own mind.

   To teach Irish and English in separate classes of our schools and
universities is surely to deepen that chasm. When Pearse decreed that
Irish and English were separate literatures, he still had visions of a
perilous but rewarding crossing to the other side of that chasm, back
to an Irish-speaking Ireland. Nowadays, it would seem more sensible
to fill the gap and unite the two traditions. Pearse's latter-day followers who persist in his belief that Yeats and Synge are not Irish
writers should learn from the mistakes of their forerunners in the
nationalist movement. All through the nineteenth century, Irishmen had fought and argued for the freedom of their country while,
at the same time, they permitted the virtual extinction of the native
language and culture—a major basis of their claim to recognition as
a separate nation. In 1892 in his classic address on 'The Necessity for
de-Anglicising Ireland', Douglas Hyde pointed to the anomaly of
'men who drop their own language to speak English . . . nevertheless
protesting as a matter of sentiment that they hate the country which
at every hand's turn they rush to imitate'.[22] By 1901, D. P. Moran
had extended Hyde's analysis and had set out to challenge 'the
accepted view that politics was the begin-all and end-all of Irish
nationality'.[23] His diagnosis was simple and devastating. Irishmen
had exalted the unending fight against England into a self-sustaining
tradition and had forgotten the very things which they fought
for—the native language, dances, music, games, a whole civilisation.

According to Moran, a nation was the natural outcome of a distinct civilisation and any power that killed the one was guilty of the death of the other. He observed wryly that his fellow-Irishmen 'threw over Irish civilisation whilst they professed—and professed in perfect good faith—to fight for Irish nationality'.[24] This may still be the case today, when some Irishmen persist in rejecting the matchless achievement of Yeats, Synge and Joyce, because they wrote in the English language. For a narrow nationalist principle, they have thrown over a major part of their inheritance.

There is, of course, misunderstanding on the other side too. Some of those who wrote in English displayed an alarming ignorance of the Gaelic tradition which they professed to mock. Patrick Kavanagh, in his role as recalcitrant peasant, even wrote a brilliant poem on the subject, entitled 'Memory of Brother Michael':

> It would never be morning, always evening,
> Golden sunset, golden age—
> When Shakespeare, Marlowe and Jonson were writing
> The future of England page by page,
> A nettle-wild grave was Ireland's stage.
>
> It would never be spring, always autumn
> After a harvest always lost,
> When Drake was winning seas for England
> We sailed in puddles of the past
> Chasing the ghost of Brendan's mast.
>
> Culture is always something that was,
> Something pedants can measure,
> Skull of bard, thigh of chief,
> Depth of dried-up river.
> Shall we be thus for ever?
> Shall we be thus for ever?[25]

The Brother Michael of whom Kavanagh wrote was one of the Four Masters who compiled the Annals of Ireland in the 1630s; and the literary period in Irish which Kavanagh contrasted unfavourably with its counterpart in England was the late-sixteenth and early-seventeenth century. In fact, this was the last age of high achievement in the native language, a period when poetry and prose enjoyed a superb revival as the ancient Gaelic order disintegrated. As a literary period, it might more aptly be compared with the Anglo-Irish revival at the start of the twentieth century, when a whole group of writers burst into a kind of swan-song as their own class suffered its final decline and disintegration. When all this was pointed out to him, Kavanagh cheerfully shrugged and announced that his lines were 'good poetry but bad history'[26]; yet the attitude which underlies his poem is still prevalent in Ireland. When Seán Ó Faoláin concluded a long essay on 'Fifty Years of Irish Writing' in 1962, he devoted only a couple of sentences to those who wrote in Irish in the twentieth century. Although the work of men like Synge, Clarke and MacDonagh testifies to the inspirational value for an artist of both languages, a lasting rapprochement between writers of Irish and English on the island has yet to be achieved.

It may be objected that such a rapprochement is of little significance when our two greatest writers in this century—Yeats and Joyce—knew little or nothing of their native language. Such an objection, however, takes little account of the deeper implications of this situation. It was a matter of constant regret to Yeats, throughout his life, that his poor skills as a linguist caused his repeated attempts to master Irish to come to nothing. The poet who finally confessed that he owed his soul to Shakespeare, to Spenser, to Blake and perhaps to William Morris was the same man who had also insisted that the Irish language held the key not only to the west but to the lost imagination of the whole nation.[27] Yeats wrote with a mixture of rue and pride: 'I might have found more of Ireland if I had written in Irish, but I have found a little, and I have found all myself'.[28] That little had been found mainly in translations such as those made by his friend, Lady Gregory. It is not surprising, therefore, that Yeats should have come to regard such translations as the 'true tradition' for the movement which he led. In the Preface to *A Book of Irish Verse* he wrote: 'It was not until Callanan wrote his naïve and haunting translations from the Gaelic that anything of an honest style came into verse'.[29] Sensing that Samuel Ferguson's knowledge of Irish gave him an intimate appreciation of Ireland's legends, such as no previous Anglo-Irishman had possessed, Yeats argued that he was 'the greatest poet Ireland has produced because the most central and the most Celtic'.[30] Translations such as Callanan's conveyed to Yeats a sense of the style and themes of Gaelic poetry, which he yearned to incorporate into his work. But, at best, Callanan's poems were only translations. Ferguson was the greatest poet because he had gone beyond mere translation. His treatment of the Deirdre legend was a powerfully original poem in

English, informed, nevertheless, by the Gaelic poetry in which he had so immersed himself. His poem was recognisably a work in the Anglo-Irish tradition, but it was also an unmistakeable recreation within the spirit of the Gaelic original, possible only to an artist with a feeling for Irish.

If Yeats and Lady Gregory achieved some sort of rapprochement with Irish literature in translation, then other writers such as John Eglinton and St John Ervine fought shy of the native language and even denounced it. Not all who abandoned it did so without scruple and James Joyce is an interesting case in point. He opted, of course, for Europe and modernism, as he playfully explained in *Finnegans Wake*: 'He even ran away with hunself and became a farsoonerite, saying he would far sooner muddle through a hash of lentils in Europe than meddle with Irrland's split little pea'.[31] Never has a writer commented more wryly on Ireland's divided mind and body. Understandably, Joyce's encounter with Gaelic Ireland in the shape of Michael Cusack, 'Emma Clery' and the pale young men of the Gaelic League had given him a restricted view of the Irish tradition. Had he followed the example of Synge in reading the work of Keating or the love songs of the folk, he might have come to share the playwright's belief in the possibility of creating a European modernist art which would nevertheless draw on the Gaelic tradition—a national art which would, for all that, be international in appeal. He might have seen that the shortest way to Tara was indeed through Holyhead. On rare occasions Joyce did turn to the native literature for an idea or an idiom, such as 'silk of the kine' (síoda na mbó) in *Ulysses*—an image of Ireland culled from the famous lyric, *Droimeann Donn Dílis*.[32] He had halting imitations of the bardic *deibhidhe* in mind when he wrote mockingly in the same book:

> Bound thee forth my booklet quick
> To greet the callous public,
> Writ, I ween, 'twas not my wish,
> In lean unlovely English.[33]

Apart from his admiration for the free translations of James Clarence Mangan, Joyce turned to the native poetry on only one other occasion—and then to use the Gaelic tradition in mockery against itself. In *A Portrait of the Artist as a Young Man* Stephen's friend, Davin, has enjoined on him 'Ireland first, Stevie. You can be a poet

or mystic after'. But Stephen is too clever for Davin. He knows the
lines of Keating, the great Gaelic poet who did put Ireland first and
who found expression for his frustration only in the most bitter of
images:

—Do you know what Ireland is? asked Stephen with cold
violence. Ireland is the old sow that eats her farrow.[34]

In Keating's poem, 'Óm Sceol ar Árdmhagh Fáil', the land is
destroyed by the greedy farrow of a foreign sow; but in Joyce's
work the image is inverted and the Irish sow consumes her own
children. It is an ingenious use of the Gaelic tradition against itself,
of a kind which we shall find often in the plays of Synge. Another
such device may be found in the burlesque of an elementary Gaelic
lesson in the Citizen passages of *Ulysses*:

—Ah, well, says Joe, handing round the boose. Thanks be to God
they had the start of us. Drink that, citizen.
—I will, says he, honourable person.[35]

Pádraic Colum has pointed out that the pseudo-Gaelic phrase,
'honourable person' (based on the Irish, 'a dhuine uasail'), has a
humour that only those who knew Dublin at the time could fully
appreciate.[36]
    The Irish Ireland which he rejected with such coldness haunted
Joyce all his life in the shape of Nora Barnacle and his liberation
from it was more apparent than real. In the final story of *Dubliners*,
'The Dead', Gabriel (the central character) is forced to come to
terms with the spiritual gulf between himself, a sophisticated Dublin
intellectual, and his homely wife from the west. He is chided by a
young woman named Miss Ivors for holidaying on the continent
rather than on Aran. As the story closes, his thoughts are moving
west, across the Central Plain over a snow-bound Ireland, to the peasant boy whom his wife had once loved. The ambiguity of Gabriel's
position in 'The Dead' is the predicament of his author. Joyce's
uneasy feelings towards the west are elaborated with an almost painful clarity in the closing pages of *A Portrait of the Artist as a Young
Man*. The reader is given extracts from Stephen's diary which cover
the days immediately prior to his departure for Paris. Stephen is
flippant about the Gael and seeks to belittle him in a European context:

April 14. John Alphonsus Mulrennan has just returned from the west of Ireland. European and Asiatic papers please copy. He told us he met a man there in a mountain cabin. Old man had red eyes and short pipe. Old man spoke Irish. Mulrennan spoke Irish. Then old man and Mulrennan spoke English. Mulrennan spoke to him about universe and stars. Old man sat, listened, smoked, spat. Then said:
—Ah, there must be terrible queer creatures at the latter end of the world.[37]

What one notices here is not just the parody of the dialect of Synge's plays in the final sentence, nor even the travesty of his conversation with a countryman about the constellations in *The Aran Islands*. Remarkable above all else is the corrosive realism in the portrayal of Mulrennan's encounter with the peasant—an encounter which was hopefully initiated in Irish, but soon lapsed (as the contents of Mulrennan's phrase-book were exhausted) into the English language. It was the first of many such encounters. Joyce has made his brilliant little joke against Synge (to be repeated and amplified in *Ulysses*) and against Mulrennan; but his treatment of the peasant, when finally he comes to him, is downright frightened, even defensive. The split-mindedness of Gabriel in *Dubliners* has now grown to near-hysteria:

I fear him. I fear his red-rimmed horny eyes. It is with him I must struggle all through this night till day come, till he or I lie dead, gripping him by the sinewy throat till . . . Till what? Till he yield to me? No. I mean no harm.[38]

Clearly, the author of this passage turned his back on Gaelic Ireland with mixed feelings and no absolute certainty that silence, exile and cunning were answers to the challenge of the native tradition. Joyce was a middle-class Dublin Catholic, born into that very society which, through organisations like the Gaelic League, was staking its claim as the logical heir to the Gaelic tradition. To deny that gospel was indeed to kick against the pricks. Joyce's rejection of this tradition did not arise out of ignorance—rather it was planned and dynamic, at once a cunning strategy of self-defence and wilful opposition. But even if, in one sense, he formally rejected this Irish tradition, there is a deeper sense in which he could not help being its beneficiary. As Flann O'Brien observed in a letter to Sean

O'Casey, every Irish writer who uses the English language with resource and imagination owes an indirect debt to his native language, whether he has learned to speak it or not: 'I agree absolutely with you when you say that the Irish language is essential, particularly for any sort of literary worker. It supplies that unknown quantity in us that enables us to transform the English language—and this seems to hold good for people who know little or no Irish, like Joyce. It seems to be an inbred thing.'³⁹ This is, of course, one of the deeper implications of a situation which urgently demands further study.

The following chapters catalogue Synge's debts to the Gaelic literary tradition, but there is a very real sense in which his work may be seen as forming a legitimate part of that tradition. The influence of *The Aran Islands* on subsequent accounts in Irish of island life is clearly discernible. Similarly, the echo of Yeats is never far from the lines of the finest living poet in the Irish language, Máirtín Ó Díreáin. These fascinating intersections between two supposedly rival traditions would repay further study, but it is difficult to see such investigations being conducted in Ireland as long as Irish and English are quarantined in separate classrooms. This book is based on a doctoral thesis written at Oxford University and the very fact that it had to be written outside Ireland is itself symptomatic of the problems confronting those writers and critics who wish to fuse the two traditions. It is customary, at the close of introductions such as this, to express the pious hope that the thesis has been adequately re-cast for the ordinary reader in a less argumentative and technical form. I should be sorry in this case, however, if some of the more polemical sentences in the text did not remain. This was a thesis written to prove a larger point, an attempt to establish Synge's debts to Irish and, in the process, to demonstrate the confluence in the work of one Irish writer of two Irish traditions. I wanted to take Irish and English out of their classroom quarantine and to show that this unfortunate division has distorted our view of Synge. Our view of him has never been more than one-dimensional. He has always been presented as a great Anglo-Irish writer and he is certainly that, but he is also a vital artist in the Gaelic tradition. Synge believed in and celebrated 'the cursed versatility of the Celt'. Until we can learn to see his work as a fusion of both traditions, we shall never truly know him at all; and until we can learn to live with both traditions on this island, we shall never truly know our-selves. We have distorted our view of ourselves in just the same way as we have permitted our scholars to distort our view of Synge. Across this small island, a partitionist mentality has divided North from South, Unionist from Nationalist, Anglo–Irish from Gael; in even the smallest parishes we have built separate Catholic and Protestant schools; and in the schools themselves, we have parcelled up the literature of the island into two separate packages. It is not surprising that our schizophrenia has assumed notorious and warlike form. Most Irish teachers and critics today are still caught in the pretence that they are the heirs to one narrow tradition; while their creative writers have told them, over and over again, that their inheritance is richer and wider than that. Every Irish person who has passed through the classrooms of the island has emerged from this educational mauling with a chronically divided mind; and at the root of his inability to live in peace with his neighbour is the inability to live at peace with himself.

Such problems are not solved in a generation, but a start must be made and scholars have a small but significant contribution to offer in this enterprise. There have been persuasive calls for integrated multi-denominational schools in Ireland and these calls will hopefully be answered. However, such schools will be self-defeating if they persist in sanctioning the current divisions in the educational curriculum. It is imperative that wide-ranging courses in 'Irish Studies' be instituted in all schools and universities now. Such courses are already pursued with success in foreign universities and they offer interdisciplinary studies of Anglo–Irish and Gaelic literature, of Irish history, folklore, politics and language. The schools and colleges of Ireland are already filled with experts trained in these various fields, so that the organisation of a course in Irish Studies, on both sides of the border, would require not so much an expenditure of money as of imagination and will. The battle will finally be won or lost in thousands of parish schools across the land, but the universities have the chance to play a leading role. Over ten years ago, Frank O'Connor called for a chair of Irish Studies which would integrate the study of the Gaelic and Anglo–Irish traditions in literature. His call yielded only a proliferation of chairs in Anglo–Irish literature, many of them held by men who knew little about Irish. Yet in his book, *The Backward Look*, O'Connor had offered a brilliant model of what such a course of studies might be. After a decade which has been filled with political violence and literary stagnation, his call seems more pressing than ever.

The present book is an attempt to apply O'Connor's method to

the work of a single Irish writer. It is not an exercise in literary
criticism, much less an interpretative study, but a catalogue of debts.
It could never hope to be a model for similar studies in the future,
for it represents only an initial investigation of totally uncharted
territory. In any case, there will be as many models as there are
writers. My one hope is that such studies will come in due course
after the establishment of a formal curriculum in Irish Studies—and
that they will be more sophisticated than this initial effort. Synge's
debts to Irish are so clear that the present writer fears that he may at
times have seemed to labour the obvious. If Synge's debts to Irish
are obvious, then previous Irish critics have been highly successful in
ignoring them or in evading their implications. This gigantic
exercise in self-deception could only have been sanctioned in a
country which preserves such artificial divisions between its writers
and which guards its cultural borders even more zealously than it
patrols its political frontiers. It is indeed ironic that those who have
fought most steadfastly to remove a political border which divides
the island have failed quite dismally to end a cultural partition of
their own making.

2 Synge's Knowledge of Irish

THE STUDY BEGINS: EARLY DIFFICULTIES

Apart from four haphazard years of schooling in Dublin and Bray,
Synge's education was conducted by a personal tutor at home. That
education was comprehensive but, in accordance with the general
practice of the time, it did not include the study of Irish. Synge's
first encounter with the effects of Irish as a spoken language probably
occurred on a walking tour in his early teens through the valley of
Glenasmole. In this spot Irish had been spoken only forty years
before and stories were still told of ancient Gaelic heroes.[1] Further
south in Co. Wicklow near Arklow town, Irish was spoken as late
as 1907, when Synge wrote that 'some of the comparatively recent
immigrants have revived Gaelic in this neighbourhood . . .'[2]

Synge studied Irish while he was a student at Trinity College,
Dublin from 1888 to 1892. In those days, what Lady Gregory
described as a 'Chinese Wall' separated Trinity from Irish Ireland.[3]
Synge studied Irish at university not for any cultural or nationalistic
reasons, but simply because the subject was part of the curriculum
for those under-graduates who were intended for a ministry in the
Church of Ireland. The Chair of Irish had been established in 1840
in order to prepare clergymen for the Irish-speaking ministry. This
work was encouraged by the Irish Society for Promoting the Education of the Native Irish through the Medium of their own Language.
The dramatist's uncle, the Reverend Alexander Synge, a graduate
of Trinity, had himself gone to the Aran Islands in 1851, in an

19

abortive attempt to convert the staunchly Roman Catholic islanders. Both sides of the Synge family had produced Anglican bishops in the past; but John Synge soon abandoned evangelical Protestantism and began to look to the culture of his native country for inspiration. In his *Autobiography*, he wrote: 'Soon after I had relinquished the Kingdom of God I began to take a real interest in the Kingdom of Ireland. My patriotism went round from a vigorous and unreasoning loyalty to a temperate nationalism, and everything Irish became sacred . . .' (*Prose*, p. 13). In keeping with this sentiment, the diaries of his college years give constant accounts of his reading in Irish history, geography, and antiquities. The study of the Irish language met with no opposition from members of his family, because it had for them no connotations of apostasy. To them Irish was one of the 'Divinity School subjects'.[4]

Synge's notebook for 1888–9, his first academic year at Trinity, includes notes from lectures on the rules for aspiration in Irish, on the derivation of the words 'Mac' and 'Ó' in Irish surnames, on the complex rules concerning the negative prefix 'ní', as well as sub-stantial lists of elementary Irish vocabulary.[5] According to his diary of March 1892, he worked slowly through the Gaelic version of *The Children of Lir*. He jotted down incidents from the narrative, as if they were happening to real people around him,[6] just as, many years later in letters to Molly Allgood, he would write about the developing characters in his plays as flesh-and-blood folk with whom he lived every day.[7] The study of Irish grammar was noted on many occasions throughout this period. In May, Synge set to work on the Gaelic version of St John's Gospel: 'May 24: Irish—finished the 1st chap. of John and studied second'.[8] Years later, when he was pro-ficient in Irish, Synge was to look back wryly upon the attitude of his professor, James Goodman, to the study of the language:

> In those days, if an odd undergraduate of Trinity . . . wished to learn a little of the Irish language and went to the professor appointed to teach it in Trinity College, he found an amiable old clergyman who made him read a crabbed version of the New Testament, and seemed to know nothing, or at least to care nothing, about the old literature of Ireland, or the fine folk-tales and folk-poetry of Munster and Connaught.[9]

This verdict on Goodman, six years after the professor's death, is uncharacteristically bitter.

Goodman was, in fact, a Protestant clergyman who came to love
the Irish language for its own sake. He was born in 1828 at Ventry
Strand, in the heart of the Kerry Gaeltacht. As Rector of Ardgroom,
another Gaeltacht parish, from 1860 to 1866, he took down many
songs from native speakers. Dr Donal O'Sullivan, an authority on
Irish folk music, has written of him that 'there can seldom have
been so Gaelic a parson'.[10] He was a member of the Governing
Body of the Ossianic Society and he owned a fine collection of
Gaelic manuscripts, one of which was edited by Standish H. O'Grady
for the Society.[11] In all, he collected two thousand traditional songs
and melodies. He held regular Gaelic parties in his rooms at Trinity,
at which he played the pipes for his friends, including John Pentland
Mahaffy, a future Provost. He must have been something of an
anachronism in the Trinity of his day. It is strange that Synge
appears to have known so little of the real Goodman, for they
would surely have been kindred spirits. Perhaps Goodman's parties
were frequented by fellow-academics only, and not by pass-degree
students like Synge, though O'Sullivan tells us that Goodman in-
vited 'all those—and they were many—who delighted to hear him
perform'.[12] It is likely that Synge, who went into Trinity as seldom
as possible, never remained long enough to make the old man's
acquaintance outside the formal setting of the lecture hall.

Inside the classroom, James Goodman appears to have been a
more than competent lecturer in Irish at a time when the standard
of teaching in that subject was very low. Synge made excellent notes
during lectures and these give us a clear idea of the high standards
set by his professor. The complex rules on aspiration in Synge's
notes for August 1891 are so clearly tabulated that they cannot
merely be the impressionistic gleanings from an average university
lecture. From the parallels with the treatment of aspiration in P. W.
Joyce's *A Grammar of the Irish Language* (1878), it might seem, at
first sight, that Synge himself has carefully copied out notes from
this text. But this cannot be, since there are important alterations
and additions to Joyce's material. In fact, the pages in Synge's notebook, in which we find these rules, are headed with the words
'Celtic Lectures 8/91 Goodman'.[13] Clearly, Goodman himself had
used Joyce's book as the basis for the lecture. It was a most popular
textbook—so much so that a special edition for the use of schools
and colleges was issued in 1879, just a year after the publication of
the original text. That Synge found it uncommonly useful is proved
by the way in which he returned to it after leaving university, as

he continued with the independent study of Irish.[14] Douglas Hyde also prized his copy of the text, which he kept in his library long after he had left Trinity College.[15]

In Synge's notes from Goodman's lecture, the rules are tabulated in much the same order as in Joyce's book—at one stage, for instance, three subsections fall in exactly the same sequence. Sometimes, where Joyce seems to go into unnecessary detail, the text is reduced and simplified; elsewhere Joyce's slender information is judiciously augmented. For example, the complex rules governing the use of prepositions are outlined by Goodman in greater, but essential, detail. He simplifies the explanation of the aspiration of the verb, by breaking it up into its different parts. He treats each of these parts separately and clearly, whereas Joyce confusingly amalgamates them. Goodman's lecture is an accomplished synthesis of one of the best grammars then available, sharpening Joyce's text where there is vagueness, reducing its excessive details, and augmenting it where the examples are inadequate for all contingencies. Synge's initial training in Irish, therefore, was manifestly of a high order for the time. His complaints against his professor, ten years afterwards, ring very hollow, since his own college notebooks bear such eloquent testimony to Goodman's excellent teaching.

In spite of his misgivings about Goodman, Synge must have pursued his study of the Gospel in Gaelic with real enthusiasm. In those days, lectures at Trinity were not compulsory. The only set of lectures which Synge attended with any regularity were those on Irish, if we are to judge from the diaries in which he recorded his activities. For example, he records his attendance at Irish lectures on 13, 16, 18, 21, 23, 25 and 30 May 1892. On the intervening days, he worked hard on the text of *Diarmuid and Gráinne* (Dublin 1884). One of the entries is as follows: '13 May 1892—Irish Lecture. St John's Gospel XV, 1–5. Got New Testament from the Irish Society gratis'. From 15 to 17 June, the continual study of Irish is recorded. The reason for this flurry of activity soon becomes clear. At the instigation of his elder brother, Samuel, who had already passed through the Divinity School, Synge sat a special examination in Irish. He wrote in his diary on 28 June 1892: 'Got Irish Prize £4'. He won this award for taking first prize in the annual tests in Irish administered by Professor Goodman. Three candidates had been judged worthy of prizes in the Senior Class, but Synge alone had been so honoured in the Junior Class.[16] His interest in Irish studies had been irretrievably aroused and the entry in the diary for the following day tells its own tale: '29 June 1892—Started *Children of Lir* again'.

So it went on. Synge read, very slowly, the Gaelic version of *Diarmuid and Gráinne*, which he bought in mid-July for study on a summer sojourn at the family's country house in Castle Kevin.[17] His nephew wrote that these tales of ancient Ireland '. . . caught his folk imagination as the Greek tales had done, but for him they had a new quality that seemed akin to the mode of expression used by his friends among the country people, a wild, fantastic exaggeration which had no counterpart in the classics of Greece . . .'[18] In 1892, also, Synge studied Standish J. O'Grady's *Red Hugh*, James Clarence Mangan's *Autobiography* and *Memoir*, Henry Grattan's *Speeches*, Thomas Davis's *Ballads* and Hardiman's *Irish Minstrelsy*. At the end of the year, in his customary summary of the progress of his studies, prominent place is given to the following entry: 'Irish; *Children of Lir, Diarmuid and Gráinne*, 12 Chaps of Testament, Some Songs'.

Both *The Children of Lir* and *Diarmuid and Gráinne* had been published in cheap editions with interlineal English translations by the Society for the Preservation of the Irish Language. This society was founded in 1876. Like its predecessor, the Ossianic Society of which Goodman had been a leading member, it desired to ensure the preservation of the old literature and language. However, its members displayed little interest in the spoken tongue of the west where, in the words of one historian of the language, 'the living sparks really lay'.[19] Synge's early interest was in keeping with this praiseworthy but restricted tradition. He studied the Society's texts diligently, but with no apparent curiosity about the living language on the western seaboard.

So, in December 1892, Synge graduated from Trinity College with a 'gentleman's degree', undistinguished but for his prizes in Irish and Hebrew. The explosion of his interest in Irish, so minutely chronicled in the diaries of his years at Trinity, cannot have been wholly accidental. It must be attributable in some degree to the stimulus and shrewd instruction of James Goodman.

For many years after his graduation, Synge continued to keep a diary. In 1893 a significant development occurred, when he began to register entries in Irish as well as in English. The script of these entries is hesitant, the sentences studded with errors of grammar and punctuation, but the meaning comes through clearly enough: '8 Jan 1893; Do ċuġ mé ṗann ċum ṛaġaṗc na leaḃaiṛ'[20] (I sent verses to the priest of the books). He had, in fact, submitted one of his earliest poems, 'A Mountain Creed', for possible inclusion in Fr Matthew Russell's journal, the *Irish Monthly*. To modern scholars of the language, the errors of grammar and spelling committed by Synge may seem elementary, especially for one who has just won a university prize for excellence in Irish. Synge confuses nominative singular and plural ('rann' should be 'ranna'), genitive singular and plural ('leabhair' should be 'leabhar'). Even long after he became competent in written Irish, Synge continued to commit the most rudimentary spelling blunders.

It is worth pointing out, lest too much be made of this defect by those who wish to deny Synge's competence in Irish, that he was also an indifferent speller in English. Edward Stephens noted with outraged fastidiousness that his uncle John 'spelt badly and his hand-writing was a scrawl'.[21] Bourgeois reports that Synge was self-conscious about this and that he always asked friends to re-check his writings, 'for he spelt badly and had no punctuation whatsoever'.[22] However, apart from this personal weakness at spelling and punctuation, there is an even more fundamental reason for Synge's poor written Irish.

It must be remembered that in the late nineteenth century there was no standardised way of writing Irish, nor any consensus as to what modern dialect forms should or should not be used. A Sizar of Trinity College, the Reverend James Murphy, experienced the same difficulty as Synge. In a letter to the *Irish Times*, he complained bitterly about the many errors in Comyn and Nolan's primer, *The First Irish Book*.[23] Many of the early textbooks were, in the words of a present-day scholar, 'stilted, unnatural, even sometimes wrong'.[24] The young Eoin MacNeill, later to become an eminent professor of Celtic history, tried to learn the language at precisely the same time as Synge. He 'soon found out how inadequate were the means then available for learning any current form of Irish'.[25]

In preparing his first publication in Irish, Douglas Hyde found that the differences between the various dialects posed grave problems in writing the language: 'In Connaught I must pronounce *leo* as *lófa*, *dóibh* as *dófa*; but it is needless to say that I have never written them so'.[26] Here, Hyde has cut through to the core of the problem—the lack of a standard spelling. It was a problem which afflicted writers of Irish at all levels. Stephen Gwynn set himself to learn Irish and found the orthography 'elaborate and cumbrous'.[27] William Larminie, like Hyde, wished to print Gaelic folk-tales in a book, but he observed that the mere sounds of western dialects 'cannot be given at all on the basis of common spelling'.[28]

The frustrations which beset Synge in his first attempts at written Irish must have been experienced by scores of other students. At Trinity College, Dr Robert Atkinson must frequently have heard such complaints from even the most gifted of his pupils. It was probably this which impelled him to launch his notorious attack on the introduction of Irish as a school subject at Intermediate level. As a professor of Old Irish, Atkinson was appalled at the diversity of modern Gaelic dialects. In his eyes, these dialects were a degeneration from the classic norms of the twelfth-century language. In January 1903, his outline of the difficulties facing the student of modern Irish was summarised, brutally but accurately, in the hostile columns of *An Claidheamh Soluis*:

I do not regard this language as in a settled state. There are numerous patois, but there is no standard of speech absolutely accepted by everybody. In these variations the child's mind must be confused . . . spelling is an extremely difficult thing in Irish. Further, one patois differs from another. It must be to a child a circumstance of the utmost confusion to find this variation in spelling.[29]

Amid the fierce enthusiasms of the time, Atkinson was attacked as being anti-Irish in attitude; but he was merely articulating the problems encountered by generations of Trinity students, including John Synge. After all, Trinity was one of the few places where Irish had been formally studied from textbooks in the nineteenth century and Atkinson was speaking from years of experience as a teacher. Like many critics of modern Irish, he exaggerated the difficulties of mastering it and his long-term influence was disastrous for the study of the modern language at Trinity College.[30] Nevertheless, many of his warnings were justified by subsequent events. For instance, *An Claidheamh Soluis* was forced to report a split in its Spelling Committee, just two years after its attack on Atkinson for exaggerating the problems of Irish orthography.[31]

Like Synge, the young Douglas Hyde kept a diary and made lists of his reading in Latin, Greek, French and German; and, like Synge, he gave himself practice in the writing of Irish. As late as 1876, Hyde was still making such elementary mistakes in his diary as the failure to distinguish the Copula 'is' from the Verb of Being 'tá'. He confused 'mhúin mé' (I taught) with 'd'fhoghlaim mé' (I learned) and, even more outrageously, he wrote 'adharc' (a horn) for 'radharc' (a view).[32] These errors, committed after three years of studying, are just as serious as those mistakes made by the young Synge in his diary. Nevertheless, this did not prevent Hyde's thinking in terms of winning the Irish Prize at Trinity College: 'Jan. 27, 1877 . . . In the end I decided to read the New Testament in Greek and in Irish, because there is a lot of talk about my going in for a Sizarship in Irish at the College'.[33] The truth of the matter must now be clear. Even prizewinners at university in those days made rudimentary mistakes in written Irish. These errors were often due to the lack of a standard spelling and to the proliferation of various dialect forms.

Well after the turn of the century, there was still no agreement on how to standardise spelling. Many of Atkinson's predictions came true. Some scholars opted to return to the standard Classical Irish orthography of the years 1200–1600; others sought a simplified spelling of those words common to the three modern dialects. Eoin Mac Neill refused to opt for any single dialect and simply exhorted students to 'be thoroughly familiar with the leading peculiarities of the usage of the different provinces'.[34] This was the course which Synge himself was to take. Although Connacht Irish became his major dialect after his sojourns on Aran, he also studied the dialects of Munster (Kerry) and North Connacht (Mayo).

All of these problems must be borne in mind when we seek to explain Synge's decision not to employ the Irish language as a literary medium. The lack of a standard spelling made the study of Irish a frustrating affair for the scholar who sought to write lucidly in the language. It will soon be seen how this difficulty afflicted even highly intelligent native Irish-speakers, who could write competent English, but who never learned to write with confidence in their own language.

THE SCHOLAR-APPRENTICE: CELTIC STUDIES IN PARIS

In 1893, one year after Synge's graduation, the Gaelic League was founded and his interest in the 'Kingdom of Ireland' grew stronger still. He continued to train himself laboriously in the reading of his native language, using as textbooks both *Diarmuid and Gráinne* and

The Children of Lir, with the aid of Joyce's grammar to clarify any difficulties. He studied the work of George Petrie on the ecclesiastical architecture and round towers of Ireland.[35] This study must have taken his fancy, for he wrote in his diary of a walking tour: 'June 4, 1893; Saw cromlech and remains of round tower—then on to Enniskerry'. And again, 'July, 1893; Went up to the cairn above Castle Kevin'. Some of Synge's notebooks for this period contain sketches of such ruins, including a round tower at Kildare.

From the ruined walls of some old churches, Synge jotted down inscriptions in the Irish language. Edward Stephens has suggested that his uncle did not understand these inscriptions because 'at that time his knowledge of Irish cannot have extended much beyond the alphabet'.[36] This is quite untenable. Stephens's mistake is due to his incorrect attribution of these notes to the year 1888, when, indeed, Synge may have known little more than the alphabet. The attribution should be 1889 at the earliest but probably much later, the year 1893 being the most likely. The early part of the notebook is filled with lecture notes of 1889. It was Synge's habit to make personal notes from his reading on the remaining pages of old lecture notebooks, such as this, no longer in academic use. This would explain the gap in time between 1889 and 1893, when his interest in antiquities really emerged.

The first inscription is taken from the entrance porch to the ancient church at Freshford, Co. Kilkenny. The church was built for St Lachtin in the eighth century. It was reconstructed in the eleventh century, as the inscription in Early Modern Irish serves to prove: 'Ór do neim igin cuirc acus do mathgamain a chiarmeic las in dernad i tempulsa.'[37] Synge was perfectly well aware of the meaning of this inscription. He noted that the building on which it was found could 'not be earlier than the 11th century, as surnames were not used before that time'.[38] This information he had gleaned from his reading of Petrie's *Inquiry into the Origin and Uses of the Round Towers of Ireland* where a similar point is made.[39] He would also have read Petrie's translation of the inscription: 'A prayer for Niam daughter of Corc and for Mathgamain Ó Chiarmeic under whose auspices this church was built'.

On the following pages of the same notebook, Synge recorded an inscription from Cormac's Chapel on the Rock of Cashel, which is recorded in the Annals of Munster, 1127 A.D. This inscription is written in the kind of Irish which Synge studied at university. It is copied into his notebook in his natural free-flowing handwriting,

and not in the tortuous letter-by-letter printing which characterises
the earlier inscription copied. It may well have been intended as an
exercise for translation:

> Sluagh mór le Toirdealbhac Ua Conchabhair go riacht Corcaigh
> agus é féin ar tír, agus cobhlach ar muir timchiol go Corcaigh,
> go ndeannaidh féin agus Donncha Mac Cárthaigh go n-a muintir
> Cormac Mac Muireadaigh, Migh Cárthaigh, d'aithríoghadh, go
> mo h-éigion dó dul a n-oilithre go Lios Mór, agus bachall do
> gabháil ann agus Donncha, mac Muireadaigh meig Carthaigh
> don ríoghadh n-a fiaghnaise.[40]
>
> (A great crowd went to Cork with Terence O'Connor, he by
> land, and a fleet by sea; and he and Denis MacCarthy, with
> their people, reinstated Cormac Mac Murray MacCarthy as king.
> He was obliged to go on pilgrimage to Lismore, and take a
> crozier there, and this in the presence of Denis MacMurray
> MacCarthy.)

The work of Petrie may have roused Synge's interest in the Aran
Islands. As early as 1889, he had read Stokes' *Life of Petrie*[41] and in
May 1892 he took notes from that book.[42] Petrie's work contained
observations on everyday life on Aran, including an account of an
old woman, like Maurya in *Riders to the Sea*, who had lost her
son to the ocean. Years later, when he first set foot on Aran, Synge
recalled 'Petrie's words that the clothing of the Irish peasant . . . has
rich positive tints with nothing gaudy' (*Prose*, p. 54).

These archaeological studies are of crucial importance in charting
Synge's path towards Gaelic literature and lore. They were under-
taken entirely on his own initiative, for there was no course in
archaeology at Trinity College. Edward Stephens had observed that
'It was through John's interest in archaeology that he began consciously to accept and to associate himself with Irish tradition. From
archaeology he was to pass on, stimulated by events and by the
people he met, to studying folk-lore, history and the Irish language . . .'[43] At this time, also, Synge read Matthew Arnold's *Irish
Essays* and his work *On the Study of Celtic Literature*. He studied
Songs of the Munster Bards. This book contained poems by the
greatest Gaelic poets of the eighteenth century, including Donnchadh
Mac Con Mara, Seán Ua Tuama, Aindrias Mac Craith, Aodhagán
Ua Rathaille, an t-Athair Uilliam Inglis, Tadhg 'Gaodhalach' Ua
Súilleabháin, Peadar Ua Doirnín, Eoin Ruadh Ua Súilleabháin, Seán

Clárach Mac Domhnaill, Seán na Raithíneach and Liam Mac Coitir. The poems were accompanied by versions in English composed by James Clarence Mangan. Synge himself was destined to translate one of the greatest love lyrics of this book, *Bean Dubh an Ghleanna*, into a fine version in English.

Synge's family were taking note of this developing interest. The study of Irish at Trinity had been unopposed, but his interest in Irish archaeology was discouraged by his mother. She regarded the lore surrounding the ancient ruins as 'foolish stories invented by local guides to obtain money from tourists'.[44] Although she did, on occasion, ask John to guide her English visitors around the antiquities of Wicklow, in general Synge was forced to look outside the immediate family circle for an encouragement of his interest. He sent many books to his cousin Emily for her opinion and on one occasion received the following reply:

> Annamoe   Monday
> My dear John,
>   Many thanks for your books which I return—*Diarmuid and Gráinne* were delightful. The game of chess under the quicken-tree especially pleased me and Matthew Arnold is very interesting— do you mean to be the first professor of Celtic Literature at Oxford? I do not care very much for the Munster bards, but perhaps the translator has not done them justice—his measures are somewhat halting and uneven.
>
> Your affectionate old cousin,
Emily R. Synge.[45]

Emily's complimentary quip about Synge as a future Celtic scholar would not be the last reference to him in this context. However, until 1893 and for some years afterwards, Synge intended to devote his life's work to music. Even in this discipline, however, his creative instincts were turning to Gaelic sources for inspiration. He composed many musical pieces for the violin and he wrote in his diary of 1893: 'May 20, Started words and music for opera on Eileen a rúin'. Once again, the Gaelic words are written in a slow and tortuous hand, when compared with the flowing upstrokes and downstrokes of his written English.

Synge continued to make cryptic entries in Irish in his diary. For him, Irish seemed to possess the status of a privileged secret language, a personal code in which he could record his feelings about Valeska von Eiken, the youngest girl of the German family with whom he stayed near Oberwerth. He probably used Irish so that nobody at home, on chancing to see the pages, might understand the intimate nature of their information. A similar desire for privacy explains the entry in Irish, already noted, recording the submission of his adolescent poem to Fr Russell's magazine. This would also explain the cryptic references to his infatuation with his English cousin, Alice Owen, in the summer of 1892, moving from expectation on 11 September ('Chonnaic mé Aleus'—I saw Alice) to disappointment on 28 September ('Do chuaidh Aleus a gcéin, ochón, ochón'—Alice went abroad, alas, alas).

The affair with Valeska von Eiken was rather more serious. On the day after his arrival in Oberwerth, he wrote 'July 30, Lá Bhaleusca'—(Valeska's day), in order to denote the day on which he made one of the lasting friendships of his life. He spent six months with the von Eikens, studying the violin, before moving on to Wurzburg: '22 January 1894; Left Coblenz by train at 11.30 and arrived in Wurzburg 5.30'.[46] Again, he felt obliged to use Irish rather than English, when expressing his innermost emotions concerning the move from Oberwerth. A year later, having just ended a stay of two months in Oberwerth, Synge wrote of his last day with Valeska: '31 December 1894; Bhaleusce, ochón, ochón' (—Valeska, alas, alas).[47] This entry stands out clearly amid all the entries in German which surround it. Synge was to use identical words, two years later, to express his anguish about the religious differences with Cherrie Matheson, which prevented her from marrying him.[48] The cryptic nature of these entries in Irish can be ascribed not—as we might uncharitably suspect—to an inability to write at greater length, but rather to that very need for secrecy which impelled him to employ the language in the first place. This is borne out by the fact that he made brief entries in French in his diary while on Aran, in order to maintain secrecy. On the islands he did not employ Irish, which could have been read by prying or inquisitive folk.

Synge quitted Coblenz on New Year's Day 1895. Four days later, Valeska wrote kindly to cheer him up: 'Nothing can destroy our friendship; time and the future will only enhance it'.[49] Having studied German with the von Eikens, Synge now moved to Paris to improve his French. He had abandoned the idea of a musical career, despairing of his ability to perform in public. From now on, he would devote himself to the study of languages.

In April 1895, Synge settled in Paris and studied comparative phonetics with M. Paul Passy.[50] Just one year later, he attended a lecture on Breton life by Anatole Le Braz. At once, he became a passionate student of Celtic lore and a keen reader of Le Braz's works on the subject—*Au Pays des Pardons, Vieilles Histoires du Pays Breton, La Légende de la Mort chez les Bretons Armoricains*. Le Braz had published Breton folklore in French (rather than Breton), capturing for it an international audience. In the introduction by Leon Marillier to Le Braz's *La Légende de la Mort en Basse Bretagne*, Synge would have read:

M. Le Braz . . . les a toutes écrites sous la dictée des conteurs dans la langue même où elles lui étaient dites, puis il a ensuite traduit en français celles qui lui avaient été contées en breton . . . C'est seulement pour ne pas trop grossir le volume et pour le faire accessible à un plus large public, que M. Le Braz n'a pas publié les originaux bretons.[51]
(From the narrations of storytellers, Mr. Le Braz . . . has written them down in the very language in which they were told to him. Next, he translated into French those stories which had been told to him in Breton . . . Mr. Le Braz has chosen not to publish the Breton originals, in order to curtail the size of the publication and to make it available to a larger public.)

It may well be that this example inspired Synge to follow suit in *The Aran Islands*, where he won a global audience for Gaelic lore by translating it into English.

Synge paid a handsome tribute to this teacher in an article in the *Dublin Daily Express* on 28 January 1899. He noted that the nature of Le Braz's relationship with Brittany was rather different from that of Gaelic enthusiasts like himself with Inishmaan. Le Braz had 'passed his childhood in close contact with the Breton peasantry' and 'now sees with a vague and unpractical disquiet the waning of much that he intimately loves' (*Prose*, p. 394). For Gaelic enthusiasts in Ireland, on the contrary, the old ways have not 'the charms of lingering regret, but rather the incitement of a thing that is rare and beautiful, and still apart from our habitual domain'. Le Braz's consuming interest in the theatre is reflected in another article by Synge in the *Freeman's Journal* on 22 March 1900. In this he praised the Celtic Theatre of western Brittany for its 'early vigour which recalls the first pre-Elizabethan dramas'. While happy to note the

growth of 'a somewhat similar movement' in the Irish Literary
Theatre, he commented tersely on the fact that the Breton players
'act in Breton', whereas 'our poets write in English' (*Prose*, p. 393).
Synge was aware, from the outset, that the concept of an Irish
National Theatre in the English language was something of a con-
tradiction in terms.

William Butler Yeats, who had met Synge in Paris in 1896,[52]
wrote to Lady Gregory in February 1899 with the news that his
friend 'is learning Breton'.[53] Not only was Synge studying Breton
in Paris, but he visited Brittany for two weeks in April, as the
guest of a student named Piquenard, with whom he frequently
exchanged letters on Celtic topics. Piquenard marked Synge's visit
with a poem in Breton, published in a local paper under a fulsome
dedication to 'Un Fils de l'Irlande.'[54] For a time, Synge thought of
becoming an interpreter of French life and literature. But this first
contact with the Celtic Revival on the continent was finally to send
him back to interpret the lore of his native land. He confided in
Yeats that he feared losing the Irish he had learned at Trinity College.[55]
So, in February 1898, he attended the lectures of Professor H. d'Arbois
de Jubainville on Old Irish and allied subjects at the Collège de
France. Synge noted such lectures in his diary: 'Feb 18; To cours de
Jubainville sur la civilization irlandaise comparée avec celle
d'Homère'.[56]

Maud Gonne, the Irish revolutionary, had introduced Synge to the
famous Celtic scholar. In her biography, *A Servant of the Queen*, she
claimed that de Jubainville had asked her if she could find him a
secretary who knew modern Irish.[57] In a letter to Maurice Bourgeois,
she said that Synge worked 'for some time'[58] with de Jubainville in
this capacity. This claim is questionable. What drew Synge to de
Jubainville's course, in the first place, was the desire to consolidate
his Irish, rather than the belief that he could act as a resident expert
on the language for a professor of international standing. There is
no evidence for such an assignment in Synge's diaries, which chronicle
his days and hours in Paris. It is, however, true that Synge felt
sufficiently confident of his knowledge of Irish to correct de
Jubainville's misconceptions concerning the pronunciation of certain
words in the modern language.[59] In a postscript to a letter to Lady
Gregory on 22 February 1902 he wrote: 'I am working at de
Jubainville's lectures now, so I shall not forget my Irish this winter.
He came to see me the other day to ask me to go and give them
the pronunciation of modern Irish. I feel rather a blind guide but

I do my best'.[60]

From a notebook kept by Synge in February 1902, it is clear that de Jubainville's lectures were mainly concerned with comparative philology, the parallels between Irish forms and those of other Celtic languages. There are detailed notes on the grammar of Old Irish—declension of nouns, conjugation of important verbs, personal pronouns, uses of the article, numerals of all types, and extensive lists of vocabulary. From these notes it is clear that Synge himself was obsessed with the European parallels to Irish grammar and vocabulary. This passionate commitment to fitting Gaelic culture into the larger European design was maintained by Synge all his life. He considered himself a European writer and he believed that the Gaelic intellectual tradition had reached its highest point in those periods when Irish writers and scholars had enjoyed comprehensive links with Europe. It was fitting, therefore, that Synge's were the first plays of the Irish dramatic movement to be produced in the major European languages.[61]

De Jubainville's method with literature and language was comparative. In literature, he made constant comparisons between the Irish Mythological Cycle and the age of Homer. In language, as Synge's notes testify, he stressed those elements of grammar and syntax common to European, and especially Celtic, languages. This comparative method dominates his major work, *Éléments de la Grammaire Celtique*. Consider, for example, his treatment of the words used in various languages to denote the cardinal number seven:

Les formes primitives indo-européennes paraissent avoir été: 1° septm, en sanscrit sapta, en grec επτα, en latin sĕptĕm; 2° sĕptŏm, en vieil irlandais secht n-, aujourd'hui seacht produisant éclipse, en gallois seith, en breton seiz, seih, tous supposant un celtique sechton, plus anciennement septom. La labiale subsiste en germanique, allemand sieben, anglais seven.[62]

(The primitive Indo-European forms seem to have been firstly septm, in Sanskrit sapta, in Greek επτα, in latin sĕptĕm; secondly, sĕptŏm, in Old Irish secht n-, today seacht causing an eclipse, in Gallic seith, in Breton seiz, seih, all of which assuming the existence of a Celtic sechton, formerly rendered septom. The labial persists in Germanic, German sieben, English seven.)

It is clear that lectures which Synge received on this subject were the raw material from which de Jubainville later produced his

textbook. On the second page of his lecture notes, Synge took down
the following list of comparisons between similar words in the Celtic
languages:

2 Jubainville   Feb 1902   Collège de France
Naktis   noks
noctium
nahts
—
nos(G)
noz(B)
noss(Man)
en noz
an noz   genitive du temps
an ocht(1)
in nocht (M.I.)
seacht(1)
seigh(B).[63]

In these notes, Synge noted the remark, 'peut-être verbe bretons
vient de l'Irlandais'.[64] Later, de Jubainville extended these comparisons dramatically to embrace other European languages, including French: 'cé tá; qu'est-ce'.[65]

This method profoundly impressed Synge and was applied in the
notes on Irish which he made during his visits to Aran. For instance,
in one notebook, beside the Irish word 'salach' (dirty) he scrawled
the French 'sale'.[66] In lectures, de Jubainville often went to Old and
Early Modern Irish in order to explain features of the contemporary
language: 'E.M.I. Accus. and nom. are assimilated in Modern Irish
and the accus. form persists—hence *Eirinn*'.[67] So persuaded was Synge
by the method that he applied it to explain a peculiarity, which he
had found in the Irish of Aran: 'th. not pronounced in Old Irish—
hence guttural in *go brath* in Aran pronunciation'.[68] This must have
been one of the cases, mentioned in the letter to Lady Gregory of
the same month, in which Synge provided his teacher with the pronunciation of modern Irish.

The study of comparative linguistics was only one of de
Jubainville's interests. He was not afraid to apply his comparative
techniques to Celtic myth and folklore. That Synge found such an
approach attractive is evident from the notes which he made from
de Jubainville's book, *Le Cycle Mythologique Irlandais et La Mythologie*

Celtique.[69] These notes are a pithy summary of de Jubainville's narrative: but whenever the author halts the narrative to make a 'European' comparison, then he is quoted *in extenso*. For example: 'Les traits commun de la mythologie irlandaise et de la mythologie grecque proviennent d'un vieux fonds de légendes grecs-celtique antérieur à la séparation des races'.[70] (The features common to both Irish and Greek mythology derive from an ancient source of Graeco-Celtic legends, existing prior to the division of the races.) This method is reflected in Synge's own work. In *The Aran Islands*, he repeatedly draws imaginative comparisons between the folk-tales of the islands and of many European countries. It will later be shown that Synge's contribution to the study of Irish folklore lay in his introduction of the comparative method to the field, a method in which other accomplished folklorists, such as Douglas Hyde, William Larminie and Lady Gregory, had displayed little interest.

Synge's attitude to de Jubainville was respectful, but not idolatrous. He reviewed R. I. Best's translation of the book on the Mythological Cycle for the *Speaker* on 2 April 1904. De Jubainville's book was published in English under the title *The Irish Mythological Cycle and Celtic Mythology*. Synge welcomes Best's accomplishment of 'a useful task', but adds:

In a sense it is, perhaps, a little to be regretted that M. D'Arbois de Jubainville has chosen to put his work in the form of a discussion of the Irish myths, as they are found in the Book of Invasions (the *Leabhar Gabhála*, a twelfth century account of the mythical colonisations of Ireland), for in following this plan he has had to begin with rather unattractive material, where the thread of Irish myth is much obscured by pseudo-classical or Biblical adaptations (*Prose*, p. 364).

Nevertheless, Synge is fair-minded enough to quote in full from de Jubainville's justification of the method and to concede that the value of the book is beyond dispute. However, he feels bound to remind his readers that there exist contrary interpretations of early Celtic pantheism and of the system of Scotus Eriugena. Synge remarks that philologists find Old Irish as important to the study of Latin etymology as Sanskrit itself. Once again, he returns to his concern with the European basis of Irish mythology: 'Irish mythology has been found to give, with the oldest mythology that can be gathered from the Homeric poems, the most archaic phase of Indo-

European religion' (*Prose*, p. 365). Once Synge has struck this obsessive note, the review, to all intents and purposes, is over. The remaining paragraphs become a catalogue of the more dramatic parallels drawn by de Jubainville. Illustrating the Greek kinship of Irish legends, Synge describes the mythical god Lug as a Celtic Hermes and he equates his victim Balor with Belleros. Even more exciting is the possibility that Irish myth may help to explain some of the most basic features of European culture. The Celtic Dagda ('good god') corresponds to the Latin Bona Dea. This god owns a magic cauldron which is to be found also in the Welsh study of Branwen, daughter of Llyr. The suggestion is that this cauldron provides the pagan source of the legend of the Holy Grail. Though Synge makes this suggestion tentatively, it is one which, on his own admission, he finds 'entrancing.' Above all, Synge values de Jubainville's work for providing the finest 'consecutive view of Irish mythology' available and points out that such a view is essential before it is possible to assign to it its true place in the whole European scheme.

Synge faithfully attended the lectures of de Jubainville twice a week, being often the only student present.[71] When he came to write an article on 'La Vieille Littérature Irlandaise' on 15 March 1902 in *L'Européen*, he paid tribute to his mentor: 'C'est à M. d'Arbois de Jubainville que revient l'honneur d'avoir éclairé par de longs travaux toute cette mythologie irlandaise, et ses cours de la littérature celtique sont d'une valeur inestimable pour tous ceux qui voudraient se renseigner sur ce sujet' (*Prose*, p. 354). (To M. d'Arbois de Jubainville goes the honour of having elucidated by sustained effort the whole of this Irish mythology; and his lectures on Celtic Literature are of inestimable value to all those who wish to learn about this subject.) It was in Paris, also, that Synge became a close friend of R. I. Best,[72] who had come to the Sorbonne to prepare himself for what was to be an illustrious career as a Celtic scholar.

There can be little doubt that it was this encounter with the Celtic Revival in France which impelled Synge to make for the Aran Islands. Too many critics have hastily assumed that his visits to Aran can be ascribed to Yeats's advice in 1896 that Synge should 'Go to the Aran Islands. Live there as if you were one of the people themselves; express a life that has never found expression'.[73] Even Synge's official biographers fall into this trap and state bluntly that 'the decision to go was made at Yeats's suggestion', while noting acidly that 'Yeats was not reticent about claiming credit for it'.[74]

There are good reasons for the failure of critics to see these events in perspective. There is, for one thing, Yeats's inaccurate scholarship, his inability to count the passing years. In 1905, when his original claim was made, he said that he had first met Synge 'six years ago'[75] (that is, in 1899). He told his new friend to go to Aran, from which he himself 'had just come'.[76] Synge had already made his first trip to Aran in 1898, but this is not to accuse Yeats of telling Synge to do something which the young man had already done. Plainly, Yeats has miscalculated. From a variety of sources it is clear that Yeats's visit to Aran was in 1896.[77] He went there to collect material for his forthcoming novel, *The Speckled Bird*, and 'had just come' from the islands when he gave his celebrated advice. Synge's diary records an introduction to W. B. Yeats in Paris on 21 December 1896. It begins to seem likely that 1896, and not 1899, is the date of the famous injunction.

This is confirmed beyond doubt by a private letter written by Yeats to Lady Gregory in 1911, with instructions for Maurice Bourgeois's forthcoming biography of Synge. On this occasion, Yeats computed the years correctly: 'Tell Bourgeois that I met Synge in Paris long before he had ever been in Aran. I met him in 1896, and our conversatoin about his going to Aran was published in the introduction to the first edition of *The Well of the Saints* during Synge's lifetime'.[78] The length 'long before' give Yeats away, for they call attention to the lengthy period between the advice in 1896 and the visit in 1898. An intense exposure to Celtic Studies filled Synge's life in these intervening years. Doubtless, the advice from Yeats was an important factor in Synge's decision; but the passionate studies in Breton culture must have awakened his enthusiasm for the Gaelic lore of his own country, to which he already held the key in his knowledge of the Irish language. It would be naïve to follow Greene and Stephens in asserting that he went to Aran at Yeat's suggestion. He was heading in that direction from the very beginning.

THE SPOKEN IRISH OF ARAN

Up to 1898, when he was twenty-seven years old, Synge's contact with the Irish language had been purely academic and literary. He may have known more than his Paris professor about the spoken language, but he cannot have known very much. On 10 May 1898, Synge landed on Inishmore, the largest of the Aran Islands. He stayed for two weeks before moving on to Inishmaan, 'where Gaelic is more generally used, and the life is perhaps the most primitive that is left in Europe'. (*Prose*, p. 53). This sentence suggests that his main reason for going to Aran was the desire to learn Irish. That impulse must have been very strong for, despite his delicate constitution and chronic asthma, he was prepared to endure great hardship in the cottage where learners lodged on Inishmaan. He remarked that 'the place looked hardly fit for habitation' (*Prose*, p. 52), yet he bore the hardship willingly because more Irish was spoken on this island.

It is worth dwelling on this point because the official biographer has written that on Aran 'Synge's real purpose was neither to learn Irish nor to record folktales' and that the islanders were unaware that he 'was more interested in their English than their Irish'.[79] This interpretation cannot be sustained. The Anglo-Irish dialect cannot be studied in any part of Ireland without an initial study of its Gaelic *substratum*. In the words of P. W. Joyce, 'by far the greatest number of our Anglo-Irish idioms come from the Irish language'.[80] Synge's knowledge of Irish was crucial in the creation of his Anglo-Irish dialect and this knowledge preceded and determined the composition of that particular dramatic language. It would have been impossible for Synge to express a life that had never found expression, without first learning the language through which the daily affairs of that life were conducted. In the words of one historian of the language, 'the tradition of the Irish people is to be understood and experienced with intimacy only in the Irish language. It would be impossible that it could be so come upon in the English language'.[81] Yeats himself wrote a letter on the subject to the editor of the *Leader* in September 1900, while Synge was on Aran. In it he held that the Irish language was the key not only to the west, but to the lost imagination of the whole nation. He insisted that 'the mass of the people cease to understand any poetry when they cease to understand the Irish language, which is the language of their imaginations'.[82]

There is ample evidence, apart from Synge's early move to Inishmaan, to support the contention that his first object in visiting Aran was to learn his native language. We have, most crucially, his own word for it. In an account of his life written in 1905 for Max Meyerfeld, his German translator, Synge wrote: 'In 1898 I went to the Aran Islands to learn Gaelic and lived with the peasants. Ever since then I have spent part of my year among the Irish-speaking peasantry, in various localities, as I am now doing once more.'[83]

Synge's constant companion during his visits to the island of Inishmaan was a boy named Martin McDonough. He had no doubts about the reasons for Synge's repeated visits and he wrote to his friend in the autumn of 1900: 'I now see that your time is comming on for the future to come to Inishmaan to learn your native language'.[84] Edward Stephens, in whom Synge often confided, testifies that during the first visit 'John's time was spent learning Irish'.[85] The very frequency with which the narrator of *The Aran Islands* returns to the successes and frustrations of this effort is itself eloquent testimony to the way in which the idea possessed his mind.

In 1898, Synge spent four weeks on Inishmaan after his fortnight in Inishmore. He returned to Aran in each summer of 1899, 1900, 1901 and 1902, spending in all about eighteen weeks on the islands. During his first stint on Inishmaan, his hostess spoke no English and few of his acquaintances spoke it with any comfort (*Prose*, p. 58). This would have given him an opportunity to achieve a reasonable fluency in Irish. The wordlists and phrases, collected in his notebooks during the visit, testify to the seriousness of his effort to master the use of the spoken language in everyday affairs. Here is the earliest list:

lánamhain: married couple	sgaoileadh: release
maol: bald	daingean: firm
fréamh: root	iolar: eagle
droch-meisneach: discouragement	sméura dubha: blackberries
ithir: arable ground	malairt: exchange
smugarle: saliva	go cneasta: honestly
créafóg: clay	cumhang: narrow
blaosg: skull	faire: watch
gáir: a cry	reithe: ram
iosgadh: thigh	

This is typical of the vocabulary required by a newcomer to an island parish, with its everyday words for married couples, dotards, clay, blackberries, rams and eagles, as well as the special recondite word for arable ground as distinct from grazing acreage.

Another notebook from this period contains two pages of basic conversation in Irish. They are the kind of stock sentences which Synge would have found useful on arrival at Aran—for instance, polite requests for permission to smoke or for letters in the post. There are also references to the learning and reading of Irish, to his photography which fascinated the folk and to the fact that his uncle had lived on the islands twenty years earlier.

An maith libh mé a bheith chaith tobac ann sa teach
bhí m'oncle in sia tá sé fiadh bliadhain ó choin
an bhfaca tú an pueso taodh astig
bhí me go fada le barr aille
codal me an fhada inniu mar bhí mé tursach
tá sé deirionnach ins an lá

bhfuil fios agad ar an fear
tá mé ag dul teacht astach
go bhfollem beagán Gaedhilge
bhfuil aon litir domsa?
is trua nach bhfuil pelati agam
thóg mé dhá phicture ar maidin indiu
tar astach
tá dhá litir agam le cuir a phosta
bhfuil aithne ar an bhfear sin agad?[87]

(Do you mind my smoking tobacco in the house?
My uncle was here twenty years ago
Did you see the pussy inside?
I was for a long time on the top of the cliff
I slept very late today because I was tired
It's late in the day

Do you know the man?
I am going/coming in
To learn a little Irish
Is there any letter for me?
It's a pity that I don't have pampooties
I took two pictures this morning
Come in
I have two letters to post
Do you know that man?)

There are, of course, grammatical errors in these sentences, which seem to have been written at speed. 'Chaith' is the Past Tense of the Verbal Noun 'caitheamh', which would be correct above; 'codal' should be 'chodail'; 'bhfuil fhios agad ar an fear' is a notorious beginner's blunder but is corrected further down the list with 'bhfuil aithne ar an bhfear sin agad'. There are also numerous errors of punctuation, especially omissions of aspiration and lengthening.

These sentences are even more remarkable for the great improvement which they show on the Irish written by Synge in his diaries of previous years. It is not simply a matter of improved spelling or longer sentences. It is more a matter of style and 'blas'. These sentences, when grammatically correct, represent idiomatic Irish at its best. Few exponents of Irish, apart from native speakers or outstanding students, would use the interjectory 'tá sé' to denote time past. That is the touch which distinguishes the stylist from the average student. In these notes, when Synge was not sure of the conventional orthography of a strange new word, he employed the International Phonetic Alphabet to reproduce the sound. In a cottage in Inishmaan, he found a use for the lessons learned from Passy in the lecture-halls of the Sorbonne during the previous winter. In a later page of the same notebook, Synge made two revealing observations which illustrate his progress:

Is tig liom Gailige léigheadh   I am able to read Irish
tá mo dhóthain léighta agam inniu   I have read enough today[88]

Naturally, during his first visit, Synge encountered difficulties in coming to terms with the rapid speech of the islanders. Of the speech of his monoglot hostess, he confessed soon after his arrival that 'I could not understand much of what she said' (*Prose*, p. 59). It is clear from the surrounding commentary in Book One of *The Aran Islands* that the staple language of Synge's conversation was still English.[89] It seems that even those whose English was very poor felt obliged to speak it to him. Throughout the Gaeltacht at the time, it was usual for the peasantry to address a stranger first in English.[90] Pat Dirane, the Inishmaan shanachie, had to tell Synge a story in English, though he pointed out that 'it would be much better if I could follow the Gaelic' (*Prose*, p. 61). Pat must have considered that Synge was progressing in his study of Irish for, some days later, he told the story of 'The Unfaithful Wife' in Irish. Synge had great difficulty with Pat's story—'unfortunately it was carried on so rapidly in Gaelic that I lost most of the points' (*Prose*, p. 70). Shortly afterwards, Synge wrote despairingly of the island birds that 'their language is easier than Irish and I seem to understand the greater part of their

cries . . .' (*Prose*, p. 73). The very frequency with which Synge
voiced his worry over this point suggests just how strongly the desire
to learn Irish burned within him.

He was, however, on the verge of a breakthrough. Some days later,
he proved himself able to understand the rapid shouting in Irish from
one boat to another. More significantly, he spoke for the first time
in a simple style to some island children.

> After some shouting in Gaelic, I learned that they had a packet of
> letters and tobacco for myself . . .
> 'Is it tired you are, stranger?'
> 'Bedad, it is not, little girl,' I answered in Gaelic,
> 'it is lonely I am . . .' (*Prose*, p. 83)

Later still, he showed that he could now understand the Irish of an
agitated old woman, perhaps even one of those monoglot women
whose fluency had previously caused him such difficulty:

> . . . an old woman . . . began a fierce rhapsody in Gaelic, pointing
> at the bailiff and waving her withered arms with extraordinary
> rage . . . 'This man is my own son.' she said, 'it is I that ought
> to know him. He is the first great ruffian in the whole world.'
> (*Prose*, p. 92)

At the end of this first visit, in the privacy of his own notebook,
Synge could not help recording his disappointment with the progress
of his studies: 'Older women are full of good fellowship but have
mostly little English and my Gaelic does not carry me beyond a few
comments on the weather and the island . . .' (*Prose*, p. 102). That
the will to learn the islanders' language was bound up with the
desire to express their life in his writing is clear from the sentence
which immediately follows: 'To write a real novel of the island life
one would require to pass several years among the people . . .'
(*Prose*, p. 102).

Whatever the reason—it may have been the winter study noted
in his diary from 1 January 1899[91]—Synge seems to have spoken
the language with far greater ease from the outset of his second
sojourn on the island in the summer of 1899. On the very first page
of Book Two of *The Aran Islands*, there is an account of a long
conversation in Irish between Synge, Martin and another islander
(*Prose*, p. 105). Later we find Synge reading Douglas Hyde's *Love*

Songs of Connacht, and knowing enough Irish to see that the islanders' versions of the songs differ from Hyde's (*Prose*, p. 112). Towards the end of the book, Synge has achieved a rudimentary mastery of the language: 'Old Mourteen is keeping me company again, and I am now able to understand the greater part of his Irish . . . (*Prose*, p. 120). The claim is proved by a report of a playful conversation which Synge had with an Irish-speaking porter in Galway, after leaving Aran (*Prose*, pp. 121–2). The Irish idioms listed in his notebook for the visit display an increasing sophistication. There is a developing preoccupation with stylish phrases such as:

cuir in iúl dhó	(inform him)
cos in airde	(at a gallop)
ní fiú e	(it's not worth it)
go bhfaghach sé a dhóthain	(he'd get his fill)
is dual dó é sin do dhéanamh	(it's natural to him to do that)[92]

So Synge's progress continued. On the third visit, he spent much time with Martin again and wrote that 'many of our evening walks are occupied with long Gaelic discourses about the movements of the stars and moon' (*Prose*, p. 128). This argues a sophistication of spoken Irish to which few learners can attain. Synge spent the last nine days of this visit on the south island, Inishere; and this sophistication is manifest in his comparison between the Irish of Inishmaan and Inishere, a comparison which cannot be made without a detailed knowledge of the spoken language and a sharp ear for its sounds.

These repeated visits to the island enabled Synge to become a competent speaker of the language. His initial slowness in learning it may be traced to his shyness in company. The islanders themselves recalled Synge as a man 'so strange and silent that no one actually knew him'.[93] This is certainly true of the narrator of Book One of *The Aran Islands*—a passive, receptive man, full of shame and regret that his poor Irish excludes him from so many of the delights of the island. In the private notebook, kept during the 1899 visit, Synge wrote of the playboys of Aran who met noisily at that time of year:

'I would have been glad to join them but till my Gaelic is more fluent I do not dare to get among the merry-makers . . .'[94]

At the end of that second visit, however, he wrote proudly:

'Another visit is over. This year I have learned little but Gaelic and nearer understanding of the people . . .'.[95]

This entry was made in a private notebook, where there was no need for him to deceive others about his knowledge of Irish and no point in deceiving himself. It was probably modesty which led him to omit this sentence from the published version of *The Aran Islands*. By Book Four, he presents himself as a man very different from the shy onlooker of Book One, for now he is an active member of the community, taking part in the arguments and furtive illegalities of the folk. Synge's nephew remarked that, by the fourth visit, 'the people had grown accustomed to his visits, and delighted him by talking freely of their own interests, of faction fights, of fairy music and of magic'.[96] Such integration could not have been achieved by a man who lacked a working knowledge of the local dialect. All through *The Aran Islands*, Synge has been scrupulously honest about the limitations to his knowledge of the language. Hence there is no reason to doubt the veracity of the claims made in the later books.

SYNGE'S WRITTEN IRISH

What of Synge's ability to write and read Irish? Early in Book Two of *The Aran Islands*, there is a competent translation of a letter in Irish from Martin in Galway to Synge on Aran:

> 22 Sept 1899
> Sgríobhaim chugad an litir seo le bród agus ríméad go bhfuair tú bealach go teach mo athair an lá bhí tú ar an long gaile . . . Agus tá mé ceapadh nach mbeidh uaigneas ort beidh cruinniughadh deas aluinn Gaedhilge agaibh gach domhnach agus beith tú a foghlaim go cumasach. Tá mé ceapadh nach bhfuil duine ar bith ag siubhal leat ó mhaidin go hoidhche acht tú féin, agus nach mór an tró . . .[97]

Synge's translation runs thus:

> I write this letter with joy and pride that you found the way to the house of my father the day you were on the steamship. I am thinking there will not be loneliness on you, for there will be the fine beautiful Gaelic League and you will be learning powerfully.

I am thinking there is no one in life walking with you now but your own self from morning till night and great is the pity (*Prose*, pp. 111–12).

From this letter, it appears that Synge, along with many of the islanders, attended weekly classes given by the Gaelic League in the reading and writing of Irish. The most interesting feature of the letter, however, is that Martin has written in the margin the following note: 'Peter Concannon will read this letter for you if you are not able'. This refers to Martin's worry about his indifferent literary Irish and poor handwriting rather than to Synge's difficulty in reading the native language. After all, Martin merely suggests that Peter can *read out* the letter to Synge, not that he need explain it in English.

Martin McDonough exchanged many letters after the first visit to Aran. These letters afford direct evidence of Synge's powers of writing and reading Irish. David H. Greene has written of this correspondence: 'In his earliest letters to Synge, Martin McDonough was dubious of Synge's ability to read Gaelic and appended English translations of what he had written'.[98] This interpretation is not sustained by a close examination of the correspondence.

Synge opened the exchange with a letter in English. Martin replied on 23 July 1898 with his own letter in broken English, appending some comments in Irish to reiterate the main points of his letter. This was not, as Greene implies, a word-for-word translation of all that he had written in English. The Irish comments are introduced with these words:

I am going to write you some Irish and tell me you will understand it. I will write this letter all in Irish but I do not know will you understand it let you write the next letter in Irish If you don't I won't look on it . . .[99]

The portion in Irish reiterates this very point:

. . . ní bfuil tada agam le rádh leat acht cuir agam litir Gaedilge gan míol cuirfinn litir a fada Gaedilge agat act tá mé a capa nac bfuil tú anaon é leabeabh act bhí fios agam air anuar a cuirfios tú agam litir Gaedilge . . .
(I have nothing to say to you but send me a letter in Gaelic without delay. I would send you a long letter in Gaelic but I am

thinking you are not able to read it, but I'll know that you are
when you send me a letter in Gaelic.)[100]

Martin's literary Irish is, if anything, even weaker than his poor
English, His request that Synge write to him in Irish would hardly
have been made, if he really considered that his friend could not
read the language.

A further letter from Martin, written wholly in English on 20
February 1899, makes the same point again, as if such a point were a
kind of formula used by the islanders in writing to cultured outsiders, to whom invariably they tried to speak and write in English:
'I will write this letter in Irish but I do not know are you able
to understand it . . .'[101] Greene notes that Synge deleted this sentence when he published Martin's letter in *The Aran Islands*.[102] The
implication is that Synge was attempting to conceal from his readers
an inability to read and write the language—an inability which
would reflect badly upon a man who presumes to interpret the life
of a Gaeltacht island. This is not the case. Martin was certainly
dubious of Synge's ability to read his Irish, but the important word
there is 'his' and not 'Irish'. Martin's written Irish was very poor.
There are twenty-four errors of grammar, syntax and punctuation
in the lines of the letter quoted above.[103] Furthermore, his handwriting was not always clear, a fact of which he was painfully self-
conscious. In a letter to Synge on 10 October 1898, he asked him to
'Excuse the bad writing . . .'[104]

It may seem strange that an intelligent native speaker could not
express himself easily in written Irish but there is a reason. It has
already been shown how difficult it was even for trained scholars
to write a standard Irish that would be free from dialectal idiosyncrasies and spelling errors. For the haphazardly educated folk of
Aran, in whose schools Irish was a forbidden language, the problem
of writing Irish was immeasurably greater. They were very conscious of this. For instance, Martin's father wrote to Synge, as late as
December 1902, apologising for his poor written Irish: '. . . bhí mé
ag fanacht go mbeidh am ag Máirtín le litir a sgríobh duit, mar atá
fhios agad nac bhfuil mise ionán Gaedilge a sgríobh'. (I was waiting
until Martin would have time to write a letter to you, since you
know that I am not able to write Irish.)[105] In fact, the errors in
the father's letter are less frequent and less serious than those in
Martin's. McDonough is using the fact that he has a schooled son
as an excuse for not writing sooner himself, for he was painfully

conscious of the limitations of his written Irish.

Let us consider the entire letter from which Martin's enigmatic comment, discussed by Greene, was taken:

> 20 Feb 99.
> Dear John Synge, I am for a long time expecting a letter from you and I think you are forgetting Inishmain altogether. Mr Kilbride died a long time ago and his boat was on anchor in the harbour and the wind blew her to Black Head after his death. Tell me are you learning Irish since you went. We have a Branch of the Gaelic League in Inishmain now and the people is going on well with writing Irish and reading. I will write this letter in Irish but I do not know are you able to understand it. But I will write the next letter in Irish to you. Tell me will you come to see us . . .[106]

Obviously, Martin was taking lessons in the League's classes on the reading and writing of Irish. He was keen to write this letter in Irish but hesitated to do so, lest his composition be so flawed that Synge would find it incomprehensible. So, he postponed the attempt at a full-scale letter in Irish until the next occasion, when he hoped to be more skilled in writing his native language. Despite his disclaimer, he did append a few sentences in Irish to his letter, as if to try out his skill and demonstrate his progress to his friend. If we compare one of these Irish sentences with the corresponding passage in the letter above, it becomes clear just how superior was Martin's written English: 'Fuair Mr. Kilbride bás tá tamal mór ó shin agus bhí a bhád ar an ród Chill Rónaín a chuir an gala sior go ceann dubh tar éis a bhás é agus tá sé briste ó céile'. These are but a few examples of a widespread phenomenon of the time. In the words of one concerned Member of Parliament, a generation in the Gaeltacht had been 'brought up without a knowledge of how to read or write Irish'.[107] The islanders were compulsorily educated by a Board of Education schoolmaster who knew no Irish. A Gaelic League pamphlet, entitled *The Case for Bilingual Education in the Irish-Speaking Districts*, called on the Board 'to permit reading and writing of Irish to be taught side by side with English'.[108] While this agitation went on, the amateur teachers of the League held weekly classes on the islands such as those attended by Synge.

Another islander, John McDonough, 'could not write Gaelic at all'. Whenever he wished to write to Synge, he 'had to dictate a letter

in English to his brother Martin, who turned it into Irish'.[109]
Martin's own literary Irish was poor and his sentences were devoid
of structure. In many letters he was forced to abandon Irish in mid-
paragraph and resort to literary English, which he handled with as
little confidence. Martin writes the letter under discussion, says Synge,
'beginning in Irish but ending it in English' (*Prose* p. 103). The
sequence is important. He was manifestly unsure of his ability to
make himself understood in Irish and provided for this contingency
by adding material in English. So, despite the opinion of Synge's
biographer, it seems wiser to see the English sentences as appendages
to explain the Irish, and not as the pith of the letter. This is certainly
the way in which Synge saw them. Those islanders of Synge's
acquaintance seemed to regard English as an easier literary language
than Irish and they wrote it among themselves when communicating
by letter. Martin wrote all letters to his mother in English, says
Synge, because 'he is the only one of the family who can read or
write in Irish' (*Prose*, p. 107). The result of all this was that the
islanders' written English in general, excelled their written Irish. This
is confirmed by a passage in *The Aran Islands* where Synge discussed the problem. He was reading a dual-language textbook with
a scholarly boy of the island: 'In most of the stories we read, where
the English and Irish are printed side by side, I see him looking across
to the English in passages that are a little obscure, though he is
indignant if I say that he knows English better than Irish. Probably,
he knows the local Irish better than English, and printed English
better than printed Irish, as the latter has frequent dialect forms he
does not know . . .' (*Prose*, p. 133).

It must now be clear why Synge omitted that crucial sentence of
Martin's from the letter quoted in *The Aran Islands*. The deleted
sentence was not germane to his purpose in reproducing the letter
and, if published, it could only have caused Martin acute embarrass-
ment about his poor written Irish. The boy-scholar became highly
indignant when Synge gently suggested that he might have known
written English better than written Irish. Martin's own feelings can
hardly have been very different. Indeed, Maurice Bourgeois was told
that 'for a long time' Martin held a grudge against Synge for having
printed the letters at all.[110] Martin had been upset at seeing one of
his letters reproduced in Synge's article, 'The Last Fortress of the
Celt', in *The Gael* of April 1901. However, Bourgeois was wrong
in suggesting that the grudge was borne for a long time, since Synge
wrote to Lady Gregory on 22 February 1902 that: 'The Inishmain

people have forgiven me at last for my indiscretion and I have just
had a very kindly letter from Mourteen . . .'[111]

Nevertheless, the whole incident would have made Synge doubly
careful not to offend Martin when the time came to publish *The Aran
Islands* in April 1907. The notorious deleted sentence should, therefore, be seen as yet another effort on Synge's part to spare Martin's
tender feelings and not as a clumsy attempt to cover up his own
inability to read Irish. This interpretation is borne out by the other
alterations which he made to Martin's letters, such as the correction
of spelling errors and the remoulding of his syntax into a more
graceful style. For example: 'I now see that your time is comming
(sic) on for the future to come to Inishmain to learn your native
language . . .'[112] is turned into the more lucid, but hesitantly
charming: 'I see now that your time is coming round to come to
this place' (*Prose*, p. 126).

In their correspondence, Martin never voiced any doubt about
Synge's ability to read Irish. Indeed, after expressing doubts about
the clarity of his own written Irish, Martin went on directly to
ask Synge to write him a letter in his native language: 'I will write
this letter all in Irish but I do not know will you understand it let
you write the next letter in Irish if you don't I won't look on it'.[113]
This is a request which Martin would not have made unless he
felt Synge equal to the assignment.

Synge proved himself able for the task, as is clear from the following draft of a letter written to Martin, probably in January 1899.
Composed in a clear though somewhat graceless style, it indicates
that Synge was a keen reader of books in modern Irish:

90 Rue d'Assas, Paris
A Mhartin dílis,
  Is mór an t-am nach bhfuil litir uait agam. Tá súil agam go
bhfuil tú agus do mhuintir go maith na sláinte. Tá mé maith go
leor fós, acht tá mórán tinneas ins an tír so anis.
  Tháinic mé ar Blauellen trí mhí ó shoin agus bhí gala an-mhór
ann an lá sin, agus ba beag nach raibh a long gaile briste ar na ail.
  Tá go leor leabh Gaeilge agam anis agus mé ag l go minic.
(Dear Martin; it's a long time since I had a letter from you. I
hope that you and your people are in good health. I am quite
well still, but there is much disease in this country at present.
  I came upon Blauellen (?) three months ago and there was a
very great gale that day—the steam-ship was almost wrecked

upon the rocks.
I have many Gaelic books now which I often read.)[114]

This letter, with its abbreviations of key words, is a model draft of the letter which Synge wrote and posted. This rough draft alone remains. If Synge could write Irish as clearly as that, then he would have had little difficulty in reading the language. Synge's use of the language is competent by comparison with Martin's halting attempts. Martin was well aware of this. Even after only one visit to Aran, Synge displayed sufficient ability in letter-writing in Irish to evoke a rambling reply in admiration from his friend:

> October 10, 1898.
> A chara ionmhuin dilis,
> Furas do litir beagán laetha o soinn agus go deimhin duit bhí brod agus lugfar orm faoi e a bheith sgriobhthadh a ngaedilge agus budh deas brodual muintric an litir é agus moran brod orm . . .
> (My dear true friend; I received your letter a few days ago and be certain that I was proud and delighted that it was written in Gaelic and it was a nice, fine, comradely letter, making me very proud.)[115]

Elsewhere in the letter, Martin remarked

> . . . an litir deirnach fuar me uait bhí se sgriobhthagh go deas le litir dhuinne air bith a chonnaic me ariamh . . .
> (. . . the last letter I got from you was written as well as any letter I have ever seen).

As Martin told Synge at the close of his letter, this is a significant compliment to come from one who had already corresponded with Patrick Pearse earlier in that summer.

THE DIALECTS OF NORTH CONNACHT AND MUNSTER

Synge never returned to Aran after 1902, the year in which he wrote *Riders to the Sea*, but the break with Aran did not imply an end to his study of Irish. It has already been remarked that Eoin MacNeill had exhorted learners of Irish to be familiar with the leading dialects of the different provinces. So, in the summer of 1905 Synge had the chance to renew his Connacht Irish, when he toured the western seaboard with Jack B. Yeats. The playwright was to write a series of twelve articles for the *Manchester Guardian*, while Yeats was to supply sketches. Synge's familiarity with the Irish of the province may have been one of the reasons why C. P. Scott commissioned him to write the articles. At all events, Jack Yeats wrote afterwards: 'His knowledge of Gaelic was a great assistance to him in talking to the people. I remember him holding a great conversation in Irish and English with an innkeeper's wife in a Mayo inn . . .'[116] Another such incident occurred in Spiddal, Co. Galway, when Synge and Yeats gave alms to an old beggar-woman. As Synge narrates: '. . . as she was moving away with an ordinary "God save you", I said a blessing to her in Irish to show her that I knew her own language if she chose to use it. Immediatey she turned back towards me and began her thanks again, this time with extraordinary profusion' (*Prose*, p. 287). The fact that Synge could speak Irish in this way was of lasting value in allowing him to achieve a rapport with the ordinary folk. On this trip, even as far west as Gorumna, the Irish of an old man posed no problems (*Prose*, p. 306).

In the summers of 1903, 1904 and 1905, Synge travelled through the Kerry Gaeltacht and studied the Munster dialect. On the last of these visits, Synge made a particular effort to improve his knowledge. His host-to-be in Ballyferriter, Mr Long, wrote reassuringly in July 1905, that 'my household all speak Paddy's language'.[117] But even while he was still journeying on the Killarney train, Synge heard a conversation in Munster Irish which he followed with ease (*Prose*, p. 237). Predictably, he experienced difficulty in speaking the Munster dialect, which has important idiosyncrasies of vocabulary and pronunciation (*Prose*, p. 248). Nevertheless, he felt sufficiently pleased with his progress to write a letter to Lady Gregory on 4 August:

I am in the centre of the most Gaelic part of Munster—10 miles beyond Dingle close to Smerwick Harbour—and I am making great strides with the Munster dialect. I have realised that I must resuscitate my Irish this year or lose it altogether, so I am hard at work . . . the people are very ready to talk Irish and be friendly which is a help. So many of the Mayo people are hard to get at, for one reason or another, that I did not have much talk up there.[118]

On the Blasket Islands, Synge was able to entertain his hosts with ghost stories in Irish (*Prose*, p. 253). It is clear that, over the intervening three years, he had retained the Irish of Aran and that he had lost little of its flavour. Its idioms sometimes puzzled his Kerry host, the 'king' of the island: 'He had little English, but when I tried him in Irish we got on well though he did not follow any Connaught forms I let slip by accident . . .' (*Prose*, p. 275). Synge's Irish was a good deal better than the 'king's' English and it was easier for them both to hold their conversation in the native language. In a letter to Lady Gregory, on 20 August, the dramatist was rather less sanguine about the problems posed by dialectal differences and complained that he had 'great trouble with it sometimes'.[119]

The notebook kept by Synge on this visit is marked 'Notes in Ballyferriter and the Great Blasket Islands'. It contains the customary lists of vocabulary but this is clearly the vocabulary of an advanced student seeking to penetrate the inner style of the language. The phrases noted are more stylishly idiomatic—'tulca báisdidh: torrent of rain'—and the mind is forever curious, seeking to put the new word to imaginative use, in accounting for the placename, 'river Tolca'.[120] Thus Synge employs an idiom acquired in Kerry to explain the name of a Dublin river. Here is a typical word-list;

> calmánta: shy
> crunca: a man bowed with age
> tarcuisne: contempt
> thug sé stinntín orm: he offended me
> scafaire: a fine fellow
> sceimhle: terror
> aicíd: disease[121]

Among his notes Synge listed the varied uses of a single idiom:

> Cia bhí'n bhur dteannta: who was with you?
> dteannta chéile: with each other
> le do cois: at your side[122]

Synge also made lists of Irish words which occur in the English of the folk, and some of these phrases found their way into *The Playboy of the Western World*, which he was writing at the time. For example, he made the entry 'strílín: conversation' in a notebook[123] and this word crops up in the play:

PEGEEN (Nodding with approval): If you weren't destroyed travelling you'd have as much talk and streeleen, I'm thinking, as Owen Roe O'Sullivan or the poets of Dingle Bay . . . (*Plays 2*, p. 81).

The employment of the original Irish word in the play is no mere affectation of style but a realistic reflection of Anglo-Irish usage. Even outside Irish speaking districts a limited number of words, among them 'streeleen', have passed directly from Irish into Anglo-Irish usage. There are traces in these notes of Synge's continuing interest in European parallels to Irish idioms: '*cravat* in Irish still is carabhat';[124] and a number of proverbs, a list of books on the Dingle peninsula and an unfinished translation of *Eibhlín a Rúin* complete this notebook. However, the most appealing item is the Gaelic Alphabet which Synge took down from 'Mr Daly of Dunquin':

A	an cúpla	N	an blathach
B	an beach	O	an fáinne
C	an crudh capaill	P	an pípín
D	leath na gealaighe	Q	an iarbhaillín
E	an mart	R	an randaimín
F	faideog	S	an phéistín
G	an spiacla	T	an maide croise
H	an droim cathaorach	U	an galairín
I	an geapa baitín	V	an cupáinín
J	an camáinín	W	na g-caidhpeanna
K	an eochar	X	na spur
L	an tuagh	Y	na gcosa caola
M	an t-im	Z	na gcosa cama

As a result of these years of study Samuel Synge wrote that John's final mastery of Irish was such that he actually thought in the language while speaking it.[126] This claim is definitely excessive. Nevertheless, it is clear that Synge knew a great deal more Irish than is normally supposed. However, a final assessment of the extent of this knowledge must await a consideration of his work as a scholar and translator of the classic works in the language.

3 Scholar and Translator

THE SIGNIFICANCE OF GEOFFREY KEATING

By 1902, when Synge had paid the last of his visits to Aran, he was not only competent in spoken Irish, but was also conversant with the literary language in all its phases from the Classical Irish of 1200 to the idiom of contemporary literature. On 8 December 1900 he had reviewed J. C. MacErlean's edition of the poems of Geoffrey Keating, *Dánta, Amhráin is Caointe Sheathrúin Céitinn*, in the *Speaker*. So pleased was the editor with the performance of this assignment that on 6 September 1902 Synge was again called upon to pass judgement on the work of Keating. On this occasion the book for review was the first volume of David Comyn's edition of *Foras Feasa ar Éirinn*: *The History of Ireland* (1902). This work was the acknowledged masterpiece of Classical Irish prose and 'not an easy book' in the judgement of Daniel Corkery, an authority on the Irish language.[1] Synge could not have gone to a more taxing or inspiring source than Keating, described by Douglas Hyde as the greatest author in the classical idiom: 'He brought the art of writing limpid Irish to its highest perfection, and ever since the publication of his history of Ireland some two hundred and fifty years ago, the modern language may be said to have been stereotyped'.[2]

In his article on the poetry of Keating, Synge showed himself fully aware of the great significance of MacErlean's publication at that time. It was, he said, ' . . . of considerable interest in the history of Gaelic literature for this volume is the first collected

54

edition of the works of a Gaelic poet that has ever been given to the public . . . ' (*Prose*, p. 356). Neither this nor any subsequent Gaelic book reviewed by Synge was 'elementary', as Pádraic Colum has suggested.[3] MacErlean's work was erudite and is still the standard text on its subject. The very existence of Synge's review makes nonsense of Colum's claim that he ' . . . did not know the learned poets who had the full Gaelic tradition—indeed, I do not think that O'Rahilly, O'Bruadair, Geoffrey Keating, had been published in any accessible form in his time'.[4] In fact, he had not only studied and reviewed the poems of Keating, but had translated many of them into English as well. As for the poet Egan O'Rahilly, he had studied examples of his work as early as 1892 in *Songs of the Munster Bards*.[5]

In the review, Synge gives a summary of the life of Keating, as given in pp. 3–7 of MacErlean's book. The shape of the review owes much to this potted biography, but the reviewer gives more details of Keating's sermon against Lady Elinor Laffin than are offered by MacErlean. This additional material was taken by Synge from *A Literary History of Ireland* by Douglas Hyde. In a chapter on Keating, Hyde told of his education at a seminary on the continent and went on to quote an account of the sorrows of the exiled intellectuals of the period:

'The same to me,' cries, in the hexameter of the Gael, some unhappy wanderer contemporaneous with Keating, driven to find refuge where he could, 'the same to me are the mountain or the ocean, Ireland or the West of Spain, I have shut and made fast the gates of sorrow over my heart'.[6]

In a footnote to the same page, Hyde gave the Gaelic source for this quotation:

Ionann dam sliabh a's sáile
Éire a's iarthar Easpáine
Do chuireas dúnta go deas
Geata dlúth an doilgheas.

Synge translated this poem from Hyde's volume in a notebook which he kept on his visit to Inishmaan in 1899. This was his first ever translation of a piece of Gaelic poetry and his version is close to Hyde's:

> The same to me mountain & the salt
> Sea Erin or the West of Spain
> I have shut and made fast
> The gates of sorrow on my heart.[7]

A Literary History of Ireland appears to be the only book in which this quatrain was ever reproduced, for its author claimed that the lines were 'copied from a MS in Trinity College'.[8] This proves that Synge not only studied Hyde's book in the year of its publication, but also that he read the section on Keating with particular interest. In this chapter Hyde proceeded to give an account of Keating's sermon denouncing Lady Laffin for her affair with the President of Munster. The lady instigated Carew 'to put the anti-Popery laws in execution against Keating'.[9] Hyde described how the persecuted priest hid for a time in the Glen of Aherlow and later travelled in disguise throughout the country, collecting material for his history of Ireland. It was from this account that Synge drew the material about Lady Laffin in his article.

It is scarcely surprising that the following notes on Keating's life may be found in Synge's Aran notebook of 1899, on the page previous to that bearing the quoted quatrain. These notes appear under the letter 'H', to denote their source in Hyde's book:

—educated on the continent
—said to have travelled about the country in disguise studying the MSS.[10]

Synge's review was written just a year after he had read *A Literary History of Ireland*. He augments it with material about the life of Keating in an attempt to supply a background to the study of the poems, for MacErlean himself had given too little information in his scanty preface. Hence Synge's paradoxical concentration on the prose of Keating, which occupies half the space in a review of the poetry.

In the article Synge shows that he is interested not only in the 'folk', but also in 'the more literary aspects of Gaelic'. He welcomes the 'new mood of intellectual patriotism', as distinct from narrow political patriotism, which has given the impulse to such studies (*Prose*, p. 356). In fact, as an exponent of literary Irish, Keating is one of the crucial influences on Synge's mind and art, an influence more palpable than that of Molière, Wordsworth or other much-canvassed mentors. The great lesson which he learned from Keating was the fusion of scholarship with the creative imagination, the incorporation of his learning into his artistic sensibility. His description of Keating, 'a man of about forty', 'wandering through the country' with 'a sombre shade to his disposition that we find in most of his poetry' (*Prose*, p. 357) might well have been applied to himself, his own wanderings and the brooding melancholy which suffused his poetry even more than his plays. Among Keating's crucial attributes, he lists 'all the scholarship of his century' and a 'remarkable literary talent' (*Prose*, p. 357). It is the fusion of these two characteristics which so attracts him. In his own art Synge was to follow Keating's method, harnessing his learning and Gaelic studies in its service.

In the work of Keating, Synge could discern the whole cast of mind of the western countryman: 'the work has many personal traits of considerable interest, which show the shrewd observation, and naïve reasoning that are common to the learned men of his age and the peasants of our own. One might almost say that it is history written in the spirit of the folktale' (*Prose*, p. 358). Synge applied this approach to literature—so much so that we might say of his work that it is literature written in the spirit of the folk-tale. His plays and prose are deeply indebted to folklore; but even those devices in his plays which do not have a source in folklore are recreations within its spirit. For instance, in *The Shadow of the Glen* Nora Burke says that she must call upon her sister to lay out the corpse of her husband, since he has forbidden her to touch it. This is a dramatic device which has no basis in Irish folklore. Nevertheless, it is entirely consistent with the taboos and prohibitions which are so much a part of the folklore traditions surrounding the dead. It was this combination of cosmopolitan, literary sophistication and folkloristic, peasant naïvety in Keating—his 'half-mediaeval, half-modern temperament' (*Prose*, p. 359)—which made him so important to the dramatist. After all, Synge wished to infuse the sophisticated forms of modern poetry and drama with the imagination of mediaeval folklore. This was an aim which he shared with most contemporary Irish writers. Time and again Yeats had pointed out that, while other writers sought the peasant, his movement sought the peasant's imagination.[11]

Synge's second article on Keating appeared in the columns of the *Speaker* on 6 September 1902. His assessment of *Foras Feasa ar Éirinn: The History of Ireland*, as edited by David Comyn, was long and scrupulous. He congratulated Comyn on his 'carefully edited' text, but astutely withheld final judgement on the grounds that 'the notes to the whole edition are to be published in the final volume, so it is not yet possible to judge of this important section of the editor's work' (*Prose*, p. 360). Synge showed himself still conscious of the need for background information on the life of Keating, in the light of which more might be inferred from his patently autobiographical poems. He gently chided Comyn:

> It is to be regretted that Mr. Comyn has not given more attention to Keating's biography in his preface, where he brings together a few localities and dates without stating on what authority they are placed. He says, in passing, that a full biography of Keating is still a desideratum, but it may be doubted whether there are materials enough for such a work, and the preface to this edition would have been an excellent place to collect the facts that can be known . . . (*Prose*, p. 360).

Synge also criticised Comyn for being 'too inclined to treat Keating as a serious historian', for acquiescing too readily to a semi-fictional view of the past, for seeming 'to compare Keating's way of dealing with his materials with the way Dr. Liddell deals with early Roman history' (*Prose*, p. 361). This was another echo from the literary history of Hyde, who had remarked that Keating, lacked 'critical faculty' in his treatment of the ancient manuscript sources.[12] Synge took issue with Comyn on this point, preferring to treat Keating frankly as 'a quaint and half-mediaeval writer with no notion of history in the modern sense of the word' (*Prose*, p. 361). Subsequent scholarship has corroborated his remark that the work is 'chiefly useful for the information it gives about MSS., to which Keating had access, but which have since perished' (*Prose*, p. 361).

Synge's fascination with the relationship between Gaelic and European literary traditions manifests itself again in this review, where he finds 'interest of a high order in the way a learned Irishman at the beginning of the seventeenth century saw Ireland in her relation to England and Europe' (*Prose*, p. 362). In writing of Keating in this way, the dramatist may well have been thinking of the parallels with his own experience. In his view, Keating differs from the other writers of his time in his combination of 'natural talent' with 'foreign studies' (*Prose*, p. 362)—that fusion of scholarly discipline and natural artistry which had initially fascinated the young playwright. In praising Keating's studies on the continent,

Synge may have been covertly hinting at the value of his own post-graduate studies in Paris under Passy, Le Braz and de Jubainville: 'In a purely intellectual sense the intercourse he must have had with men who had been in touch with the first scholarship of Europe was of great use in correcting the narrowing influence of a simply Irish tradition' (*Prose*, p. 361).

Synge was no mere Gaelicist but a man who brought a thoroughly European sensibility to bear on the native literary tradition. He modelled himself on writers such as Keating, who had managed to Europeanise Irish writing without making it any less Gaelic. This was also true of the contemporary Irish writers whom Synge numbered among his friends. Yeats endlessly urged the writers of the Gaelic League to study Molière and the European classics,[13] while Stephen MacKenna consistently refused to measure modern writing in Irish by any other than European standards.[14] Similarly in this review, Synge praised Keating for his correction of 'narrowing' or 'simply Irish' traditions. This spirit informs each of Synge's later attacks on the chauvinism of the Gaelic League. For him, Keating was more than a writer whose books had to be reviewed. He was a vital model in whose work he detected vital parallels to his own previous experiences and current literary sensibility. The comparison of Keating's work with that of other Gaelic writers of his age recalled for Synge, 'in a curiously remote way, the difference that can be felt between the work of Irish writers of the present day who have spent part of their life in London, and the work of men who have not left Ireland' (*Prose*, p. 361). The contrast between Keating and the other writers of his time emphasises the contrast between Synge and many minor Irish writers of his era. Synge perceived that only those who leave Ireland for a time can truly interpret her, or, as Joyce was later to write, that the shortest way to Tara is via Holyhead.

One of the great problems for the writers of the Irish revival lay in the fact that their movement had been accompanied and explained by no critic of commensurate stature and ability. In this review, Synge sought to provide the kind of criticism by which the contemporary movement could be assessed—the judgements on a writer implicit in every line written by the ancestral authors of the language. His programme for Irish writers was utterly traditional. The incorporation of the European into the Gaelic sensibility goes back more than a thousand years to St Columbanus and the Irish missionaries of the sixth century who founded centres of learning on the continent. This tradition reaches back also to the learned men at home who attracted students from all parts of Europe, earning for Ireland the title 'Island of Saints and Scholars'. In the period of Classical Irish from 1200 to 1600, the native love poets assimilated the themes of 'amour courtois' poetry into those syllabic metres which had already been exploited for centuries by the professional bards. Keating was one of the very last links in that thousand-year-old chain of young scholars who had studied at the great universities of Europe and returned to apply this erudition within the disciplines of native art.

In a real sense, Synge can be seen as having revived that tradition. After the collapse of the Gaelic aristocracy about the year 1600, the professional bards lost their patronage. Like Keating, they were left to wander through the countryside, plying a redundant and increasingly debased art. The two poems of Keating, which Synge translated in his review, were wrought in the intricate stanzas of the ancient bards; but the long-lined poems by the same author, which Synge later came to translate, in private versions, represent the looser order of poetry which was soon to rout the strict bardic metres from the modern language. Keating stands at a focal point in Gaelic tradition, one of the last great writers to employ bardic forms and one of the first to turn to the looser metres of popular poetry. With the disintegration of the bardic orders and the plantations of the seventeenth century, the Gaelic tradition lost its European dimension, turned in upon itself and had no Renaissance. Irish literature in the late-eighteenth and nineteenth centuries is filled with a sense of its own weakness and intellectual introversion. Therefore, to Synge's audience in Ireland at the start of the twentieth century, the fusion in his art of Gaelic and European elements was strange and new. For his critics in the Gaelic League and Sinn Féin, 'Europe' meant only the 'cynical decadence that passes current in the Latin Quarter'.[15]

In this context, Synge's article on Keating assumed crucial proportions. In it, he sought to remind Irish writers and readers of their own lost European tradition. He explained that this was the classic Gaelic tradition, the central intellectual inheritance of his fellow-countrymen. So committed was he to this concept of a lost intellectual life in Irish that he returned to it later in the review: 'In another way, the traditional knowledge of old or, at least, of middle Irish which Keating shares with the Four Masters, Duald Mac Firbis, and others, proves that an independent intellectual life existed in Ireland till that time, quite apart from the shifting political life that is seized by the historians' (*Prose,* p. 362). This distinction between 'independent intellectual life' and 'shifting political life' is a development of an idea first expressed in the earlier review of Keating's poetry. There, Synge had commented on the 'new mood of intellectual patriotism' which had led to the revival of interest in 'the literary aspect of Gaelic'. This juxtaposition of the words 'intellectual' and 'patriotism', while it may have surprised the nationalists of the time, clearly insists that patriotism is not mainly a matter of national politics. Synge may well have taken the concept of an independent political life persisting amid the political turmoil of the age from the following sentences in Hyde's *A Literary History of Ireland*:

> . . . It was indeed an age of national scholarship which has never since been equalled. It was this half century which produced in rapid succession Geoffrey Keating, the Four Masters, and Duald Mac Firbis, men of whom any age or country might have been proud, men who amid the war, rapine and conflagration, that rolled through the country at the heels of the English soldiers, still strove to save from the general wreck those records of their country which to-day make the name of Ireland honourable for her antiquities, traditions and history, in the eyes of the scholars of Europe.[16]

In making precisely the same point as Hyde, it is no accident that Synge should have cited the Four Masters, Mac Firbis and Keating as his examples too.

The similarities between Synge and Keating are endless. Both were from 'outside' stock, Keating from an Anglo-Norman family[17] and Synge from the Anglo-Irish. Both returned to Ireland to travel the country, collecting manuscript, folk-tale and anecdote from a culture that was fast dying. Both were dogged by 'physical and moral sufferings' (*Prose,* p. 357). Both incorporated their erudition into their artistic productions. Both adopted identical positions in respect of the national culture. Both worked admirably in poetry as well as in prose.

THE TRANSLATION OF KEATING'S POETRY AND PROSE

The most significant feature of Synge's review of the poetry of

Keating in December 1900 was the publication of his own translations of four stanzas by the master. These versions mark the development of an interest first exemplified in the translation of the four-line stanza from Hyde's text in 1899. In style these translations are quiet, even tame. They catch the simplicity of Keating's work, the direct language praised in the review, but not the sinuously intricate rhythms. Synge is still nervous enough about his knowledge of Irish to allow concern for linguistic accuracy to overcome any desire to render the spirit of a text in a freer translation. The scholar is as yet in control of the artist:

KEATING	SYNGE
A bhean lán do stuaim	Oh woman full of wiles,
Congbhuig uaim do lámh.	Keep away from me thy hand.
Ní fear gníomha sinn,	I am not a man for these things,
Gé taoi tinn d'ár ngrádh.	Though thou art sick for my love.
Ná síl mé go saobh,	Do not think me perverse,
Arís ná claon ceann,	Do not bend thy head,
Bíodh ár ngrádh gan gníomh	Let our love be inactive
Go bráth, a shíodh sheang.[18]	Forever, oh slender fairy.

(*Prose*, p. 357)

At no point in his commentary does Synge claim these versions as his own work, but they are, having been painstakingly drafted in his notebooks. There were no English versions in MacErlean's volume.

Synge trades with Keating, line for line and word for word. His third line, with its appropriately dismissive 'these things' (dignifying them with no specific mention), nicely solves the dilemma posed by the poetic ambiguity of 'gníomha', a learned technical term for copulation used in the ancient medical tracts. Although he remains close to the Irish text, he is close in a free way. His simple lines are not a crib, but rather they constitute a poem in its own right. The concentrated classical idiom of Keating does not deter him, and the rich ambiguity of 'gníomha' does not paralyse his mind, which responds freely to the challenge. The short monosyllabic lines of the English are sufficiently close to the Irish to evoke its terse tight-lipped rhetoric of renunciation. Such literal attention to the details of a poem results in a competent translation when the original text is a simple lyric, composed of short lines and direct statement. It is to Synge's credit that he chose a lyric such as this for his first public exercise in translation from Classical Irish. For the clear idiom of this lyric is delightfully susceptible to a literal translation, especially by a man who was possessed of a sensibility very much in harmony with Keating's. A longer poem by some other Gaelic poet, in a figurative idiom or a more complex syntax, might not have translated itself so obligingly. For his earliest translation, Synge shrewdly selected a simple but powerful lyric, rightly one of the most famous in the language.

Just how guarded he was in this version, however, is made clear by a cursory glance at the 'Vocabulary of the Poems' at the back of MacErlean's book. Synge relied heavily on this for translation of the more ambiguous or 'poetic' words in the piece. This explains the rather muted sense of correctness which pervades his rendition. It is clear that he has closely followed some key words of MacErlean's vocabulary:

p. 191 stuaim f.	ingenuity, wiles
p. 126 congbhaim	I keep
p. 183 saobh	silly, perverse
p. 122 claonaim	I incline, bend down
p. 188 síodhaidhe síoghda	fairy
p. 186 seang	thin, slender, graceful[19]

Nevertheless, Synge did display real discretion and his version is much more than a beginner's exercise. 'Wiles' is better by far than 'ingenuity', offered as first choice by MacErlean. 'Wile' was, in fact, the word finally employed by Frank O'Connor in the most famous translation of all, many years after Synge's.[20] 'Keep away' is more insistent and menacing than 'keep', while 'perverse' is far more resonant than MacErlean's rather weak 'silly', which is too light-hearted an adjective in this context. Synge wisely omits the translation of 'arís', opting to open the second line with the emphatically repeated 'do not'. It must be admitted, however, that the final two lines let the whole translation down into bathos. As a translator Synge shows that he is still a novice, capable of under-mining his best effects. 'Inactive' is far too journalistic a word, without being sufficiently literal a translation—'unfulfilled' or 'untold' would be better. The bathos is complete with 'oh slender

fairy'. The problem with the last line is, of course, that no single
translation of 'seang' can convey all the nuances of beauty, physical
excitement and menace conjured up by the word in Irish poetry.
'Seang' was an adjective which came to be applied to beautiful
women so often, and in so many contexts, that eventually it assumed
the functions of a noun.

Synge's second translation, published in the review, is of *Mo
Bheannacht Leat a Scribhinn*:

KEATING

Mo bheannacht leat, a scríbhinn,
Go hinis aoibhinn Ealga.
's truagh nach léir dom a bheanna
Gidh gnáth a dteanna dearga.

Slán dá huaisle is dá hoireacht,
Slán go roi-bheacht dá cléirchibh,
Slán dá bantrachtaibh caoine,
Slán dá saoithibh re héigse.[21]

SYNGE

My blessing to you my writing,
To the pleasant noble island:
And it is pity I cannot see her hilltops,
Though usual their red beacons.

A salutation to her nobles and to her clan meetings,
A particular salutation to her clerics,
A salutation to her weeping women,
A salutation to her learned men of poetry.   (*Prose*, p. 356)

'Leat', at the opening, would be more satisfactorily and more literally
translated as 'with you'. 'Usual' is banal in just the way that
'slender fairy' was in the earlier poem, though both are literal
equivalents of their originals. The third line is, however, strangely
impressive. Apart from proving that Synge did not myopically
follow MacErlean's vocabulary, it displays imaginative grammatical
idiosyncrasies. 'Léir' is rendered by MacErlean as 'visible, evident,
clear', but Synge opts for the more directly dramatic 'see', sub-
stituting a verb for an adjective. For 'beanna' he offers 'hilltops'

and not 'mountain peaks'. Above all, the line is notable for the suppression of the clausal relative 'that'. This was to become a feature of Synge's Anglo-Irish dialect, being a literal translation of the syntax of the Irish language. 'Weeping women' is a nicely alliterative example of onomatopoeia, obtained, however, at the cost of a mistranslation. The rhythm and movement of the second stanza are vastly improved, largely because the stanza is built around the repetition of the ringing 'salutation'. This feature of Irish poetry was to be increasingly used by Synge in his plays, where a whole speech is often built around the steady repetition of a key word or phrase. For example, in *The Shadow of the Glen*, Nora Burke angrily chides her husband who has thrown her out of the house: 'What way will yourself be that day, Daniel Burke? What way will you be that day and you lying down a long while in your grave? For it's bad you are living, and it's bad you'll be when you're dead (*Plays 1*, p. 55).

Once again, to see how closely Synge still relied on MacErlean's vocabulary in this version, the following list may be useful:

p. 185 scribheann m. writing, letter, document
p. 106 aoibhinn pleasant
p. 142 ealga noble ms Inis Ealga i. Eire
p. 165 leir visible, evident (with *do*) clear
p. 111 beann f. peak, mountain peak
p. 195 teann neut. fire, beacon
p. 189 slan noun (1) salutation, welfare
p. 176 oireacht f. gathering of the clan
p. 123 cleireach m. clergyman, cleric, d.pl. cleirchibh
p. 110 bantracht m. (collect.) company of women, women-folk
p. 183 saoi m. sage, savant, nobleman, d.pl. saoithibh
p. 143 éigse, f. art, skill . . . 'saoi re héigse' learned in poetry[22]

So, in the winter of 1900–1, Synge's interest in translation from Irish had been irrevocably aroused and tested. He was manifestly less than satisfied with these early attempts, although he included them in his published review in the *Speaker*. It is clear that he retained his reviewer's copy of MacErlean's edition and that he continued to develop his skill as a translator. The notebook which he kept on Aran in 1901 is dominated by his translations from the poetry of Keating. Significantly, he also began to translate the oral literature of Aran into English, for it is in this notebook that the Irish text and translation of *Rucard Mór* first appear. His studies on this visit to Aran must have been devoted totally to translation for, during this holiday on the islands, he also made his translation into English of *Oidhe Chloinne Uisnigh*. This was the text which would form the basis of his final play, *Deirdre of the Sorrows*.

The poems of Keating, rendered in the 1901 notebook, are a great deal more complex than those translated in the review of the previous winter. Synge's versions display an increasing independence of spirit and a greater sense of the artistic potential of a translation. There is much less reliance on the supporting vocabulary of MacErlean. Even when he does consult the list of words, the translation frequently improves upon the editor's own version:

KEATING

Táin óig-fhear ar feodh dá bhfír-sheirc
's as dul i dtáimh do ghrádh na síoghan;
Cáidhe an t-ól ó thós gach laoi ghil
Go fuineadh gréine um néall na hoidche.

Scor marc-shluaigh ag athnuadhadh a gcraoiseach
D'éis a dtaisteal ó chreacha gach críche,
Drong don éigse is dréacht-ghlan díoghlaim
Ag déanamh duan don tsluagh dá ngríosadh.

Uch! mo nuar! cá huair do-chífead
'san riocht chéadna an glé-bhrugh gnaoi-gheal?
Mar baintear a thuir ó thigh dá aoirde,
Leigthear mar sin a thruil go híseal.

Truagh mo chúrsa, a chú na mí-chean,
A shaoghail shanntaigh mheabhlaigh bhaoisigh,
An mur do-chonnarc i n-uraidh go líonmhar
Mar tá sé i mbliadhna 'na siabhra síthe.[23]

SYNGE

Band of young men withering with deep love
And going unto death for the love of queens
Where is the drinking from the beginning of each
   bright day

Till the setting of the sun in the cloud of the night?

Troop of horse-men renewing their spears
After a journey for the plunder of every country.
Throng of poetry and [untranslated]
Making poems for the inciting of hosts.

Alas my woe what time shall I see
In the same state the bright castle of gay aspect?
When a tower is taken off from a house however
high
There is left thus a summit that is low.

Wretched my course, hound of evil
[untranslated]
The castle I saw last year in abundance
Now it is this year in haunted desolation.[24]

The second line of the final stanza is left untranslated. There can
only be two possible deductions from this, both of them pointing
towards Synge's increasing independence of MacErlean. Either he
deliberately refrained from consulting the key, in order to test his
powers of Irish more fully than ever; or he did consult MacErlean's
key and found the proposed translations unsatisfactory. This line
contains three sonorous onomatopoeiac adjectives of the type denounced in Synge's review of Keating's poetry. Each of the
adjectives is rendered in English at the back of MacErlean's book,
but perhaps Synge felt that they were not thus translatable. His
complaint in the original review may have arisen from a difficulty
akin to his problem here; for even in Irish it is hard to define
what each adjective might mean. 'Covetous, deceitful foolish life'
is offered by MacErlean, but this seems top-heavy. Seán O'Casey
encountered an identical problem when he sought to provide an
English version for the following sequence of adjectives from a
Gaelic poem:

> tá m'urla sgainneach,
> bachallach, búclach . . . [25]

He despairingly concluded that these adjectives were 'untranslate-
able'. Over a century earlier, Charlotte Brooke had been painfully

aware of the bluntness of English in its attempt to render complex
Gaelic adjectives: 'One compound epithet must often be translated
by two lines of English verse, and, on such occasion, much of the
beauty is necessarily lost: the force and effect of the thought being
wrecked by too slow an introduction into the mind.'[26] Edward
Walsh, probably the most brilliant and neglected translator of the
last century, cited this as the insuperable problem posed by Gaelic
poetry, 'a pyramid of words upon a single thought', such as the
proliferation of adjectives in Keating's line. Walsh asserted that the
translator 'seeks, in vain, for equivalent terms in the English tongue
to express the graceful redundancies of the original'.[27]

The emergence of the Anglo-Irish dialect of Synge's plays is clear
in such literal translations as 'going unto death' or in the beautiful
imagery and rhythm of the line:

> Till the setting of the sun in the cloud of the night.

This is a perfect example of the way in which two threadbare poetic
conceits in Irish are magically revitalised by the simple expedient
of translating them into English. This is one of those delightfully
unexpected rewards which, now and then, raise the heart of a
translator—the power suddenly acquired by worn phrases when they
are literally rendered in a second language. This was a lesson which
the dramatist was to apply in his plays, many of which turn conventional clichés of Gaelic verse into speeches of lyric beauty.[28]
George Moore once wrote rather wickedly that Synge was
responsible for the discovery that, if one translated Irish word for
word into English, then the result was poetry.[29] Moore knew no
Irish whatsoever and could scarcely have known just how true this
quip was.

Other improvements by Synge include the use of 'band' instead
of MacErlean's 'crowd, swarm, tribe,'; 'inciting' instead of the less
precise 'exciting' or the less dramatic 'encouraging'; 'of gay aspect'
instead of 'of bright countenance, fair face'. In the whole translation,
which is only an unfinished exercise, there is not a single error,
despite the fact that Synge's dependence on the glossary was minimal.

These tendencies are increasingly evident in other translations,
for example, *Om Sceol ar árd-mhagh Fáil*:

KEATING
Óm sceol ar árd-mhagh Fáil ní chodlaím oíche,

's do bhreodh go bráth mé dála a pobuil dílis,
Gidh ró-fhada atáid 'na bhfál re broscar bíodhbhadh,
Fá dheoidh gur fhás a lán don chogal tríotha.

A Fhódhla phláis, is nár nach follus daoibh-se,
Gur córa tál ar sháir-shliocht mhogail Mhíleadh;
Deor níor fágbhadh i gclár do bhrollaigh mhín-ghil,
Nár dheolsad ál gach crána coigríche.

Gach treod gan tásc tar sáil dar thogair síneadh
Go hoir-shliocht álainn ársaidh Chobhthaigh Chaoilmbreagh,
Is leo gan ghráscar lámh ár ndona-bhruidhne,
Gach fód is fearr dár n-áitibh eochar-aoibhne.[30]

SYNGE

From my coming to the smooth plain of Fail I do not sleep
    in the night
And the conditions of her dear people destroyed me forever,
Although it is very long they are in ramparts against
    multitudes of enemies,
In the end there grew up a full measure of tares.

Oh deceitful Fodla, it is shame that it is not plain to thee,
That it is juster to give milk to the noble race of the seed
    of Mile,
A drop is not left in the plain of your smooth bosom
Which is not sucked up by the brood of every foreign sow.

Every land without reputation beyond the water which
    choose a stretching out,
To the royal race that is ancient and beautiful of
    Cobhtach Caol mBreagh
Our hapless castles are theirs without a contest of hands
And every sod that is finest of our beautiful border places.[31]

This version marks an attempt by Synge to catch the style, as well
as the meaning, of the original. So he opts for what was to become
one of his favourite Anglo-Irish idioms, 'destroyed' for 'breodhadh',
instead of MacErlean's cliché, 'crushed'. MacErlean offers the stilted
'level expanse of thy bosom' for 'clár do bhrollaigh mhínghil',

while Synge's 'in the plain of your smooth bosom' shows a more
precise awareness of the original image and of its underlying rhythm.
One could multiply such instances: 'multitudes' for 'broscar' rather
than 'crowd, rout, crew'; 'plain' for 'follas' rather than 'clear';
'hapless castles' for 'dona-bhruidhne' rather than 'unhappy castles'.
In fact, this could almost be called a free rather than a literal
translation. Synge not only improves MacErlean's favoured version,
but he deliberately alters the meaning of the text itself. So 'from
the story' becomes 'from my coming to'; and 'árd mhagh' is given
as 'smooth plain', though it is clear from the second stanza that
Synge knew that the Irish for 'smooth' is 'mín'. Now and then,
despite his fidelity to the Irish, Synge experiments with a phrase
for the sake of self-expression. It must be remembered that the poem
he gives us is finally his own and that he has a right to interpret
the Irish in a personal way. The points of deviation from the original
are often the points of real interest, since they bear the personal
seal of the translator. At times, a literal word-for-word fidelity to the
Irish serves only to obscure the real meaning of a line. After all,
Synge was trying to find an equivalent in English, not for an order
of words, but for the ideas and images which those words embodied.
There are some idioms in any language which cannot be translated
and it is essential that a translator be granted occasional indulgence
in order to simplify an idea or a description.

These are far from great translations, though they have their
high moments. They do establish Synge's ability to comprehend the
most intricate Classical Irish poetry; and they are a testimony to his
growing interest in translating the elements of Gaelic culture into
English, a language not expressly of that culture. His lines try to catch
something of the atmosphere, as well as the bare meaning, of their
originals. The Anglo-Irish dialect is the logical outcome of this
process and it was to become the triumphant medium of his major
plays.

By 1902, in his review of David Comyn's edition of *Foras Feasa
ar Éirinn*, Synge was sufficiently sure of his own feeling for the
complex syntax of Keating's prose to take issue with Comyn for the
stiltedness of his translations into English. These were, he said,
'not always as pliant to the movement of Keating's language as could
be wished' (*Prose*, p. 360). He must have had no difficulty in
reading through a piece of Keating's prose, if he could make so
confident a public assertion against the acknowledged expert on the
subject. He substantiates the assertion by providing his own trans-

lation of Keating's text. He sets his version alongside Comyn's, pointing out that 'I translate a little differently from Mr. Comyn in order to keep closer to Keating's tone' (*Prose*, p. 361). To translate such a text into a simple English, as Comyn did, requires a scholarly grounding in Classical Irish. To recreate the evanescent tone of Keating's prose, as Synge does here, would demand an intimate feeling for the lilt and rhythms of the original. Synge here displays his belief in a creative translation, which would fuse the scholar's precision with the style of the artist, making him a kind of co-author with Keating. This is the belief of a man who would finally create his own cadenced Anglo-Irish dialect out of a translation from Irish.

Synge's concern to catch the tone as well as the mere meaning of the words is a result of his encounter on Aran with an old sailor. The islander had volunteered that 'a translation is no translation unless it will give you the music of the poem along with the words of it' (*Prose*, p. 149). This was the criterion employed by Synge one year later in his review of Comyn's translation of *Foras Feasa*. The sailor had pronounced himself unsatisfied with Archbishop McHale's translation into Irish of *Moore's Irish Melodies* and had offered his own alternative versions. Now Synge, unsatisfied with Comyn, offers what he considers to be superior translations. There can be no doubt as to the accuracy of that judgement.

Short as Synge's alternative paragraphs are, they are an impressive outcome of his years of translation and tortuous study. All the work of the notebooks has been brought to a triumphant conclusion and Synge can publicly flaunt his ability to catch the fugitive nuances of formal Irish prose. As an incidental outcome of this process, he has forged his desired Anglo-Irish dialect. We have only to compare his paragraph with Comyn's to note the difference in tone:

KEATING

. . . óir atáim aosda, agus, drong díobh-san óg; do chonnairc mé agus tuigim prímh-leabhair an tseanchusa, agus ní fhacadarsan iad, agus dá bhfacdís, ní tuigfidhe leo iad. Ní ar fhuath ná ar ghrádh droinge ar bioth seach a chéile, ná ar fhuráileamh aonduine, ná do shúil re sochar d'fhághbhail uaidh, chuireas romham stair na hEireann do scríobhadh, acht do bhrígh gur mheasas ná'r bh'oircheas chomh-onóraighe na hÉireann do chrích, agus comh-uaisle gach fóirne d'ar áitigh í, do dhul i mbáthadh, gan luadh ná iomrádh do bheith orra . . . [32]

COMYN

. . . for I am old, and a number of these were young; I have seen
and I understand the chief historical books, and they did not
see them, and if they had seen them, they would not have understood them. It is not for hatred nor for love of any set of
people beyond another, nor at the instigation of anyone, nor
with the expectation of obtaining profit from it, that I set forth
to write the history of Ireland, but because I deemed it was not
fitting that a country so honourable as Ireland, and races so noble
as those who have inhabited it, should go into oblivion without
mention or narration being left of them . . . [33]

SYNGE

. . . I am old, and a number of these people are young. I have
seen and I understand the head-books of history, and they have
not seen them, and if they had seen them they would not have
understood anything. It was not for hatred or love of any tribe
beyond another, nor at the order of anyone, nor in hope to get
gain out of it, that I took in hand to write the history of Ireland,
but because I thought it was not fitting that a country like
Ireland for honour, and races as honourable as every race that
inhabited it, should be swallowed up without any word or mention
to be left about them. (*Prose*, pp. 361–2)

In every alteration, Synge opts for a concrete rather than a
needlessly abstract translation. He realises the hardness that is the
genius of the Irish language. For each of Comyn's rejected translations, he substitutes forms from that Anglo-Irish dialect which he
was to use so effectively in the plays. Indeed, what makes Synge's
plays memorable for so many critics is this very dialect, 'his wonderful
language which pleases us not as a heightened form of the language
we ourselves use, but as a picturesque deviation from it'.[34] It is
precisely this deviation which Synge proposes for public approval,
in his alterations of Comyn's translation. It is almost as if, in the
columns of a literary journal, he is rehearsing on a select audience
the future dialect of his plays and flaunting its colourful deviation
from standard English. Let us examine some of these deviations:

SYNGE	COMYN
head-books of history	chief historical books
they have not seen them	they did not see them

anything	them
tribe	set of people
at the order of anyone	at the instigation of anyone
in hope to get gain out of it	with the expectation of gaining
I took in hand	I set forth
I thought	I deemed
a country like Ireland for honour	a country as honourable as Ireland
should be swallowed up	should go into oblivion
without any word or mention	without mention or narration being
to be left about them	left to them.

It is not simply a question of syntax, vocabulary or even tone. Synge's paragraph, as a paragraph, *reads aloud* far more impressively, having a subtler, more periodic and more flexible rhythm than Comyn's. This is difficult to prove conclusively on paper. Leonard Foster has shown that, in order to judge the success of a version, we must finally resort to 'the translator's most simple and obvious way of testing style: reading aloud'.[35] If this test is applied, there are clear suggestions of an iambic line running through Synge's reconstructed paragraph. His alterations of phrase have a nicely rounded ring, when compared with Comyn's original words. Note that:

a) 'thĕ hēad-bŏŏks ŏf hĭstŏrў' is in the alliterative prose, so common in Gaelic;

b) the emphatic closure of 'anything' to drive home the sentence, in preference to the diminuendo effect of 'them' in Comyn;

c) ŏf ānў trĭbe bĕyōnd ănōthĕr
ăt thĕ ōrdĕr ŏf ānўŏne
ĭn hōpe tŏ gēt gaĭn ŏut ŏf ĭt
Ĭ tōŏk ĭn hānd;

d) 'thought' is more directly colloquial than the sentenious 'deemed';

e) 'a country like Ireland for honour', with the concrete effect reinforced by the use of the Gaelic preposition.

The only degeneration is in the second alteration. The Perfect Tense 'they have not seen' seems not to exist in the Anglo-Irish dialect, whereas the version given by Comyn, 'they did not see', certainly does.[36]

Consider now the second paragraph in Irish, Comyn's version and the alternative translation by Synge:

KEATING

Mar atá, iomorro, go moltar an fonn leis gach staraidhe d'a scríobhann ar Éirinn, díonmoltar an fhoireann leis gach Nua-Ghall-staraidhe d'a scríobhann uirre, agus is leis sin do gríosadh mise do chum na stair seo do scríobhadh ar Éireannchaibh, ar mhéid na truaighe do ghabh mé fá'n eagcóir fhollusaigh doghnítear orra leo. Dá dtugadaois, trá, a bhfír-theist féin ar Éireannchaibh, ní fheadar créud as nach cuirfidís i coimhmeas re haoin-chineadh 'san Eoraip iad i dtrí neithibh, mar atá, i ngaisgeamhlacht, i léigheantacht, agus i n-a mbeith daingean i san gcreideamh Catoileaca . . . [37]

COMYN

If, indeed, it be that the soil is commended by every historian who writes on Ireland, the race is dispraised by every new foreign historian who writes about it, and it is by that I was incited to write this history concerning the Irish, owing to the extent of the pity I felt at the manifest injustice which is done to them by those writers. If only indeed they had given their proper estimate to the Irish, I know not why they should not put them in comparison with any nation in Europe in three things, namely, in valour, in learning, in being steadfast to the Catholic faith . . . [38]

SYNGE

If it happens, indeed, that the land is praised by every historian who has written about Ireland, the people are dispraised by every new foreign historian who has written about them, and the thing that stirred me up to write this history of the Irish is the greatness of the pity I felt at the plain injustice that is done to them by these writers. If only, indeed, they had given their true report about the Irish, I do not know why they should not have been put in comparison with any race in Europe in three things, as they are in bravery, in learning and in being steadfast to the Catholic faith . . . (*Prose*, p. 362)

In Synge's version, 'indeed' is more gracefully placed after the verb; and 'happens', better than 'be', catches just that innocently surprised note of accidentality which Keating clearly wished to convey in the original sentence. Synge chooses the more colloquial 'praised' over Comyn's 'commended' and this is only just—'mol', after all, is the normal Gaelic word for 'praise' and there are equivalent words such as 'mórtar' for the more sonorous 'commended'. This is just the type of alteration which greatly affects the tone of a piece of writing. In one idiom, Comyn is closer to the syntax of the original:

κ. is leis sin do gríosadh mise do chum na stair seo do scríobh
c. it is by that I was incited to write this history
s. the thing that stirred me up to write this history

Comyn's correctness is at the cost of clarity. Like many scholars who have translated from Irish, he seems to forget that English is a wholly distinct language with its own consistent sense of style. While the fresh charm of a translation from Irish may lie in its deviations from standard English, too great a divergence ruins this delicate balance and causes only confusion and awkwardness.

Synge always avoids such pitfalls. This is a tribute to his sure sense of English style and his shrewd awareness of the limits to the resources of his medium. Not all who have used the literary dialect have been so sure in touch. Lady Gregory, on the opening page of *Cuchulain of Muirthemne,* is guilty of a clumsy construction remarkably similar to Comyn's: 'It is what I have tried to do, to take the best of these stories'.[39] This awkward phrase is often employed by Gaeltacht folk in writing, and even sometimes in speaking English. There is, however, no reason for blindly following the folk in the vices as well as the virtues of their language, for the translator will merely reproduce that awkwardness. The reason for employing the dialect in the first place is its charm and freshness; but when it ceases to charm and starts to confuse, then it is not to be imitated. This Synge wisely saw. The lapses of style in Comyn's version and the painstaking apprenticeship of Synge as a translator prove that the ability to write smoothly in Anglo-Irish dialect was not easily acquired.

Elsewhere, Synge's tendency is to favour a concrete colloquialism, for example, 'people' rather than the more academic 'race'. 'Méad' can mean either 'greatness' or 'amount, extent', but in the context Synge's rendition is more likely. He translated 'follus' as 'plain', whereas Comyn preferred 'manifest', a more ponderous word. 'True report' would not sound strange from the lips of a countryman, but Comyn's 'proper estimate' certainly would. These translations capture that idiom of shrewd concrete observation, which Synge believed Keating had in common with the western peasant. Máirtín Ó Cadhain, the greatest writer of modern Irish prose, instilled the same precept into his translation classes at Trinity College, Dublin—that the translator must be careful to express the most abstract ideas as concretely as possible, so that a Connemara man might be able to understand every word, even if the subject were existentialism. For 'cine' Comyn gives 'nation', but Synge offers the more precise 'race'. Here the precision is justified by the pointed nature of the original Irish word.

Implicit in Synge's prose translations are ideas about the subject which were very close to those held by Douglas Hyde. Hyde also aimed at a close and literal rendition in English, with no unwarranted interference by the translator. His claim in the introduction to *The Religious Songs of Connacht*—that he has rendered the text 'exactly as I got it myself, without my adding anything to it, nor taking anything from it'—is similar to the declaration of 'inventing nothing, and changing nothing that is essential' with which Synge introduces his material in *The Aran Islands*. Hyde further believed that, even when the medium was prose, the translator must seek to catch the style of the original in 'just the kind of language which the narrator would have used, had he told or been able to tell the story in English'.[40] The style desired was the brand of English spoken by native speakers of Irish, an almost literal translation into English by Irish-thinking people. This was the prose vehicle which Hyde pioneered, which Lady Gregory refined, and which Synge perfected as a literary dialect. It is no accident that all three of them first forged it while engaged on works of translation from the native language.

Synge's two articles on Keating were written at a time when careless essays on the Irish language and literature in English journals were pounced upon by Patrick Pearse in the columns of *An Claidheamh Soluis*.[41] Synge's plays were frequently denounced by Pearse and the Gaelic League, but they could never criticise him for his Irish scholarship. In that field, at least, there was no discernible weakness.

THE TRANSLATION OF *RUCARD MÓR* AND *OIDHE CHLOINNE UISNIGH*

In the notebook which contains Synge's versions of the poems of Keating, we find also the text in Irish of a folk poem, *Rucard Mór*, along with a translation. This translation is not credited with an author in the notebook, but it is clearly an earlier draft than that published in *The Aran Islands*. Being written in Synge's hand, it is probably his own initial attempt at the version in English later published in his book. This ballad was given to him by John Joice, the storyteller of Inishere. In the notebook the transcript of another ballad, *The White Horse,* is credited to John Joice.[42] It is also credited to Joice in *The Aran Islands,* where Synge reproduces it, but he is at pains to make clear that this 'extraordinary English doggerel rhyme' is 'singularly incoherent' and not of his own making (*Prose,* p. 167). However, when he comes to reproduce *Rucard Mór* one page later in *The Aran Islands,* Synge makes it clear from the outset that the translation is his own work, 'as near to the Irish as I am able to make it' (*Prose,* p. 172). The normally unobtrusive narrator of *The Aran Islands* engages in some uncharacteristic self-admiration, as he relays the old man's admiring comments on his translation: 'The old man who tells me the Irish poems is curiously pleased with the translations I have made from some of them. He would never be tired, he says, listening while I would be reading them, and they are much finer things than his old bits of rhyme.' (*Prose,* p. 172) In placing this comment directly before the twenty-eight stanzas of his poem, Synge is clearly inviting his readers to make the comparison between his poem as a finished article and the old man's doggerel in *The White Horse.* There is doubt about the superiority of his version. With the aid of his notebook, however, we can do more than compare the two books. We can go further and judge the success of *Rucard Mór* as a translation.

The virtues of Synge's translation of *Rucard Mór* are those of the original—narrative fluency, conversational rhythms and a powerful monosyllabic urgency. His version, while not myopically close to the original, does not lose the easy comprehensibility and terse rhythms of the Irish. Indeed, the rhythms of Synge's version in English often serve to reproduce those of the source line. This is especially true of the dead-pan fourth line of each stanza with its tight-lipped shortening. Consider the following example of a whole stanza which closely follows the rhythms of its original:

I ran on in my walking	Do ghread mé lion chun siubhal
I followed the road straightly	Do lean mé an bóthar go díreach
I was in Glenasmoil	Bhí mé in Glen na Smól
Before the noon was ended.	Sul má bhí an meadhan lae
	críochnadh.

Synge's verse has, of course, its own inner consistencies, which are quite independent of the original. The dominant metre of the second couplet of most stanzas appears to be the regular balladic English:

> And they all making merry
> Before the noon was ended.

However, as with the Gaelic original, this is not invariable. A great deal of the charm of Synge's version lies in its subtly controlled tension between the strict patterns of poetry and the comparatively loose patterns of conversation. The translation, like the Gaelic verse, trembles on the brink of system. T. S. Eliot has said that the most interesting type of verse is that which threatens constantly to fall into a pattern, but never actually does so.[43] This quality of *Rucard Mór* is due to the fact that the ballad springs from a predominantly oral culture, which relies heavily on the repetition of key lines and stanzas. Synge shows himself to have been deeply aware of this in his translation. It is in the crucially repeated stanzas that he keeps closest of all to the rhythms and words of the original, as in the repeated four-liner quoted above.

Perhaps the most appealing feature of such songs is the way in which the singer, after a very short line, has to fit a much longer line into the limited space which the regular metre will allow. This is a standard device of traditional Irish 'sean-nós' singing and another instance of the delicate balance between freedom and system which characterises folk art. Twice in his writings Synge discusses this method. Firstly, he describes the men's rendition of *The White Horse*: 'These rhymes are repeated by the old men as a sort of chant, and when a line comes that is more than usually irregular they seem to take a real delight in forcing it into the mould of the recitative'. (*Prose*, p. 167) In another work, *In West Kerry*, he explains how the long loose lines are teased into the regular mould of recitation: 'when one makes the obvious elisions, the lines are not so irregular as they look, and are always sung to a measure . . . ' (*Prose*, p. 267).

In *Rucard Mór* this tension between pattern and freedom is exemplified by the juxtaposition of lines vastly unequal in length. Both in Synge's version and in the Irish, a short line is often marooned among long ones:

> Do labhair mise leis an bhfear
> Crutach grádhna
> Muna fhaghfheadh sé dom an láirín
> Go mbriseann trian dá cnámhadh.

The two short pounding adjectives, surrounded by longer flowing lines, are intensely dramatic. The translator is a poetic dramatist with a dramatist's sense of the effects that can be achieved by specific alignments of words. Other examples of long and short lines in juxtaposition are:

Féuch Rucard Mór	Look at Rucard Mor
Agus é ag tosnuigheadh a láirimh	And he looking for his little mare
Do labhair mé lobh	I spoke to them
Má bhí innti ceart do dhéanamh	If it was in them to do a right thing

Synge even creates this effect in two stanzas where it does not occur in the original. In the second stanza he actually breaks up the line

> Is sé an tsluagh sigh chuir mé le seachrán

into two new lines and he sets these short, dramatic lines against a long final line:

> It is the fairy host
> Put me a-wandering
> And took from me my goods of the world.

The dramatic suppression of the English relative 'that' helps to concentrate the meaning of this sentence in the minimum number of words. This will later become a feature of Synge's dialect.

Many other elements in the translation of *Rucard Mór* might be noted. The half-rhymes, with their persistent suggestion of a fully schematic rhyme and their stubborn refusal to submit to it, increase

our sense of the clash between freedom and system. Half-rhyme can
be found in successive lines:

> The men and women of the *country*
> And they all making *merry*.

Even more subtle, and more characteristic of the conventions of
Gaelic poetry, is the simultaneous appearance in a couplet of
ordinary rhyme, internal rhyme and alliteration:

> Do you hear, Rucard *Mór*
> It is not *here* is your *mare* . . .
> She is in Glenasmoil
> With the fairy-men these three months.   (*Prose*, p. 173)

That the words in each case should yield only half-rhymes (more/
mare/here) adds to the delicacy of balance held by Synge in the
translation. It is only a suggestion of order. Anything more
definitely patterned would be too obvious and vulgarly unfaithful to
the original. The alliterating *m* of the two final rhyming words of
the couplet achieves closure in the word 'months'. This word
concludes the stanza, having been waited for throughout the long
fourth line.

    This is, however, to ignore the greatest significance of *Rucard Mór*,
which is its use as a vital Anglo-Irish idiom. This idiom emerges
almost as an accidental and unexpected result of a sensitive and literal
translation. Many words, which are tired poetic conventions in
Irish, emerge with a freshness and vitality in English, which they
could never have possessed in the original. For instance, the stock
threat in Irish, 'go mbrisfinn trian dá chnámhadh', acquires a
disturbing pointedness, a kind of vicious precision, in the English
'I would break a third of his bones'. So a translation from one
language to another, though made at a certain cost to the original,
has its unexpected and surprising improvements on the source.
Another fine example is the richly ambiguous 'on me' in the fifth
stanza: 'the devil a hill is not searched on me for my mare'. In
two short words, this concentrates all the force of the Gaelic Dative
of Disadvantage, allied with the standard English sense of 'on my
behalf'. The Dative of Disadvantage has been used already in the
opening lines, 'on me the shameless deed was done', and again in
'took my little horse on me'.

This kind of ambiguity, between the meaning of standard English and the sense of the Irish original, is a primary virtue of the Anglo-Irish dialect. Synge exploited such ambiguities for he was shrewdly aware that the dialect stands in medial position between the two languages. There is a superb example of this in *Riders to the Sea*, when Nora says of Bartley, who has left for a dangerous sea-voyage without taking any bread: 'And it's destroyed he'll be going till dark night, and he after eating nothing since the sun went up' (*Plays 1*, p. 11). On one level, 'destroyed' is used in the idiomatic Gaelic sense of being 'destroyed with hunger, thirst, work etc.', a sense which normally denotes great discomfort. However, on another level, there are echoes of the standard English meaning of 'destroyed', suggesting dissolution and death. At the early stage in the play when the word is used, the Gaelic echo is the dominant one; but, as the play continues and as the sense of fated doom grows, the word uttered in all innocence becomes grimly prophetic.

Many other features of Synge's dialect appear, often for the first time, in this translation—the frequent suppression of the relative 'that', 'which', 'where', to introduce a subordinate or relative clause, as in 'it is the fairy host put me a-wandering'; the use of 'it is' to emphasise the words immediately following, as in 'it is not here is your mare', which also involves the suppression of the relative 'that'; the use of ancillary 'and', rather than 'when' or 'where' to introduce an adverbial clause, as in 'and he looking'; and, finally, the use of stock phrases, later to become mainstays of the dialect, such as 'the black fall of night', 'before the noon was ended', 'the devil a hill or a glen', 'in my walking' and, of course, the Dative of Disadvantage 'on me'. The crucial part played by these translations in the evolution of Synge's literary dialect has been overlooked by scholars and would repay even deeper study.

On the envelope which contains Synge's Irish version of *Oidhe Chloinne Uisnigh: The Fate of the Children of Uisneach*, the following note has been written in the handwriting of Edward Stephens: 'If MS. was written in Aran (1901)—it may have been taken from some book belonging to "The Scholar"'. The scholar was John Joice of Inishere. The book, based on an earlier text by Andrew MacCuirtin (1740), was published in Dublin in 1898 by the Society for the Preservation of the Irish Language with a translation, notes and vocabulary by Richard O'Duffy. Synge may well have owned a copy of the book himself, since he had already purchased *Oidhe Chloinne Lir*, an earlier publication in the same series.

As an exercise in translation, Synge's work is spirited, vivid, but by no means flawless. It contains a fair number of mistakes and errors. The very opening words, 'Is fada do bhí cogadh . . . ' (7)[44] are mistranslated as 'it is long since . . . ' (3) and such mistakes are quite frequent. In spite of these intermittent errors, however, Synge's version is written in a charming, concrete and slightly circumlocutory style which is close to the dialect of his major plays.

The Irish language is a concrete, noun-centred medium, with a marked preference for the specific in its mode of expression. One of the virtues of Synge's translation, which makes it sometimes superior to O'Duffy's, is its avoidance of unnecessary abstractions. Synge always relies on concrete forms of expression, even when these involve some degree of circumlocution.[45] To take a simple set of examples, 're linn' (7) is given by Synge as 'at the time' (3) rather than 'when' (49); and 'cá háit' (32) is rendered as 'in what place' (41) rather than 'where' (76). It will immediately be seen that this a matter of giving a literal translation of the original Irish. Often, in keeping with his distrust of adjectives, Synge scorns to translate an adjective as such, opting for a more concrete, but circumlocutory, relative clause. 'An duine bréagach' (16) is given not as 'the deceitful man' (58), but as 'him who is a liar' (13). Similarly, 'thógaibh Conchobar a ollghuth ríoghdha ós árd' (12) is rendered as 'Conor lifted up his great voice that was the voice of a king' (4), whereas O'Duffy prefers 'his great royal voice' (54). 'An aithne díbh uireasbaidh ar bith orraibh féin?' (12) is rendered by O'Duffy as 'do you know of any want on yourselves?' (54); and by Synge as 'Is there knowledge among you of anything that is wanting?' (4). Thus 'any want' is expanded by Synge to become the circumlocutory 'anything that is wanting' and the subtle drift towards Anglo-Irish dialect is manifest in such a transformation. We can see that this trend is deliberate if we compare O'Duffy's and Synge's respective translations of 'dá mbeith gan a bheith d'Ultaibh ann acht an triúr sin féin amháin' (12). O'Duffy's 'even did there not exist in it of Ultonians but that triad alone' (55) seems almost a pastiche of the stilted versions of Standish H. O'Grady in *Silva Gadelica*. On the other hand, Synge's 'if there were men of Ulster in it but those three only' (6) is the authentic idiom of *Riders to the Sea*, with its repeated use of 'in it' and its sentences which end on displaced, wailing adverbs: 'what is the price of a thousand horses against a son when there is one son only?' (*Plays 1*, p. 9). The play was written scarcely a year after this translation.

This example is just one of a host of improvements made by

Synge on O'Duffy's translation. There are many others. 'Thógbhas' (19) is rendered by Synge as 'raised up' (18), rather than the limp 'built' (62). 'Tréan tráigh' (19) is given as 'firm beach' (19) rather than 'stern strand' (62). 'Beacht' is given its specific meaning in this context as 'precise' (26), rather than the generalised 'excellent' (68). Synge realises, also, that there are times when too literal a translation may rob a text of its life. When Lavarcham says 'is truagh liomsa an gníomh do dhéanfar anocht a n-Eamhain . . . ' (27), O'Duffy translates this correctly but lifelessly as 'I grieve for the deed which will be done to-night in Eamhain' (71). Synge, by a subtly dramatic change of tense, in which the future has caught up with the present—'the deed that is being done to-night' (32)—catches the overpowering sense of fate in the story. We sense that, even as Lavarcham utters the sentence, men are at work elsewhere sealing that fate. By such deft manoeuvres, Synge translates not only the words before his eyes, but something of the spirit that suffuses the whole tale.

Many of Synge's improvements illustrate his capacity to dramatise the translated phrases. 'Endless destruction' (9) is much more telling than the vague 'eternal dissolution' (56) to catch the violence at the heart of 'bith-éaga' (14). More often, it is a matter of the translator's capacity to dramatise syntax. 'Adubhradar dá dtigeadh seacht gcatha Uladh ann, go bhfaghaidís uile a sáith ann' (26) is stiltedly expressed by O'Duffy as 'They said if there came the seven battalions of Ulster they would all get their sufficiency of it' (69). By removing the cumbersome conditional clause, and by replacing the awkward 'got their sufficiency of it' by the tersely effective 'be satisfied', Synge manages to simplify and heighten the impact of the figure of speech—'They said that seven champions of Ulster might come into it and they would all be satisfied' (29). O'Duffy, despite his superior grasp of Classical Irish vocabulary, offers us a parallel text. Synge, despite his intermittent mistakes, often leads us to an experience in creative translation.

Some critics may argue that scholars such as Comyn and O'Duffy did not aim to provide imaginative translations, but were content to produce parallel texts or 'cribs'. It could be alleged that, in this context, such comparisons between the creative translations by Synge and the scholarly versions are scarcely illuminating. Nevertheless, it was Synge who first made the public comparison between his own versions and those of MacErlean. He did so because he felt that many reputable Celtic scholars, who had produced admirable scholarly editions of Irish texts, had failed to meet the more exciting challenge of making the native literature live again in English. The deserved academic reputations of Comyn and O'Duffy had given their English versions of classic works of Irish literature an undeserved immunity from criticism. Despite the self-confessed limitations to his own knowledge, Synge was willing to offer criticism and to support it on occasion with alternative translations which caught the tone as well as the meaning of their originals. His own work as a translator from Irish may be seen as the apprenticeship of an artist whose major aim was to express the psychic state of the Gael in the English language.

SYNGE AS CRITIC OF OTHER TRANSLATORS

Synge's ideas on translation continued to develop in the years after 1901 and 1902. This was due to his continuing experiments with Anglo-Irish dialect and to his work as a reviewer of newly-published translations. His review of A. H. Leahy's *Heroic Romances of Ireland,* published in the *Manchester Guardian* on 28 December 1905, gathers together many of his basic perceptions on the subject. In it he discusses the perennial problem of whether to translate poetry into verse or prose. This problem was compounded for Leahy by the fact that he had to work on a Gaelic text in which terse elliptical verse alternated with ordinary discursive prose. Synge states that 'a plain literal version' can be 'somewhat unattractive', a view most likely prompted by disappointment with his early literal translations of Keating's lyrics. A consistent translation of the romance, which could sustain at once the concentrated lyricism of the poetry and the free simplicity of the prose, would have demanded from any scholar 'the greatest literary tact'. The alternative adopted by Leahy, of translating Irish verse into English verse, is even more perilous. Synge does not scruple to show that the odds are heavily weighted against such an experiment: '. . . it may be doubted whether . . . almost the whole mass of English translations, from the time of Pope down, is not a dreary and disheartening exhibition of useless ingenuity which has produced hardly anything of interest for those who care most about poetry' (*Prose*, p. 371). This judgment is, of course, informed by Synge's own experience of translating Keating's poetry and prose and by his far greater success with the prose translations. It is also conditioned by the experiments

of Douglas Hyde in *Love Songs of Connacht,* which Synge studied
assiduously. In his book, Hyde had provided English translations of
the love poetry both in prose and verse. He had done this in the
belief that a literal prose version could assist learners of the language.
He added that the 'English prose translation only aims at being
literal, and has courageously, though no doubt ruggedly, reproduced
the Irish idioms of the original'.[46] Hyde's verse translations attempted
the impossible—to keep faith with their originals in the strictest of
metres. The stilted poetic diction in which they are couched robs
them of any life. His prose versions, on the other hand, were
wrought with comparative freedom and are far more vital and
arresting. In them he has translated directly from Irish to English,
keeping deliberately close to the words of the text for the benefit'
of learners who may use his book. Examining these respective
versions, Yeats decided that Hyde's literal rendition had yielded a
cadenced idiom of surpassing beauty. In a preface to the limited
edition of Hyde's collection published in 1904, Yeats wrote: 'Dr.
Hyde's prose translations printed at the end of this book are I think
even better than his verse ones; but even he cannot always escape
from the influence of his predecessors when he rhymes in
English . . . '[47]

It is no coincidence that, just one year later, Synge repeats this
very point. He applies it more comprehensively to most of the
translations made from Irish poetry in the nineteenth century. He
quotes a stanza of Leahy's poem on Deirdre which, like many such
translations, is a 'facile parody' of late-Romantic English poetry.
He accuses all this verse of 'the provinciality which—at least till
quite lately—has distinguished a good deal of Anglo-Irish taste'.
Gaelic poetry is full of the 'most curious individuality and charm',
but 'there is probably no mass of tawdry commonplace jingle quite
so worthless as the verse translations that have been made from it in
Ireland during the last century' (*Prose,* p. 371). This strenuous
disapproval of the work of Anglo-Irish translators and versifiers in
the nineteenth century, especially the writers of Young Ireland, is
a measure of his former passion for their work of which he
'repented bitterly' (*Prose,* p. 13).

There were, of course, some noble exceptions to the proponents
of this worthless jingle, most notably Samuel Ferguson and Edward
Walsh. Indeed, Ferguson anticipated Synge's attack by seventy years.
Perceiving in 1834 how desperate the situation was, he launched
his attack on the contributors to Hardiman's *Irish Minstrelsy.* These

men, he said, were 'actuated by a morbid desire, neither healthy nor honest, to elevate the tone of the originals to a pitch of refined poetic art altogether foreign from the whole genius and *rationale* of its composition'.[48] The genius of Irish poetry was altogether different from that of refined contemporary poetry in English. Ferguson complained that Hardiman's versifiers persisted in dressing the homely songs of Gaelic Ireland in this alien garb. It is exactly the same complaint which Synge makes against Leahy's translations. Ferguson would have preferred Hardiman's translations to have been faithful to 'the poetic fact of the original'.[49] His own versions, no less than Synge's, display what seems at times an almost disingenuous fidelity to the Gaelic text; but in both cases this may be seen as a deep reverence for 'the poetic fact of the original'.

Synge's amazement that Leahy should submit a Tennysonian pastiche as a serious translation from the stark idiom of the *Book of Leinster* is couched in unambiguous terms. He writes that it is 'hard to imagine a more deplorable misrepresentation of the spirit of these old verses' (*Prose*, p. 372). Once again he has returned to his obsession, the need to catch the spirit as well as to translate the word. He sees clearly that such a task, difficult enough in prose, is almost impossible in poetry. He repeats and extends Yeats's perception about Hyde's translations: 'Those who know no Irish can get some idea what Gaelic poetry has suffered in this kind of treatment by comparing the beautiful prose translations which Dr Douglas Hyde wrote of the *Love Songs of Connacht* with the verse translations—in themselves often pleasing enough—which he put in the same volume' (*Prose*, p. 372). This problem is compounded when the translation is of a poem eight hundred years older than the songs rendered by Hyde. The only saving grace which Synge can detect in the versions comes when Leahy 'keeps to the strictly trochaic or iambic movement' (*Prose*, pp. 372–3). We recall just how useful Synge found this device and how he relied on it in his own prose translations.

The flaw which Synge isolated in Leahy's work was, therefore, the same flaw which Ferguson had detected in Hardiman's *Minstrelsy*—the fatuous attempt to translate the homely idioms of Irish poetry into an alien English poetic tradition. Like so many translations from minor into major languages, these versions proceeded from the wrong premise. All through the nineteenth century, most translators had tried to turn Irish into English, instead of turning English into Irish—that is, they had a greater reverence for the conventional usage of their target language, English, than for the spirit of the Irish. This was part of a wider European pattern in the nineteenth century, affecting many of those who translated into imperial languages. In *Die Krisis der europäischen Kultur,* Rudolf Pannwitz accused German translators of turning Hindi and Greek into German, instead of converting German into Hindi and Greek. He went on: 'The basic error of the translator is that he preserves the state in which his own language happens to be instead of allowing his language to be powerfully affected by the foreign tongue'.[50] All of this Synge clearly saw. He did not convert the half-medieval idioms of Keating into the conventions of late nineteenth century English poetry. Instead he injected toxins of Irish idiom, the cadences and syntax of Gaelic poetry, into English. He allowed his translations in English to proceed unrestrained by the conventions of that language. His English versions, were, therefore, 'powerfully affected by the foreign tongue', though in this case the 'foreign' tongue was Irish.

Synge reserves his unstinted praise for Leahy's prose versions and provides us with a brilliant description of the qualities of a true translator, 'fearlessness, enthusiasm, and the scholar's conscience' (*Prose,* p. 373). Once again he celebrates a fusion of artistic imagination and scholarly scruple. Finally, he sounds a warning note about the way in which 'needlessly archaic' phrases creep into Leahy's text. This was a mistake common in translations of the time, a mistake which Synge sought always to avoid.

Scarcely three months later in a review of the second volume of Leahy's work, Synge returned to the point. Leahy had claimed that the tales were given a rapid prose recitation in Irish, but that English prose could not similarly bring out their character. So he chose to represent them in English by the narrative ballad, as had been done so often before. Synge corrects this error, pointing out that: 'in numberless villages in the west and south of Ireland there are now storytellers who have a large store of folk-tales which they tell indifferently in English or Irish, and those of them who have fairly good English often give the same characterisations in both their versions' (*Prose,* p. 374). This is true but it would have been fairer of Synge to point out, as he did in *The Aran Islands,* that the English versions were usually inferior to the Irish ones in the judgement of those who knew best, the reciters (*Prose,* p. 61). Nevertheless, Leahy would have been better advised to employ English prose rather than the form of the ballad. With its connotations of 'literary' Romanticism, the ballad was 'by no means

in harmony with the spirit of Irish story-telling' (*Prose*, p. 374).
Again, Synge decries the failure of a translation, wrought in English
Romantic moulds, to catch the spirit of a work forged in an oral
culture.

It is no accident that the vast majority of Synge's scholarly
reviews are scrupulous assessments of the work of other translators,
for he was obsessed with the pleasures and problems of their
enterprise. One of the main propositions of this work is that Synge
had a genius for translation. His literary sensibility found its truest
expression in the manoeuvre between two languages, Irish and
English. His own poetry, composed in English, seems all too often
to be a stilted pastiche of second-rate contemporary styles, whereas
the brilliant translations from continental languages into Anglo-Irish
dialect give us a sense of the man himself. The dialect in which
he finally found his desired medium was the bilingual weave produced by this manoeuvre between two languages. There is a sense
in which it was also the language of his innermost being—what
George Steiner has recently called 'the poet's dream of an absolute
idiolect'.[51] In the years of dramatic success from 1903 to 1909,
Synge's interest in translation never declined but was compounded
by his desire to test the resources of the Anglo-Irish dialect. Even
towards the end of his life, he translated the works of Petrarch,
Walter Von der Vogelweide and other continental writers into his
dialect. These translations were far more successful than many
standard English versions of the work of these poets.

This genius for translation went far deeper than a conventional
flair for turning a piece of Irish poetry or prose into English. It
involved a capacity to project a whole Gaelic culture in English,
a language ostensibly alien to that culture. Each one of Synge's works
is an act of supreme translation. This is true on a linguistic as well
as a thematic level. It will later be shown that the language of his
plays is a translation, based not upon the English spoken in rural
Ireland but on the peculiar brand of English spoken in Gaeltacht
areas. This English is an instantaneous and literal translation from
Irish.

Renato Poggioli has argued in an inspired paraphrase that the
translator is a 'character in search of an author', in whom he can
identify a part of himself. His translation of such an author's work
is no masquerade in which he deceives his audience by mimicking
the original writer; rather ' . . . he is a character who, in finding
the author without, finds also the author within himself . . . Nor must

we forget that such a quest or pursuit may intermittently attract the original writer also, when he too must search anew for the author in himself.[52] In the image of Keating, Synge found a reflection of himself and his own concerns. In the native literature and lore, he found all those characteristics for which his artistic soul had longed— intensity, homeliness, wry irony, sad resignation, sensuality and the love of place. His years of writing in Paris had yielded nothing but morbid and introspective works; but the discovery of Aran, and the challenge to project its life to the world in English, signalled his discovery of himself as a writer. The English in which he had tried and failed to express himself in those Paris writings had been mannered, weary and effete; only when that language was vitalised by contact with a 'backward', oral culture did it offer him the chance of real self-expression.

The rigorous standards which Synge applied to the translations of David Comyn were maintained in his assessment of Lady Gregory's *Cuchulain of Muirthemne*. This was a version in Anglo-Irish dialect of the stories of the Red Branch Knights which he reviewed in 1902. He received the book warmly, but added that 'it would be possible to criticise certain barbarous features, such as the descriptions of the fury of Cuchulain' (*Prose*, p. 370). He concluded with a warning to students that 'for their severer studies they must still turn to the works of German scholars, and others, who translate without hesitation all that has come down to us in the MSS'. Here, Synge displays his knowledge of the original texts and scholarly translations. Making clear that Lady Gregory has not always been true to them, he shows that he would not allow personal friendship to compromise his integrity as a scholar. He might write to Lady Gregory in 1904 saying that he had read her 'great' book with 'intense delight', but even in the privacy of a letter he is firm enough to add: 'There are a very few details that I would like differently managed—I will tell you about them if I may when I see you again'.[53] The distinction between the literary and scholarly value of such a book had been forced on Synge in conversation with de Jubainville some weeks earlier, for he tells Lady Gregory: 'I told old Jubainville about what you were doing a few weeks ago and he was very much interested, but I am afraid he looks at Irish things from a too strict point of view to appreciate their literary value as fully as we do . . .'[54]

Evidently, the tension in Synge between artist and scholar, which had been maintained for so long, was now resolved. In this letter, he refused to allow the rigours of scholarship to obscure the larger claims of art. At the very period when he wrote that letter, he was beginning to harness his own scholarship in the service of his plays. We shall see how even in his last play, *Deirdre of the Sorrows,* he borrows features from *Cuchulain of Muirthemne* which never ceased to fascinate him. Two years after the original review of her book he wrote to Lady Gregory: '*Cuchulain* is still a part of my daily bread'.[55]

Nevertheless, Synge's demand in his review for scholarly precision was influential and was echoed by other experts in the field. Standish J. O'Grady was in sympathy with Lady Gregory's attempt to simplify and collate the diverse elements of the saga, but he criticised her prudish omissions: 'One of the greatest stories of the whole world ought to be printed and published in the very words that our ancestors thought fit to use, with all the barbarism and the very loose morality of the age set down exactly as those people thought and wrote'.[56] Synge's review appeared two months before O'Grady's in June 1902. O'Grady knew little or no Irish,[57] and had constructed his own *History of Ireland: Heroic Period* (1878–80) from translations. He may well have relied on Synge's textual knowledge in this case. Certainly, he echoed the dramatist's insistence on the 'barbarism' of the original. That this was no idle insistence on Synge's part is shown by the way in which his own *Deirdre of the Sorrows* restored to that legend the starkness of the Gaelic original, which had been lost through centuries of romantic- isation and translation into well-bred English. Kuno Meyer was asked by Lady Gregory if he had any criticisms of her book, which could be utilised in the preparation of a new edition. He complained that she 'ought not to have left out the description of Etain's naked body when King Eochaid caught sight of her beside the well'.[58] Douglas Hyde, too, felt of the work that only a strict scholar should have done it.[59]

Lady Gregory was self-conscious about the frequency of such comments and in her autobiography she strove to justify herself: 'I was not scholar enough to read ancient manuscript, but the Irish text of most of the stories had already been printed, and I worked from this text with the help of the translations given . . . '.[60] The admission in the final words of that sentence seems to give the game away. In fairness, however, there may be reasons other than an excessive reliance on polite translations for the softening of barbarism in Lady Gregory's edition. In her 'Dedication of the Irish Edition to the People of Kiltartan', Lady Gregory wrote that

'I have left out a good deal that I thought you would not care about for one reason or another'.[61] Her work was intended not for scholars but for the common reader, to whom Irish myth and legend had been a sealed book. Clearly, she did not wish to shock the moral sensibilities of the folk for whom the book was intended. More important than this, however, was the fact that *Cuchulain of Muirthemne* was produced as an answer to Professor Atkinson of Trinity College, who had attacked Irish literature on moral grounds in evidence to the Commission of Intermediate Education. He said: 'It is almost intolerably low in tone—I do not mean naughty but low; and every now and then when the circumstance occasions it, it goes lower than low'.[62] If the book is a rebuttal of Atkinson's allegation, it is no wonder that Lady Gregory was at pains to omit from it any passage which might be considered low in tone. This interpretation is confirmed by Lady Gregory's 'Dedication', where she speaks of the need for 'more respect for Irish things among the learned men that live in the college at Dublin, where so many of these old writings are stored'.[63] In her autobiography many years later, she pointed out that the laudatory reviews of her book 'showed that the enemy could no longer scoff at our literature and its want of idealism'.[64]

It is a little surprising that Synge criticised Lady Gregory so bluntly for her omissions, without displaying any awareness of the reasons for them. He did express the hope, however, that her book 'will give new impetus to many lukewarm Irishmen who have been unsympathetic towards their country because they were ignorant of her real tradition' (*Prose*, p. 367). This may be a veiled reference to those who supported Atkinson in the debate. Once again, we note Synge's emphasis on the need to re-establish a link with the lost Gaelic tradition.

Yeats pronounced himself pleased with Synge's review and wrote to him to say so. In the same letter he also advised Synge to write regularly on topics of Gaelic interest. He suggested *An tÚr-Ghort* (1902), the Irish translation of George Moore's stories in *The Untilled Field* (1903), as a starting point: 'There should be a good opening now for a critic of Irish books and you ought to step in— You might also do them a "middle" on plays in Irish—articles in *The Speaker* might probably lead to your doing work in the *Daily News* or *Chronicle*.'[65] For some years after his meeting with Synge in 1896, Yeats had regarded him not as a potential dramatist but as a budding Celtic scholar. On 14 February 1899 he had written to

Lady Gregory: 'He (Synge) is really a most excellent man. He lives in a little room which he has furnished himself. He is his own servant. He works very hard and is learning Breton. He will be a very useful scholar . . . '[66] Yeats was not the only one to gain the early impression that Synge might be destined for a distinguished career in Celtic studies. We have already noted his Cousin Emily's quip about John becoming the first Professor of Celtic at Oxford. All his life, Synge maintained his friendship and correspondence with Breton scholars such as Le Braz and Renan, and with Irish scholars such as R. I. Best and J. G. O'Keeffe. In Ireland, long after his genius as a dramatist had far surpassed his skill as a scholar, Synge still retained his interest in Old Irish literature and commanded the respect and friendship of the most eminent Celtic experts of the time. As late as 1906, J. G. O'Keeffe wrote to him:

12 Charleville Road, Rathmines   31 Jan 1906
My dear Synge,
    Hearing your beautiful play, *Riders to the Sea*, the other evening revived in me a promise I had made to you some time ago. In tardy fulfilment I am now sending you the beautiful old Irish love tale of *Liadan and Curithir* knowing that you are sure to like it . . .

Sincerely yours,
J. G. O'Keeffe.[67]

It may reasonably be deduced from the evidence presented concerning Synge that:

1. His spoken Irish was of good quality; that he could understand and converse in the two major dialects of Munster and Connacht, though he would always have a strong bias in favour of the Connacht Irish learned on Aran.
2. His written Irish was only moderate; that he was capable of writing a lucid letter but had a poor grasp of the syntax and spelling of the language, these being widespread deficiencies at the time. We are told that he considered writing a play in Irish, but there is no evidence that such a play was attempted and his written Irish would scarcely have been equal to the task.[68]
3. His academic Irish was of a high quality, comprehending the history of the language and literature in all its major phases,

from Old Irish taught by de Jubainville, through the Classical Irish of Keating, right up to such modern works as Hyde's *Love Songs of Connacht*.

Some may object that Synge translated only those works in Irish which contained English versions or comprehensive lists of vocabulary. This is not true. He also translated folk poems such as *Rucard Mór* and the love songs heard on Aran. Furthermore, it has been shown that he often consulted the parallel texts and vocabularies only to spurn the versions which they offered. By current standards this may seem a fair but not outstanding degree of knowledge. Synge embarked upon the study of Irish when he was eighteen, a late age for anyone to begin grappling with the grammar and syntax of a new language. He was twenty-eight before he actually heard the living language spoken. His achieved competence in Irish was certainly greater than that possessed by the average school-leaver in Ireland today, after fourteen years of intensive daily exposure to the language with all the aids to learning provided by a technology unknown at that time.

In order to appreciate the magnitude of Synge's success with Irish, it must be judged against the prevailing conditions and attitudes of the time. It was a period of brief cultural idealism, in which many writers and revolutionaries undertook the study of Irish, only to find that it was beyond their capacities. Yeats repeatedly attempted Irish but never even achieved an elementary mastery of the language,[69] and lived to regret it.[70] His famous advice to Synge to live on the Aran Islands and express a life that had never before found expression may be seen in terms of his own inability to master the language which held the key to that life.

Even Lady Gregory, for whose expertise in Irish extravagant claims have been made, was forced to admit in her autobiography that she was not a 'real Irish scholar', being 'imperfect, stumbling'.[71] Judged against this depressing background, Synge's command of the various types of Irish seems impressive, especially when we consider the social class to which he belonged. The Protestant ascendancy had in the main set its face against Gaelic revival. Synge's mother was not alone in her opposition to Irish. Lady Westmeath confided in her friends that 'the study of the language may create bad feeling in the country'.[72] Lady Gregory told how she was often sneered at by fellow-aristocrats for her interest in the subject.[73] Doubtless, Synge incurred similar abuse from his social peers for the same reason. However, all this never deterred him from the continuing study of a language which the veteran Fenian, John O'Leary, in a warning to young Irishmen, had judged to be beyond the powers of the human brain.[74]

This accumulation of evidence should go some way towards correcting T. R. Henn's mistaken assumption that Synge had but 'a little Gaelic'[75] and David H. Greene's defeatist belief that 'it would be impossible to estimate the fluency he ultimately developed in the language'.[76] These assumptions are shared by a great number of scholars, all of whom have had no training in Irish and impute a similar ignorance to Synge. Perhaps, because they know no Irish themselves, they have a vested interest in denying its importance to Synge and to an understanding of his writings. The consistent attempt by successive scholars to minimise the explosive potential of Synge's exposure to the Irish language is, to say the very least, disturbing.

4 Synge and Irish Literature— Saga, Myth and Romance

INTRODUCTION

The Irish Literary Revival at the close of the nineteenth century heralded, among other things, the publication, translation and development into new forms of ancient literature in the native language. Yeats and Synge realised that the best way of coming to terms with the Gaelic tradition was not to write crude plays of nationalist propaganda, but rather to revitalise in their art the finest features of the old literature in Irish. Despite this, few of the major writers of the Revival proved themselves equal to the task of mastering modern Irish, not to mention the ancient literary language. Even Lady Gregory's successful *Cuchulain of Muirthemne* was based on previous English translations. Yeats was in an even less happy position when he set about his treatment of the wanderings of Oisin. Harold Bloom has cruelly exposed the poet's real distance from his Ossianic sources, as he based his material on a translation of an eighteenth-century poem by Mícheál Ó Cuimín which he had found in the *Transactions of the Ossianic Society*: '. . . he sits in the British Museum, himself knowing no Gaelic (he never bothered to learn any) and he reads a version of a version. He is so far from mythology, and indeed in every sense so far from Ireland, that we need not be surprised to discover that his poem, despite its Celtic colourings, is in the centre of the English Romantic tradition . . .'[1]

Yeats's failure in 1889 to do anything more in *The Wanderings of Oisin* than produce another English Romantic poem is bitterly ironic,

but he learned from the experience. As a young man, he had praised
the ballads and poems of the Young Ireland movement; but by 1895
he had come to see the translations from the Irish by Mangan,
Callanan and Ferguson as the true tradition and to regard the Young
Ireland poets as pale imitators of the English Romantics. Synge's own
development, as critic and writer, offers an uncanny parallel to Yeats's
changing opinions, for the dramatist wrote in his *Autobiography*:
'The Irish ballad poetry of 'The Spirit of the Nation' school engrossed me for a while and made me commit my most serious
literary error; I thought it excellent for a considerable time and then
repented bitterly . . .' (*Prose*, p. 13). There were good reasons for
repentance. Yeats complained that Davis and the poets of Young
Ireland had '. . . turned away from the unfolding of an Irish tradition,
and borrowed the mature English methods of utterance and used them
to sing of Irish wrongs or preach of Irish purposes. Their work was
never wholly satisfactory, for what was Irish in it looked ungainly in
an English garb and what was English was never perfectly mastered,
never wholly absorbed into their being'.[2] The themes of the Young
Ireland poets might have been Irish, but their forms and metres
were borrowed from the English Romantics. That *The Wanderings
of Oisin* should fail in exactly the same way, almost fifty years later,
is a measure of the constraints upon all Irish writers in the nineteenth
century. Clearly, the only solution to this problem was to adopt the
forms of the older literature in Irish. That is why Yeats's critical
reinstatement of Callanan is so excitedly unqualified.

It was in precisely this context that Synge embarked on his *Vita
Vecchia* between 1895 and 1897. With its alternating fragments of
prose and verse, this work was a conscious return to the characteristic form of medieval Irish romance. Synge's knowledge of the native
literature came to him unmediated by the screen of translation. So,
he was in a superb strategic position to carry out Yeats's programme
and exploit the forms of the native literature, no less than its themes.
With his thorough academic grounding in Irish and his developing
mastery of English prose, he was uniquely fitted to make the great
breakthrough, forestalled so long by the false start given by the Young
Ireland writers. He was about to fuse two vigorous literary traditions—the one in Irish, the other in English—which had seemed for
centuries to be heading in contrary directions.

VITA VECCHIA AND THE FORMS OF GAELIC ROMANCE

If Synge had turned to the Old Irish sagas and romances simply for plots and themes, he would have done no more than many contemporary writers of the time. But he drew from these sources new forms and techniques and it is this which sets him apart from his fellow-artists. *Vita Vecchia*, composed of fourteen autobiographical poems bound together by a prose commentary, is the clearest example of this. This form was built around the alteration of fragments of prose and verse. Synge had encountered this mode in many works, most notably in *Oidhe Chloinne Lir* and *Oidhe Chloinne Uisnigh*. He had read and studied these works closely. These tales played a crucial role in the development of the form employed in *Vita Vecchia*. In the judgement of Alan Bruford: 'The normal pattern of mixing prose with verse was probably established by the "Three Sorrows" (Oidhe Chloinne Uisnigh, Oidhe Chloinne Tuirinn, Oidhe Chloinne Lir) which, it is suggested, were worked over by a single hand some time before 1500'.[3] Synge had always wished to become a master of poetry as well as of prose, so he was strategically positioned to renew the form in Irish writing, albeit in the English language.

Synge's alternation of prose and verse in *Vita Vecchia* was, therefore, the result of his deep study of those medieval Irish tales in which that form had been employed with greatest success. Nine years after writing *Vita Vecchia*, he was still so obsessed with this unique form that he saw fit to open a review of A. H. Leahy's *Heroic Romances of Ireland* with the words: 'Most of the early Irish romances are written in alternating fragments of prose and verse, like the old French take of *Aucassin and Nicolette*' (*Prose*, p. 371). He was greatly impressed by this exploitation of the form in French romance, for he gave a copy of *Aucassin and Nicolette* to his fiancée, Molly Allgood. His comparison between Irish and French romances was shrewd, in its day, and has subsequently been corroborated by Terence McCaughey's demonstration that the poems of the Irish tales and the 'chant fable' of Medieval French Romance perform identical recapitulatory functions.[4] In the review, he went on to make a valuable contrast between the concentrated style of the poems and the more flexible manner of the prose: 'The style of the verse portions is usually of a rather stiff elliptical kind . . . Prose versions, on the other hand . . . can give the reader a sense that he is reading sometimes rather highly-pitched verse and sometimes a simple prose, and

are still natural and pleasing' (*Prose*, p. 371). So it is in Synge's own
use of the form. His prose is simple, direct and explanatory. At times
it becomes conversational, as the writer acquaints the reader with the
circumstances in which each poem was composed. The poems, on
the other hand, are tight of form and elliptical in statement. They are
full of inversions and oblique turns of phrase, which imply but do
not immediately disclose a meaning. The oblique and elliptical
character of these poems is the main source of their emotional
power. This is wholly in keeping with the traditions of medieval
Irish romance. Alan Bruford points out that in the Irish romance the
poems are 'nearly always put into the mouth of a character: if a
druid or *file* is present he is responsible for many of them . . .'[5]
Likewise in *Vita Vecchia* Synge is constantly in the foreground and
takes responsibility for all the poems recited. Bruford says that such
poems 'may be resumés of dialogue or even narration'[6] and the
poems of *Vita Vecchia* perform both of these functions. Some
merely recapitulate situations already described in the commentary.
Others actually introduce new action into the narrative, of which
there has been no previous account in the prose—'I curse my bearing',
'Wet winds', 'Through ways I went', 'Five fives', 'Thrice cruel' and
'A Dream'.

    The poems of *Vita Vecchia* deal with such themes as love, solitude,
pain, dream and death. They are concentrated and evocative renditions of the joys and sorrows of love, of meetings and partings, and
of loneliness. Their oblique lines, which work on a number of levels,
would be impossible in discursive or narrative prose. These qualities
are in keeping with those detected by Bruford in the finest poems
of medieval Irish romance. He admits that most of the romance
poems are dull elegies on dead heroes, repetitive lists of victories and
battles. This was a tradition which Synge wisely eschewed, opting
instead to emulate only the more sincerely impromptu works in the
genre. As Bruford observes of the romances: '. . . the best poems
come at moments of emotion; laments, farewells, welcomes, or
declarations of love. To some extent these may serve, like the verse
in Icelandic sagas, to express emotions too complex or unrestrained
for prose speeches: but they seldom throw much light on the speaker's
character'.[7]

    Bruford points out that in the incidental poems, in which a persona
speaks, 'the normal procedure in that case is to give the gist of the
conversation in prose before saying that a poem was made out of it'.[8]
As a characteristic example of the lines used to introduce a poem, he

gives the formula 'agus do rinne an laoi' (and he made this lay). This is exactly the procedure followed by Synge:

In the morning I wrote these lines . . .
I made many simple poems the day that I saw her . . .
I made these lines . . .
This is the end of the poem I made in the morning . . .
I wrote in a notebook by a river . . .
I wrote this little verse . . . (*Prose*, pp. 17–21)

Bruford notes that in the late tales we often come upon 'poems in stress metres', as opposed to the strict syllabic metres of bardic poetry.[9] Perhaps, it is permissible to see Synge as developing this tendency of the late romances, and turning to the stress metres of ballad, song and sonnet for his own poetic forms. Bruford detects 'a tendency to regular stress' in the corrupt later manuscripts of the romances; and he suggests that the long lines of the *amhrán* would have been the logical development of this tendency.[10] It is such a development that we find in the final poem of *Vita Vecchia*, with its long lines in iambic pentameter and its increased length. In general, however, the poems of *Vita Vecchia* are much shorter, only one of the eleven numbering more than twelve lines. This is in keeping with the observation that 'nearly all the poems in the romances are short by bardic standards, between three and twelve lines'.[11]

When we recall Synge's youthful passion for the violin, it comes as no surprise that he should have employed in *Vita Vecchia* metres of ballad, song and sonnet, all of which were born in music. In 1894, only a year before he embarked on *Vita Vecchia*, he had abandoned his ambition to become a concert violinist on account of his nervousness. As late as 20 May 1893, he had started to compose the words and music of an opera on 'Eileen A Rúin'. So even at the height of his musical passion, he was turning to Gaelic literature for inspiration. Two years later, in *Vita Vecchia*, he showed himself keen to draw on the forms of song for his poetic material. In Synge's imagination, literature and music were brought into a creative and mutually enriching fusion. Poised in 1895 between his frustrated ambitions to become a violinist and his awakening desire to become a writer, he found the form of Gaelic romance entirely appropriate to his purpose in *Vita Vecchia*—a group of poems or operatic arias, in the metres of song, linked by a prose narrative. Once again, this fusion of the arts of literature and music was clearly sanctioned by the tradition of Gaelic romance. In these romances, Bruford points out that the poems 'vary the flow of the narration of prose recitative' and that 'like bardic eulogies, they were sung or chanted in public performance'. Thus, 'they would break up the prose fairly considerably' and the poem, usually sung at the end of an episode, 'would make an effective musical finale of the evening's entertainment'.[12]

The very defects of *Vita Vecchia* may be attributed to the fidelity with which it reproduces the elements of Gaelic romance. This is not simply a matter of local vices of style, such as intrusive alliteration but, more crucially, a problem of structure. The greatest single flaw in a work such as *Buile Shuibhne* is the increasing redundancy of the prose narrative as the story progresses. This is due to the fact that the narrative is merely a later device, invented as a frame for the pre-existing body of poems. The prose sections of the work merely rehearse or repeat the subjects in the verse. They provide the reciter with a period of relaxation between each concentrated poem and a valuable mnemonic method of retaining the poems in his memory in correct sequence. As *Buile Shuibhne* progresses towards a conclusion, so there are fewer poems to remember and less explanation is necessary. The prose narrative is severely attenuated, at times threatening to disappear altogether. Similarly, with *Vita Vecchia*, where the poetry is clearly the pre-existing basis of the work, the prose sections are short, poorly written, and all too frequently decline into such one-line introductions as:

> After many months I find these lines in my note-book . . .
> I wrote in a book by a river . . .
> Later I thought I was better and returned to Paris. I wrote this little verse . . .
> At this time also I wrote this sonnet . . .
> I find two short poems at the end of my note-book . . .
> (*Prose*, pp. 19–22)

Finally the poet, bored by this charade, admits the redundancy of the prose device. He introduces the penultimate poem with a perfunctory 'and again'; and he prints the last poem with no words of introduction.

Synge's attempt to re-create a romance of the Gaelic mode in modern English was high-minded and idealistic. It was the earliest sign in his writings that he would look for inspiration to the forms, as well as the themes, of Gaelic literature. Apart from one or two isolated stanzas, its poetry is a dismal failure, a derivative and confused mixture of cloyed sensuousness, pseudo-Wordsworthian nature mysticism and crippling Gaelic alliteration. The prose narrative is uninspired, wrenching the reader from circumstantial detail to ponderous philosophy. These defects are in the main the defects of the author's Gaelic sources. While this in no way extenuates the failure of *Vita Vecchia* as a work of literature, it proves that Synge from the very outset of his career was trying deliberately to set his work within the Gaelic tradition.

TOWARD A NATIONAL DRAMA

In his playlet, *National Drama: A Farce*, through the character of Jameson, Synge expressed his belief in a literature which projects the beauty of Ireland, without being 'wilful' in its cultivation of national feeling. He had Jameson make a spirited sally against the Young Ireland poets and their latter-day disciples: 'I do not say that all artistic production is national—Gaelic adaptations of fourth-rate English poetry are not national . . . But any art work that is in any sense the product of a few minds working together, the work is and cannot help being national . . .' (*Plays 1*, p. 225). Jameson goes on to outline the attitude adopted by Synge and Yeats to the previous literature of Ireland, written both in Irish and English: 'Isolated imitations of some foreign form do not make national art, but when two or three people use the infinite number of influences from the past and present of the country, that gives their work a local character which is all a nation can demand . . .' This is exactly what Synge did in fusing the techniques of Gaelic literature with the preoccupations of contemporary Anglo-Irish writing.

Synge's Breton friend and mentor, Anatole Le Braz, must have encouraged him in this brave manoeuvre. The dramatist was an avid student of Le Braz's books and in one of these, on the history of Celtic theatre, he would have come upon the following description of the problem which confronted him and of the manner in which he was to solve it:

Or, en réalité, il n'y a qu'un seul peuple celtique chez lequel on ne conaisse aucun vestige de théâtre, et—par un anomalie qui, au premier abord, a de quoi surprendre—c'est le peuple irlandais. Nul autre, on l'a vu, ne fut naturellement mieux doué pour inventer des situations fortes, créer des caractères d'une trempe peu banale, mener avec entrain une action pleine de mouvement et de vie. 'A la fois violent et sensible, imaginatif et batailleur', il a prodigué le drame dans l'épopée. Oui, mais il ne semble pas qu'il l'en ait jamais fait sortir. Alors que, peu à peu, au cours des âges, les genres littéraires en germe et comme en suspens dans l'ondoigante matière, épique—jurisprudence, médecine, géographie, histoire— finissaient par s'isoler, se dégager, s'organiser, se développer chacun d'une existence propre, le genre dramatique ne parvint pas a se dissocier de la gangue primitive où il flottait à l'état de dialogues et de scénarios épars . . .[13]

(Now in reality there is only one Celtic people among whom one can find no traces of theatre and—by an anomaly which in the first instance is somewhat surprising—it is the Irish people. We have seen that no other people was better endowed by nature to devise striking situations, to create characters of a remarkable stamp, and to conduct with zest an action full of movement and life. 'At once violent and sensitive, imaginative and pugnacious', they have lavished all their drama on the epic form. Un- doubtedly—but it does not seem as if they could ever have detached it from that form. While, gradually through the ages each of the literary genres which were suspended in embryo in the undulating epic material—jurisprudence, medicine, geography and history— ended up by being isolated, detached, organised and developed with a life of its own, the genre of drama did not succeed in detaching itself from the primitive matrix in which it had floated in the form of dialogues and random scenarios.)

Le Braz went on to explain that an Irish theatre never developed, because it could only do so in a settled, urbanised and peaceful society. He argued that the Irish people had suffered from far too much real drama in their lives to feel the need to create a theatre of fictional tragedy. His major point was that the various genres of modern writing, as we know them, derive from common sources in ancient literature and folklore. He felt that in the 'agallaimh' or dialogues of Old Irish writing lay the basis of a modern national drama. It was simply up to a writer like Synge to set in train the process which years of political turmoil and social upheaval had prevented—to hasten the detachment of the old themes from their ancient genres into the newer dramatic form. In the dialogues between Oisín and St Patrick lay the seeds of that debate between pagan and Christian which dominates *The Tinker's Wedding* and *The Well of the Saints*. In a brief folk story lay the basic plot of *The Shadow of the Glen*. In one phase of the story of the Sons of Usnach lay the plot of *Deirdre of the Sorrows*. In the decline and fall of the Irish Heroic Cycle lay the spiritual history of Christy Mahon.

Lady Gregory, too, was not slow to sense the possibilities of a Gaelic drama. She noted shrewdly that 'Irish speakers . . . have an inborn love of drama'.[14] Like Le Braz, she perceived an incipient drama in such long dramatic dialogues as those between Oisín and St Patrick: 'At country gatherings, those old dialogues, and the newer ones between Death and Raftery, or between the farmers of two provinces, are followed with a patient joy; and the creation of acting plays is the natural outcome of this living tradition'.[15]

In an article introducing Irish literature to a Fresch audience in March 1902, Synge had implied a criticism of his fellow-writers for their neglect of Irish. He wrote that his native literature fell into two categories: '. . . la littéarature ancienne, écrite en celtique, et la littérature moderne, écrite en anglais par de jeunes ecrivains qui ignorent à peu prés complétement la langue originaire de leur pays . . .' (*Prose*, p. 352). (. . . the ancient literature, written in Celtic, and the modern literature, written in English by young writers who are almost completely ignorant of the first language of their country.) He went on to suggest that, while there were important links between the two traditions, it would scarcely be possible for him to treat them together. With a polite compliment on the beauty of some modern Irish writing in English, he emphasised the greater value of the ancient literature in the native language: 'c'est la vieille littérature et elle seule qui a une veritable importance européenne' (it is the ancient literature and that alone which is genuinely significant at a European level). So, as late as 1902, Synge still had no very great opinion of Irish writing in English. As a critic, he showed himself painfully conscious of the gulf between the two traditions. As an artist, he had already set about the fusion of these traditions in his own writing, so that some day future critics might be able to treat them together.

His first sustained attempt at such a fusion in the drama was a failure. This was *Luasnad, Capa and Laine* which was inspired by an anecdote from Geoffrey Keating's *Foras Feasa ar Éirinn*. This play was worked on between March 1902 and January 1903. Synge had reviewed Comyn's edition of the first volume of *Foras Feasa* in the

Speaker on 6 September 1902; and it is clear that this long critique was written, published and, no doubt, discussed in the months when he was at work on the play. Here is Comyn's translation of the extract:

> Some others say that it is three fishermen who were driven by a storm of wind from Spain unwillingly; and as the island pleased them that they returned for their wives to Spain; and having come back to Ireland again, the deluge was showered upon them at Tuaigh Innbhir, so that they were drowned: Capa, Laighne, and Luasad their names. It is about them the verse was sung:—
>
>> Capa, Laighne, and Luasad pleasant,
>> They were a year before the deluge
>> On the island of Banbha of the bays;
>> They were eminently brave.[16]

Keating saw fit to mention the story of these men because they are reputed to have been the very first inhabitants of Ireland. His account provided Synge with the characters and setting of a uniquely symbolic play. Fishermen from the continent were no strangers in the west of Ireland and, although it is not so named in the story, one of the Aran islands may have been the rocky setting which pleased the three men. At all events, the theme of this play is the same theme which permeates *The Aran Islands* and *Riders to the Sea*, Synge's other studies of island life. That theme is the assertion of man's will to live and procreate in the face of death and decay all around him— or, as Capa says 'We shall live / In spite of all this deluge' (*Plays 1*, p. 196). In Keating's terse narrative, Synge may have discerned the original pattern on which all later island life was based. His play dramatises not only the founding of the Irish race (and, by implication, the source of the native cultural tradition), but also the very origins of that life on Aran which had so fascinated him. By his treatment of these prehistoric protagonists, he shows how nothing in that life had changed over the centuries. He frequently called Inishmaan a rock in the Atlantic and in this play he places his characters on a similar rock, battling for life against wind, water and sun. This drama is informed by all he had witnessed on Aran, by the keens and laments of the folk, by his share in their terror at the prospect of death by sea, by the astringent quality of their gaiety—their sudden outbursts of joy in the face of mist or death. All this is compounded by feelings from Synge's personal life, by his consistent refusal to believe in a merciful God, by the consequent frustration of his sexual desire for Cherrie Matheson, and, above all, by the Flood which had formed so crucial a part of his mother's evangelical Protestantism.

These elements might have combined to give us a work of art, as Synge's intentions were of the best. He had tried to tackle these themes as introspective fiction in *Étude Morbide*, but had failed to achieve clarity because of the excessive subjectivity of its form. Subsequently, in *The Aran Islands* he had found in the world of the fisherfolk so many external images that conformed with his inner mood that the desired balance between the subjective and objective was persuasively achieved. In *Luasnad, Capa and Laine* he sought to carry this process a stage further and to cast the same themes within the absolute objectivity of the dramatic form. He failed yet again; but on his return to Ireland in the same year, he embarked on *Riders to the Sea* which would project those themes in what many critics regard as the most perfect one-act play of all time. *Luasnad, Capa and Laine* fails primarily because the rigid formality of the verse does not sort with the extremity of the situation. We have only to witness *Riders to the Sea* to measure the extent of Synge's failure in blank verse drama and the stunning progress in his art between the writing of both plays. *Luasnad Capa and Laine* is *Riders to the Sea* in the making, *Riders* written without a time or a location; and without it the great one-act play might never have come to fruition. Although it is a failure, this early verse play contains significant hints of the techniques and themes of Synge's later masterpieces. It is revealing, for example, that Keating's source offers the dramatist nothing but the basic situation for his play, certainly nothing as elaborate as a plot. This was the scale on which he was to choose the source materials for later dramas such as *The Tinker's Wedding* and *The Well of the Saints*. These works, also, were based on brief anecdotes, whose simple situations left the author's spirit free to create at will within the basic outlines. It is also remarkable that, even at this early stage in 1902, Synge's instinct should have been so unerring in choosing an occurrence which allowed him to dramatise his primary preoccupations. That he should have seized upon a very short anecdote in the midst of Keating's long narrative proves that, from the very outset, he sought to found his plays on material taken from his native literature.

On the night of the riots at *The Playboy* on Monday 28

January 1907, Synge gave an interview to a young reporter of the
Evening Mail. In this conversation he gave a pithy account of his
artistic practice: 'I wrote the play because it pleased me, and it just
happens that I know Irish life best, so I made my methods Irish'.[17]
It is his allegiance to these methods that we must trace. We shall see
that it was his deliberate cultivation of the methods of classic works
of Irish literature which outraged the so-called Gaels of his time. It
was his honesty in confronting the native tradition in all its aspects,
sweet and sordid, that brought him into disrepute with the selective
revivalists of his own day. He was unique among the Anglo-Irish
writers of his age in his total commitment to the Gaelic literary
tradition; and he was unique among the Gaels of his day in his total
commitment to the primacy of literature and the rigours of its craft.
Other Gaelic writers emulated the ancient bards in their love of
Ireland and praise of its people; Synge alone followed the bards in
the lonelier discipline of literary craft. He was very much alone.

THE PLAYBOY AND ALLITERATIVE ROMANCE

In 1878 Standish James O'Grady had published a book entitled
History of Ireland: Heroic Period, a work which helped many Irish
writers to come to terms with the ancient literature. In his autobiography Yeats claimed that to O'Grady, 'every Irish imaginative
writer owed a portion of his soul'.[18] Synge came early to the study
of O'Grady's works, as we note from his diary for 1892.[19] However, O'Grady knew no Irish, taking his material 'from the dry
pages of O'Curry and his school'.[20] His work, therefore, can have
had only a limited value for Synge, although, like other young
writers, he was fired by it at the time. O'Grady had proved that the
legends were not solely the possession of editors and translators, but
could be exploited richly as a source for contemporary Irish writing.

Synge, for his part, had gone straight to the original sources in
the Irish language. At Trinity College he had studied 'some epic
literature'[21] along with *Oidhe Chloinne Lir*, which exploited a heavily
alliterative style both in poetry and prose. This he sought to emulate
not only in the poems of *Vita Vecchia* but also in the speeches of
his plays. In Standish H. O'Grady's introduction to *Tóruigheacht
Dhiarmada agus Ghráinne* (a tale based on a manuscript taken down
from oral recitation), he came upon an analysis of this technique:
'the genius of the Gaelic seems to impel to alliteration, and its

numerous synonyms invite to repetitions which, properly used, strengthen, and, being abused, degenerate into jingle and tautology. The Irish speakers of the present day very commonly, for emphasis' sake, use two synonymous adjectives without a conjunction, instead of one with an adverb, and these they almost invariably choose so that there shall be alliteration'.[22] O'Grady offered as an example of alliterating synonyms 'suan ná sámhcodla', which he translated as 'slumber or sweet sleep'. His argument that such alliteration is essentially an oral device would not have been lost on Synge who realised that in drama, rather than in the novel or the modern short story, the status of the spoken word is much the same as in oral storytelling. So in *The Playboy of the Western World* he repeatedly employed such alliterating synonyms: 'powers and potentates' (*Plays 2*, p. 79), 'cot and cabin' (81) 'prayers and paters' (149); or closely related words such as 'cup and cake' (87), 'wealth and wisdom' (95), 'next and nighest' (137); or even contrasting words such as 'wakes or weddings' (59), 'judge or jury' (71), 'fasting or fed' (101).

Synge also encountered this alliterative technique in the opening lines of *Oidhe Chloinne Uisnigh*, which he translated into English in 1901: 'Fleadh mheadhar-chaoin mhór-adhbhal do righneadh le Conchobhar, Mac Fachtna Fathaigh, mhic Rosa Ruaidh mhic Rudhraighe . . .'[23] Although he seldom tried to recapture such effects in his version of the prose narrative of this text, he did seek to reproduce the alliteration of the poems. Two years later in Lady Gregory's *Cuchulain of Muirthemne*, however, he found ample evidence that this alliterative prose could be translated gracefully into the English of rural Ireland. All the women of Ulster loved the young Cuchulain, wrote Lady Gregory, 'for the lightness of his leap, for the weight of his wisdom, for the sweetness of his speech'.[24] This was a style fitting for heroics—and for mock-heroics. It had been parodied most notoriously in a seventeenth-century satire in Irish on the peasantry, *Parlaimint Chloinne Tomáis*, whose author—a master of the literary language—burlesques the style of the heroic romances. The traditional use of alliteration in the hero-tales was taken to an absurd extreme in this work, the better to mock the convention; and this style became even more dramatic when used in abrasive conversations between churls: 'Mo mhallacht ort, a ladruin láinbhréin na leathbhróige lobhtha, nach raibh riamh acht lán do chiorum-cárum'.[25] This is a compelling fusion of the noble alliteration of the hero-tales and the ignoble alliteration of seventeenth-century slang (ciorum-cárum). The noble idiom jostles with the base to mock-heroic effect all through the work. It was in just such a style that Synge had Sara Tansey celebrate the latter-day heroism of those comrades-in-carnage, Christy Mahon and Widow Quin: 'Drink a health to the wonders of the western world, the pirates, preachers, poteen makers, with the jobbing jockies, parching peelers, and the juries fill their stomachs selling judgements of the English law' (*Plays 2*, p. 105). Here the dramatist has applied an insight first gleaned from O'Grady's introduction to *Tóruigheacht Dhiarmada agus Ghráinne*, where that scholar had praised the graceful cadence of such alliterative devices, while warning at the same time of the 'sacrifice of sense and strength for sound' in the romances: 'and this taste never having been corrected, the Irish peasantry, albeit they make in their conversation a pleasing and moderate use of alliteration and repetition, yet admire extravagance and bombast in their romances'.[26] It is this extravagance and bombast which Sara Tansey employs with delight as a fitting toast to the romantic heroes of the Mayo village.

These ancient romances had been studied closely by Synge in his student years at Trinity; but later in Paris he sought to extend his knowledge by attending the lectures of de Jubainville on the place of Irish heroic literature in the mythology of Europe. His deepest interest was in the Cuchulain saga, as is clear from this reading list taken from a notebook kept in the winter of 1898–9:

> The Cuchullin Saga   Hull
> For the birth of Conachar see Rev. Cel. VI. 173, 182, ix, 1.
> Wooing of Emer   Rev. Cel. IX 442
> Siege of Howth   Rev. Cel. VIII 49.63.
> Goudor   Études de Mythologie Gaulois   1886
> Táin Bó Cuailgne   see Zimmer   Kel. Stud.   O'Curry.
> (Compare Cuchullin's cutting of an oak sapling using but one foot, hand and eye with the initial feats in folk tales.)[27]

Considering that Synge's work under de Jubainville 'formed no part of the critical studies to which he planned to devote himself during his stay in Paris',[28] this investigation of Irish mythology was impressive. In subsequent years he became an avid reader of Lady Gregory's English language version of the story of Cuchilain. He urged his fiancée, Molly Allgood, to read the volume and wrote to Lady Gregory herself with the news that 'your *Cuchulain of Muirthemne* is part of my daily bread'.[29] It was this version of the heroic saga which most excited and inspired the dramatist. Not only did it provide him with a confirmation of the power and grace of alliterative peasant dialect, but it also proved that this idiom could fittingly project the lives of ancient heroes as well as well as the preoccupations of the contemporary peasant. In the words of Synge's biographer: 'Lady Gregory had boldly written her stories from ancient Irish saga in the language of a modern English-speaking peasant. Whatever Synge may have owed her for his mastery of the same medium, there is no doubt that she had shown him the possibility of making the personages of the past speak like peasants while still remaining heroes'.[30] Such an idiom was the ideal language for Christy Mahon, the peasant boy who was destined to become a hero; and Synge's parody of the Cuchulain saga in *The Playboy* owes much to these earlier studies and, in particular, to Lady Gregory's *Cuchulain of Muirthemne*.

THE *PLAYBOY* AS HEROIC PARODY

The Playboy of the Western World evokes the action and excitement of the Cuchulain cycle at many points, the better to mock the puny latter-day reality of life among the peasantry. The peasants still delight to tell stories of a heroic past, but even the saga has been scaled down in the process. Marcus Quin, the man who was 'a great warrant to tell stories of holy Ireland' (*Plays 2*, p. 59), never appears onstage. He is dead, having been jailed for the rather less holy, less heroic offence of maiming ewes. The folk who once listened spell-bound to the saga now regale each other with tales of Daneen Sullivan who 'knocked the eye from a peeler' and 'the mad Mulrannies were driven from California and they lost in their wits' (*Plays 2*, p. 59). Tales of the bodily excellence of Cuchulain are replaced by anecdotes of Red Linahan who 'has a squint in his eye, and Patcheen is lame in his heel' (*Plays 2*, p. 59). Nevertheless, if Synge depicts these farmers and publicans as folk fallen from the heroic past, he does allow his outsiders, such as Christy Mahon to retain some of the glamour and lyricism of the epic heroes. If Synge evoked the great-ness of the saga life, the better to mock the littleness of the contemporary peasant, then the irony works both ways, mocking also the portentous bearing and blind violence of the ancient pro-tagonists. This ambiguous two-way irony is at work also in Joyce's *Ulysses* and Eliot's *The Waste Land*.

That the attributes of a godlike Cuchulain should re-appear in a feckless peasant is entirely in keeping with the thrust of ancient Irish literary tradition. The *Lebar Gabála* (*The Book of Invasions*) was a twelfth-century work which set out with the intention of reducing the deities of pagan Ireland to the status of mere mortals. This work was well known to the dramatist who had taken notes about its contents in the winter of 1898/9. He was later to criticise de Jubainville for relying too heavily on the plan of the *Lebar Gabála* in his own book on *The Irish Mythological Cycle and Celtic Mythology*. In Synge's case, familiarity with the contents of the *Lebar Gabála* bred contempt. He complained of its 'rather unattractive material, where the thread of Irish myth is much obscured by pseudo-classical or Biblical adaptations'; but he praised de Jubainville's facility in tracing the euhemerised figures of Irish myth back to their sources in gods common to Greek, Gaulish and Celtic legend (*Prose*, p. 364). At all events, the process of reducing deities to mere mortals was performed for Irish mythology by the *Lebar Gabála* and Synge noted it. This tendency was widespread in Gaelic literature. It persists still in the Fenian ballads of Donegal, where one song, heard by the present writer, depicts Fionn performing amazing feats as a construction worker on a local railway. This transition in the native literature may be attributed to a change in its audience from noblemen to farmers; but, Gerard Murphy has observed that 'though the tendency to give prominence to buffoonery in Fenian poetry is late, the roots of that tendency may be ancient'.[31] Professor Murphy supports the contention (made famous by the Chadwicks in *The Growth of Literature*) that the gods were frequently dealt with 'in a rough humorous way markedly different from the respectful way in which nobles were treated'.[32] Because Fionn was seen originally as a god, he was liable to humorous treatment at first by unlearned storytellers and later on, with the decay of the heroic tradition, by learned writers as well.

Many contemporaries of Synge, such as Standish James O'Grady, attacked historical dramas such as George Russell's *Deirdre* or Synge's own *Deirdre of the Sorrows*, because it was alleged that these plays made the ancient kings and queens talk like peasants.[33] Such critics plainly failed to see how these works developed an inherent tendency of the native literary tradition. To dress Conchubor and Naoise in peasant garb was no crime, since the story itself had come down in peasant idiom anyway, narrated and moulded by successive generations of countrymen. There is a demonstrable relation between the regal personages of the legends and the rural Ireland where these tales lingered. By reducing kings and warriors to speakers of his rustic dialect, Synge was merely the exponent of a tradition which had already reduced the gods to mortals and thence to day-labourers on the railroad.

In a famous letter to Stephen McKenna, the dramatist wrote: 'I do not believe in the possibility of "a purely fantastic unmodern ideal breezy springdayish Cuchulanoid National Theatre". We had the *Shadowy Waters* on the stage last week and it was the most distressing failure the mind can imagine—a half-empty room with growling men and tittering females.'[34] This declaration has been interpreted to signify that Synge 'resolutely set his face against the use of myth in his plays' and that 'he was certainly too little interested in it to write his greatest work as parody'.[35] This is a myopically literal interpretation of the letter and takes no account of the force with which its lines were written. It is certainly true that Synge set his face against myth, but it is not true that he was little interested in it. So obsessed was he with heroic myth and with the lies which it seemed to foster among his fellow-dramatists, that he sought to expose it fully in *The Playboy*. Here he attacked the idea of heroism with its own inner contradictions. We may call this a parody if we choose, but that is no disgrace. A good parody can transcend its immediate occasion and become, like *Don Quixote* or *Buile Shuibhne*, a masterpiece.

P. L. Henry has written of Christy Mahon as a 'Playboy-Hero' and has pointed out those details which the play has in common with *Beowulf* and the heroic Irish sagas.[36] T. R. Henn rightly described the play as 'a semi-parody of the Celtic heroic cycles: of the violent hero who attains his stature by giving good blows. And as the epic narrative becomes subject to improvement, the violence increases in those primary virtues of epic: ferocity, courage and strength'.[37] This is all very well, but Henn does not explain why Synge should have chosen to parody the accounts of ancient heroes. To ask this question is to ask how, exactly, the parody works. There are, in the author's own words, several sides to *The Playboy*. One of them may well be a satire on the hero-cult which was growing among the nationalists and even among the writers of Synge's own day. A whole book has been devoted to an analysis of Yeats's obsession with the heroic ideal.[38] So potent a paragon was Cuchulain for Patrick Pearse that one of his pupils at St Enda's remarked that the school had Cuchulain as 'an important if invisible member of

the staff'.[39] Pearse's motto was one of the aphorisms attributed to
the ancient hero: 'I care not though I were to live but one day and
one night, if only my fame and my deeds live after me'. Standish
James O'Grady had made Cuchulain the central figure of his historical
books and Lady Gregory had devoted her finest work to the
exploits of the hero.

In all of these works, the central theme was the skill of Cuchulain
in glamorised combat, his capacity to make violence seem heroic.
Synge was a staunch pacifist and took exception to this. He had
objected to the militarism of *Irlande Libre* during his time in Paris;
and he could not have viewed the increasing glorification of heroic
violence in Ireland with anything other than grave concern. He saw
that along with the spirituality of the peasantry, upon which writers
of the revival seemed wholly to dwell, went a streak of brutality to
man and beast alike. He saw Yeats and Pearse glorify the blind
violence of the heroes in mythology, but conveniently ignore the
same mindless brutality in the lives of the peasants who yet revered
these tales. In *The Aran Islands*, Synge confronted the truth about
violence in rural Irish life: 'Although these people are kindly towards
each other and to their children, they have no feeling for the suffering of animals, and little sympathy for pain when the person who
feels it is not in danger. I have sometimes seen a girl writhing and
howling with toothache while her mother sat at the other end of the
fireplace pointing at her and laughing at her as if amused by the
sight' (*Prose*, p. 163). There are numerous references in *The Playboy*
to the sinister pleasure taken by country folk in cruelty to animals.
One of Marcus Quin's sports was maiming ewes and other folk
travelled miles to see the hanging of a dog. Susan Brady reminds
Sara Tansey that she is 'the one yoked the ass cart and drove ten
miles to set your eyes on the man bit the yellow lady's nostril on
the northern shore' (*Plays 2*, p. 97). Violence to animals reached such
alarming proportions in Connacht in the last century that Richard
Burke, a famous landlord, was given the mocking nickname
'Humanity Dick', because of his campaigns in defence of animals.
According to the historian, Nicholas Mansergh, Synge's bleak portrayal of this violence is not exaggerated:

In the early years of Queen Victoria's reign, the French traveller,
de Beaumont, had spoken of the 'vindictive cruelty', of the 'savage
violence' of the Irish peasant in his acts of revenge. For some
seventy years from the time when he first visited Ireland, outrage

and reprisal disturbed the peace of the countryside. A tradition was established, men became accustomed to brutal scenes, and, as those who have read the opening scene of *The Playboy of the Western World* will recall, revenge even on helpless animals might in certain circumstances be referred to with pride.[40]

Other violent sports casually referred to in *The Playboy* include the challenge to 'slit the windpipe of a screeching sow' (*Plays 2*, p. 71) and the story of a dying dog 'screeching and wriggling three hours at the butt of a string' (*Plays 2*, p. 73).

If there was ambiguity in the attitude of Yeats and Pearse to heroic violence, there was a similar ambivalence in the peasant's indulgence of savagery. The Mayo folk revere Christy for his tale of a violent death and they thrill to the increasingly lurid narrations of his parricide. Philly Cullen sports with a skeleton and Jimmy Farrell talks bravely of skulls, each in pursuit of the vicarious thrill; but when real violence erupts before their very eyes, as Christy tries again to murder his father, their true feelings emerge with a sudden clarity and peasant cunning overwhelms all other considerations. Pegeen's pithy words convey the popular response, as she exclaims that 'there's a great gap between a gallous story and a dirty deed' (*Plays 2*, p. 169). There is self-deception, as well as forthright honesty, in those words. Violence must be committed in the past to qualify as a 'gallous story', but current violence is 'a dirty deed'. Synge's unsentimental view of things, his desire to give in his plays 'the entire reality of life',[41] demanded that the evasions of Pearse and Yeats be exposed. He saw behind the cult of the hero to the eternal truths about military violence that lay beneath the superficial glamour of action—to the fact that heroes are brave only because they are so frightened and that violence is at best only 'a sneaky kind of murder' (*Plays 2*, p. 89). The ancient heroes committed immense acts of violence and bravery, which were applauded by ordinary men, too timid to think of emulating them. The bravery manifested by Christy Mahon in the initial slaying of his father may be of a similar variety; but the heroism which he displays in attacking his father a second time is of a higher plane, for, on this occasion, he knows that his act will win no social acclaim. He has now established himself as a real hero, who, like Synge, can openly confront the paradox on which society exists—the violence which ordinary folk feel to be necessary but which society, as such, cannot afford to condone.[42]

Even today, the descendants of Jimmy Farrell and Philly Cullen vicariously taste this violence in crime thrillers and bar-room ballads in celebration of the IRA; but if the violence is to be glamorous, it must happen only in fiction, or at least, a hundred miles away on the other side of a patrolled political border. Funds for the men of violence are not lacking as long as the campaign is waged elsewhere; if it erupts in one's own back-yard, then it becomes a 'dirty deed'. The rebellion of 1916 and its bloody aftermath forced men like Yeats to face this paradox. He had to admit that he could no longer separate his poetic celebration of the savagery of the ancient heroes from his obvious political distaste for the contemporary violence, which he saw all around him. His confession of this split-mindedness is made with compelling honesty in 'Easter 1916'.

In the Ireland of Synge's time there were two schools of writing, one following O'Grady in its evocation of a heroic past, which can have existed only in men's imaginations—the other dedicated to an equally spurious vision of the western peasant as a kind of secular Gaelic mystic. Synge's evocation of Christy as a mock-Cuchulain provides an ironic commentary on the evasions of both these schools of writing. By making an ancient warrior live again in the person of Christy Malon, Synge provides an example to both schools of how they might shape a serious and mature art, which probed the similarities and disparities between the Irish past and present. The play is not simply a critique of Yeats's and Lady Gregory's Cuchulain, nor is it just another sally against the Gaelic League's idealisation of the countryman. It is a challenge to both schools to concede the essential continuity of both traditions and to recognise the savagery, as well as the beauty, which lies at their heart. In the words of Martin Lamm, Synge's peasants do not need much disguising to serve as the legendary heroes of a thousand years ago.[43] This is the method pursued in full seriousness in his next play, *Deirdre of the Sorrows*. In *The Playboy*, we get a first mocking hint of this technique, when the legendary hero of a thousand years ago needs little disguising to pass muster as a shiftless young peasant. In this play we find, for the first time in the English language what Máirtín Ó Cadhain's *Cré na Cille* offered, for the first time in the Irish language, four decades later— the deglamorised version of life in the west of Ireland. These works pandered to no sentiment, but provided the long-awaited answer to a felt need, especially in the west itself. An old shoemaker in the 1870s had confided in a boy named William Yeats that for him the attractions of Kickham, Griffin and the other sentimental Irish novelists had begun to pall. He longed, he said, for a work in which the people would be 'shown up in their naked hideousness'.[44]

Some possible points of contact between Synge's play and the Cuchulain cycle will now be outlined. These may prove helpful to a fuller interpretation of *The Playboy* as mock-drama and of Christy as mock-Cuchulain. However, it is wise to make clear from the outset that this is not a question of one-to-one correspondence. Synge was free to use the story to his own devices, taking a point here, inverting a point there, as all writers must. The test of a true artist is not what he borrows from literary tradition, but how he deploys these borrowings. The Cuchulain legend is a palpable force at work in Synge's play; but the debasement of the ancient heroes, set in train in the native literature as early as the tenth century, is carried even further by Synge, who is clearly conscious of his strategic role in such a process. Christy retains many of the virtues of the ancient hero. If he displays some unheroic vices, that may well be part of Synge's jibe against 'Cuchulanoid' drama. In this play we witness Synge's wry delineation of the real face of herosim and, in the words of Maxim Gorki, 'a subtle irony on the cult of the hero'.[45] The fact that the author should have mentioned a 'Cuchulanoid drama' in the famous letter to Stephen MacKenna proves that the Cuchulain cycle was never far from his mind as he wrote. That his use of 'Cuchulanoid' was pejorative should make us doubly alert to the possibilities of a mock-heroic approach in his finest play.

CHRISTY AND CUCHULAIN

The tales of the Ulster Cycle are framed by Bricriu, the satirist who steers his heroic characters in and out of trouble, frequently with mocking intent. Only one of Bricriu's heroes, Cuchulain, escapes the satirist's ridicule and survives the narrative with dignity intact. Synge arrogates to himself Bricriu's ancient function and deals his characters the rough blows of the mock-heroic, as all contrive in various ways to make themselves ridiculous. Like Cuchulain, Christy is not immune to the satirist's lash. However, both protagonists stand head-and-shoulders above their respective communities. The attitude of society to these heroes oscillates between fear and admiration; and both men go on to win a higher and lonelier kind of self-respect in the end.

This is only to emphasise the similarity in the general situation of the two protagonists. In matters of detail, Synge is as likely as not to invert in the character of Christy Mahon the virtues and triumphs of the Ulster hero. Cuchulain in early youth was renowned for his athletic ability, his comely face and pleasant speech, all of which made him so attractive to women that the men of Ulster decided to safeguard their wives and daughters by forcing him to wed.[46] Even as a lad, he was master of the boy-troop at Emain.[47] Christy Mahon, on the contrary, is first described as cowering in terror in a ditch; and he is neither athletic, nor handsome, nor sweet of speech. Instead, he is seen as 'a lier on walls' (*Plays 2*, p. 51), 'a slight young man' (p. 67), 'a talker of folly' (p. 51) and so ridiculous to the local girls that they call him 'the laughing joke of every female woman where four baronies meet' (p. 123). However, attempts are made by his father to marry him off to the Widow Casey. The Ulstermen had wished to marry off Cuchulain because his charismatic appeal to women was a threat to all the men; Old Mahon wishes to marry off Christy to a withered hag in order to earn some money from the transaction which will subsidise his drinking. Cuchulain's initiation as a warrior occurs when, attired in King Conchubor's borrowed arms, he defeats the three brave sons of Nechtan and returns with their three heads as trophies.[48] Christy, too, attired in the borrowed wedding-suit of Shawn Keogh, defeats all comers at the local sports, returning also with three trophies.

Despite the opposition of her father, Emer was wooed by Cuchulain, clad 'in his rich clothes'[49] like Christy in the borrowed wedding-suit. Emer was famed for her looks, her chastity, her sweet voice, her way with words, and, curiously, her ability at needlework.[50] In Pegeen Synge recreates these virtues in his own subtly ironic way, inverting the parallels even as he invokes them. She is, according to the stage directions, 'a wild-looking but fine girl' (*Plays 2*, p. 57). According to Widow Quin, her only fragrance is 'the stale stink of poteen' (p. 127); but Christy sees her as 'a lovely, handsome woman' (p. 111). She is, of course, chaste; but her chastity is ambiguous, the result of circumstances rather than conscious will. Even in her frightened enumeration of the many threats to her chastity, she betrays a colourful awareness of the excitement, as well as the dangers, posed by 'the harvest boys with their tongues red for drink, and the ten tinkers is camped in the east glen, and the thousand militia—bad cess to them!—walking idle through the land' (p. 63). She displays no scruples whatever about passing a night alone with a man who has murdered his father. In her speech, Christy hears only 'sweetness', but she herself admits being 'the fright of seven townlands for my biting tongue' (p. 151). Like Emer, she is adept with the needle and proudly covers Christy with a rug 'I'm after quilting a while since with my own two hands' (p. 91).

Like Pegeen, Emer is surrounded by other girls, whom she dominates.[51] Emer has another suitor named Lugaid, just as Pegeen has her Shawn Keogh; but both men retire from the contest, despite having the initial support of the girls' fathers, on hearing of the physical feats of their opponents.[52] Cuchulain persists in his suit despite this opposition, because of his pride in his aristocratic background, training and warlike prowess. Pegeen discerns the sure signs of the aristocrat in Christy's appearance: 'the little small feet you have and you with a kind of quality name, the like of what you'd find on the great powers and potentates of France and Spain' (*Plays 2*, p. 79). Like Cuchulain, Christy justifies his suit with references to his background: 'We were great, surely, with wide and windy acres of rich Munster land' (p. 79). He is finally emboldened to seek Pegeen's hand, when he triumphs like Cuchulain at the games.

Shawn Keogh's terror-stricken description of his fear to face 'a leppin' savage the like of him has descended from the Lord knows where' (p. 155) seems to cast doubts on Christy's pedigree and background. The same doubts exist about Cuchulain, whose father was never named. However, Shawn Keogh's sentence may also have been worked in by Synge as an indirect reference to the godly origin of the ancient heroes. Pegeen, at all events, has no difficulty in believing that Christy has lived the life of a personage from the saga, 'the like of a king of Norway or the Eastern world' (p. 83). In his book, *Saga and Myth in Ancient Ireland*, Gerard Murphy has observed that many of the chief protagonists in such tales 'are identifiable with Celtic gods known to us from other sources: Lug, for instance, with the god who gave his name to Lyons (Lugdunum), Laon, Leyden and other continental towns'.[53] This point had been noted by Synge himself, many years earlier, in his review of de Jubainville's book, *The Irish Mythological Cycle and Celtic Mythology*: 'In the early Irish myths a god is met with who is known as Lug the Longhanded, a name that is also found in Gaul in the first portion of the place-name Lugudunum, which has given us Lyon in modern French' (*Prose*, p. 365). T. F. O'Rahilly, in his invaluable *Early Irish History and Mythology*, has no doubt that Cuchulain was once a god-figure, in fact, that very Lug to whom Synge referred:

. . . Cuchulain, who in the *Táin* is assigned the role of defender of the Ulaid against their invaders, can be shown to be in origin Lug or Lugaid, a deity whom we may conveniently call the Hero, provided we bear in mind that he was a wholly supernatural personage, and not a mere mortal. The other leading characters, such as Cú Roi, Fergus, Bricriu and Medb, are likewise euhemerised divinities.[54]

So, if Christy is a latter-day Cuchulain, then Shawn Keogh is fully entitled to quake at his origins 'from the Lord knows where'. Christy himself seems inclined to believe that, like Cuchulain, he is a euhemerised god. He recalls his divine origins and subsequent degradation when he confides in Widow Quin that he is 'a kind of wonder was jilted by the heavens when a day was by' (*Plays 2*, p. 127).

Pegeen goes on to tell Christy that for her he evokes the ancient world of the poet and its heroic virtues—'it's the poets are your like, fine fiery fellows with great rages when their temper's roused' (p. 81). Oisín, the son of Fionn, was at once a great warrior and a poet, the reputed author of ballads and tales of the Fianna. In more recent centuries, writers such as Eoin Rua Ó Súilleabháin were not only great poets, but also brave warriors and soldiers-of-fortune. In *Cuchulain of Muirthemne* we learn that its hero, too, exemplified the twin virtues of poetry and bravery in battle. His poetic training was of the finest: 'I stood by the knee of Amergin the poet, he was my tutor, so that I can stand up to any man, I can make praises for the doing of a king'.[55] Christy's 'great rages' are an echo of Cuchulain's notorious 'battle-rage'. Because of this battle-rage, Cuchulain could not be allowed into Emain Macha until his ardour cooled. In the end the Ulstermen solved this problem in novel style. Thirty of the most beautiful virgins were sent naked from the fort to meet the hero. When Cuchulain saw them, his reverence for womanhood caused him to bow his head and the battle-rage left him. Christy, too, is innocent of woman, as we soon see:

JIMMY: He's a wicked-looking young fellow. Maybe he followed after a young woman on a lonesome night.

CHRISTY: (shocked) Oh, the saints forbid, mister; I was at all times a decent lad (*Plays 2*, p. 69).

He, too, is filled with the battle-rage of triumph after the sports and his frantic speech recalls the parade of chosen virgins at Emain

Macha: 'It's Pegeen I'm seeking only, and what'd I care if you brought me a drift of chosen females, standing in their shifts itself, maybe, from this place to the Eastern World?' (p. 167). It is ironic that this speech, a modest remoulding of the great scene of the national saga, should have been the immediate cause of the nationalist attack on the play. Synge had clad his maidens demurely in 'shifts', to appease the prudish members of the Abbey audience—but to no avail. Cuchulain was permitted the vision of thirty naked virgins in the native manuscripts and in Lady Gregory's version; but the latter-day disciples of Cuchulain could not tolerate the vision of a peasant boy, whose fury was soothed (if only in his imagination) by females standing in shifts. That the audience should have broken up in disorder at the use of the word 'shift' was ironic indeed and Synge commented bitterly on this in a letter to Stephen McKenna.[56]

Cuchulain wooed Emer in words culled from traditional mythology and literary metaphor, so that 'the young girls with her might not understand what I had come for'.[57] Similarly, Christy woos his Pegeen in speeches and images taken from the love poems of the folk.[58] Such a use of riddles and literary allusions to test a bride or suitor is widespread—it occurs, for example, in Fionn's wooing of Ailbe. The Tartars employed this device in many stories; and the testing of the suitor by literary riddles was a living custom in Russia, as late as the nineteenth century.[59]

Before he finally wins Emer by his championship of the Ulstermen, Cuchulain encounters the famed warrior-druidess, Sgathach. She tutors him in the ways of the world and prepares him for his warrior feats, in return for certain services which include the defence of her family against her enemies.[60] Likewise, Christy encounters the Widow Quin who is also famed for her feats—most notably, she 'destroyed her man' (*Plays 2*, p. 131). She offers Christy shrewd assistance in his suit, in return for certain services such as 'a right of way I want, and a mountainy ram, and a load of dung at Michaelmas, the time that you'll be master here' (p. 131). As Sgathach prepared Cuchulain for his tests as champion of Ulster, so the Widow Quin enters Christy for the local sports.

In overcoming all the obstacles set before him, Cuchulain came to a valley 'and only one narrow path through it, but he went through it safely'.[61] So, Christy negotiates a dangerously narrow gap in the horse-races:

JIMMY: It's the last turn! The post's cleared for them now!

MAHON: Look at the narrow place. He'll be into the bogs! (with
a yell) Good Rider! He's through it again! (*Plays 2*,
p. 141)

The Widow Quin is the first to pronounce Christy 'with the shade
of a smile', 'the champion playboy of the western world' (*Plays 2*,
p. 139). Some moments later, she dubs him 'the wonder of the western
world' (p. 143). In the heroic cycles, championship is always expressed
in terms which are superlative or even global. For example, in
Cuchulain of Muirthemne, Cuchulain and Ferdia, who fight at the
ford, are referred to as 'the two champions of western Europe'.[62]
For winning the Championship of Ulster, Cuchulain is awarded the
triple headship of warriors, poets and musicians.[63] For becoming
Champion of the Western World, Christy is himself given three
awards—a blackthorn stick (sign of the small-town warrior), a fiddle
(played by a poet in the years gone by), and bagpipes (symbol of
ancient Gaelic music).

It would not be wise to seek for one-to-one correspondence
between the narrative of *Cuchulain of Muirthemne* and the incidents
of *The Playboy*; nor would it be right to think that the influence
of the Ulster Cycle on Synge's work can be limited to a single
play. It is clear, for example, that there are many resonances from the
Sweeney legend in the story of Christy Mahon;[64] and it is common
knowledge that a section of Lady Gregory's narrative was an important, if secondary, source for some of the speeches in *Deirdre of
the Sorrows*. It should not be suggested, however, that the echoes
from the Sweeney legend in *The Playboy* discount in any way
the points of contact with the Ulster Cycle. Too many critics have
reduced this multi-faceted masterpiece to an analogue of one legend
and one alone. It is all too easy for the critic to seize upon a model
legend, to show its correspondences in the play, and to go on to
assert that this tale—and this alone—is the crucial model for that
work. That, however, is not the way in which the imagination of
an artist works. A writer like Synge, who steeped himself in Irish
myth and legend, will not be influenced by one work at a time. He
may not be consciously influenced at all. Rather, all his reading has
been subsumed into his imagination, becoming a part of his complex
personality until, in Coleridge's valuable phrase, his thoughts have
become incorporated into his feelings. *Cuchulain of Muirthemne* was
Synge's 'daily bread'. He took it with him everywhere. In such a
happy position, a writer will seize upon a situation here, an image

there, borrowing as widely as his plot demands. He will not scruple to mingle resonances from the Bible, pagan mythology, newspaper reports and peasant gossip. The debts to these sources need not be 'debts' at all in any conciously acquired sense. However, that does not negate the critic's right to search for such sources, if a knowledge of such material can lead to a more resonant reading of a work. 'Influence' and 'debt' are perhaps too strong as words to describe this process; it is wiser to think of 'points of contact', remembering Ezra Pound's useful formulation that the best criticism provides fixed points of departure.[65] To claim any more is spuriously to re-write the work under consideration; to claim any less is wilfully to ignore the richness of a writer's imagination. In this context, with echoes in *The Playboy* from myth and romance, it might be wisest to view the play not as an analogue of the stories of Cuchulain or Sweeney, but as a wholly new myth in itself—a creation within the tradition of a wholly new legend.

5 The Songs of the Folk

POPULAR LOVE-SONG

The love-songs of the folk in Ireland are closely related to the *Dánta Grá*, the poems of love composed by professional poets and aristocrats between the years 1350 and 1600. The earliest *Dánta Grá* were perfected by aristocrats like Gerald 'The Rhymer' Fitzgerald, an earl who fused the forms of bardic poetry with themes of love and passion. Although there are traces of the French *amour courtois* tradition in his sighing and disconsolate lovers, his poems finally owe far more to the native traditions of popular love-song and love-story. It was only in the fifteenth century that the *amour courtois* tradition became a significant element in the *Dánta Grá* and, even then, its philosophical background was reduced in scale and importance by the Irish writers. Nevertheless, many conventions of the genre entered Irish aristocratic poetry and some even went underground to live even more vibrantly in the songs of the folk. This popular tradition was a crucial source of inspiration for the poetry and plays of Synge.

The conventions of *amour courtois* had been developed in Provence in the south of France, where many of the themes and situations of popular love-song were given an intellectual and theological basis. These themes and situations had long been part of the unlearned folk tradition in Ireland as well as in most parts of Europe;[1] but it was in Provence of the twelfth century that they were given, for the first time, a sophisticated codification. 'Sexual feeling was raised to the level of a transcendent emotion, and the theme of ideal love, unknown to the poets of Greece and Rome, was added to those of great poetry.'[2] The genre gave rise to many heresies, most notably that of the mystic Avicenna. He taught that sexual love was a virtue in itself, as long as it had a spiritual basis, because it taught man to rise to the love of God. In the love of a man for a woman he saw an image of Christ's love for the soul. The desire for unity with the beloved became a crucial factor, for it was the main way for the soul to attain virtue.[3] This insight is to be found at many points in Synge's work. In *The Well of the Saints,* for example, Martin Doul utters a rare prayer in thanksgiving for the beauty of Molly Byrne:

> . . . and every time I set my eyes on you, I do be blessing the saints, and the holy water, and the power of the Lord Almighty in the heavens above. (*Plays 1,* p. 111)

Martin is a latter-day Avicenna, whose love for Molly's beauty increases his virtue. The Saint in the same play, on the other hand, would 'walk by the finest woman in Ireland . . . and not trouble to raise his eyes to look upon her face' (*Plays 1,* p. 89). His hell-fire threats have failed to inspire reverence in Martin Doul. That the beauty of Molly should do so is beyond his comprehension. Even Molly herself cannot comprehend this particular heresy: 'I've heard the priests say it isn't looking on a young girl would teach many to be saying their prayers' (*Plays 1,* p. 111).

A fundamental feature of the *chanson d'amour* was the ennobling power of earthly love.[4] Synge himself, in his courtship of Molly Allgood, constantly sought to validate his emotion by the use of godly adjectives concerning their 'divine love'[5] and its 'divine moments'.[6] In his poems and plays he could seldom describe an earthly love without invoking the concept of an over-watching God. In an early poem 'In Dream', he subscribes to the idea that the love of a man for an unattainable woman is an image of Christ's love for the soul:

> Again, again, I sinful see
>   Thy face, as men who weep
> Doomed by eternal Hell's decree
>   Might meet their Christ in sleep   (*Poems,* p. 18)

This brief poem illustrates the three fundamental conventions of courtly love poetry—1) the ennobling power of human love 2) the consequent elevation of the beloved above the lover and 3) the conception of love as unsatiated desire, always increasing.[7] These conventions had a personal poignance for Synge in 1896 when the poem was written. His comparison of the apprehension of a lost lover with the guilty starts of a sinful man was painfully apt. He had just been rejected by Cherrie Matheson, the woman whom he wished to marry, on the grounds of his unbelief.

The heresy of Avicenna was but one convention of courtly love and it never gained much support in Ireland. On the contrary, the author of one famous song wrote of sexual love as a challenge to the moral order of God and his church. In Lady Gregory's *Poets and Dreamers,* Synge would have read in 'The Grief of a Girl's Heart' the hapless maiden's declaration to her lover that 'you have taken God from me'.[8] It was with this tradition that he identified in composing such poems as 'In Rebellion', 'L'Échange', In Spring', 'Dread' and 'Abroad'. In the last poem, he developed the idea of an earthly love as an ecstasy superior to any offered by religion. In the final line, God is brightened by a kiss from the earthly woman whom he has long coveted from the loneliness of his throne in Heaven. In *The Playboy,* during his courtship of Pegeen, Christy similarly expresses pity for a God who cannot know the joys of sexual love. Encouraged by Pegeen's praise of his eloquence, he launches into an even more heretical speech. The day on which Christ died shall henceforth be the day on which man learned to live, as Christy woos his girl with the traditional promises in the songs of the folk:

> Let you wait to hear me talking till we're astray in Erris when Good Friday's by, drinking a sup from a well, and making mighty kisses with our wetted mouths, or gaming in a gap of sunshine with yourself stretched back unto your necklace in the flowers of earth. (*Plays 2,* p. 149)

This invitation to elope to the countryside is a classic theme of Irish love poetry. In an earlier speech to Pegeen, Christy conjured up its most characteristic image, a walk by night across a dewy mountain:

> . . . when the airs is warming in four months or five, it's then yourself and me should be pacing Neifin in the dews of night, the times sweet smells do be rising, and you'd see a little shiny new moon maybe sinking on the hills. (*Plays 2,* p. 149)

This symbol of the dew has been invariably associated with virginity[9] and in many Irish love-songs the dew is paced by virgin lovers at night. Probably the most famous example occurs in the poem entitled 'Éamonn an Chnoic', which Synge studied in *Poets and Poetry of Munster*:

> A chumainn's a shearc,
>   Rachamaoid-ne seal,
> Faoi choilltibh ag spealadh an drúchta:
>   Mar a bh-fhaghmaoid an breac,
>   'S an lon ar a nead,
> An fiadh 'gus an poc a búithre . . . [10]

(My love and my dear, we shall for a while go pacing the dew by the woods, where we shall find the trout and the blackbird in the nest, the deer and the bull bellowing . . .)

Christy has recourse to this lyric, not just for the image of the dew, but also for his promise to Pegeen that they too will catch fish by night in illicit rivers:

> . . . you'll be an angel's lamp to me from this out, and I abroad spearing salmons in the Owen or the Carrowmore. (*Plays 2*, p. 149)

When Pegeen, moved by these lyrical outbursts, asks 'I'd be nice so, is it?', he replies by ascribing to God's prophets in Heaven the restless desire for a mortal woman. Heaven has now become a prison which cages lonely souls, who cannot know the delights of the body:

> If the mitred bishops seen you that time, they'd be the like of the holy prophets, I'm thinking, do be straining the bars of Paradise to lay eyes on the Lady Helen of Troy, and she abroad pacing back and forward with a nosegay in her golden shawl. (*Plays 2*, p. 149)

The imagery of this speech is clearly related to that used by Synge in 'Is it a Month?', the poem in which the splendour of the lady's beauty makes Paradise seem impoverished by comparison (*Poems*, p. 52). This idea is culled from the courtly poetry, with its roots in Provençal and even further back in Arab tradition—for example, in

The Arabian Nights: 'I should not delight in life without seeing you, even were I in Paradise or the Garden of Eternity'.[11] Christy's reference to the prophets straining the bars of Paradise is taken straight from the conventions of Irish love-songs, where the lover repeatedly avows: 'B'fhearr liom bheith ar láimh leat ná ar ghlóir Fhlaithis' (I had rather be beside you than in the glory of Paradise).[12] So, in the love scenes of *The Playboy* the Almighty has been finally vanquished by the poet.

Courtly love could not by definition exist between husband and wife. Averroes' Heresy of Two Truths taught that there were two rules—one of faith and theology, the other of reason and philosophy—which could co-exist. A man could, therefore, be satisfactorily married by faith and theology, but yet retain a secret love for another woman according to philosophy and reason. J. M. Cohen explains that this could happen because a man did not 'love' his wife as we today understand it:

> Passion to the eleventh or twelfth century moralist—even a man's passion for his own wife—was sinful. The sexual relation was an obligation, subject to the laws of contract and physical pleasure; it must not involve emotion.[13]

In aristocratic poetry, including *Dánta Grá*, the beloved was a noble-woman, wife of a chieftain or prince; but in the love-songs of the people she might be any woman unhappily wed. In the type of song known as 'Chanson de la malmariée', the woman complains of her marriage to the insensitive old man. Seán Ó Tuama has given the formula of this situation:

> Tá sé docht, dúr; batrálann sé í. Ní shásaíonn sé a mianta collaí. Éiríonn sí amach i gcoinne an phósta sin (gurab iad a tuismitheoirí go minic faoi deara é). Ba bhreá leí a bhás—d'imeodh sí le leannán (a bhíonn aici cheana féin de ghnáth) . . . [14]

(He is hard and dour; he batters her. He fails to satisfy her sexual needs. She strikes out against the marriage [which has often been occasioned by her parents]. She would love her husband to die— she would make off with a young lover [whom she usually has already] . . .)

This might serve as a perfect description of the situation in *The*

Shadow of the Glen, which John Butler Yeats described as a satire on a loveless marriage.[15]

The play opens with the woman's wish already granted. Her aged husband is dead and her young lover waits expectantly in the wings. Nora speaks of her dead husband as 'an old man, and an odd man' and adds the most telling indictment of all, as she looks uneasily at his body:

> Maybe cold would be no sign of death with the like of him, for he was always cold, every day since I knew him—and every night, stranger . . . (*Plays 1*, p. 35)

This is the selfsame complaint of the wife in the 'chanson de la malmariée' about the 'géaga fuara' (cold limbs)[16] of her husband:

> Straoill gan bhrígh 'na bhallaibh . . .
> Ach ceasachdacht fhada do shíor dá chrádh . . .
> 'Na ghnaoi níl maise ná lúth 'na chnámha[17]

> (A clumsy old fellow with no life in his limbs, eternally breaking his heart with long complaints; there is no beauty in his features or agility in his bones.)

Similarly, Nora's husband has been 'complaining a while back of a pain in his heart' (*Plays 1*, p. 35). He had a shake in his face, his teeth were failing, and his white hair unkempt (*Plays 1*, p. 51). He was to her no more than an 'old fellow wheezing the like of a sick sheep close to your ear' (*Plays 1*, p. 57), like the dotard of the song:

> Críonán claoidhte atá fillte crapaithe . . .
> Bhíonn de choidhche ag cneadaigh a's ag síor-chrannráil.[18]

> (A withered old man who is bent and shrunken; who is ever groaning and eternally stooping . . .)

One of the crucial features of the 'chanson de la malmariée' is an argument between the aged husband and his restless wife. Invariably he loses patience and vows to cast her onto the roads, without clothes or food.[19] In Synge's play Dan Burke discovers his wife's planned alliance with a younger lover and launches into the conventional threat:

> You'll walk out now from that door, Nora Burke, and it's not
> to-morrow, or the next day, or any day of your life, that you'll
> put in your foot through it again. (*Plays 1*, p. 53)

Even the details of the genre, such as the threat to leave the wife
seeking alms ('Go bhfeicfead ag iarraidh déirce thú')[20]—or to
abandon her to the charity of the crossroads ('Bí ar na cros-
bhóithribh'),[21] are reproduced in Dan's speech: 'Let her walk round
the like of Peggy Cavanagh below, and be begging money at the
crossroads, or selling songs to the men' (*Plays 1*, p. 53). The stock
threat is that the wife will die for lack of clothes, shelter and food;
and Dan's outburst is no exception: 'let you not be passing this way
if it's hungry you are, or wanting a bed' (*Plays 1*, p. 55).

The courage with which Nora Burke meets her husband's threat
is entirely in the 'chanson' tradition. Like the girl in the song
who said:

> Dob fhearr liom an t-óig-fhear . . .
> Mar bhí mo chroidhe ceangailte ann, a's tá[22]

(I would prefer the youth, for my heart was with him and is . . .)

Nora decides that 'you've a fine bit of talk, stranger, and it's with
yourself I'll go' (*Plays 1*, p. 57). Normally, in the 'chanson de la
malmariée', the girl concludes by cursing the husband and expressing
the hope that he will soon die. Synge subtly alters this convention,
weighting it even more in favour of the girl by giving her a final
speech full of humanitarian concern rather than vengeance. Instead
of wishing the death of her husband, Nora voices the fear that death
will overtake him all too soon: 'And what way will yourself live
from this day, with none to care you?' (*Plays 1*, p. 57). To this
subtle reversal Synge adds a further ironic twist, since the young
man who waits in the wings for Nora turns out to have none of the
passion of the conventional 'leannán', but is in fact motivated by the
same sordid economic motives which forced the original match.
Deliverance comes for Nora not through Michael Dara, the youth,
but through a tramp of indeterminate age who still has the spirit of
youth alive in him. So Synge altered the convention of the
'malmariée' even as he espoused it; and that alteration may be seen

as a characteristic criticism of the black-and-white options of the genre. Seán Ó Tuama has written that the treatment of *amour courtois* themes in Ireland showed a tendency to 'personalise any stock situation'.[23] Synge is merely carrying this process to its logical conclusion, offering the essential criticism of the convention which he exploits, lest it decline into smugness.

HYDE'S *SONGS OF CONNACHT*

Douglas Hyde's *Love Songs of Connacht* was published in 1893 and greeted warmly by W. B. Yeats in the October issue of the *Bookman*. Yeats praised Hyde's translations from the Irish as being 'very much better than the bulk of Walsh's and beyond all measure better than any of Mangan's in *The Munster Poets*'.[24] Synge had always been interested in translations from Irish poetry and he took Hyde's book with him on his visits to Aran. He made detailed notes about certain songs which he found striking or useful; and there are so many echoes in the plays from the songs of Connacht that they cannot be accidental. Consider these famous lines from 'Una Bhan':

> B'fhearr liomsa bheith ar leabaidh léi 'gá síor-phógadh
> 'Ná mo suidhe i bhFlaitheas i g-cathaoir na Tríonóide.

> I had rather be beside her in a couch, ever kissing her,
> Than be sitting in heaven in the chair of the Trinity.[25]

This image is fused by Synge with the feeling of compassion for a lonely God who is jealous of the intimacies of earthly love. The idea of a jealous God is expressed in many of his love poems, including the final lines of 'Dread' (1906–8):

> Now by this window, where there's none can see,
> The Lord God's jealous of yourself and me   (*Poems*, p. 40)

The fusion of the image from Hyde's song and the idea from Synge's poem is made in a speech of Christy to Pegeen:

> . . . and I squeezing kisses on your puckered lips till I'd feel a kind of pity for the Lord God is all ages sitting lonesome in his golden chair. (*Plays 2*, p. 147)

Synge has made the kissing even more sensuous by the infusion of
the adjective 'puckered' and the verb 'squeezing'. In the play he
transfers the sense of eternity from the lovers' kiss to the loneliness
of God; and introduces a note of faintly patronising compassion that
is altogether lacking in his poem. In Hyde's song the poet had
imagined himself in two antithetical positions—one by the side of the
woman, the other on the throne of Heaven—as if he had to make
a choice. In Christy's speech the question of choice never arises. The
lad never bothers to imagine what it would be like for himself to
sit on the throne of Heaven, for he has already imagined in terrified
detail how lonely it must be for God. In the same scene Christy
promises Pegeen that soon they will 'be pacing Neifin in the dews
of night' (*Plays 2*, p. 147); and it is on Neifin also that he plans to kiss
her puckered lips. In *Love Songs of Connacht* Neifin is the traditional
spot for such a lovers' assignation; and in the opening lines of 'Mala
Neifin' (The Brow of Neifin), a woebegone youth imagines:

Dá mbeidhinn-se air Mhala Neifin
'S mo chéud-ghrádh le mo thaoibh . . .

If I were on the brow of Neifin and my hundred loves by my
side . . .[26]

Clearly, Christy has chosen the appropriate location, no less than the
virginal dew, with scrupulous regard for the poetic tradition.

In a discarded draft of *The Playboy*, Synge attempted a scene in
which Christy tells Pegeen about all the girls whom he could have
had:

PEGEEN: How many girls had you beyond in the south?

CHRISTY: There was Kitty Kinsella, I rarely ever spoke to and
there was his Lordship's daughter a rich lovely lady
had a big window with a yellow blind in it looking
out on the park . . . (*Plays 2*, p. 110)

The idea of listing the names and grades of other women who had
sought the poet's love is taken from the poem conventionally titled
'Bean Dubh an Ghleanna' (The Dark Woman of the Glen). Two
versions of this poem are given by Hyde, one titled 'Mall Dubh an

Ghleanna' and the other 'Pol Dubh an Ghleanna'. To the first of
these, Hyde added the comment that John O'Daly, in his *Poets and
Poetry of Munster,* had published a version of 'Bean Dubh an Gleanna',
part of which 'is very like this poem'.[27] He noted that there were
'two verses in O'Daly's song, which are like two verses in my one . . .
The two songs are altogether different from one another, except in
these two verses'.[28] The verses in question deal with the girls in the
south of the country whom the poet might have won. It was on these
verses that Synge modelled Christy's reply, even down to points of
detail. Hyde's second version, 'Pol Dubh', is even closer to that of
O'Daly and it also contains the crucial two stanzas.

Synge studied the versions in Hyde's book during his visit to West
Kerry in 1905, for he wrote in a notebook kept throughout the
sojourn:

hair compared to sea-weed　　Hyde's songs　　feamainneach[29]

This is taken directly from a footnote appended by Hyde to a line
from 'Mall Dubh an Ghleanna': ' "Feamuinneach" in the third verse
means "clustering like sea-weed", a word often applied to hair . . .'
We have seen that Synge had already read O'Daly's *Poets and Poetry
of Munster,* with Mangan's English versions, in *Songs of the Munster
Bards.* His subsequent study of Hyde's book (and of the implied
comparison with O'Daly's version) must have sent him back to a
closer analysis of O'Daly's 'Bean Dubh an Ghleanna'. For, in a notebook which contains early fragments of *The Playboy,* there is a
translation by Synge of 'Bean Dubh an Ghleanna'. Here is O'Daly's
text of the final stanza:

> Gheabhainn-se bean san Mumhain,
> Triúr ban a Laigheann,
> 　Agus bean ó righ gheal Seoirse,
> Bean na lúbadh buidhe
> D'fháisgioch mé le na croidhe
> 　Bean agus dhá mhíle bó léi.
> Inghíon óg an Iarladh
> Atá go teinn dubhach diacrach
> 　Ag iarraidh mise d'fhághail le pósadh!
> 'S dá bh-fhaghainnse féin mo rogha!
> De mhná deasa an domhain
> 　As í an Bhean Dubh ó'n n-Gleann do b'fhearr liom.[30]

This is Synge's translation:

> I would get a woman in Munster
> Three women in Leinster
>   And a woman from King George
> A woman with yellow hair
> Who would press me to her heart
>   A woman and she with two thousand cows
> The young daughter of an earl
> Who is pleasant and seemly
>   Who is trying to get me for a marriage
> And if I would get my own choice
> Of the women that are most beautiful in the world
>   It is herself I would choose, the black woman of the Glen.[31]

Let us compare this with the translation by Mangan:

> In Momonia I could find
> Many damsels to my mind
>   And in Leinster—nay, in England, a many.
> One from George, without art,
> Who would clasp me to her heart,
>   And a beauty is the lass among many.
> The daughter of the Earl
> Who walks in silks and pearl,
>   Would fain have netted me in her thrall yet.
> But could I have my choice
> How much would I rejoice
>   To wed thee, my Dark Maiden, of all yet![32]

No doubt, this was one of the *Songs of the Munster Bards* to which Emily Synge felt that Mangan might not have done justice with his 'halting and uneven' measures.[33] Synge's own translation far excels Mangan's, for it captures that combination of homeliness and intensity which Seán Ó Tuama has found peculiar to the love songs of the folk in Ireland.[34]

In terms remarkably similar to those of the quoted stanza, Christy Mahon lists for Pegeen the other women who were his for the asking, beginning with Kitty Kinsella. He then goes on to name 'his Lordship's daughter, a rich lovely lady', who is modelled on 'The young daughter of an Earl/Who is pleasant and seemly'. Perhaps, also, the ironic image in *The Playboy* of the love-sick Shawn Keogh, vainly chasing east and west after ewes, is modelled on the distracted lover of the opening lines of 'Bean Dubh an Ghleanna' in Synge's version:

> I have a cow on the mountain
> And I am a while going after her
> Since I lost my sense about my companion
> I went east and west
> Every place the sun does be going . . .[35]

This same image was used in *The Shadow of the Glen*, where the Tramp mocks Michael Dara, the nervous young lover of Nora:

> . . . I'm thinking it's a poor herd does be running back and forward after a little handful of ewes the way I seen yourself running this day, young fellow . . . (*Plays 1*, p. 47)

Like the disconsolate herdsman of the poem, Michael Dara freely admits his incompetence and links it with his love for Nora Burke, another dark lady who lived in 'the last cottage at the head of a long glen' (*Plays 1*, p. 31):

> It's no lie he's telling. I was destroyed surely . . . They were that wilful they were running off into one man's bit of oats, and another man's bit of hay, and tumbling into the red bogs till it's more like a pack of old goats than sheep they were . . . Mountain ewes is a queer breed, Nora Burke, and I'm not used to them at all . . . (*Plays 1*, p. 47)

There is a beautiful ambiguity about that last sentence. The name of Nora Burke, inserted as its central pause, reminds us that she herself is of a frisky mountain breed. Michael, 'an innocent young man (*Plays 1*, p. 45), will be no match for her'.

In his introduction to 'Cailín Beag an Ghleanna' (Oh, Youth Whom I Have Kissed), Hyde reminds us that on this occasion a girl is the speaker of the poem. He draws particular attention to her comparison of her sweetheart's arrival with the emergence of a star through mist. Here, as so often elsewhere, it is significant that the image borrowed by Synge is the one singled out by Hyde in his commentary. Hyde recalls a similar image from Hardiman's

Minstrelsy:

> I saw her come towards me through the middle of the mountain
> As a star shines through the mist[36]

In 'Cailin Beag an Ghleanna', the girl tells her man that he has come 'mar realtán tríd an g-ceo' (like a star through the mist).[37] Although it is normally Christy who borrows images from the love songs, it is no accident that in this case Pegeen should marvel at his sudden arrival in terms similar to the girl's:

> . . . and I not knowing at all there was the like of you drawing nearer like the stars of God. (*Plays 2*, p. 151)

Nor is this Pegeen's only borrowing from the girl's poem. Some moments later in the same act, she turns upon Shawn Keogh with the complaint that 'it's sooner on a bullock's liver you'd put a poor girl thinking than on the lily or the rose' (*Plays 2*, p. 155). Similarly, in 'Cailín Beag an Ghleanna', the girl complains to her lover that she is upset by his concern for his animals at the expense of their love:

> 'S gur chuir tú do dhúil i n-airgiod 's i mbuaibh
>   Agus i seafaideadhaibh dubha an tsléibhe.
>
> Thou hast set thy affection on money and on kine
>   And on black heifers of the mountain.[38]

The contention between the lily and the rose—the modesty of the lily and the blushing passion of the rose—is a feature of Irish love songs and may be found in the work of Eoin Rua Ó Súilleabháin.[39] The girl in 'Cailín Beag an Ghleanna', like Pegeen, would prefer a sprightly lover to a man who owned cattle but showed no tenderness:

> B'fhearr liom go mór bheith ar taoibh bhuachaill óig
>   'Ná sealbhán bó ar taebh chnuic.
>
> I should greatly sooner be at the side of a young bohal
>   Than have possession of cows on the side of a hill.[40]

This is the voice of Nora Burke, as she welcomes a young lover and bemoans her marriage for reasons of prosperity to a cold man:

I do be thinking in the long nights it was a big fool I was that time, Michael Dara, for what good is a bit of a farm with cows on it, and sheep on the back hills, when you do be sitting, looking out from a door the like of that door, and seeing nothing but the mists rolling down the bog . . . ? (*Plays 1*, p. 49)

One of the most famous poems of Hyde's collection is 'A Ógánaigh an Chúil Cheangailte' (Ringleted Youth); and this is its most quoted stanza:

> A's shaoil mé a stóirín
>   Go mbudh gealach agus grian thú
> A's shaoil mé 'nna dhiaigh sin
>   Go mbudh sneachta ar an tsliabh thú,
> A's shaoil mé 'nn a dhiaigh sin
>   Go mbudh lóchrann ó Dhia thú,
> Nó gur ab tú an réult-eolais
>   Ag dul romham a's mo dhiaigh thú.

And I thought, my storeen, That you were the sun and the moon, And I thought after that, That you were snow on the mountain, And I thought after that, That you were a lamp from God, Or that you were the star of knowledge going before me and after me.[41]

Christy clearly draws on the image of the 'lamp from God' when he tells Pegeen that 'you'll be an angel's lamp to me from this out' (*Plays 2*, p. 149). He employs the final image of the stanza even more spectacularly, late in the play, when he cries out in despair: 'Amn't I after seeing the love-light of the star of knowledge shining from her brow?' (*Plays 2*, p. 125) The final lines of the poem, in which the abandoned lover is left 'like a bush in a gap',[42] were also used by Synge as an image of rejection in *The Shadow of the Glen*, as Dan Durke spurns Nora: '. . . your head'll be the like of a bush where sheep do be leaping a gap' (*Plays 1*, p. 55).

Synge seldom borrowed an image from Irish poetry without altering it in some fashion. In the poem the phrase 'star of knowledge' refers directly to the beloved—she herself is the star of knowledge. But in Synge's lines the star is not a personification, since it is 'shining from her brow' as an attribute of the lady. Such a use of the image may be found elsewhere in Hyde's book, for example in 'Teig and Mary': 'A love-spot thou hast on thy brow'.[43] This is but one of a host of instances in Irish song and story where lovers bear a sign of their passion on the brow. Synge fuses this idea with the star-image to brilliant effect. Instead of the traditional 'ball seirce', he places the shining star of knowledge on the girl's brow. This newly-wrought image is further invoked at the climax of the play, when Christy is betrayed by Pegeen: 'But what did I want crawling forward to scorch my understanding at her flaming brow?' (*Plays 2*, p. 163) This particular reference to the star of knowledge which shines in her brow is all the more powerful for being oblique. Taking the idea of the brightness of the star, it compounds it with the suggestion of a heat that becomes intolerable if one ventures too close.

Nicholas Grene has complained that this phrase 'degenerates into a purely decorative image' and argues that Synge 'can fairly be accused of overstrained rhetoric'.[44] This is unfair. Firstly, Grene fails to distinguish between Synge and his creation. It is entirely appropriate that Christy's language at this moment should be overstrained. He is at his wit's end, hopelessly in love with Pegeen and terrified that the re-appearance of his father will jeopardise that love. His earlier speeches in the scene, in which he thundered against his revived father, were vicious elaborations of Gaelic cursing rituals. Now, all of a sudden, in an equally strained rhetoric of tenderness, he bursts into the time-honoured imagery of the rejected lover in Irish poetry. This brilliant verbal contrast between rival Irish poetic traditions is entirely appropriate. If the idiom is strained, it is only because literary histrionics have cut Christy off from reality. He may justly be accused of strained rhetoric, but Synge cannot. In fact, the idiom of Christy is all times a register of his moral growth. As the play proceeds, it becomes less ornamental and more functional until, at the end, the languages of actuality and the imagination are one.

The final poem of Hyde's collection, 'The Roman Earl' tells the story of an earl who asks his wife what she would do if he happened to die. She vows that she would wrap him in satin, bury him in a gorgeous tomb and give the rest of his wealth to the poor. So he feigns death only to find that, on the contrary, she stints his funeral expenses and keeps all the wealth for herself. He rises from the shroud and denounces her. This work is of interest for two reasons. Firstly, the scene in which the man asks the woman how she would behave at his funeral, if he were to die, may well have been in Synge's mind when he composed 'A Question' in 1908:

> I asked if I got sick and died, would you
> With my black funeral go walking too,
> If you'd stand close to hear them talk or pray
> While I'm let down in that steep bank of clay   (*Poems*, p. 64)

Molly Allgood told Yeats that Synge often joked with her about death. One day he asked 'Will you go to my funeral?', to which she replied 'No, for I could not bear to see you dead and the others living' (*Poems*, p. 64). Her reply was as emotional as that given to the Roman Earl:

> Och! och! dá bhfuighfeá-sa bás
> Budh bheag mo chás ionnam féin . . .
>
> Och! och! if thou wert to die
> Little would be my regard for my own life.[45]

This is dramatised even more strikingly in Synge's poem, where anguish turns suddenly into blind fury.

> And, No, you said, for if you saw a crew
> Of living idiots, pressing round that new
> Oak coffin—they alive, I dead beneath
> That board,—you'd rave and rend them with your teeth
> (*Poems*, p. 64)

Secondly, 'The Roman Earl' proved useful to Synge and Yeats in their defence of the authenticity of *The Shadow of the Glen* against attacks from Arthur Griffith in the *United Irishman*. Griffith had alleged that Synge's play was no more Irish than the *Decameron* and that it was inspired by 'the decadent cynicism that passes current in the Latin Quartier and the London salon'.[46] When *The Well of the Saints* was about to be staged early in 1905, Griffith renewed his attack on Synge's earlier play:

Mr. Synge's adaptation of the old Greek libel on womankind— *The Widow of Ephesus*—has no more title to be called Irish than a Chinaman would have if he printed 'Patrick O'Brien' on his visiting card . . .[47]

Yeats and Synge replied quietly to these allegations. They were
concerned to show that the play had an Irish source and that this was
no isolated tale but a story whose variants were widespread in Ireland.
Yeats remarked in a letter to the *United Irishman* on 28 January that
'I can remember several Irish poems and stories in which the husband
feigns death for precisely the reason the husband does in Mr. Synge's
play'.[48] He re-read *The Widow of Ephesus,* but denied that it
contained significant parallels with Synge's plot. Synge's play was
wholly native, he argued. From the 'several Irish poems and stories'
available, Yeats clinched his argument by citing 'The Roman Earl':

> Ireland may, I think, claim all the glory for Mr. Synge's not less
> admirable tale. The only parallels I can remember at this moment
> to the husband who pretends to be dead that he may catch his wife
> and his wife's lover are Irish parallels. One is a ballad at the end of
> *The Love Songs of Connaught* . . . [49]

'The Roman Earl' is, fundamentally, the same story as that of Synge's
play. A morose old man feigns death, in order to find out how his
wife would dispose of the wealth which she inherits. Admittedly, the
old man of whom the story is told is a Roman earl—perhaps this
was the echo in Griffith's mind when he ascribed Synge's plot to a
writer of the Roman decadence. But the story of 'The Roman Earl'
is only an illustration of the poet's moral. The poet himself and his
idiom are wholly Irish and so is the situation which he envisages.
He simply seizes on the story of the Roman earl to show that women
throughout the world are as faithless as this.

   Hyde's collection proved of similar service to Synge after the
Playboy disturbances. He told the *Freeman's Journal* in an interview
that 'shift' was 'an everyday word in the West of Ireland, which
could not be taken offence at there, and might be used differently by
people in Dublin. It was used without any objection in Douglas
Hyde's *Songs of Connaught,* in the Irish, but what could be published
in Irish perhaps could not be published in English.'[50] This bitter
quip turned out to be even more apt than Synge suspected. Count-
less critics of his play took grave exception to Christy's scenes of
courtship with Pegeen, without realising that almost all the con-
troversial lines of the speeches were culled from Gaelic poetry and
song. The Gaelic Leaguers protested that Christy's free and passionate
idiom misrepresented the peasants of the west. They did not realise

that it was from the songs of the folk that Christy's most passionate lines had been looted.

On 13 July 1905 Synge wrote to Stephen MacKenna with the information that he had been reading the poetry of 'Rafferty' (sic).[51] This was, no doubt, Hyde's *Songs Ascribed to Raftery*, which had been published in 1903. MacKenna may have helped to arouse his interest in this poet, for he wrote to Synge in the Spring of 1904:

> I see of late much in the New York *Nation* and in the *Athenaeum* of Irish things—Lady Gregory and Douglas Hyde upon Raftery among the rest. I wish Plotinus had been a bare-legged Irish tramp. But indeed Raftery seems to have had a quaint and powerful soul. If he had not existed, he would have had to be invented. He makes things plausible. Did he exist?[52]

Raftery was something of a cult-figure among Irish writers of the time, including Yeats, Lady Gregory and even Joyce.[53] Synge's interest in the poet would have been increased by the attention given to his work by Lady Gregory in her *Poets and Dreamers* (1903). For him, no less than for Yeats and Lady Gregory, Raftery was an enigmatic but powerful exemplar. Hyde's boast that Raftery 'has not so much as a word that he did not get from the people themselves'[54] seems to lurk behind the claim in the Preface to *The Playboy* that 'I have used one or two words only, that I have not heard among the country people of Ireland' (*Plays 2*, p. 53). There is, furthermore, some evidence to suggest that Synge drew upon the life and writings of Raftery, as revealed in Hyde's collection, in his portrayal of Christy Mahon.

Hyde revealed that Raftery was a small, thin man[55] and Synge's stage-directions describe Christy as 'a slight young man' (*Plays 2*, p. 67). Despite his small stature, Raftery was amazingly strong and not shy of proclaiming his agility.[56] Christy, too, was possessed of great strength and a corresponding boastfulness. At the Mayo sports Christy won prizes for 'leppin' and Raftery displayed a similar agility at competitive jumping. Like Christy and all of Synge's heroes, Raftery was a wanderer whose only home was the highway. The most striking similarity is, of course, that both men are poets. Christy is celebrated for his lyricism and 'poet's talking'. Raftery was praised, in identical terms, not only for his formal poetry but for his adroit conversation.[57] According to Hyde, Raftery emulated the satiric function of the ancient bards: 'There is no doubt that the people were afraid of him, and he who would not give to him through friendliness would give through fear . . .'[58] In the same fashion, the village girls offer Christy gifts from pure affection and friendship. For contrary motives of fear and terror, Shawn Keogh tries to bribe Christy with 'my new hat', 'my breeches with the double seat', 'my new coat is woven from the blackest shearings for three miles around' and 'the half a ticket to the Western States' (*Plays 2*, pp. 113–15). Shawn proves that he is motivated by fear, when he confides to Widow Quin: 'I'd inform again him, but he'd burst from Kilmainham and he'd be sure and certain to destroy me' (*Plays 2*, p. 117).

Many of Christy's elaborate promises to Pegeen seem to draw upon Raftery's songs. For example: 'Let you wait to hear me talking when we're astray in Erris when Good Friday's by . . . or gaming in a gap of sunshine with yourself stretched back unto your necklace in the flowers of the earth' (*Plays 2*, p. 149). The idea of Erris as the location for an illicit tryst is suggested in Raftery's 'Nancy Walsh'.[59] Furthermore, the idea of being 'sínte' or 'stretched' romantically beside a lover may be found in these lines:

> . . . And I should rather be stretched beside you
> with nothing under us but heath and rushes.[60]

—although Synge turns the heath and rushes into more exotic flowers.

Charles McKinley has complained that Christy's reference to Helen of Troy, in the course of a speech wooing Pegeen, is 'incongruous coming from this lout who has spent his days working in the fields'.[61] This naïve judgement takes no account of the way in which classical Greek and Roman learning had been incorporated into folk poetry and song. As George-Denis Zimmerman has observed in his study of Irish songs:

> On the whole, the common people of Ireland often enjoyed non-popular style, which included pseudo-learned references as well as unusual vocabulary. They were pleased to name Venus or Flora, to compare their heroes with Hector, Alexander, Caesar and Pompey, or to recall the destruction of Troy.[62]

It was the very lack of formal education in the lives of the folk which had caused classical learning to be so highly prized among them. Precisely because he was a 'lout', Christy Mahon would have been doubly anxious to retain and exploit any scraps of learning that came his way. The mingling of the names of classical and Gaelic protagonists is a major feature of Raftery's poetry. It cannot have escaped Synge's notice, especially when we recall his passionate interest in the European associations of Irish poetry and prose. In Raftery's 'Máire Standún' (Mary Staunton), Helen and Deirdre are mentioned in the same quatrain as paragons of beauty:

> Tá pósaidh glé geal ar bhruach na céibhe
>   Agus bhuail sí Deirdre le sgéimh a's gnaoi,
> 'S dá n-abrainn Helen an bhainríoghain Ghréagach
>   Ar thuit na céadta d'á barr 'san Traoi.

> There's a lovely posy lives by the roadway
>   Deirdre was nowhere beside my joy,
> Nor Helen who boasted of conquests Trojan,
>   For whom was roasted the town of Troy.[63]

In Christy's speech, Synge brilliantly evokes the confusion wrought by Helen on earth and transfers it to the heavens:

> If the mitred bishops seen you that time, they'd be the like of the holy prophets, I'm thinking, do be straining the bars of Paradise to lay eyes on the Lady Helen of Troy, and she abroad pacing back and forward with a nosegay in her golden shawl. (*Plays 2*, p. 149)

There, he imagines, Helen still wreaks havoc among the austere prophets. Once again in his work, he asserts the joys of earthly love as a challenge to the heavens and to the pious composure of the saints.

In *The Winged Destiny*, which Synge reviewed for *The Academy and Literature* on 12 November 1904, William Sharp ('Fiona Macleod') demonstrated how the Gaelic poetic tradition has assimilated the Greek. He remarked how it was natural for an Irish poet to mention the graciousness of Helen in the same breath with the Gaelic queens of beauty.[64] This insight seems to inform Synge's working-out of the poem 'Queens' which, although conceived in 1902, was painstakingly reworked in successive drafts from 1903 to

1907. 'Queens' is informed, also, by his reading of the poems of
Raftery in the collections of Hyde and Lady Gregory. At times,
indeed, the classical and Gaelic names joined by Synge in a couplet
seem remarkably close to those used by the Gaelic poet. In *Poets and
Dreamers*, Lady Gregory had drawn attention to Raftery's 'habit of
mixing comparisons drawn from the classics with those drawn from
nature';[65] Synge's poem begins:

> Seven dog-days we let pass
> Naming queens in Glenmacnass,
> All the rare and royal names
> Wormy sheepskin yet retains,
> Etain, Helen, Maeve and Fand,
> Golden Deirdre's tender hand . . .   (*Poems*, p. 34)

Synge never exploited a literary device without developing it in some
way. Here he takes up where Raftery left off, incorporating into
his list not only the queens of classical literature, but also the
heroines of subsequent writers. He sees himself as a poet working
in what he insists is a living tradition, and not merely as an
antiquarian versifier offering a clever pastiche of Raftery's mode.
Rather, he seizes upon the central techniques of that mode in a poem
which is at once a re-working of Raftery's characteristic device and
a liberation of its hidden potential. Even the brutal realism of the
closing lines is a re-working, with characteristic Syngean bluntness,
of Raftery's devices. Consider Synge's lines:

> Queens who wasted the East by proxy
> Or drove the ass-cart, a tinker's doxy,
> Yet these are rotten—I ask their pardon—
> And we've the sun on rock and garden,
> These are rotten, so you're the queen
> Off all are living, or have been.   (*Poems*, p. 34)

This is precisely the point to which Raftery returned in the stanza
of 'Máire Standún' quoted earlier—the belief that no paragon of
beauty in classical Greece or ancient Ireland can equal the girl
celebrated by the poet. Inevitably, Synge has added a new twist to
the judgement. Raftery had used the comparison, by which Deirdre
and Helen were found wanting, as a means of claiming, if not
actually describing, the beauty of his love. But Synge employs the

device to altogether different effect. He sees behind the tired old comparison a truth no one, not even Raftery, had faced—the fact that the girl in your arms is superior just because she is living, while all the Deirdres and Helens are rotten in clay. Behind the conventional ornament, Synge detects the bitter underlying truth of the image. Synge can only evoke past beauty amid an overpoweringly honest realisation of its death, decay and current rottenness. He makes no claim for the beauty of his girl. For him, the fact that she lives and that the others are dead is enough. Raftery's comparison holds good in the brutal existentialist poetry of Synge and his images still retain their currency—but in ways of which he would never have dreamed.

Hyde's third collection, *Religious Songs of Connacht,* was published in 1906, after appearing in serial form in previous years in the *New Ireland Review.* Many of the songs are an indictment of the avarice of the clergy and Synge may have drawn on them for *The Tinker's Wedding.* One poem in particular, 'An Siota agus a Mháthair' (The Lout and His Mother), contains material which was definitely exploited in the play. In Hyde's poem the Lout questions the sincerity of priests:

> Till the Bishop is paid the 'Nobis' is not read,
> And, you hag, isn't it a dear business, the 'Ego Vos'?[66]

In the play the tinkers approach the priest with the request that he marry them according to the laws of the Church. In theory, the priest should be gratified that an errant tinker couple wish to solemnise their liaison by a Catholic wedding and he should be glad to perform the ceremony with no charge to poor folk. In fact, as the Lout insisted, the priest is less anxious to solemnise the marriage than to extract maximum profit from the transaction: ' . . . If you want to be married, let you pay your pound. I'd do it for a pound only, and that's making it a sight cheaper than I'd make it for any one of my own pairs is living here in the place' (*Plays 2,* p. 15). When the tinkers protest inability to pay, he sweeps them aside.

A similar point is made by the Lout concerning funerals:

> Sure if you were dead to-morrow morning
> And I were to bring you to a priest tied up in a bag,
> He would not read a Mass for you without hand-money . . .[67]

Synge exploited this situation in the climactic scene of *The Tinker's Wedding,* where the priest is tied in a sack as a punishment for selfishness. In the play the occasion is not a death but a wedding; and the priest is tied in a sack not before but after his refusal. However, this is entirely in keeping with Synge's technique of ironic reversal, by which he frequently inverts material borrowed from the Irish language. It must be admitted, however, that there is a certain ambiguity in the lines quoted, as to whether it is the mother (the 'you' of the second line) or the priest who is tied in the bag. This ambiguity exists in the Irish and in the English versions. It is more likely that it is the dead mother who is tied in the bag, as poor people in the last century often could not afford coffins and were buried in canvas. But this has not prevented many scholars from subscribing to the other interpretation[68]—by which the priest is trapped in the bag—and Synge in all innocence may have interpreted the lines in this way himself. It is more probable, however, that he took the basic situation—the mother in the sack and the priest free— and inverted it, so that in his version the priest ends in the sack and the woman is free. This would be in keeping with his delight in reversing the basic situations of his source text.

'An Siota agus a Mháthair' ends with a palinode in which the Lout retracts all his blasphemies and this retraction is given the sanction of the poet: 'If there is folly in it—Christ make it right!'[69] This poem bears out the thesis that Irish anti-clericalism is purely verbal, a matter of word rather than deed. We begin to suspect that this long dialogue has been a tongue-in-cheek revolt by a fundamentally devout soul.

The Tinker's Wedding was never staged in Synge's lifetime, because it was feared that the assault on the priest might offend members of the Abbey audience. It is ironic that the very scene which Yeats feared might outrage the Gaelic Leaguers was itself based on an incident taken from a Gaelic poem, published by Douglas Hyde, the President of the League. The folk could tolerate the idea of violence to a priest as long as it was kept on a verbal level; but to have this violence enacted physically on stage was quite another matter, so Yeats's caution was justified.

Moreover, Synge's play contains no palinode. The Lout of the poem was permitted to blaspheme because his auditors were good Christians who knew that he would retract all heresy at the end. This foreknowledge gave him a license to hit out freely at priest and saint alike. But the blasphemies of the tinkers are neutralised by no palinode and they never repent of their violence to the priest. However, in his Preface to the published play, Synge himself offered a kind of palinode in the final paragraph:

> In the greater part of Ireland, however, the whole people, from the tinkers to the clergy, have still a life, and view of life, that are rich and genial and humorous. I do not think that these country people, who have so much humour themselves, will mind being laughed at without malice, as the people in every country have been laughed at in their own comedies (*Plays 2*, p. 3).

An unpublished typescript of this Preface, written on 20 November 1907, is even more explicit in its apologies, which are offered solely to the priesthood. Synge makes the point that anti-clerical humour does not betoken atheism or apostasy:

> I do not think these country clergy, who have so much humour— and so much heroism that everyone who has seen them facing typhus or dangerous seas for the comfort of their people on the coasts of the west must acknowledge—will mind being laughed at for half an hour without malice, as the clergy in every Roman Catholic country were laughed at through the ages that had real religion (*Plays 2*, pp. 3–4).

Hyde himself had occasion to publish a number of songs which contained blasphemous material in his collection. He excused this in *Religious Songs of Connacht* with a similarly pitched defence of the role of the priesthood in the countryside: 'When we see that the bards were so ready to speak their minds openly about the priests in cases where they had occasion for censure, our respect for that priesthood which gained and preserved the reverence and love of the people must be all the greater'.[70] Synge may well have modelled the apology in his own Preface on these lines, for the point which he makes is identical. The suspicion is confirmed when we examine the dates of publication. Hyde's collection was published as a book, complete with Irish text and English translations, in 1906; and Synge completed his Preface to *The Tinker's Wedding* in December 1907. Furthermore the idea of ending the play with the priest tied in a sack appears only in the fourth draft 'D' of the play, which Dr Saddlemyer has dated 1906. It is even possible that Synge had already read Hyde's material in its serial publication in the *New Ireland Review* or that he had heard many of the songs in his own sojourns in the west. However, given his enthusiastic response to Hyde's earlier collections, it seems most likely that he would have closely studied *Religious Songs of Connacht* on its publication in 1906; and it can scarcely be an accident that, in the following year, it seems to have conditioned his final work on *The Tinker's Wedding*.

HYDE, SYNGE AND DRAMATISED FOLKSONG

Hyde's three collections of Connacht song represent only one aspect of his work which was studied with profit by Synge. Like Synge, Hyde was an artist as well as a scholar and, in particular, a pioneer of the one-act peasant play. His *Casadh an tSúgáin* (The Twisting of the Rope) was based on one of his love songs of Connacht, 'An Súisín Bán' (The Soosheen Bawn); and this may have given Synge the idea of turning to the songs of Connacht for dramatic material. Synge recalled the first performance of *Casadh an tSúgáin*, which took place on 21 October 1901, in an article in *L'Européen* on 31 May 1902, where he showed himself aware of the long-term significance of the occasion: 'Ce fut la première fois qu'on joua une pièce en irlandais sur une grande scène' (*Prose*, p. 381) (This was the first occasion on which a work in Irish was played on a large stage). In an unpublished article, he pointed out the pioneering artistic value of Hyde's play as a model for the short peasant dramas which followed it. Under the title 'The Dramatic Movement in Ireland', Synge considered the productions of the Irish Literary Theatre in the autumn of 1901:

> . . . The Irish Literary Theatre wound up its career by giving two plays in the Gaiety Theatre Dublin, *Diarmuid and Grania*, written by Mr. W. B. Yeats and Mr. George Moore in collaboration, and a small one-act comedy in Gaelic written by Dr. Douglas Hyde. The first play was acted by Mr. Benson's company and the second by amateurs with Dr. Hyde himself in the principal role as the wandering folk-poet. This little play was in some ways the most important of all those produced by the Irish Literary Theatre, as it alone has had an influence on the plays that have been written since, and have made up the present movement. The other plays had many good qualities but none of them had the germ of a new dramatic form or seemed to have found any

new store of the materials of drama. *The Countess Cathleen* differed more in the peculiar beauty and distinction of its writing from the many verse plays that were written than in its essentially dramatic qualities. The plays of Mr. Edward Martyn and Mr. George Moore, on the other hand, were closely related to those produced by the school of Ibsen. *The Twisting of the Rope* however (Dr. Hyde's play), slight as it was, gave a new direction and impulse to Irish Drama, a direction towards which it should be added the thoughts of Mr. W. B. Yeats, Lady Gregory and others were already tending. The result has been a series of little plays dealing with Irish peasant life which are unlike, it is believed, anything that has preceded them.[71]

For Synge, the importance of *Casadh an tSúgáin* lay in its creation of a model for short peasant comedies and not in the fact that it was written in Irish, which he mentions only briefly. This short drama provided Yeats, Lady Gregory and 'others' with a model of the type of play towards which they had been working. By 'others', Synge may have been hinting with characteristic reticence at himself; for Hyde's play represented a genuine resolution of his personal dilemma as a playwright. He was caught between the realistic problem play, the 'joyless and pallid' work of Ibsen, on the one hand, and the lyrical abstractions of *The Countess Cathleen* on the other—yet he could not bring himself to admire either mode. What Synge wanted was a drama of the peasantry that was not just lyrical but realisitc, a drama that avoided abstract concepts but captured the concrete poetry of country dialect. In the critical and popular acclaim for Hyde's play, he detected a way forward for himself and for the national theatre.

Casadh an tSúgáin was not only performed in October 1901, but in that month also it appeared in the first number of *Samhain,* both in Hyde's original Irish text and in an unsigned translation by Lady Gregory. That date marks a crucial point in Synge's development as a playwright. Before it, he had written only a few unsatisfactory fragments and a disappointing play, *When the Moon Has Set.* In September 1901 he had completed a draft of that work, a play which represented an uneasy fusion of the Yeatsian lyricism of *The Countess Cathleen* with an Ibsenite study of the problem of a professed nun confronted with an earthly lover. Synge brought this work to Coole in the same month, but nothing came of it (*Plays 1,* p. xiv). The rich dramatic potential inherent in the clash of character and of linguistic styles—between polite English and rustic dialect—is never developed, merely hinted. After the success of Hyde's play, however, Synge concentrated on peasant drama and the comedy of rural manners. In the twelve months after the acclaimed production of *Casadh an tSúgáin*, he embarked on *Riders to the Sea, The Tinker's Wedding* and *The Shadow of the Glen*. No contemporary play by other Irish writers assumes such strategic importance in the evolution of Synge's art as *Casadh an tSúgáin*, for, as he wrote in 'The Dramatic Movement in Ireland', 'it alone has had an influence on the plays that have been written since and have made up the present movement'.[72] Yeats, Lady Gregory and Synge followed the example of Hyde not just in treating comic peasant themes, but also in their emphasis on the one-act play centred on a very few characters. Naturally, the one-act play was extended to two and even three acts as the size and scope of the company grew; but the preoccupation with peasant comedy survived the transition to full-length drama and has persisted to this very day.

So impressed was Synge by Hyde's comedy that he recalled it often in the following months when he sat down to write of the literary revival. Not only did he mention it in his article of May 1902 in *L'Européen,* but in an early draft of 'The Old and New in Ireland', finally published in *The Academy and Literature* on 6 September 1902, he complained that Irish humour had been 'pitifully interpreted' by Anglo-Irish writers of the nineteenth century. For Synge, Hyde's play represented a breakthrough to a more genuine tradition: 'At the last representations of the Irish Literary Theatre a little drama by Dr Douglas Hyde was acted in Irish and in this little drama there was a trace—a first rather tentative trace—of the real Irish humour' (*Prose*, p. 383). In a private notebook of the period, devoted to an analysis of the various 'unities' of drama, Synge saw fit to place Hyde's play in the most distinguished dramatic company. The plays of Shakespeare and Calderón possess 'great diversity held together by strong action', whereas in Ibsen's *The Master Builder* he detects a 'weak action—given power by a strange atmosphere'.[73] Yeats's *Where There is Nothing* has 'diversity of action held together by a single character'.[74] Clearly, Synge was willing to hold Hyde's little play up against these classics of drama, if only to discover in what ways it was open to improvement. So we find: 'Shakespeare's comedies given unity by an action; Molière's by an idea. In *Twisting of Rope* the idea of poet expelled by people is hardly developed enough to make it a play.'[75] At least three of Synge's comedies— *The Shadow of the Glen*, *The Well of the Saints* and *The Playboy of the Western World*—represent an attempt to develop this idea of a poetic figure who is expelled by a hyper-conventional society. The response evoked by Hyde's Hanrahan is similar to that obtained by the Tramp, by Martin Doul and by Christy Mahon: 'They say that there is no place that he'll go to, that the women don't love him and that the men don't hate him'.[76] Like Synge's three heroes, Hanrahan arrives into a settled community, offers his love to a fair woman already engaged to a nondescript law-abiding man, only to find that the penalty for this behaviour is that he must again become a social outcast. Synge was conscious that the rich potential of the theme had not been fully exploited by Hyde. This dissatisfaction is apparent in the phrases with which he qualifies his praise for the play. It offers humour, but in a 'rather tentative' treatment; its underlying idea is excellent but 'hardly developed'. It was left to him to develop the full resonances of Hyde's theme in his peasant comedies.

Casadh an tSúgáin represents a dramatisation of a folk-story and folk-song; and this was a technique followed by Synge in some of his subsequent plays. *The Tinker's Wedding*, like *Casadh an tSùgáin*, drew inspiration from one of Hyde's songs of Connacht; and in both plays, songs of the folk are sung on stage. *The Playboy* was based upon a folk anecdote of Aran and many speeches in that work are inspired by the songs of Connacht. The crucial importance of Hyde's short plays in the evolution of Synge's major dramas has yet to be fully appreciated.

Synge's other debts to the work of Douglas Hyde have already been outlined, in particular, his scholarly use of *A Literary History of Ireland*. It would not be fanciful to argue that his artistic debts to *Casadh an tSúgáin* and to the three collections of Connacht songs are even more palpable. It is not surprising that the work of Hyde should have so interested the playwright, for the similarities between the roles played by the two men in the Irish Revival are striking. Their respective paths to Irish Ireland were almost identical. Delicate sons of Anglo-Irish families, they were both sent for convalescence to the countryside, where Irish was still spoken by some servants. Each was sent to Trinity College, where he competed for the Irish prize. Each rejected a family wish that he take Holy Orders, opting instead for a life devoted to art and scholarship. The broken Irish of Hyde's youthful diaries parallels the crude entries in the native language made by Synge in his own journals. In his early years, Hyde shared Synge's belief that the most they could hope for was 'to save the Irish language from death'.[77] Like Synge, he was obsessed with the lore of his friends among the peasantry and made long lists of the tales he had heard in his notebooks. His early reading in Irish literature was almost identical to the dramatist's. For some years, Yeats looked to Hyde as the scholar-in-waiting to the Irish Renaissance; but after he was drawn into the propagandist campaigns of the Gaelic League, Yeats began to cast Synge in this role. Hyde, finally, chose to devote his energies to Gaelic scholarship and propaganda, whereas Synge concentrated on art and the theatre. But, to the very end, Synge was always keen to exploit the scholarship of Hyde in the service of his dramatic art.

6 Synge and Folklore

> There was a legendary character we called 'Squirely' who was a
> sort of folk-lore creation. We could spend hours inventing
> adventures for him to pass through. I was a sort of poet with
> the frank imagination by which folklore is created . . . We
> were always primitive. We both understood all the facts of life
> and spoke of them without much hesitation but a certain pro-
> priety that was decidely wholesome. We talked of sexual matters
> with an indifferent and sometimes amused frankness that was
> identical with the attitude of folk-tales.
>
> *The Autobiography of J. M. Synge*

SYNGE AS A FOLKLORIST

With the publication of Douglas Hyde's *Beside the Fire* in 1890, Irish
folklore was significantly advanced. Unlike most of his predecessors,
Hyde provided the original text in Irish for six of his fourteen tales
and he cited sources for all his material. In the preface to the book,
he called for collectors who would use the methods perfected by
Iain Campbell of Scotland. Synge took *Beside the Fire* with him to
Aran, where its methods served as a model on which to base his
own collection of folk material. Following Hyde's advice, he also
took notes from Campbell's work in the winter of 1898/9.[1] Most
crucially of all, he accepted the doctrine that, wherever possible, tales
should be collected in the Irish language and he remarked in the

notebook which he kept on Aran: 'I have given up my attempt to collect the tales till I am more perfect in Irish as the English version they give me is very poor and incomplete'.[2]

Synge's study of folklore was most intensive in 1898 and 1899. Here is a sample reading list from that period, which shows how keen he was to relate the study of Irish folklore to that of the continent:

Grant Allen   Attis
Cosquin   Miss Cox   Cinderella
Friend, *Flowers and Folk Lore*   London 1884
Jacobs   (J)   *Celtic Fairy Tales*
Legrand   Gipsy Sorcery   London 1891
Popol   Vie de L'Abbé Brasseur   Paris   1861
The Science of Fairy Tales   E. S. Hartland   London 1891
Sabillot   *Contes Populaires*
Spitta Bez   *Contes Arabes*   Leipzig   1883
Hibbert Lectures on Celtic Heathendom   1888
Professor Rhys   . . .   Arthurian Legends
Elworthy   *The Evil Eye*
MacInnes   *Waif and Stray*   Celtica   No. 11, 1890[3]

This is the same notebook which contains accounts of de Jubainville's lectures on the Irish Cycle. The comparative method is clear in such sentences as the following: 'Les traits communs de la mythologie irlandaise et de la mythologie grecque proviennent d'un vieux fonds de légendes grecs-celtique antérieur à la séparation des races'[4] (The features common to Irish and Greek mythology derive from an ancient basis in Graeco–Celtic legends which pre-dates the separation of the races). It was but a short step from a commitment to comparative mythology to an espousal of comparative folklore. That French sentence from de Jubainville's lecture appears, in an almost literal English translation, in an article by Synge in the *New Ireland Review* of November 1898. Under the title 'A Story from Inishmaan', he published the story of 'The Faithful Wife' (later to appear in *The Aran Islands*) and ended with the passage: 'It is hard to assert at what date such stories as these reached the west. There is little doubt that our heroic tales which show so often their kinship with Grecian myths, date from the pre-ethnic period of the Aryans'.[5] In his reading, no less than in de Jubainville's lectures, Synge found sanction for the comparative method in the achievement of Sir James

Frazer in *The Golden Bough*, a work which treats of folk customs
in many countries. One of Synge's notes will serve to illustrate the
use which he made of Frazer's research:

> Frazer   Golden Bough   Ch 11
> Iron . . . disliked by the spirits, a superstition dating perhaps
> from the time when iron was a novelty[6]

This perception found its way into *The Aran Islands*, along with
additional information gathered by the author during his sojourn in
Brittany. On Aran Pat Dirane had tried to ward off evil fairies with
a needle and Synge comments: 'Iron is a common talisman with
barbarians, but in this case the idea of exquisite sharpness was
probably present also, and, perhaps, some feeling for the sanctity of
the instrument of toil, a folk-belief that is common in Brittany'
(*Prose*, p. 80). All this folk scholarship is finally put to creative use
in *The Shadow of the Glen*, where the tramp is afraid to watch a corpse
and asks Nora for a needle:

> TRAMP (moving uneasily):   Maybe if you'd a piece of grey thread
> and a sharp needle—there's great safety in a needle, lady of the
> house—I'd be putting a little stitch here and there in my old coat,
> the time I'd be praying for his soul, and it going naked up to the
> saints of God (*Plays 1*, p. 41).

It is precisely this emphasis on comparative study which distinguishes Synge's contribution to Irish folklore. Even *Beside the Fire*
has been attacked because of 'the insufficiency of comparative references to outside Gaeldom'.[7] A similar fault has been found with
Lady Gregory's *The Kiltartan Wonder Book* (1910) on the grounds
that 'no notes comparing her tales with others are given, for she was
never the comparative folklorist'.[8] Hyde and Lady Gregory were
more caught up than Synge in the national movement and this
may explain the inward-looking nature of their folk studies. In her
writing, Lady Gregory repeatedly allied her work as a folklorist
with her efforts for the Gaelic League, of which Hyde himself was
president.[9] Although Hyde and Lady Gregory's love of folklore
was wholly innocent, recent history has taught us to be watchful
when folklore is used for propaganda by political movements. Seán
Ó Súilleabháin vindicates the wisdom of Synge's approach when

he argues that 'folklore is international in its main implications rather than regional or national'.[10]

Synge's notes on folklore include material from William Larminie's *West Irish Folktales and Romances* (1893). He noted Larminie's remarks on the common Aryan origin of the tales and he made a list of those stories which seemed to him to have variants elsewhere in Connacht or even in Europe. For instance, he notes that 'The Servant of Poverty' is a 'poor variant of the Cymbeline story without the pound of flesh'. Similarly, he remarks that the sea-serpent in 'The Son of the King of Prussia' is 'perhaps the worm of Pat Dirane'[11]—a reference to an account of a sea-monster given by Pat in his version of the classic tale 'The Dragon Slayer'. Making experimental comparisons, including parallels with the lore of Brittany, he continues his musings over the differences between Larminie's giant dragon and Pat's worm:

> The Son of the King of Prussia
>   a variant of Pat Dirane's tale of the Three Fomors and the Sea Serpent. Three giants come in in ships and are killed. Three daughters. The giants are put down . . .
>   bird   serpent—dragon? wings were on Pat D worm

> 'The King who had Twelve Sons' a variant of Pat Dirane's tale again. The hero cures horses instead of killing the giants who milk the cows.

> Red Pony enchantments like Breton tales.[12]

Such speculations on comparative folklore are to be found even in Synge's diary during the first visit to Aran. On 22 May 1898, he records in French a story by Pat Dirane and suggests illuminating continental parallels: 'Histoire de P. Dirane. Jack the Giant Killer and Perseus mélangés'. Pat had told the tale of the dragon-slayer mentioned above as a variant of 'The King who had Twelve Sons'. At much the same time in his stay on Aran, Synge took notes from Hartland's study of *The Legend of Perseus*, which sought to prove the identity of that classic myth with modern renditions of 'The Dragon Slayer'.[13]

Not all of the jottings in this notebook ended in idle speculation. In particular, Synge's notes on the variants of the 'Story of the Faithful Wife' proved very useful when he came to include Pat

Dirane's variant, 'The Lady O'Connor', in *The Aran Islands*. He had already found in 'The Servant of Poverty' a variant of the Cymbeline story without the pound of flesh. He added to his knowledge in the following notes taken on Aran:

Story of Decamerone 11. 9. History of Fiction 11.74.
Note. Has considerable resemblance with the French *Roman de la Violette.*
Another French romance of the 13th century entitled *Del Conte de Poitiers.*
Another romance cited by M. Michel Doit. *Roi Flore et de la belle Jeanne.*
The Two Merchants and *the Faithful Wife of Ruprecht von Wurzburg* is an interesting variant of the same story. It is in verse and published by Von der Hagen in his *Gesammtabentener* Vol. 3. Here the wager is laid by Bertram, the husband. The latter corrupts the servants.

English story in *Western Highlands.*
Story of pound of flesh—exists in a Persian form in the *Gesta Romanorum.*[14]

From Campbell's *Popular Tales of the Western Highlands*—mentioned in these notes—he actually took down a variant of the legend. This wealth of material is merely cited to illustrate the complex erudition with which Synge underpinned his remarks on the folktales narrated in *The Aran Islands*. In that book he was wary of stifling the common reader with pedantry, so he deliberately underplayed his extensive scholarship:

The incident of the faithful wife takes us beyond Cymbeline to the sunshine on the Arno, and the gay company who went out from Florence to tell narratives of love. It takes us again to the low vineyards of Wurzburg on the Main, where the same tale was told in the middle ages, of the 'Two Merchants and the Faithful Wife of Ruprecht von Wurzburg'.
    The other portion dealing with the pound of flesh, has a still wider distribution, reaching from Persia and Egypt to the *Gesta Romanorum*, and the *Pecorone* of Sir Giovanni, a Florentine notary.
    The present union of the two tales has already been found

among the Gaels, and there is a somewhat similar version in Campbell's *Popular Tales of the Western Highlands. (Prose*, p. 65)

The pages of careful annotation and shrewd speculation in the Aran notebooks have been reduced to these four elegant sentences.

The work of Anatole Le Braz, the Breton folklorist, had a deep influence on Synge, who became his friend and pupil. In particular, the dramatist found much of interest in *La Légende de la Mort en Basse Bretagne* (1892), which proved just how close the links between beliefs on Aran and Brittany really were. Le Braz shared Synge's conviction of the pagan origin of many Christian festivals, such as fire rituals on the Feast of St John:

> les Bretons s'imaginent de très bonne foi que les cérémonies qu'ils accomplissent pendant les nuits claires de la Saint-Jean d'été autour des bûchers d'ajoncs petillants, ou dans la chaumiere close que bat le vent sinistre du mois noir, sont des cérémonies chrêtiennes'.[15]
> (The Breton folk believe in all good faith that the rites—which they perform on the bright nights of the summer feast of St John around the crackling gorse fires, or in the dark thatched cottages beaten by the grim wind of the black month—are Christian ceremonies).

Synge noted the same custom in *The Aran Islands*, where the burning turf from bonfires was carried in ancient times in order to increase fertility: 'Last night, St John's Eve, the fires were lighted and boys ran about with pieces of the burning turf, though I could not find out if the idea of lighting the house fires from the bonfire is still found on the island' (*Prose*, p. 102). This is just one of those many ceremonies in which he detected a fiercely defiant paganism underneath a thin film of Christian belief. His remarks on the keening at an island funeral register this dualism with an amused and affectionate irony akin to that of Le Braz: 'There was an irony in these words of atonement and Catholic belief spoken by voices that were still hoarse with the cries of pagan desperation' (*Prose*, p. 75). This paradox may have been first suggested to Synge by the introduction to Le Braz's collection, in which he read:

> Il est peu de circonstances de la vie qui ne soient marquées par quelque cérémonie symbolique qui a revêtu maintenant des apparences chrêtiennes, mais qui porte les marques indeniables de

manières de sentir et de penser bien antérieures au christianisme.[16]
(There are few events in life which are not marked by some
symbolic ceremony which has now assumed a Christian guise, but
which bears the undeniable marks of a way of feeling and thinking which considerably pre-dated Christianity.)

The introduction to *La Legende de la Mort en Basse Bretagne* draws
a classic distinction between two types of folk narrative. On the one
hand, there is the 'conte', a tale of international provenance with a
durable form which scarcely varies from one country to the next. On
the other hand, there is the 'légende', which is infinitely variable
and which deals with more local and homely matters.[17] The tellers
of the 'contes' put little of their own personalities into their remote
other-worldly tales, but the 'légendes' arose from the lives of
ordinary people and were rooted in a particular place.[18] Into this
second category fell the stories recounted by Le Braz. In Ireland
the same distinction holds good and is used to discriminate between
two different types of storyteller. The 'sgéalaí' enjoys the higher
status as narrator of the international tale (sean-sgéal), while the
'seanchaí' narrates local tales, family genealogies and lore concerning
places, fairies or ghosts.[19] The 'sgéalaí' was always a man but the
'seanchaí' could be male or female. The tales told by the 'sgéalaí'
were long and difficult to remember, filled with adventures and
remote wonders narrated in the third person. The 'seanchaí' narrated
his story as if he himself had witnessed it. Synge kept these distinctions, which he had first learned from Le Braz, clearly in his
mind while gathering folklore on Aran. The situation on the islands
was somewhat confusing and some storytellers, including Pat Dirane,
did not distinguish one genre from another but were adept at both
types of tale. However, Synge himself keeps the distinctions clear
for the reader. In *The Aran Islands*, after Pat's story of 'The Unfaithful
Wife', Synge emphasises that this falls into the repertoire of the
'seanchaí' known as *seanchas*: 'In stories of this kind he always speaks
in the first person, with minute details to show that he was actually
present at the scenes that are described' (*Prose*, p. 72). In a letter
to Arthur Griffith, the editor of the *United Irishman*, Synge defended
the authenticity of *The Shadow of the Glen* by supplying the story
of 'The Unfaithful Wife', which he had heard on Aran in 1898. He
ended his letter with the same scholarly point: 'As you will see, it
was told to me in the first person, as not infrequently happens in
folktales of this class'.[20] Other informants on Aran were humbler in

status than Pat and could narrate only *seanchas*. Synge is careful to
remind the reader of *The Aran Islands* of the limited material of
'seanchaí': 'Another old man, the oldest on the island, is fond of
telling me anecdotes—not folktales—of things that have happened
here in his lifetime' (*Prose*, p. 95). In such an anecdote, he found
the plot for *The Playboy of the Western World*, for, immediately
after this observation, he goes on to narrate the old man's story
about 'a Connaught man who killed his father with the blow of a
spade' (*Prose*, p. 95).

The collection of folklore was a major object of Synge's visits to
Aran. In his first conversation with Old Mourteen on Inis Mór, he
was told that the old man had given material to Petrie, Sir William
Wilde, Jeremiah Curtin, as well as Finck and Pedersen. Like Pat
Dirane, Old Mourteen was both a 'sgéalaí' and a 'seanchaí', for,
although he 'talked continually of the fairies and the women they
have taken' (*Prose*, p. 54), he could also unfold 'a long folktale which
took more than an hour to relate' (*Prose*, p. 120). Synge was
fascinated by the formulaic 'run' with which Mourteen ended his
tale: 'They found the path and I found the puddle. They were
drowned and I was found. If it's all one to me to-night, it wasn't
all one to them the next night. Yet, if it wasn't itself, not a thing
did they lose but an old black tooth' (*Prose*, p. 120). Synge speaks
of this as a nonsense ending, mainly 'gibberish'. Such formulaic
'runs' are a feature of Irish storytelling and particularly of romances.
Jeremiah Curtin found it impossible to translate these 'runs' adequately and James Delargy has argued that 'no Irish storyteller, no
matter how gifted he may be, can hope to do justice in a foreign
idiom to a Gaelic wonder- or hero-tale, with its characteristic "runs"
or tricks of narrative'.[21] 'Runs' are characterised by a bombastic
series of alliterating adjectives, which are often made deliberately
incomprehensible in order to mystify and impress a credulous and
illiterate audience.[22] A trace of such alliteration may be found in
'path' and 'puddle' and the formulaic character of the words is
attested by the conscious parallelism of the sentences. Synge was
correct to call it 'gibberish', for Professor Herzog has observed
that in such formulas 'you will always come upon several phrases
which are unintelligible at the present time'.[23] Indeed, this particular
'run' is astonishingly similar to one noted by Larminie in *West Irish
Folk-Tales and Romances*: 'They found the ford and I the stepping-
stones. They were drowned, and I came safe'.[24] The dramatist
read this book about the time of his second visit to Aran. In it

Larminie notes that 'these nonsense endings frequently contain untranslatable words'.[25] The suspicion that Synge may have used this formula and attributed it to Mourteen, for his own purposes, is given added conviction by his repetition of Larminie's term 'nonsense-ending'.

Although not a professional collector, Synge was deeply read in folklore by the standards of his time. His treatment of his material was at once scientific and imaginative, so that even today his approach seems refreshingly contemporary. Lady Gregory and Yeats were far more interested in the lore of fairies and spirits than was Synge. After reading the typescript of *The Aran Islands*, Lady Gregory advised its author that 'the book would be greatly improved by the addition of some more fairy belief'.[26] Paradoxically, her own work on supernatural and fairy lore is not rated among her highest achievements as a folklorist[27] and Synge may have been wise to underplay this element in his book. He was far more interested in folk-tales and in the stories of *seanchas*, upon which he could base plays and incidents in the knowledge that his art was securely rooted in the reality of peasant life.

FOLKLORE AND LITERATURE

If Yeats believed that all literature was but the perfection of an art that everybody once had practised, then Synge had his own way of expressing it when he wrote that 'there exists yet in lonely places the unlettered literature which was the real source of all the art of words'.[28] He did not wish to create a folk literature for a peasant audience, but he did want to incorporate the methods and themes of folklore into his plays and poems.

Although Yeats often dreamed of creating poems and ballads which would pass into the lore of the folk, he realised that a more sophisticated art was required for Dublin audiences. By 1893 he was no longer content to imitate folk ballads, but called for a sophisticated poetry which would nevertheless draw upon folklore. He attributed the power of sophisticated poets like Shakespeare and Keats to the fact that they had used 'the folklore of their own day'.[29] He believed that the clash of oral and literary elements in the work of a modern writer could be endlessly creative.[30] He declared that the task of artists was to strike a balance in their work between oral Gaelic and English literary traditions.[31] In his own poetry, Yeats never quite achieved this fusion, for the dialect of ballads such as 'Moll Magee' and 'The Fiddler of Dooney' remains extraneous and is not subsumed into the rhythm of the poem. In the judgement of Jon Stallworthy, these poems owe 'more to literary than peasant sources'.[32] In Synge, however, Yeats discovered and encouraged an artist who achieved this fusion of literary traditions.

For his part, Synge had always been convinced of the artistic potential of folklore. In the winter of 1897–8, he wrote an unpublished essay 'On Literary and Popular Poetry'. He remarked that, with the growth of folk studies, 'men began to realize that the song and story of primitive men were full of human and artistic suggestion, that the official arts were losing themselves in mere technical experiments while the peasant music and poetry were full of exquisitely delicate emotions'.[33] The literature of Ibsen and Zola was joyless and pallid, realistic without being beautiful. In the folk idiom, on the contrary, Synge found a language that was both beautiful and real, in which a writer could give full expression to his feelings in a language which was not so overbred that it robbed them of all their force. In his essay he held that folk poetry was characterised by 'a certain brusqueness of attack',[34] an insight which he later immortalised in the injunction that poetry might have to become brutal before it could become fully human. He praised the poetry of Yeats, not as a slavish imitation of folklore, but as a skilful recreation within its spirit, using its methods of expression: 'Then a new school arose. The new poets did not copy the productions of the peasant but seized by instinct his inner mode of work. This I may observe is what Mr. Symons means when he says that Mr. Yeats' poems have the brevity of folklore.'[35] Synge has understood Yeats's intentions with extraordinary clarity in this passage. The poet himself had written in a letter to Katharine Tynan that they should turn to ballads not for the purpose of imitating them, but rather to find 'new methods of expressing ourselves'.[36] According to Synge, the great advantage enjoyed by the folk was that they were 'indifferent to rules which tend to hamper the direct expression of emotion'.[37] Yeats himself had envied the spontaneous inspiration of the anonymous songsters of Connacht, for 'the very difficulty in writing as a modern man made him more acutely aware of the beauty of folk poetry than the folk who had created it'.[38]

Turning finally in his essay to the theatre, Synge described Maeterlinck as the last master of this modern school whose dramas 'are directly related to the feeling of the folksong'.[39] The example of Maeterlinck's use of folklore to dramatic purposes was not lost on him. It is impossible to over-estimate the importance which Synge's discovery of folklore in the late 1890s had in shaping his future literary career. Before the winter of 1897–8, in which this article was written, he had devoted his life to the production of mawkish poems and brittle essays which (like this very essay on literary and popular poetry) went unpublished. His study of the relationship between literary and oral literature, especially in the drama of Maeterlinck, marked a great breakthrough. In the following years, Synge went on to write his major plays which exploited folk plots and techniques. In retrospect, this hardly seems surprising, for of all the literary genres drama is that which most closely combines both written and oral elements. From his study of the writings of Anatole Le Braz, Synge had learned that Irish folklore was full of dramatic situations, which lay in wait for the genius who might exploit them. According to Le Braz, Irish folktales were characterised by 'des situations fortes' and 'une action pleine de mouvement et de vie'.[40] Synge shared this conviction, for he wrote in *The Aran Islands* of how an islander's account of a meeting had 'the dramatic emphasis of the folk-tale' (*Prose*, p. 107).

Synge exploited the creative antagonism between folk and literary idiom in his plays and poems. A poem like 'Queens' aligns such archaic phrases as 'coifed' with such colloquial idioms as 'tinker's doxy' (*Poems*, p. 34). Its author believed that style came from the shock of new material and, in the violent juxtaposition of folk and literary idioms, he achieved the brutal effect which he sought. By placing a word like 'coifed' alongside the robustly colloquial 'doxy', he provided his readers with a measure of the distance which he had travelled from the effete diction of contemporary poetry. Similarly, many of the most powerful speeches in *The Playboy* are built around the clash between images from literary and oral traditions. Critics have falsely seen this as a clash in Synge's idiom between oral Irish and English literary conventions. In fact, that clash is a vital part of the native Gaelic tradition. James Delargy has pointed out that for centuries Ireland possessed independent oral and literary traditions until 'by force of circumstances, the two streams of tradition were joined'.[41] This fusion of traditions had a vitalising effect on both. The sagas gained a wealth of motifs from oral tradition, while the richness of medieval Gaelic romance can be adduced to its tense combination of oral and literary elements, both native and foreign.[42] Having studied the medieval Gaelic romances, Synge was aware that their vitality came from this dynamic alignment of images from rival traditions. The same vitality may be found in his own work. For example, the following speech by Christy Mahon opens with images from courtly love poetry in Irish (star of knowledge) and devotional manuals (holy Brigid):

Amn't I after seeing the love-light of the star of knowledge shining from her brow, and hearing words would put you thinking of the holy Brigid speaking to the infant saints . . .

but it ends in homely folk colloquialism:

. . . and now she'll be turning again, and speaking hard words to me, like an old woman with a spavindy ass she'd have urging on a hill. (*Plays 2*, pp. 125–7)

Synge exploited his own role as mediator between the 'literary' and 'folk' cultures of his fellow-Irishmen, dramatising the oral lore of the west for a sophisticated Dublin theatre. By employing folk devices in a modern theatre, he radically transformed the character of both. In introducing folk elements into the theatre, he subverted the Ibsenite drama of ideas, but he also transformed the oral materials with which he worked. However, it is wrong of Joseph Wood Krutch to argue that his drama 'turns away from "modern ideas" and assumes that such modern ideas are not the business of literature at all'.[43] Synge's plays are, in fact, a rejection of drama which merely discusses ideas rather than subsuming them into the action, a rejection of plays which enunciate ideas rather than dramatise them. *The Playboy* may be as justly termed a problem play as any by Ibsen, but it is a problem play in a folk medium. It is a tribute to the playwright's art that it could assimilate so many folk themes and techniques without ever becoming patronising or 'folksy'. In rejecting the temptation to imitate folk forms and in pursuing a more difficult art which sought to wed folk techniques with modern forms of literature, Synge was at one with the most progressive contemporary writers in the Irish language. He would have agreed with Pearse who called for 'the standard of definite art form as opposed to the folk form'.[44]

FOLK BELIEFS IN *RIDERS TO THE SEA*

Any folklorist who watched a performance of *Riders to the Sea* would feel no surprise at its tragic ending, for the play is filled with premonitions of catastrophe. It was considered unlucky for a traveller to return for something he had forgotten,[45] as Bartley returns for the rope. It was even more dangerous not to return a blessing;[46] and on Aran even compliments to another person were considered harmful unless they were rounded off by the precautionary words 'God bless you'.[47] Hence, when Maurya fails to return Bartley's blessing as he leaves the house, Cathleen turns upon her mother in fearful indignation: 'Why wouldn't you give him your blessing and he looking round in the door? Isn't it sorrow enough is on everyone in this house without your sending him out with an unlucky word behind him and a hard word in his ear?' (*Plays 1*, p. 11)

Maurya thereupon tries to save her son by catching up with him at the spring well in order to give him her blessing and bread for the journey. In the positive life-giving images of bread, blessing and spring well, there are strong signs of hope. But this is soon to be dashed. At the well Maurya has a vision of 'the fearfullest thing'— Bartley riding his red mare with her drowned son Michael following on a grey pony: 'Bartley came first on the red mare; and I tried to say "God speed you", but something choked the words in my throat. He went by quickly; and "the blessing of God on you", says he, and I could say nothing' (*Plays 1*, p. 19). Something rather similar happens in Shakespeare's *Macbeth* when the murderous hero tries to pray and the words are choked in his throat:

Listening their fear I could not say 'Amen'
When they did say 'God bless us'.[48]

Synge may well have had this in mind as he composed Maurya's speech. It is more likely, however, that he got the idea from a folktale collected by Lady Gregory and later published in her *Visions and Beliefs in the West of Ireland*. Here, too, a mother tries and fails to bless her son: '. . . she wanted to say "God bless him", but it was like as if a hand took and held her throat, and choked her that she couldn't say the words'.[49] In the same collection by Lady Gregory, one storyteller remarks that 'there's something not right about a grey horse'.[50] It is significant, therefore, that Maurya should continue her account of the vision with these words: 'I looked up then, and I

crying, at the grey pony, and there was Michael upon it—with fine
clothes on him, and new shoes on his feet' (*Plays 1*, p. 19). This grey
pony is the 'púca' which appears in the form of a horse to lure
people to death.[51] It is no surprise that Maurya should see Michael
on the grey pony, following hard upon Bartley. This is wholly in
keeping with the tradition by which a dead soul is believed to
return soon after death, in order to carry off its former partner.[52]

The power of the priest in rural Ireland was proverbial, especially
his alleged capacity to perform miraculous cures such as that in *The
Well of the Saints*.[53] However, the powers associated with priests did
not always operate in man's favour. It was considered unlucky to
mention a priest in the context of fishing.[54] Nora foolishly does
just this when she consults the young priest for his opinion as to
whether Michael was drowned while fishing. She had also asked the
priest if he would try to prevent Bartley from making the hazardous
sea-crossing to Galway. She tells Cathleen of his reply: ' "I won't stop
him", says he, "but let you not be afraid. Herself does be saying
prayers half through the night, and the Almighty God won't leave
her destitute", says he, "with no son living" ' (*Plays 1*, p. 5). Here
Nora expresses the widespread folk belief that one male member of
each island family will be spared by God from drowning, in order
to provide for the remaining women-folk.[55] We can get some idea
of the fear of Maurya, which the priest sought to assuage, from Pat
Mullen's observation that 'a lone woman in a house by herself on
these islands is a very very helpless creature'.[56] Hence Maurya's
question: 'What way will I live and the girls with me, and I an old
woman looking for the grave?' (*Plays 1*, p. 11) At the end of the
play, it is no surprise to find that it is Maurya, and not the hardy
young men, who has survived; for on Aran, according to Lady
Gregory, the folk remark that 'it's not often the old are taken'.[57]
However, the death of a young man in such a small rural community has a catastrophic effect and the mourning for his is 'deep
and prolonged'.[58]

Old Maurya has a presentiment that, if Bartley makes the sea-
crossing to sell the horses in Galway, he will be drowned. We can
appreciate the dire financial straits of this family which has to sell
its horses in order to survive. Pat Mullen was told by his dying
mother: 'Keep the horse . . . and you will always have a chance to
earn a shilling'.[59] Such was the value of a single horse on Aran. Old
Maurya, also, tries to make Bartley keep the horses. She is even more
concerned to point out that money is less important than a man's

life: 'If it was a hundred horses, or a thousand horses you had itself, what is the price of a thousand horses against a son where there is one son only?' (*Plays 1*, p. 9) This stern grasp of priorities—humans before horses—is reflected also at the end of a story in *Visions and Beliefs in the West of Ireland*:

'Pat is well', says he, 'but the horse he brought with him is dead in the stable'. 'So long as Pat is well', said Mr Gregory, 'I wouldn't mind if five horses in the stable were dead'.[60]

In one early draft of the play, Maurya recalls that 'in three nights it is Martin's night' (*Plays 1*, p. 244). The Feast of St Martin in Ireland occurs on 11 November and the festival is observed also on the vigil of the feast. It is clear from the final draft that the play's action falls about this time in November, for Maurya looks ahead to the nights after Samhain, that is, the long mid-winter nights after November has ended. According to Seán Ó Súilleabháin, a traditional practice of the festival was for each family to sacrifice an animal to St Martin.[61] It was at this time of year that animals were slaughtered to provide meat for the winter. The custom of dedicating the slaughtered animals in honour of Martin was ancient, for the *Tripartite Life of St Patrick*, written five centuries ago, tells how the saint killed a pig and dedicated it to Martin. Old Maurya and her children seem to have neglected this observance. Their pig with the black feet, far from being slaughtered, roams the house nibbling at ropes. According to Irish mythology, pigs are sacred both to the moon-goddess of the sea and to the death-goddess. Pigs were sacrificed to Manannan Mac Lir, the god of the sea, in order to ward off evil, including death by drowning.[62] By neglecting this duty, the island family has exposed itself to the danger of drowning, for Seán Ó Súilleabháin has observed that 'many stories have as their basis the punishment meted out to those who failed to fulfil the traditional custom of sacrifice'.[63]

The customs of the feast are transgressed at the very start of the play. According to the stage directions, Cathleen 'finishes kneading cake, and puts it down in the pot-oven by the fire; then wipes her hands, and begins to spin at the wheel' (*Plays 1*, p. 5). This is a violation of the rule which forbade bread-making or spinning during the festival.[64] The family, by neglecting the duties of the feast, invite retribution by death. The 'pig with the black feet'—and the black-

ness of the feet is repeatedly insisted upon—is the symbol linking
all the references to death. In folklore, black was the colour of evil
and death[65] and in Irish mythology the pig was an eater of corpses.[66]
In this play the pig has been eating the new coffin rope and will
soon be sold to the jobber for slaughter. Both of these references
link the pig with death. In this way, the linguistic and folkloristic
elements of the work are mutually reinforcing.

   Many minor gestures in the play could be interpreted as folk forebodings of Bartley's doom. When Cathleen rounds upon her mother
for failing to bless her departed son, Maurya turns to the fire and
rakes it 'aimlessly', until it is almost extinguished. Nora cries out
in alarm: 'You're taking away the turf from the cake' (*Plays 1*, p. 11).
In Irish folklore 'the fire is symbolic of human life' and must not be
allowed to die down:[67] 'As the prosperity of the house and farm was
thought to be closely associated with the fire, every effort was
made . . . to keep the fire intact'.[68] In raking the fire aimlessly,
Maurya gives us a vital clue to her spiritual condition and a premonition of the disaster which will soon overtake her household. Bartley
shows a similar carelessness when he puts on a flannel shirt, formerly
owned by the drowned Michael, before setting out on his journey.
It is a common belief that 'the departed still owns whatever property
he once possessed' and that he may 'be jealous of his heir, who now
enjoys its possession'.[69] So it comes as no surprise when the spirit
of the dead Michael returns to carry off to death the brother who
now wears his fine shirt. Nor was it wise of Maurya to employ
Michael's old walking stick on her ill-fated journey to the spring
well. Many tribes, in fact, bring the possessions of a dead person
with him to the grave, in fear that if ever his goods were used by
the living, his ghost would appear to snatch them away.[70] An
awareness of such customs gives a far deeper poignancy to the ritual
enacted by Maurya over Bartley's dead body before the end. Synge
explains in his stage directions that 'Maurya drops Michael's clothes
across Bartley's feet, and sprinkles Holy Water over him'; and again,
a little later, she 'spreads out the pieces of Michael's clothes beside
the body, sprinkling them with the last of the Holy Water'
(*Plays 1*, p. 25). The drowned Michael can no longer return to
haunt the brother who succeeded to his clothes—for those clothes
now drape that brother's dead body. Through succeeding to the
possessions of the deceased, Bartley has soon joined the ranks of the
dead. This all gives a poignant irony to Maurya's ensuing speech, in
which she draws attention to the normal pattern by which the old

leave things after them for the young.

At the close of the play, Michael is known to have been drowned and Bartley's body is laid to rest in the kitchen. It was a touch of genius which led Synge to insert the stage direction by which Maurya 'puts the empty cup mouth downwards on the table, and lays her hands together on Bartley's feet' (*Plays 1*, p. 25). This simple gesture, by which a cooking vessel or a cup is turned upside down, is a common practice in many countries.[71] Its origins may be based on the idea that the cup from which the dead person has drunk must be emptied of its dangerous content and taken out of common use.[72] Again we note the danger implied in the improper use of a dead man's possessions.

All through the play, therefore, members of the family have violated folk prohibitions. This heightens our sense of the inevitability of Bartley's death. Even the arrival of the keening women at the end is a violation of the customary belief that the corpse 'should not be keened over for two hours after death lest the sleeping dogs of the Devil be roused along the path which the departed soul had to follow'.[73] Maurya's final prayer that the Almighty God have mercy 'on my soul . . . and on the soul of everyone is left living in the world' (*Plays 1*, p. 27) may be an echo of a remark of a woman in one of the tales collected by Lady Gregory: 'But God have mercy on all the mothers of the world'.[74] In those words of prayer, Maurya succeeds in giving the blessing to Bartley which earlier had been so painfully withheld.

Despite this blessing on Bartley and the world, Maurya's closing speech holds no orthodox Christian promise of a life to come. There is no talk of awards or punishments to be meted out in the next life in accordance with a person's behaviour in this. This is entirely in harmony with Synge's own observations of life on Aran and with his study of early Irish literature. In 1898 he had read an old Irish tale from the Mythological Cycle, *The Voyage of Bran*, edited and translated by Kuno Meyer; and he had made summaries of the chapters in the notebook which also contained his notes from de Jubainville's lectures comparing ancient Irish and Homeric civilisation. Meyer's volume contained an essay by Alfred Nutt entitled 'The Irish Vision of the Happy Otherworld and the Celtic Doctrine of Rebirth'. Synge cited this essay and Meyer's text in an essay written in French in 1902 to support his thesis that Old Irish and Greek literature shared a position of major importance in the Indo-European scheme:

Rien, par exemple, dans la littérature n'est aussi primitif que cette foi commune aux Grecs et Irlandais, foi en un autre monde où les morts continuent une vie semblable à l'existence terrestre sans espoir d'être récompensés pour leurs virtus ni l'appréhension d'être punis pour leurs méfaits' (*Prose*, p. 354).

(For example, nothing in literature is as primitive as that common faith of the Greeks and Irish, faith in another world where the dead continue a life similar to their terrestrial existence, without the hope of being recompensed for their virtues or the fear of being punished for their misdeeds).

This essay was written in the same year as the play and it explains a great deal about the world-view implied in Maurya's closing lines—a vision of life which can assert a belief in an all-powerful God but not in a life to come.

THE SHADOW OF THE GLEN AS A WAKE

The wake was essential to Synge's dramatic conception of death. The *Irish Times*'s critic at the first performance of *Riders to the Sea* complained that it 'developed into something like a wake. The long exposure of the dead body before an audience may be realistic, but it is certainly not artistic'.[75] In *Deirdre of the Sorrows*, when Deirdre and Naisi decide to return to Ireland, the other sons of Usna, along with Fergus and Lavarcham, come in; according to Synge's stage direction, they 'are all subdued like men at a queen's wake' (*Plays 2*, p. 233). These words forecast the dominant visual image of the closing act, during most of which an open grave is exposed to the audience, as Deirdre wails for her dead Naisi. Pádraic Colum asked Synge if this heightening of the tragic feeling by means of an open grave was not too obvious: 'but he said that he had been close to death, and that the grave was a reality to him, and it was the reality in the tragedy he was writing'.[76] However, it was in *The Shadow of the Glen* that Synge most fully effected a dramatic presentation of the wake. It turns out, of course, to be a mock-wake, for the corpse like that of the illustrious Finnegan is very much alive. But that is not clear at the start.

The folk tale which forms the basis for the plot of this play ends with the enraged husband beating the lover of his wife to death.

In that version (told by Pat Dirane) the tramp was only an onlooker, but Synge tightens the structure of the plot by making him also the lover. To this simple tale the dramatist also added minor characters and local intensity, as well as new themes such as man's relationship to nature. His most significant alteration is to the ending, which he makes at once more ambiguous and more optimistic than it is in the source. There is no grotesque assault on the lover. Instead, the wife leaves with the tramp to an uncertain but challenging future; and the outraged husband subsides into a quiet life of drink and self-deception. In giving his tale this ironic twist, Synge was acting within the traditions of the folk tale, which permitted each teller to mould the story in keeping with his own character, provided that the alterations kept 'a kind of harmony with what is already there'.[77] Synge remarked to Edward Stephens that 'people are entitled to use these old stories in any way they wish'.[78] In conferring on his tale a subtly ambiguous ending, he was giving his primitive vehicle a sophisticated impact, converting folklore into literature before his audience's very eyes. It would scarcely be excessive to claim that this play cannot be understood without an appreciation of his folk studies and, in particular, of the folk beliefs surrounding the wake.

The drama opens with the following scenario: 'Cottage kitchen; turf fire on the right; a bed near it against the wall with a body lying on it covered with a sheet' (*Plays 1*, p. 33). This is the correct setting for a formal wake. Seán Ó Súilleabháin, in a pioneering study of the wake in rural Ireland, remarks that the body is normally left on 'a bed in the kitchen'[79] and that 'sheets are hung over the bed'.[80] He emphasises that lighted candles stand on a table for the duration of the wake,[81] just as Nora Burke is 'lighting candles on a table' (*Plays 1*, p. 33). Nora remarks to the tramp that 'it's a wild night, God help you, to be out in the rain falling' (*Plays 1*, p. 25). Normally, men congregate out of doors at a wake, but they move 'inside the kitchen if the weather is inclement',[81] which is why Nora urges the tramp to 'come in out of the rain' (*Plays 1*, p. 33). The tramp expresses surprise that Nora should have left the corpse on the bed 'not tidied, or laid out itself' (*Plays 1*, p. 33). This task is usually performed by neighbouring women, as soon as it is clear that death has supervened.[83] Although the tramp marvels at it, Dan's injunction to his wife not to touch his dead body might be seen simply as an expression of the common belief that a wife should not have to lay out the body of her husband. However, his threat to put a black curse on her if she violates his wish proves that his injunction arose from a deep antagonism. So there is a real ambiguity about the prohibition. It has no direct sanction in folk custom, yet it is consistent with the many taboos governing the treatment of the dead. It is a dramatic device of Synge's own making, yet it is a device created within the spirit of folklore.

Nora tells of her husband's character and last hours, in keeping with the tradition by which the personality of the deceased is recalled at wakes. The tramp says 'God rest his soul' and crosses himself (*Plays 1*, p. 35), for a visitor to a wake-house is expected to pray briefly for the departed soul.[84] Nora then pours the tramp a glass of whiskey and gives him a pipe and tobacco with the polite excuse: 'I've no pipes saving his own, stranger, but they're sweet pipes to smoke' (*Plays 1*, p. 35). Normally, at a wake the guest is given whiskey and new clay pipes[85] and that is why she apologises for having only used pipes on hand. Emboldened by this hospitality, the tramp remarks sardonically that he has 'never seen a wake till this day with fine spirits, and good tobacco, and the best of pipes, and no one to taste them but a woman only' (*Plays 1*, p. 37). Nora quickly explains that her husband died at sunset 'and how would I go out into the glen and tell the neighbours and I a lone woman with no house near me?' (*Plays 1*, p. 37) In this situation her duties were twofold and contradictory. On the one hand, she was obliged to send news of the death to distant relatives such as Dan's sister as soon as possible.[86] On the other hand, this could not be done without violating 'a strict traditional rule that at no time during the wake should the corpse be left alone'.[87] This rule arises from the folk belief that 'in the intermediate period between death and interment the deceased is in a way still present'.[88] This is the reason for holding the wake, with the conviction that the deceased is still alive and should be made the centre of many activities, honoured with company before his long journey of the soul.[89]

During the course of a wake, it was the custom that 'current topics were discussed'.[90] So Nora and the tramp recall the recent death of Patch Darcy, the manly shepherd who went mad in the hills. After these courtesies Nora asks the tramp to remain with the corpse for a while. She wishes to pass on her news to a neighbour 'the way he can go down into the glen when the sun goes up and tell the people that himself is dead' (*Plays 1*, p. 41). Here again she obeys the strict duty that news of the death should be sent to relatives as soon as possible; and she seizes the opportunity provided by the tramp who can stay with the corpse. Unhappy at this prospect, he rejoins: 'It's

myself will go for him, lady of the house, and let you not be destroy-
ing yourself with the great rain' (*Plays 1*, p. 41). His uneasiness is
due to fear of the dead body, but it may also arise from the belief that
it was usually women, more appropriately than men, who sat with
the corpse. Nora goes out and the tramp, who has taken a needle as
a protective talisman, recites the *De Profundis*, a prayer for departed
souls. At this moment Dan rises from his death-bed and strikes terror
into the tramp by asking for a drink. In the folklore of the world
there are, of course, many similar cases in which a corpse was reputed
to have sat up in order to rebuke the mourners for their jollity.
Christiansen reports one instance from Telemark, where the convivial
company were terrified when 'the deceased half rose in the coffin and
looked reprovingly at the guests'.[91] From the outset of Synge's play,
the tramp had been uneasy with the corpse, having remarked on
his arrival: 'It's a queer look is on him for a man that's dead' (*Plays 1*,
p. 33). According to Crofton Croker, in Ireland the body lay with
face uncovered and folk were obsessively curious about the expression
on the dead man's face.[92] A stiff face was a sign of damnation. Terror
at the prospect of hell was believed to be the cause of a protracted
death agony; hence 'it was a merciful action to cover the eyes and
shut out the terrible vision'.[93] Old Dan's face does not impress the
tramp as having the authentic marks of death.

Dan has a hurried drink of whiskey and takes out the stick with
which he intends to beat his wife. He swears the tramp to silence
on her return and retreats into the bed, still feigning death. Nora
returns with her young lover, Michael Dara. She tries to usher the
tramp into an adjoining room for a sleep, while she and Michael are
free to court. The tramp will have none of this: 'Is it go away and
leave you, and you having a wake, lady of the house? I will not
surely. And it's none of your tea I'm asking either' (*Plays 1*, p. 45).
He is within his rights, for the guest at a wake normally expected
to 'remain for at least a few hours',[94] during which he might choose
between 'tea or some stronger beverage'.[95] Drunkenness was common at wakes because men were not always used to drinking spirits
in such quantities and women sought to sober them with tea.[96] The
tramp has shrewdly observed Nora boiling the kettle on the turf, so
he forestalls her ploy by asserting his traditional rights. Michael Dara,
'looking at the tramp rather scornfully' (*Plays 1*, p. 45), criticises his
coat and his tailoring. The traveller counters with a spirited attack
on Michael's clumsiness as a shepherd, which he had observed earlier
that day. Such taunting and mocking exchanges were a feature of

wakes and, although they often began in fun, 'still malice and insult were present on occasions. The relatives of the deceased had often to intervene when this form of entertainment was in danger of passing the bounds of propriety and giving rise to ill-feeling and violence . . .'[97] So Nora warns Michael 'in a low voice': 'Let you not mind him at all, Michael Dara. He has a drop taken and it's soon he'll be falling asleep' (*Plays 1*, p. 47). However, Michael admits his poor prowess as a shepherd and it is noteworthy that mock contests of shepherding were a practice at some wakes.[98]

A common feature of wakes was the playing of games of court-ship. In one game known as 'Doctoring', a man asks a girl to cure his sickness by marrying him; she then considers, refuses and gives herself to another.[99] This is precisely what happens in *The Shadow of the Glen*, where the whole plot may be seen as a variant of the game. Michael asks Nora to marry him in the chapel of Rathvanna, only to be rejected unexpectedly in favour of the tramp. Another wake amusement called 'Downey' offers an even more apt analogue to the other elements of Synge's plot, especially the irate behaviour of Dan Burke. 'Downey' was the man whose corpse was waked. The mourners lamented his death and just as they were about to take his body for burial, Downey 'would come to life and ask them for a drink'.[100] This is exactly what happens in the play, where Dan Burke comes suddenly to life, asking the tramp to 'bring me a drop quickly' (*Plays 1*, p. 43). In some versions of this game, mourners who had not spoken respectfully of the deceased were rounded upon by Downey, who beat them with a strap or rope.[101] So in the play Michael and Nora, who have spoken disrespectfully of Dan, are attacked by his risen corpse complete with 'the stick in his hand' (*Plays 1*, p. 53).

According to Thomas Dineley, unruly conduct was the rule at the wakes of old people;[102] and the wake of Dan was no exception. Dineley noted that courting was a common practice at wakes where the young, like Nora, Michael and the tramp seized the opportunity to 'make love and matches'.[103] So prevalent did this custom become that in the very year in which the play was first performed (1903), the Bishop of Ardagh and Clonmacnoise made an order forbidding unmarried men or women to attend wakes thenceforth from sunset to sunrise.[104] Not all of this love-making was romantic, however, for financial considerations were paramount in rural Irish matches. Marriages based on hard economic considerations were often ar-ranged at wakes[105] and it is into this tradition that the proposed marriage of Michael and Nora falls. As she muses on the loneliness of her past life and her romantic longings, he imperviously counts out the money which Dan left to her: 'That's five pounds and ten notes, a good sum, surely' (*Plays 1*, p. 51). This money and the farm will be added to Michael's own stock and the twenty pounds which he earned for his lambs. In the end, however, Nora's emotional longing must be satisfied. Her acceptance of the tramp is wholly within the convention of the wake amusement known as 'marrying', by which a girl was 'married' to the first man who came into the house from outside. Nora finally chooses to leave with the tramp because of his fine talk. By comparison, her husband is a poor talker and a worse listener—all he does is to repeat in barren mockery the sentences which had passed with such vitality between the tramp and Nora.

Many other conventions associated with wakes are observed by Synge in the play. It often happened that a guest became drunk and dozed off to sleep as the night wore on.[106] Nora predicts to Michael that this will happen to the tramp: 'He has a drop taken and it's soon he'll be falling asleep' (*Plays 1*, p. 47). At wakes those who drank too much first grew aggressive, as the tramp became belligerent to Michael and impolite to Nora, in refusing tea. Later, the drunkards often grew drowsy, just as Synge's tramp settles himself to sleep in the chimney corner. Ecclesiastical opposition to wakes was always strong, partly because of the unruly violence and love-making, but mainly because of the widespread drunkenness which characterised such events.[107] Another reason for this opposition was that the conception of death underlying the wake was pagan in origin. As Christiansen has commented: 'The dead were somehow still belonging to the world of man, hovering on its outskirts in a kind of frontier zone . . . In the doctrine of the church, the deceased were re-born into a new kind of existence, essentially different from that of the living.'[108] In keeping with this view, there is no reference by Nora to the consolations of Christian belief; it is rather the tramp who crosses himself and utters a prayer. The vague frontier between life and death is brilliantly projected in the reactions to Dan's two revelations that he is alive. On the first disclosure, the tramp asks doubtfully 'Is it not dead you are?' (*Plays 1*, p. 43) On the second revelation to the assembled company, Nora questions the tramp: 'Is it dead he is or living?' (*Plays 1*, p. 53)

The function of a wake was to honour the memory of the departed soul and so the main topic of conversation was usually 'praise of the

deceased'.[109] By this criterion, *The Shadow of the Glen* must finally
be seen as a mock-wake, for Dan Burke's faults rather than his
virtues are recalled. Moreover, it is often difficult to tell whose wake
this really is. The admired Patch Darcy is recalled far more often
and more poignantly than Dan. Nora was Darcy's particular friend
and, it is hinted, lover. The tramp praises Darcy's prowess as a
shepherd and chides Michael Dara for his clumsiness with sheep.
Nora adds: 'He was a great man surely, stranger, and isn't it a grand
thing when you hear a living man saying a good word of a dead
man?' (*Plays 1*, p. 47) That question holds the ultimate irony of this
vastly inverted wake.

It may be objected that most of these folk beliefs would be lost on
a modern theatrical audience, unaware of such old-world customs.
Nevertheless, it can be argued that many of the folk practices in the
play are powerfully dramatic in their own right. When the tramp
takes out a needle to protect himself or when the corpse sits up and
asks for a drink, these actions have a spine-chilling power, even for
the uninitiated. Obviously, the imaginative power of such ritual
actions is one reason why they have been hallowed by folk practice.
For the same reason they have a strong theatrical impact onstage,
even for those audiences who know little of folklore. Furthermore,
it should never be forgotten that Synge wrote each of his plays
with a specific theatre in mind, the Irish National Theatre. *The
Shadow of the Glen* was explicitly designed for the slender resources,
tiny stage company and unique audience of that infant theatre. In
the early years of the Abbey, before the splits with the nationalists
in 1906 and 1907, many members of both the company and the
audience were drawn from the Gaelic League, an organisation
pledged to restore the Irish language and lore. According to the Abbey
actress, Máire Nic Shiubhlaigh, these audiences brought to any play
on a Gaelic theme an accumulation of ideas drawn from literature
and folklore.[110] *The Shadow of the Glen* was first performed on 8
October 1903 before such an audience, with Miss Nic Shiubhlaigh
in the role of Nora Burke. Although some critics denounced it as a
slur on Irish womanhood that Nora should leave her lawful husband
for a new life with the tramp, John Butler Yeats rightly rebutted such
attacks by seeing the work primarily as an attack on that very Irish
institution—the loveless marriage. Many other lovers of the native
language and lore rallied to Synge's defence, among them Máire

Nic Shiubhlaigh. They believed that the play was a magnificent achievement, for in it Synge had achieved his major aim of transmuting ancient folk beliefs into modern dramatic art.

7 Deirdre of the Sorrows

THE DEIRDRE LEGEND IN ANGLO-IRISH DRAMA

The pioneering work of Standish J. O'Grady in his *History of Ireland: Heroic Period* (1878) had made the legends of Ireland available once again in popular form. The legends were no longer the sole preserve of scholars but could now be exploited for the purposes of art. O'Grady encouraged George Russell ('AE') in just such an enterprise and published the first act of his dramatic version of the Deirdre legend in the *All Ireland Review* of July 1901. This gave Russell the impetus to write a second act for publication in October and November of that year.[1] His version begins in springtime, with the elopment of the lovers to Alban. His play emphasises the burden of prophetic doom carried by Deirdre, who is shown as weak and passive, while Naisi is strong and brave. There is a lack of psychological motivation in Russell's mystic interpretation of the legend and a corresponding obsession with the supernatural and with fate. We are never permitted to forget that Deirdre will destroy the Sons of Usna and, finally, the Red Branch Knights themselves.

In Yeats's *Deirdre* (1906), the outlines are even more vague. The tone is elegiac. The poet has dramatised a mood, more than people of flesh and blood. The plot opens with the lovers already in Scotland, so there is less emphasis on action. Where Russell sought for a sense of the epic, Yeats seeks a lyric quality through the use of choric musicians. Hence he frames his play with a *protasis* in order to provide the expository information so necessary to a work which begins *in medias res.* The lyric texture is evoked from the outset by the first Musician:

> I have a story right, my wanderers,
> That has so mixed with fable in our songs
> That all seemed fabulous.[2]

Throughout the play, Deirdre herself repeatedly refers to the story's status as legend. Yeats's version is also notable for its portrayal of King Conchubhar as, at once, a brutal and pathetic figure. All the time, however, he bears himself like a king and his lofty demeanour impresses itself on all around him.

On 12 September 1907, Synge wrote to Frederick Gregg, an American journalist, with the news that 'I am half-inclined to try a play on Deirdre—it would be amusing to compare it with Yeats and Russell's—but I am a little afraid that the Saga people might loosen my grip on reality'.[3] He had in fact already tried his hand, for the earliest draft of the play is dated 5 September 1907. Yeats's version of the legend had been performed at the Abbey in 1906 and this may have stimulated Synge to begin writing his own play. In some respects, he learned from the example of Yeats and Russell. Like Yeats, he simplified the demands of the plot by reducing the number of its characters; but he followed Russell in retaining the three main episodes—elopement, life in Alban and tragic return to Ireland—within the three-act form. However, Synge's play is at once more dramatic and more faithful to real life than that of Yeats or Russell. Where Yeats had seen the play as an elegiac essay on fame and Russell had filled his work with nature-mysticism, he saw the plot as a crisis in human relations. His play is at all times true to the way trapped and terrified people would act under intolerable strains. Yeats and Russell had viewed the legend though the lens of nineteenth-century adaptations into English poetry and prose. Synge must have been aware of the shortcomings of this approach, for when asked by Edward Stephens if his play might be spurned as an imitation of their work, he replied: 'Oh, no—there isn't any danger of that. People are entitled to use those old stories in any way they wish. My treatment of the story of Deirdre wouldn't be like either of theirs!'[4] Later, he wrote somewhat caustically of Russell's play to Molly Allgood.[5] Dissatisfaction with the rather unreal characters of Russell's play was widespread and prompted George Moore to ask wickedly after a performance: 'Who are his people? Ours were cattle merchants'.[6]

The fundamental differences between Synge's play and the other works may be explained by the fact that, unlike Yeats and Russell, Synge did not rely on nineteenth-century English translations. Instead, he went back to the original texts of the legend in the Irish language. There had been many Gaelic versions of the tale, from the stark and primitive text in the *Book of Leinster* down to the sentimental and romantic version published by Douglas Hyde in Synge's own lifetime. Synge understood the development of the legend and the characteristic qualities of each of the major versions. Many members of the audience at the Abbey Theatre were enthusiastic students of the native literature, as well as of the work of Anglo-Irish writers. They brought to a play about Deirdre an accumulation of ideas, drawn not only from the earlier dramas of Yeats and Russell, but also from the contrasting versions of the legend in the native language.[7] It will be seen that the unique character of Synge's play—its blend of sentiment and brutality—owes much to his exploitation of the legend in its native forms. He went back to the true source of the tale in oral and manuscript versions in Irish. This is why he was so confident from the start that his play would stand alone. In the very choice of his title he was at pains to emphasise his intentions. *Deirdre of the Sorrows* is a deliberate echo of that formula in Gaelic tradition which classed 'The Fate of the Sons of Uisneach' as one of 'Trí Truaighe na Scéalaíochta' (The Three Sorrows of Storytelling). Myles Dillon has argued that the combination may have been effected by a medieval monk who wrote down the three legends together.[8] Lest the point of his title should be lost on the audience, Synge repeats it at the climactic moment of the opening act of his play. Deirdre comes in dressed as a queen and her first words to Naisi are: 'Do not leave me, Naisi, I am Deirdre of the Sorrows' (*Plays 2*, p. 207). It soon emerges that Naisi knows 'what is foretold, that Deirdre will be the ruin of the Sons of Usna' (*Plays 2*, p. 209). Her name is repeatedly emphasised in this exchange, for 'Deirdre' in the Irish language means 'alarm' and signifies the warning prophecy at her birth of the wars and suffering which she would cause.[9]

It now remains to make a closer investigation of those versions of the legend which find echoes in the play by Synge.

THE VERSION IN THE *BOOK OF LEINSTER*

In the twelfth-century *Book of Leinster*, the tales of Ireland were classified into types. The story of Deirdre and Naisi was listed among thirteen *aitheda* (elopements).[10] The same manuscript contains the story of *The Exile of the Sons of Usnach*. This version is untitled, but is referred to in the colophon as *Longas* (Exile). At a later stage an amplified version of this particular rendition became known as *The Tragic Death of the Sons of Usnach*. This narrative is spare, terse and even harsh in tone. It consists of prose sections which may date from the eighth or ninth century;[11] two obscure but dire prophecies usually described as 'rhetorics'; and three lyric poems of sorrowful nostalgia. Deirdre is briefly described and emerges as 'a barbarian woman, rude and passionate in her speech and savage in her actions'.[12] Lavarcham, her nurse, is a satirist and musician, the confidante of Conchobar, and a monstrous woman who can fly across Ireland by means of her strangely twisted legs. The tone of the version is ominous, with a repeated insistence on the inevitability of fate and constant prophecies of the tragedy to come. The protagonists are characterised by a savage energy and a brutal courage at the moment of death. The title, *The Exile of the Sons of Usnach*, shows where the emphasis of the story lay, as the narrator relied on the three doomed brothers to carry the weight of the tragedy. There was no attempt, as in later versions, to have Deirdre moan and commit suicide on her lover's grave. The style of the narration is austere, restrained and dispassionate, with no emotional speeches by the protagonists and no attempt to analyse character. There was no need to supply psychological motivation in a tale whose heroes perform all important actions under a *geis*. A *geis* was a solemn injunction, laid upon one person by another, to perform some act on pain of punishment. Deirdre asks Naisi to escape with her to Alban; but he is reluctant to break faith with the king, until she places him under *geis* to take her. In the *aitheda* (elopements), it was always the woman who initiated the action and compelled the man to submit to her will.[13] This version ends with the death of the sons of Uisneach, after which Deirdre is forced to live for a humiliating year with the enemy of Naisi, Eoghan Mac Dúrthacht. The concrete ferocity of the narration is nowhere more clear than in the ending, where Deirdre flings herself from Eoghan's chariot and dashes her brains out on a rock.

Synge knew this version and was struck by its bleak honesty. On 28 December 1905, he reviewed A. H. Leahy's *Heroic Romances of*

Ireland, which included a version of the tale based on that in the *Book of Leinster*. He took Leahy to task for his 'deplorable mis-representation' of the starkly prophetic verses uttered by Cathbad the Druid on the occasion of Deirdre's birth. He regretted that this 'characteristically wild touch' should have been translated by Leahy into well-bred Tennysonian verse (*Prose*, pp. 371–2). The duty of assessing Leahy's book gave the dramatist a timely reminder of the earliest form of the Deirdre legend. Its sharp and desolate outlines offered a telling contrast to the mystic version of Russell, to the elegiac tone of Yeats's play (then in preparation for the Abbey) and to the Victorian metrics of Leahy. The example of Leahy had a negative value for Synge, since it demonstrated what not to do with the legend.

The playwright's fear that 'the Saga people might loosen my grip on reality'—as they had done in the case of Russell and Leahy—was understandable, but unnecessary in a writer who had studied the saga life in this earliest version of the tale. Here the mode of narration is intensely realistic, at times almost mercenary. Deirdre and Naisi do not swoon into love at first sight. Instead, Deirdre's first thoughts are shrewd and calculating, for she decides that Naisi can help her to escape. There is romance in this, however, for she tries him only when Lavarcham has refused assistance and she is at her wit's end. All her thoughts concentrate on the need to escape and not on the handsome youth whom she met on the hills. He is, as yet, just a pawn in her game. In Synge's play, therefore, she traps him by the device of appearing 'royally dressed and very beautiful' (*Plays 2*, p. 207). There is a brilliant ambiguity in Deirdre's act of donning the robes of a queen. To Lavarcham, this action seems to suggest assumption of the role of Conchubor's wife and queen; but, in reality, Deirdre adorns her body for the impending seduction of Naisi.

Synge restores the realism of the old tale in his treatment of Deirdre and Naisi. She is decisive, purposeful and able to seize the main chance—she is the one who takes the initiative in escaping from Ulster. As in the old tale, Synge's Naisi is at first reluctant to go. He reasons sensibly with Deirdre, pointing out that 'when you're queen in Emain you will have none to be your match or fellow' (*Plays 2*, p. 209). He is anxious not to violate his duties to his uncle and so he suggests the time-honoured solution of thwarted lovers: 'Wouldn't we do well to wait, Deirdre, and I each twilight meeting you on the side of the hills?' (*Plays 2*, p. 211) But Deirdre is intent on flight and will have her way. She initiates every major action in the play—the decision to elope and the later resolution to return. It is she who speaks the first harsh word that severs the happy alliance with Naisi and it is she who bravely decides to join the sons of Uisneach in the grave. Eleanor Hull has written of 'the savagery of an untamed nature' in the Deirdre of the original version.[14] Something of this untamed nature persists in Synge's heroine who first 'comes in poorly dressed with a little bag and a bundle of twigs in her arms' (*Plays 2*, p. 189). Lavarcham emphasises to Conchubor that Deirdre has grown up with the wildness of nature—'she has the birds to school her, and the pools in the rivers where she goes bathing in the sun' (*Plays 2*, p. 187). Her entry bearing twigs strengthens our conviction that this wild and natural girl will be no fitting mate for an aged monarch.

Many critics of the play have argued that its blunt peasant idiom is inappropriate on the lips of noble personages; but this robust idiom is an integral part of the barbaric tale in the *Book of Leinster*. We might cite the following translation to demonstrate just how crude and primitive the original text actually was. This is the scene where Deirdre meets Naisi and puts him under *geis* to go to Alban:

'Fair is the heifer that goes past me', he cried. 'Well may the heifers be great', she said, 'in a place where there are no bulls'. 'You have the bull of the whole province, the king of Ulstermen', said he. She replied that she preferred a young bull like him, and when he demurred, she sprang upon him and seizing his two ears, cried: 'These will be two ears of shame and mockery unless you take me away with you'.[15]

Compared with this blunt passage, Synge's scene where Naisi reminds Deirdre that she could marry the king of Ulster seems mute enough. Nevertheless, the basic similarity is there. Alone among the Abbey dramatists, Synge succeeded in recapturing the vivid and robust idiom of the *Book of Leinster*. It was this version of the tale which he had studied with Henri d'Arbois de Jubainville as part of his course in Celtic Studies in Paris. In an article in *L'Européen* on 15 March 1902, Synge expressed his gratitude to this mentor and singled out his treatment of the Deirdre legend for particular praise. Writing of the Ulster Cycle, he said:

Plusieurs récits qui y appartiennent, tel que le *Sort des Fils d'Uisneach*, sont tous imprégnés de cette poésie particulièrement celtique qui réunit d'une facon inattendue une tendresse timide, un héroisme rude et mâle et un amour infini pour les beautés de la nature (*Prose*, p. 353).

(Several of its tales, such as *The Fate of the Sons of Uisneach*, are all filled with that particularly Celtic poetry which fuses in an unexpected fashion a shy tenderness, a primitive and manly heroism, and an infinite love for the beauty of nature.)

Scholars of the native literature have not been slow to point out Synge's fidelity to the spirit of the original version. Daniel Corkery believed that this play recaptured that note of intensity, 'the chiefest note in Irish literature', which, he said, had been lost in English literature with the Renaissance.[16] The quarrel which finally separates Deirdre and Naisi, at the end of the play, has been criticised as too harsh, but it had to be savage to divide two intense lovers. Synge was not afraid to put into his play that note of hardness and austerity which typified the narrative of the *Book of Leinster*. This realism pervades his treatment of all the major characters—for example, he does not fall into the trap of turning King Conchubor into a stock villain of sentimental melodrama. Instead, Conchubor is made to excite a complex pity in his associates and in the audience at the close. He is no villain but a person, like Deirdre and Naisi, who has tried to do his best within an impossible situation. This is the tough-minded character of the play and Corkery finds it adequate to the ancient tale. 'The ancient literature must really, one thinks, have released for him his deeper self'. Commending the 'savagery' with which Synge set about his work, Corkery asserts that he 'roughened the tale, acting surely more wisely than those who watered the hot blood that is in all Irish tellings of it'.[17] It is in the depiction of Deirdre that the dramatist keeps faith most notably with this ancient source. Corkery observes that in the play, 'as in the old saga, she is the huntress; it is she who entices Naisi to her, whatever his own thought may be'.[18] That combination of 'un tendresse timide' and 'un héroisme rude' which Synge detected in the ancient version is to be found also in his own work.

MEDIEVAL VERSIONS: THE EMERGENCE OF DEIRDRE

As the tale was retold through the middle ages, many folk elements

were added. In the Glen Masain manuscript (1238), episodes were
elaborated and the narrative style grew more expansive and verbose,
in keeping with the techniques of oral story-telling.[19] Alfred Nutt
has pointed out that the legend gained many beautiful details in its
medieval elaborations.[20] Most noteworthy was the increased incidence of symbolic dreams and ominous visions by Deirdre of her
future tragedy. No longer is the action narrated on a purely physical
level, but the protagonists are provided with feelings and stated
motivations. A character such as Conchubor is torn by conflicting
responses to his dilemma. He sends Lavarcham to find out if Deirdre
retains her beauty and is happy to discover that she does not. Then
he suspects deceit, becomes miserable and sends a messenger to spy
on the sons of Uisneach with tragic results. So, the medieval narrator
makes clear that Conchubor destroyed the sons of Uisneach not
because he felt that Naisi had violated his prerogative as king, but
because of his jealous desire for the beauty of Deirdre.

The increasing complexity of characterisation is even more apparent in the case of Deirdre, whose initially minor role has been
vastly expanded. In the earliest version, she had been little more
than a human token of ill fortune, confined to a passive role after
her initial imposition of the *geis* on Naisi. Now, however, she relies
not on an arbitrary *geis*, but on her loveliness and charm, to move
the young warrior. She has become more feminine and sensitive. In
the earliest version, she did not appear at the scene of Naisi's murder,
but now she is presented as the suffering wife and tragic witness to
that scene. The medieval storytellers saw the legend not primarily
as a tale of warlike honour but as a love story, with Deirdre its
tragic heroine. This reflects the growing importance of women,
both as characters and as an audience, in medieval literature. The
increasing gentility of Deirdre over the centuries reflects the changing norms of the society in which the tale was told. Eleanor Hull
has observed that 'it is curious to find the wild woman of the twelfth-
century *Book of Leinster* transformed into the Lydia Languish of a
later age'.[21]

Synge's play eschews the exaggerations of the medieval narration,
but it does retain the emphasis on the fated doom to come. Every
major character speaks ominous words based on foreknowledge.
Lavarcham refers to the prophecy at Deirdre's birth that 'she'd bring
destruction on the world' (*Plays 2*, p. 189). Conchubor ponders 'the
great troubles are foretold' (*Plays 2*, p. 193). Deirdre reminds Naisi
on their first meeting of the prophecy that 'Deirdre will be the ruin

of the Sons of Usna, and have a little grave by herself, and a story will be told forever' (*Plays 2*, p. 209). Even Naisi, though swept inexorably into Deirdre's plans, can grimly prognosticate that 'we've a short space only to be triumphant and brave' (*Plays 2*, p. 20). All of these statements are made in the first act of the play, which opens with a premonitory storm. Later still, Naisi's brothers, Ainnle and Ardan, express deep distrust of the king's reasons for demanding their return. No evidence exists to suggest that Synge made a particular study of any one of the medieval versions of the tale. Nevertheless, from the lectures and classes of de Jubainville, as well as from his readings of Lady Gregory's version, he would have been aware of these basic developments.

THE VERSION OF GEOFFREY KEATING

Geoffrey Keating included an influential version of the legend in his *Foras Feasa ar Éirinn*, an edition of which Synge studied and reviewed in 1902. Keating relied on the Old Irish version and followed closely the sequence of events in the *Book of Leinster*. The medieval version in the Glen Masain manuscript had been the most popular, but it began *in medias res* with Conchubor's demand that Fergus bring back the Sons of Uisneach from Alban. In Ireland, Keating's version gave the legend a more widespread currency. It also had the merit of filling in the beginning of the story, with its account of the elopement. The more refined society of Keating's period is clear in his version, where Deirdre makes no violent advances to Naisi, but is a shy and tender girl. It is also to be noted that Keating omits the account of the wooing of Deirdre by the king of Alban.

One of the most striking features of Keating's spare but elegant narrative is his use of the motif of blood-on-snow. Lavarcham kills a calf for meat and, as the blood falls onto the snow, a black raven alights to drink it:

Agus mar thug Deirdre sin dá haire, adubhairt re Leabharcham gomadh maith lé féin fear do bheith aice ar a mbeidís na trí datha at-chonnairc, mar atá, dath an fhéich ar a fholt, dath fola laoigh ar a ghruaidh, agus dath an tsneachta ar a chneas.[22]

(When Deirdre saw that, she remarked that she would like a man with the three colours which she saw—the colour of the raven in his hair, the colour of the calf's blood in his cheek, and the colour of snow on his skin.)

This motif is widespread in international folk-tales and has been found in such Irish tales as 'The King of Ireland's Son' and in 'The Giant and the Fair Man-Servant'.[23] Indeed, so prevalent was it in Ireland that Alfred Nutt believed it to be of Irish origin.[24] Synge would have found this motif linked with the Deirdre legend not only in Keating's text, but also in the version published by de Jubain-ville, who describes Deirdre's cry: 'Le seul homme que j'aimerai aura ces trois couleurs: les cheveux noirs comme le corbeau, les joues rouges comme le sang, le corps blanc comme la neige'.[25] (The one man whom I shall love will have these three colours: hair black as the raven, cheeks red as blood, and body white as snow.) This particular passage was quoted with admiration by Synge's friend, Anatole Le Braz, in his *Essai sûr l'Histoire du Théâtre Celtique*.[26] While regretting the lack of a dramatic tradition in Celtic Ireland, Le Braz pointed to the great dramatic potential in such a scene. While this motif las been somewhat 'overdone' in folklore, it retains its effectiveness on the stage.[27] Synge adds to the dramatic impact, putting his speech into the mouth of a defiant Deirdre, who faces not her indulgent nursemaid (as in the tale), but the aged king: 'A girl born, the way I'm born, is more likely to wish for a mate who'd be her likeness . . . a man with his hair like the raven maybe and his skin like the snow and his lips like blood spilt on it' (*Plays 2*, p. 191). This description, thrown up in the heat of an angry exchange with Conchubor, is too exact to be mere female whimsy. Deirdre has in fact seen and desired just such a man on the hillside. In this way, Synge gives point and resonance to the literary motif, in keeping with his avowed aim 'to make the whole thing drama instead of narrative'.[28]

So popular was Keating's text that it was incorporated into trans-lations of longer versions made by Theophilius O'Flanagan[29] and Whitley Stokes.[30] These versions are fundamentally similar to that transcribed by Aindrias MacCuirtin in 1740. This last version was Synge's major source in the composition of his play.

OIDHE CHLOINNE UISNIGH: THE MacCUIRTIN TEXT

In July 1901, the first act of Russell's *Deirdre* had been published in the *All Ireland Review*. This may have inspired Synge to embark

on a deeper study of the legend. During his sojourn on Aran from
21 September to 9 October of that year, he translated into English
MacCuirtin's text, *Oidhe Chloinne Uisnigh*. This had been published
by the Society for the Preservation of the Irish Language in 1898
and had been edited by Richard O'Duffy. According to Edward
Stephens, the copy of the book from which Synge made his translation may have belonged to the boy named in *The Aran Islands* as
'the Scholar'.[31] It may not be a coincidence that, already in January
1901, Lady Gregory herself had translated the legend into English
as an experiment.[32] On his way to Aran on the night of 19 September,
Synge stayed with her at Coole and may have received encouragement from his friend to work on the legend during his period on
the islands.

This version of the tale has been most popular, especially in the
translations of O'Flanagan and Stokes, which supplied many writers
(including Lady Gregory) with the basis for their recreations of the
story. Rudolf Thurneysen regretted this tendency,[33] but it is not
hard to see the attractions of this version for the modern mind.
It begins with Conchubor's command that the brothers must return
from Alban. The elopement section had been omitted, probably on
the grounds that it was already known and taken for granted; but
Thurneysen felt that writers should rely for their sources on a more
complete version. The great benefit of this approach, however, was
that it permitted an extension in the duration of specific scenes and
a deepening in the motivation of the protagonists. It was no longer
enough for the narrator to explain an action by asserting that it was
performed under *geis*. With the passing years the audience had grown
more sophisticated in its demands on the storyteller, who had to
provide the tale with some psychological analysis. This innate tendency of modern versions was reinforced by Synge in the plotting of
his play and in providing his characters with adequate motivation.
On 3 January 1909 he wrote to Lady Gregory with the news that
'I have done a great deal to Deirdre since I saw you—chiefly in the
way of strengthening motives and recasting the general scenario'.[34]

How did Synge achieve this strengthening of motive? In Mac-
Cuirtin's *Oidhe Chloinne Uisnigh*, Conchubor sends Fergus to ask for
Naisi's return to Ireland. Deirdre senses the king's treachery, but
her warnings to Naisi are futile, for he is homesick and insists on
returning. Clearly, this interpretation of events allows both Deirdre
and Naisi only a passive role. Naisi is a prey to homesickness and
to his trust in Fergus, who assures a safe passage. Not for a moment

does he wonder if Fergus himself has been deceived by Conchubor. Deirdre is doomed to an even more passive role in this scheme of things and remains a helpless prophetess of the doom to come. Synge, therefore, decided to strengthen the motivation by giving the lovers reasons of their own for the return from Alban. It was not enough for him that Naisi should be tricked and Deirdre should be a secondary victim of this deceit. So, he has his lovers decide of their own free will to return to Ireland in order to escape the inevitable decay of their passion with the onset of old age in Alban. Furthermore, it is Deirdre, rather than Naisi, who makes that final choice. From the start of Act Two, Deirdre betrays her anxiety that the love she has known might fade. More than Naisi, she realizes just how constricted their choice really is, when she confides to Lavarcham that she is 'wondering all times is it a game worth playing, living on until you're dried and old, and our joy is gone forever' (*Plays 2*, p. 219). She senses that their over-intense love may contain the seeds of its own destruction. Fergus unconsciously recalls this submerged fear of the lovers, when he advises Naisi not to 'be lingering until the day that you'll grow weary, and hurt Deirdre showing her the hardness in your eyes' (*Plays 2*, p. 227). Naisi replies in thoughtful agreement that 'I've had a dread upon me a day'd come I'd weary of her voice . . . and Deirdre'd see I'd wearied'. But she has overheard this very conversation and thereupon decides that they should return.

This is Synge's brilliant innovation, for it makes Deirdre the motive force of the play. Naisi agrees reluctantly to return, only at the end. This is a total reversal of all other versions including Mac-Cuirtin's, in which Naisi opted to return and it was Deirdre who was reluctant to do so. Naisi worries that someday he may grow weary of Deirdre and hurt her. It is more for her sake than his own that he finally yields to Fergus's persuasion. When his lover begs him to return to Emain Macha, he finally consents: 'You're right, maybe. It should be a poor thing to see great lovers and they sleepy and old' (*Plays 2*, p. 233). In this way, the lovers become truly tragic and play an active part in their own destruction. They are not merely tricked into returning, but deliberately opt for death rather than the decay of youthful love. In strengthening the motives of characters in this way, Synge further developed the tendency, evident in Mac-Cuirtin's version, to explain the action of the protagonists. Consequently, the final quarrel of the lovers on the edge of the grave is brutally ironic. They lapse, before death, into that very disharmony which the sacrifice of their lives was designed to avoid.

Naisi sighs that the grave is 'putting a great space between two friends that love' (*Plays 2*, p. 251), as the pair quarrel bitterly. Fergus had given him two contradictory reasons for the return to Ireland—firstly, to prepare for a secure old age, but, secondly, to fulfil the duties of a hero. Now that very ambiguity has caught up with the hero. Fergus had promised the lovers that there is 'no place but Ireland where the Gael can have peace always' (*Plays 2*, p. 225)—but now those words have a cruel hollowness. The couple bicker before an open grave which brings no peace. Here Synge has probed very deep, explaining that this is what happens to lovers who come face to face with their own mortality. In the presence of his own grave, how can a man remain true to his own humanity? Deirdre believes that the grave will close over them, uniting them forever in the earth; but events overtake the lovers as Ainnle and Ardan die in their defence and Naisi turns to Deirdre and 'throws her aside almost roughly' (*Plays 2*, p. 255). He is torn between his warrior loyalty to his dying brothers and his love for Deirdre; but she merely offers the cold comment that 'the hardness of death has come between us' (*Plays 2*, p. 255). Those critics who pronounce this quarrel to be too bitter and harsh have failed to appreciate fully the most tragic moment in the play. The clash had to be violent, if Naisi were to tear himself away from Deirdre, ignoring her final plea: 'Do not leave me, Naisi. Do not leave me broken and alone' (*Plays 2*, p. 255). Naisi is aghast that he should go out to a certain death with a hard word from his lover's lips—but that is Deirdre's only way of unleashing her fury against a world which offers so cruel a choice. If she had held him back she would have emasculated her man, who was delaying fatally, poised between duty and love. So she does not send him out to fight—rather she drives him out, heaping scorn upon him and upon the trap they are in. She is cruel, but only to prove her selfless love: 'It was my words without pity gave Naisi a death will have no match until the ends of life and time' (*Plays 2*, p. 257). In this moment and in Deirdre's character, Synge has once again fused brutality and tenderness—those qualities which he had always most admired in the legend.

Synge followed the example of MacCuirtin in many important details. For example, the first meeting of Deirdre and Naisi takes place in the forest and not on the lawns of Emain. In MacCuirtin's text, Deirdre had a premonitory dream that, if the returned lovers were lodged in the house of the Red Branch, this would be a sign of treacherous intent. In Synge's play, Deirdre has the premonition that 'our own blood maybe will be running away' (*Plays 2*, pp. 229–31) and 'it's in the quiet woods I've seen them digging our grave' (*Plays 2*, p. 231). In the final act, the lovers are informed that the Red Branch house is being aired and swept for them and they know that the end is near. Within minutes, Naisi has uncovered the intended grave.

The dramatic potential of the story was more fully exploited in later versions, such as MacCuirtin's. This explains their greatest innovation—the fact that Deirdre dies on Naisi's grave, rather than living on for a year as the partner of an enemy of Naisi. In Mac-Cuirtin's text, Deirdre laments over the dead body of her lover, and pressing a knife to her heart, flings herself into his grave. Synge reproduced this scene faithfully in the play. Herbert Howarth has complained that Deirdre's suicide is a projection of Synge's own sentimentality,[35] but this scholar cannot have been aware that there was sanction for this ending in Synge's source, *Oidhe Chloinne Uisnigh*.

In the speeches of the play, Synge sometimes borrows a word or phrase from his own translation of MacCuirtin's text. This is quite in keeping with the practice of previous authors who re-worked the legend. Keating, for example, had employed the *Book of Leinster* as his source, not only for plot, but also on occasion for idiom, 'echoing most effectively the phraseology of the original'.[36] In similar fashion, Synge repeated many phrases from songs in MacCuirtin's text, including Deirdre's Farewell' ('Woods of Cuan . . .') and her lament over Naisi's grave. The three songs of the *Book of Leinster* version had been increased in number to seven in MacCuirtin's manuscript and stanzas from these songs were woven into the lyric fabric of Synge's play—for example, the lament over Naisi's grave at the close. One stanza from Synge's translation of MacCuirtin reads:

> That I will live after Naisi
> Let no one think upon the earth
> After Ainnle and Ardan
> My soul will not be in me.[37]

In the play this becomes: 'It is not I will go on living after Ainnle and Ardan. After Naisi I will not have a lifetime in the world' (*Plays 2*, p. 263).

In the earlier drafts of the play, the debt to MacCuirtin is even more clear. For example, consider the following draft of a speech by Deirdre concerning her premonitory vision: 'I'm in dread Naisi. I've seen a cloud of red blood over the greenness of Ireland. I've seen three birds coming over with drops of honey in their mouths, and it was the drops of our own blood they took away with them' (*Plays 2*, p. 230). This is deeply indebted to a passage from Synge's own translation of *Oidhe Chloinne Uisnigh*:

> 'I saw a vision in the evening', said Deirdre, 'and there were three birds coming to us from Emain Macha with three mouthfuls of honey and they left them with us and took away three mouthfuls of our blood'.[38]

In general, it is not too much to claim that MacCuirtin's text was the source without which Synge's play would never have been written.

FOLK RENDITIONS

The popularity enjoyed by the legend at all levels of society made it inevitable that it would enter the folk tradition, where it remained enormously popular, even in Synge's own day. An oral version entitled *The Death of the Sons of Usnach* was taken down by George Dottin from Thomas Ford of Galway in 1891.[39] Synge must have heard many similar versions during his sojourns in Connemara and Aran. The fact that he spent the 1901 visit on Aran working on a translation of *Oidhe Chloinne Uisnigh* must have induced the island storytellers to provide him with their own accounts of the tale.

The folk version was simpler in outline than the manuscript versions, having fewer characters in the plot. No details of Deirdre's birth or parentage were given. The narrator did not resort to the use of *geis* and the supernatural element in previous renditions of the tale was forgotten. In this version royal personages were scarcely distinguished from commoners. All this is in keeping with the treatment of the plot in Synge's play, for he was very attracted by the folkloristic elements of the legend. His Conchubor is never shown in pomp at court, but is seen always as irretrievably alone. He is not a confident king, but a senile old lover. Even the mild-mannered Lavarcham speaks to the spent monarch as a fellow-crone: 'It's a poor thing the way me and you is getting old, Conchubor, and I'm thinking you yourself have no call to be loitering this place getting your death, maybe, in the cold of night' (*Plays 2*, p. 241). Unlike Russell and

Yeats, Synge followed the folk example and removed almost all traces of supernatural power from the story. Only once is there any reference to such a power, when Deirdre calls out at the end: 'Keep back, Conchubor, for the high king who is your master has put his hands between us' (*Plays 2*, p. 269). Apart from this, however, Synge humanised his characters and allowed them to act of their own free will. The folk tellers delighted in describing Deirdre's minute and credibly human response to her difficult plight. For example, they cause her to ask Conchubor for a further year's grace when he comes to seek her in marriage. Synge added this feature to the play, when Deirdre pleads: 'Leave me a year, Conchubor, it isn't much I'm asking' (*Plays 2*, p. 195).

Like the folk storytellers, Synge grasped the relationship between the heroic world of the ancient legend and the peasant Ireland in which the story still lingered. Conchubor and the other leaders of the Ulster Cycle were euhemerised gods who had been reduced by the storytellers to the status of mortals.[40] This process was at work in the twelfth-century *Book of Invasions*. More recent folk versions reduced Conchubor still further in status, until he was almost indistinguishable from commoners in language and bearing; but they gave such regal characters a credible human personality which they had lacked in the older versions. Like the folk narrators of his day, Synge rejected the vagueness in the ancient legend. On 4 January 1908, he wrote to John Quinn:

> I am trying a three-act prose *Deirdre* to change my hand. I am not sure yet whether I shall be able to make a satisfactory play out of it. These saga people, when one comes to deal with them, seem very remote; one does not know what they thought or what they are or where they went to sleep, so one is apt to fall into rhetoric.[41]

This falling into rhetoric had sullied Leahy's version and Synge was resolved not to repeat that mistake. So he gave his characters a robust, personal idiom, in keeping with their status as fallible mortals. Furthermore, he mocked the rhetoric and fustian of previous exponents of the legend in the intermittent pomposity of Conchubor: 'I've let build rooms for our two selves, Deirdre, with red gold upon the walls, and ceilings that are set with bronze' (*Plays 2*, p. 259). This is not the authoritative tone of a king, but the windy self-importance of a bad translator.

Finally, Synge followed the folk narrators in removing an account of Deirdre's birth and in drastically reducing the numbers of characters. This allowed him to proceed even further with their attempt to endow each character with a credible personality. Even after completing an eighth version of the play, he could write to Molly Allgood on 1 December 1907 that 'it wants a good deal of strengthening, of making personal, still before it will satisfy me'.[42]

THE TEXT OF DOUGLAS HYDE

The last significant version was that in a manuscript discovered in Belfast by Douglas Hyde. It was published in part in *Zeitschrifte für celtische Philologie, 2* (1899), with a summary of the remaining unpublished sections. The wild and barbarous girl of the *Book of Leinster* now appears as a sensitive and reticent child. Synge read Hyde's analysis of this version in *A Literary History of Ireland*. He may well have also read the version in the *Zeitschrifte*, of which he was a keen student.[43]

Hyde noted how his manuscript followed the trend of modern versions in 'the rather minute portrayal of Deirdre's feelings'.[44] The dominance by Deirdre of the later versions reflects the increasing importance of women in post-medieval Irish society. Where once the Sons of Usna had dominated the tale, now the lady is the focus of attention. Synge recognises this tendency and carries it further by giving Deirdre the title role, rather than the two-dimensional sons of Usna. This was not done without consideration and forethought. The dramatist agonised a great deal over the amount of emphasis to be placed on the major characters of his play. His deliberation, through several drafts, betrays a curious fidelity to the history of the legend itself. On 9 November 1907, he seemed to endorse the emphasis in the earliest versions, when he wrote to Molly Allgood that 'I finished a second rough draft of the Sons of Usna today'. Five days later he displayed a certain indecision as to what the title of his play should be: 'I am working myself sick with Deirdre or whatever you call it'. However, two days later, he happily referred to his work as 'Deirdre'.[45] In keeping with this alteration of title, he wrote in a final summary of the plot that the character of Deirdre must be 'very central and strong'. This summary emphasises the movement of his play from act to act. The first act must express 'determination for love and life in spite of fate'; the second act should capture the 'inevitable sweeping into current of life'; and the third act should offer a 'final summing up in death of Deirdre'.[46] This patient reconstruction of events over three acts distinguishes Synge's play from the one-act drama by Yeats on the same theme. The three-act structure allows for a steady revelation of Deirdre's personality not possible in Yeats's shorter work.

THE PROBLEMS OF DRAMATISING LEGEND

The use of a famous legend as the basis for a modern play is fraught with dangers and constrictions. The plot will be so well known as to deny all possibilities of excitement or surprise. This problem is particularly acute when the play deals with a prophecy of ultimate tragedy. Francis Bickley made such a complaint against Russell's *Deirdre*: 'Deirdre and the rest are too consciously people out of a story'.[47] Forrest Reid found a similar fault with Yeats's *Deirdre* which gave 'the fatal impression that the lovers are posing for posterity, are tasting in anticipation the beauty of their own story and its sadness'.[48] When a famous legend, which ends in a predicted massacre, has already been dramatised by two eminent writers, there must surely be little scope for invention or experiment. When the sense of foreknowledge is pervasive in the plot, there can be little room for resistance against fate. Insofar as there are artistic possibilities with such a plot, they will be lyrical rather than dramatic. In the work of a dramatic genius like Synge, however, this foreknowledge is turned into a virtue, since it encourages a critical attitude in the audience towards the production. The interest now lies not so much in what is done, as in how it is done—in the author's personal interpretation of the action. Here Synge's triumph is complete. Where other versions of the tale had emphasised the betrayal and death of the lovers as the final disaster, Synge, more subtly, locates the real tragedy in the death of their love. His play gains power from suspense rather than surprise. Since both audience and protagonists know the inevitable outcome, all interest centres on the brave attempts of the lovers to snatch some happiness despite the tragedy to come. In dramatising this clash between the free will of the lovers and the forces of necessity, Synge adds a new and exciting dimension to the legend. The tragedy of their foretold death at the end seems of minor importance in comparison with the disaster of their lost love.

Nevertheless, many criticisms of the play arise from an embarrassing foreknowledge of its action. Darrell Figgis, for example, has argued that the scene in which Deirdre begs the king to spare the lovers is inconsistent with their deliberate return to a sure death, in order to escape the decay of love.⁴⁹ In reply, one might argue that their passion was failing precisely because of the artificial nature of their life in Alban. There, the very fact that their love meant everything was itself a threat to its survival. As Deirdre shrewdly observed in Alban: 'There are as many ways to wither love as there are stars in a night of Samhain' (*Plays 2*, p. 233). Figgis was even more critical of Deirdre's lament over Naisi's body, when she complains of the miserable life ahead of her. He argues that this is redundant and that Deirdre is simply being kept alive for the return of Fergus and the burning of Emain.⁵⁰ The audience, he asserts, knows that she will die by suicide. Against this, it could be argued that Deirdre's forebodings of a wretched life to come provided the best possible justification for her resorting to suicide. Nevertheless, Figgis's complaints illustrate the difficulty facing those who would dramatise this legend: it was almost impossible to create the effect of a traditional story whose action was revealed for the first time.

A further problem in dramatising a famous legend is the danger that the playwright will make unwarranted assumptions about the knowledge of his audience and that aspects of his play will be clear only to the initiated. When Conchubor tells Lavarcham in Act Three that 'I'm waiting only to know is Fergus stopped in the north' (*Plays 2*, p. 243), these words are meaningless to those unfamiliar with the legend. Again, near the close of the play, when Fergus hurries onto the scene and says to Conchubor, 'It's I surely will stand against a thief and a traitor' (*Plays 2*, p. 267), this outburst has not been adequately prepared for by any preceding remarks in the act. The motives of Fergus, in turning so suddenly against the king, have not been made fully clear. We must allow, however, that we are dealing with an unfinished text and that Synge would certainly have clarified such issues in subsequent drafts of his work. It is significant that many puzzling allusions in the play become clear after a reading of the dramatist's major source, *Oidhe Chloinne Uisnigh*.

It may be argued that the fact that the play's style and themes are authentically Irish does not make them dramatically valid. Nevertheless, when Synge reworked a motif from the ancient literature in his modern play, he did so in the knowledge that such motifs had persisted in the native tradition precisely because of their vividness and power. In his play, for example, the motif of blood-on-snow retains all of its original visual impact. It is, however, no longer merely a fetching picture, but an iterative image of the whole drama. Deirdre's threefold description of her ideal man is, as has been remarked, too exact to be mere fancy. She has already seen just such a man and the vivid accuracy of her sketch of him is full of psychological and dramatic implication. When she utters these words, she has already begun to possess Naisi in her own mind.

For the translators and versifiers of the nineteenth century, the Deirdre legend had been the occasion for Tennysonian pastiche. To Russell, the tale had presented itself as a mystic reverie and to Yeats as a symbolic problem. For Synge alone, it had all the dimensions of a distinctly human crisis. Where dramatists like Yeats and Russell had to rely on collated English versions of the legend, Synge drew his inspiration directly from a Gaelic source, *Oidhe Chloinne Uisnigh*, and indirectly from his study of the evolution of the legend. This directness of approach is one reason why his play is more faithful to the legend itself and, finally, more exciting as drama.

8 Anglo-Irish as a Literary Dialect—The Contribution of Synge

TOWARDS A BILINGUAL STYLE

The idea of an Irish National Theatre in the English language is something of a contradiction in terms. Synge was well aware of this, but by the end of the nineteenth century the pressures on Irish writers to produce their work in English were overwhelming.

Earlier in that century, the great populist leader of the peasantry, Daniel O'Connell, had grown up a fluent speaker of the Irish language. However, he used English in all his speeches to mass meetings, recognising that he needed to make his cause comprehensible to British liberals as well as to the Irish peasant.[1] The few writers who sprang from the people, such as Carleton and Griffin, chose to write in English for the same reason that O'Connell spoke in it. They wrote mainly for a British audience, since the native Irish were mostly illiterate and the literate Irish were never enthusiastic buyers of books. O'Connell's radical young adversary, Thomas Davis, warmly advocated the preservation of Irish as a spoken language and literary medium, but he was caught in a cruel paradox. As a son of the Protestant Ascendancy, he knew no Irish; but he lived to see his patriotic songs, written as a 'second-best' in English, spread like wild-fire among a peasantry which was rapidly abandoning the native language.[2]

With the foundation of the Gaelic League in 1893 under the leadership of Douglas Hyde, a major attempt was made to save the dying language. Hyde actually produced songs in Irish and heard them sung

with delight by the folk in Galway. But he, too, was a prisoner of
the same paradox. In his most successful collection, *Love Songs of
Connacht*, he printed the Irish text on one side of the page and his
own translation into Anglo-Irish dialect on the other. The translation
was included simply to help the student who found difficulty with
the Irish, for the object of the work was to popularise the spread of
Irish literature. It soon became clear, however, that the main appeal
of the book to Yeats and his contemporaries lay in Hyde's own translations, and especially in those translations written in Anglo-Irish
prose rather than in verse. The very success of the book caused the
defeat of its primary purpose. Instead of popularising Irish literature,
it made the creation of a national literature in English seem all the
more plausible. Furthermore, it provided Irish writers of English
with one of their finest literary mediums, the Anglo-Irish dialect.
Hyde's position was ambiguous. In one sense, he was seen as the
leader of the movement to save Irish; in another, he was the first
exponent of the Anglo-Irish literary revival. Subsequent literary
history was to emphasise the cruelty of the paradox. It was unfortunate for Hyde that his twenty-year campaign to save Irish should
have coincided with the emergence of a group of Irishmen destined
to write masterpieces in English.

All this is obvious only in retrospect. In its time, Hyde's doctrine
was highly influential. It was supported by Frank J. Fay, the drama
critic of the *United Irishman*, who called for a National Theatre and
boldly declared: 'I must say that I cannot conceive it possible to
achieve this except through the medium of the Irish language'.[3] Fay
was taken seriously. Hyde wrote successful plays in Irish, as did Tomás
Mac Domhnaill, P. T. MacGinley and other minor dramatists. But
Synge was the only playwright who possessed an undeniable creative
genius and a knowledge of Irish; and he never answered Fay's call.
However, he took that summons sufficiently seriously to feel the need
to justify his work in English. In his opinion, the Irishman was
now master enough of English to write well in it, whereas 'Leinster
and Ulster would take several centuries to assimilate Irish perfectly
enough to make it a fit mode of expression for the finer emotions
which now occupy literature' (*Prose.* pp. 385–6). This, however, was
to gloss over some of the difficulties which confronted those who
wished to produce a national drama in English rather than Irish. Yeats
pointed to a major problem, remarking in *Samhain* (1903): 'We who
write in English have a more difficult task, for English is the language
in which the Irish cause has been debated and we have to struggle

against traditional points of view . . .'[4] Over five decades later in a similar colonial situation in Algeria, Frantz Fanon, the revolutionary and psychiatrist, had to struggle againt the 'traditional points of view' embedded in French, 'a language of occupation'.[5] He did this by broadcasting in French, the programmes of Radio Fighting Algeria, as he explained, 'liberating the enemy language from its historic meanings'.[6]

Synge faced a similar problem and solved it in a similar fashion. Irish was the historic language of the nation, but it was not his mother tongue, spoken from the cradle. He knew that he could write better in English, in which he would command a world-wide audience, whereas Irish offered only a dwindling rural community with no theatrical tradition. As late as 1902, he judged that he must write with an eye as much on an English as an Irish audience: 'The Irish reading public is still too limited to keep up an independent school of Irish men of letters' (*Prose*, p. 386).

The question still remained as to what kind of English Synge should employ. His writings in Paris in the mid-1890s had been morbid, introspective and totally unpublishable. Except for a poem in a college magazine, he had not managed to write a publishable line in five years of exhausting effort.[7] The decision to quit Paris and live on the Aran Islands may be taken as a measure of his frustration in 1898. But the years in Paris had not been wasted. The example of Guy de Maupassant, George Sand and Anatole France had convinced him of the artistic potential of dialect. In one of his many unpublished articles of this period, Synge praised Anatole France for his 'mastery of the Paris dialect' and his 'fine sense for the shades of spoken language'.[8] France's achievement was all the more remarkable because 'the half-recognised words and changes of grammar, that are usually to be found in the idiom of the cities, make it particularly difficult to form from a dialect of this kind a pliant and beautiful style'.[9] The dialect of cities fascinated Synge in this period and his admiration for the achievement of Anatole France in *Histoire Comique* may arise from his own sense of failure with 'Ballad of a Pauper', probably written in 1895. This conversation poem, composed partly in Dublin dialect, failed to achieve publication, much less a pliant and beautiful style. That disappointment did not threaten Synge's belief in the potential of dialect. M. Paul Passy, his Parisian lecturer in phonetics, had shown him that *patois* could have a literary, as well as a purely philological, value.

This conviction was strengthened by the leading theorists of the

Gaelic League back home in Ireland. Eoin MacNeill, writing in the *Gaelic Journal* of 1897, spoke of 'the absolute necessity of basing all literature on the living usage' and held that writing in Irish 'must strike its roots into the living vernacular'.[10] This was the start of a crusade for the introduction of *Caint na ndaoine*, the 'deft and sinewy and versatile Irish'[11] of the common folk, into the written literature. Over a period of three years from 1894 to 1897, MacNeill published An tAthair Peadar Ua Laoghaire's *Séadna* in the *Gaelic Journal* in order to demonstrate the validity of common speech as a basis for the literary language. What was true of the Irish spoken by simple peasants might just as easily be true of their English. The lesson was not lost on Synge.

While doodling in one of the notebooks which he brought to Aran in 1899, he hit upon a solution to the problems which had worried the founders of the National Theatre. It was also the solution to his own, more personal, artistic difficulties in the search for a valid medium. Although he did not write in Irish, Synge felt that the native Gaelic literary tradition could be a powerful source of strength and inspiration for the contemporary Irish writer. In the Aran notebook, he wrote: 'American lack of literary sense due to the absence in America of any mother tongue with a tradition for the whole population'.[12] Lower down on the same page, he scrawled with a sputtering nib a question to which his later dramatic masterpieces provided fitting answer: 'Has any bilingual person ever been great in style? crois pas?'[13]

It was, unwittingly perhaps, a succinct statement of a problem which he was to solve by developing an idiom which would make him famous through the world and notorious for a time in his native land. If he must write in English, Synge was resolved to write in an English as Irish as it is possible for English to be, an English into which toxins of the Gaelic mode of speech and syntax had been injected. In this way he could defeat the 'traditional points of view' embodied in English, which so worried Yeats and which threatened to smother the national literary revival. That Synge was acutely conscious of the dangers for a writer in these 'traditional points of view' is clear from the concluding sentence of an article written in 1902:

... it may be hoped that we have seen the last of careless writing addressed to an English public that was eager to be amused, and did not always take the trouble to distinguish in Irish books between what was futile and what had originality and merit' (*Prose*, p. 386).

Synge's dialect was not simply the solution to a national literary problem. It was also the source of his international fame. He was convinced that if Irish writers were to make a lasting contribution to world literature, they must seek to express the native mode:

> It is difficult to say how far the Gaelic atmosphere which is now so powerful all through Ireland will bring a new note into the English language. Every new movement of literature has a new note in language and every language that is spoken widely has these notes potentially without stint . . .[14]

Not long after Synge wrote those lines, George Moore confidently predicted that, from universal use and journalese, English would soon be so coarsened as to lose all power as a literary medium.[15] With deeper insight, Synge had foreseen that English would receive a renewal of life from her regional dialects. For him the use of dialect was intimately bound up with the artist's sense of place. This feeling for a known locality has been designated by Robin Flower as a crucial part of the Gaelic literary tradition.[16] Synge held that a profound work of art was 'always inimitable' (*Prose*, p. 349) in its depiction of a particular period and location. In a notebook he wrote:

> No personal originality is enough to make a rich work unique, unless it has also the characteristic of a particular time and locality and the life that is in it. For this reason, all historical plays and novels and poems . . . are relatively worthless. Every healthy mind is more interested in *Tit-Bits* than in *Idylls of the King*.[17]

The search for a language which might convey this sense of place was not merely the preoccupation of Synge the adult writer. It had become an obsession at a very early age, as he recalled in his *Autobiography*: 'I had a very strong feeling for the colour of locality which I expressed in syllables of no meaning, but my elders checked me for talking gibberish when I was heard practising them' (*Prose*, p. 5). Years later, when he attempted to express his feeling for the colour of peasant locality in dialect, a number of Dublin critics also hailed that language as gibberish. Throughout the plays, Synge does, in fact, use quite a number of words which have no objective existence in any Irish dialect and which are clearly his own invention. These include such nouns as 'dreepiness' and 'pitchpike', verbs such as 'swiggle' (a portmanteau word combining 'swing' and 'wriggle'), and adjectives such as 'louty'. He also uses unprecedented phrases such as 'string gabble', 'curiosity man' and 'puzzle-the-world'; and constructions such as 'turn of the day' which have definite roots in Irish. Many of his notebooks contain numerous inventions of his own—on the very first page of one book he wrote 'quibblers and querry-heads—JMS'[18], addint his initials to indicate that he had created the phrase himself.

These words and phrases offer further evidence of the dramatist's close affinity with the Gaelic folk-song and story-telling tradition, which delights in the composition of nonsense-words, difficult phrases and even outright gibberish.[19] But Synge's elders at home repressed this tendency in him at an early age and it was only much later in his art that he found a use for this childish genius for invention. Indeed, it may not be altogether fanciful to ascribe the earthy dialect of his plays to his rejection of the linguistic standards of his mother, who taught him that all strong language and exaggerations were sinful. She had 'sought divine aid in confining the already restricted speech of the period and class she represented, in which expression of feeling was almost paralysed'.[20] In *The Playboy of the Western World* Synge extended his war against the linguistic Victorianism of his mother, when he battled against the equally restricted language of the contemporary stage.

If Synge had a strong sense of the power of locality, then a corollary of this was his conviction that the artist must submit to the circumstances in which he found himself. 'Each work of art must have been possible to only one man at one period and in one place' (*Prose*, p. 349). The problem faced by nineteenth-century Irish writers was the linguistic disorder resulting from the rapid loss of Irish and the yet imperfect assimilation of English. That problem, in Synge's opinion, was solved by 1902, when he wrote that 'the linguistic atmosphere of Ireland has become definitely English enough, for the first time, to allow work to be done in English that is perfectly Irish in essence' (*Prose*, p. 384). The value for him of the Irish peasant's English lay in its vitality, a living antithesis to the threadbare journalese of English writers, so roundly condemned by Yeats and Moore. He chose to write in the language of the peasantry, whose discovery of English still had the freshness and excitement of surprise. Into this dialect, the country folk had absorbed phrases, images and cadences from spoken Irish. In the years of the revival, however, Irish in its written form suffered acutely from over-use by poor journalists who relied on spent images and clichés. Synge warned that the 'rareness and beauty' of peasant Irish might be 'sophisticated by journalists and translators', with the result that the language could 'lose all its freshness' (*Prose*, p. 386). So, the objections which Yeats and Moore raised against the pollution of Standard English by journalese could with equal justice be raised aganst much written Irish.

It was no wonder, therefore, that Synge's inspired compromise in fashioning his unique Anglo-Irish dialect seemed so attractive. Strategically poised between two literary languages, this dialect could exploit the poetry of both traditions, without submitting to the clichés of either. Thomas Davis had argued that a truly national tradition could exist in two languages, Irish and English. But Synge went one better and exploited the very clash between the two cultures. He forged an art of surpassing beauty out of the very fusion of these languages and thereby achieved his aim of a bilingual style. The more perceptive writers in the Gaelic League conceded the truth of Synge's analysis. Thomas MacDonagh admitted that he was losing faith in the League. By 1904 he had confided in Yeats his belief that its writers were 'infecting Irish not only with English idiom but with the habits of thought of Irish journalism, a most un-Celtic thing'.[21] MacDonagh soon came to share Synge's opinion of the Anglo-Irish dialect as an ideal literary medium. In his epoch-making study, *Literature in Ireland*, he asserted that 'the dialect at its best is more vigorous, fresh and simple than either of the two languages between which it stands'.[22]

Synge's five years in Paris as a writer of introspective 'literary' prose had ended in frustration. Yet almost as soon as he turned to writing in dialect, after his visits to Aran, he produced a number of dramatic masterpieces. Why the sudden blossoming? It was not as if the nature of his thematic interests had changed. In the *Autobiography*, which deals with his youth and which was written between 1896 and 1898, certain words recur—'radiance', 'sacred', 'primitive', 'divine', 'glory',—but these words occur with the same frequency in the writings about Aran and the peasantry. However, there is a great difference in the way the words are used. In the early work, they are vehicles of an introverted, formless and utterly subjective prose—even Synge's planned novels petered out into subjectivity and incoherence after twenty pages or so.[23] In the prose written after Aran, such words are no longer used subjectively, but have found an objective social context in the language of the island folk. For the first time in his life, Synge had found a language which mirrored his concerns, but which he could submit to objective analysis, before transmuting it into art. Yeats offered a brilliant explanation of the process:

> Whenever he tried to write drama without dialect he wrote badly, and he made several attempts, because only through dialect could he escape self-expression, see all that he did from without, allow his intellect to judge the images of his mind as if they had been created by some other mind. The objectivity he derived from dialect was technical.[24]

Dialect formed an ideal medium for Synge the dramatist; but he was much less successful as an exponent of dialect in verse or prose. In retrospect, the range of options open to him as a writer seems extraordinarily limited. It says much for Synge as self-critic that, having found his medium, he had the good sense to write only dialect plays. He would have achieved little in ordinary English.

As a contribution to international drama, Synge's dialect, based as it was on a living language, was consciously revolutionary. His *Prefaces* illustrate this attitude. He believed that the writer should convey 'the entire reality of life'.[25] In the contemporary drama of his time, he complained that he found only a distorted one-sided version of reality—either a sordid and unimaginative realism or a strained hyper-aestheticism which:

> . . . is far and away from the profound and common interests of life. One has, on the one side, Mallarmé and Huysmans producing this literature—on the other Ibsen and Zola dealing with the reality of life in joyless and pallid works. On the stage, one must have reality, and one must have joy, and that is why the intellectual modern drama has failed . . . (*Plays 2*, pp. 53–4).

The dialect of the folk offered a solution to that problem, because it reconciled these opposed modes, the cult of the beautiful and the cult of realism. It was based on the spoken language of living people, so it was realistic. The country folk had poetry in their souls, so their language was beautiful: 'in Ireland, for a few years more, we have a popular imagination that is fiery and magnificent and tender' (*Plays 2*, p. 54).

The very strength of that language may have intensified the hostility of the first Dublin audiences. They may even have thought that they were listening to another version of stage-Irish 'brogue'. But they

were not. Synge was fully aware of the dangers of what he called
the 'rollicking note'. As early as 1902, in a review of Seumas
MacManus's *Donegal Fairy Stories*, he criticised the author for failing
to 'bring out the finer notes of the language spoken by the peasants'
(*Prose*, p. 376). He went on to complain that 'the language of several
of the stories has a familiarity that is not amusing, while it is without
the intimate distinction good humorous writing requires' (*Prose*,
p. 376). His own plays spelled the death of stage-Irish 'brogue'. Even
those reviewers of *The Playboy* who attacked its bizarre plot were
forced to concede that its 'peasants' talk is racy of the soil', 'a far cry
from the stage Irishman'.[26] Synge had seized the crude stage-Irish
idiom of the nineteenth-century music hall and refined it. He blended
it with the idioms and cadence of native Irish, creating 'perhaps the
most authentic examples of poetic drama which the modern stage
has seen'.[27]

'A FAKER OF PEASANT SPEECH'?

It was St John Ervine who made the notorious allegation that Synge
was 'a faker of peasant speech'.[28] Synge's dialect was, he claimed,
'contrived literary stuff, entirely unrepresentative of peasant speech'.[29]
Synge must have anticipated such criticism, for he wrote in his Preface
to *The Plapboy* on 21 January 1907: 'I have used one or two words
only, that I have not heard among the country people of Ireland'
(*Plays 2*, p. 53). There is a direct contradiction between these two
statements, yet, in a sense, both men were telling the truth. No
peasant ever talked consistently in the cadenced prose employed by
Synge's peasants. Synge may have used few words that he had not
actually heard, but this does not mean that he wrote down *all* that
he heard in a truly representative way. Nor does it mean that the
speech of an average Synge peasant is that of an average Irish countryman. Yeats acutely described the difference when he remarked:
'Perhaps no Irish countryman had ever that exact rhythm in his voice,
but certainly if Mr Synge had been born a countryman, he would
have spoken like that'.[30] Synge used mostly the striking phrases
culled from the folk and this was only natural in a writer on the
look-out for the colourful sentence. He had an interest, characteristic
of a mind formed in the 1890s, in the creation of 'an art more
beautiful than nature',[31] as he phrased it in a private notebook late
in that decade. His language is a heightened version of natural peasant

speech. The heightening is achieved by emphasising those aspects of peasant dialect which have their sources in Gaelic speech and syntax. Because Irish country people had, in the main, learned English from each other—rather than from English people—the influence of the Irish language on their acquired idiom was immense. It has recently been noted that 'even in those areas where Irish has long ceased to be spoken, its influence on pronunciation, on vocabulary, and above all, on syntax, is paramount'.[32] In the remoter parts of Wicklow, where the young Synge first heard the Anglo-Irish dialect, the Irish language had been spoken within living memory, just forty years earlier.[33] The native Irish *substratum* in the English of the folk was what really excited and inspired the dramatist.

The language of Synge's plays is often a direct translation from the Irish of Aran, rather than a representation of the English spoken by the peasantry. After all, Synge had heard the dialect of the Wicklow peasants from earliest boyhood, but this had no immediate effect on his writing in the 1890s. It was only when he went to learn Irish on the islands that he developed the idiom of his major plays. That language often owes more to the Irish of Aran than to the English spoken by the folk of Wicklow. A simple example will serve to make this clear.

The crucial lines of *Riders to the Sea* are those with which Maurya closes the play:

> Bartley will have a fine coffin out of the white boards, and a deep grave surely . . . What more can we want than that? . . . No man at all can be living for ever, and we must be satisfied . . . (*Plays 1*, p. 27).

This stoic utterance has been repeatedly traced to Sophocles by many critics.[34] In fact, the precise words of this sentence were used in a letter written in Irish by Martin McDonough, Synge's young friend on Inishmaan. The letter to the dramatist was written on 1 February 1902 and the play was written later in that year. Here is the relevant extract:

> . . . do thit amach go bhfuair bean mo dhearbhráthair Seaghan bás, agus bhí sí curtha an domhnaigh déinach do mhí na nodlag agus féuc gurab brónaçh an sgéul é le rádh, acht má sadh féin caithfidh muid a bheith sásta mar nac féidir le aon nduine a bheith beo go deo.

(it fell out that the wife of my brother Seaghan died, and she was buried the last Sunday of the month of December and look! that it is a sad story to tell, but if it is itself, we must be satisfied because nobody can be living forever . . .)[35]

Far from composing an idiom unrepresentative of peasant dialect, Synge has here translated into English the simple idiom of a young island boy for the climatic scene of his most tense play. In lines such as these, he allowed the islanders to speak directly for themselves. This gives an unexpected point to George Moore's flippant observation that Synge was responsible for the discovery that if anyone translated Irish word for word into English, then the inevitable result was poetry. Moore, who knew no Irish, could not have known just how closely his jibe described Synge's actual mode of composition.

A certain amount of confusion has surrounded that important letter by Martin McDonough. A version of the letter was given, in a poor English translation, in the biography of Synge by David H. Greene and Edward Stephens: 'But at the same time we have to be satisfied because a person cannot live always'.[36] 'At the same time' is incorrect as a translation of 'má sadh féin' and 'always' is less satisfactory a rendition of 'go deo' than Synge's own 'for ever'. However, the flaws of this version in broken English are of no long-term concern. What is important—and disturbing—is the implication that these are the actual words of Martin's original letter, as written by him. How did this mistake come to happen? The most plausible explanation is that Edward Stephens, who had access to this Irish letter in the Synge papers, translated it into English as literally as he could. His Irish was clearly defective—like his uncle, this solicitor member of the Protestant Ascendancy had no schooling in the subject—but his translation caught the gist of the sentences. After Stephens died, his wife gave all the Synge papers over to David Greene who wrote the final version of the biography. Greene probably saw Stephen's translation and mistook it—understandably enough, because of its broken English—for Martin's actual letter. He reproduced it as such in the biography.

These unfortunate mistakes have led scholars to construct ostensibly intelligent arguments on a false basis. For example, Nicholas Grene has praised Synge's 'poetic re-ordering of the words' in Maurya's speech, whose last sentence ends on the word 'satisfied'.[37] According to Grene, this closing sentiment of resignation, reinforced by the use of 'satisfied' as the last word of the play, cuts dramatically against the dominant mood of despair induced by the action. This plausible argument is based on the misconception that Martin's own use of 'satisfied' occurred only in the middle of the sentence quoted above. Had this been the case, then Grene's argument would be wholly valid. In fact, however, Martin repeated the sentiment at the close of his paragraph about his brother's bereavement, concluding, on this occasion, with the word 'satisfied':

Atá Seaghan go rímhaith acht deirim leat go bhfuil sé brónach go leor act mar deir mé chana caithfidh sé a bheith sásta

(Seaghan is very very well, but let me tell you that he is unhappy enough. However, as I said before, he must be satisfied.)[38]

It was more likely this moving repetition of the word by Martin at the end of his paragraph, rather than any desire for a poetic re-ordering of the earlier sentence which led Synge to close his play on the word 'satisfied'. This is not to deny Grene's point about its dramatic effect in undercutting the mood of despair which dominates the play. Martin had already used the word on two occasions in the letter in just that manner, as he strove to suppress his despair at his brother's tragedy.

There are other clear examples of how the letters from Aran helped Synge to forge his dialect. John McDonough, for example, could not write his native language so he dictated a letter in English to Martin, who then turned it into Irish. This John was the elder brother 'Seaghan' of whom Martin had written in the previous letter. If Synge could use a sentence of Martin's to conclude *Riders of the Sea*, then he had no qualms about using a sentence from John's letter at a lyrical moment in *The Shadow of the Glen*. Here is the crucial passage:

. . . is ógnach a bhí muid an t-am a d'imigh tú, ar fead tamal maith, acht anois atá muid ag faghail as, anuair atá muid cleachta anois a bheith ógnach. . . .

(it is lonely we were the time you left, for a long while, but now we are getting out of it, when we are used to being lonely.)[39]

This becomes the voice of Nora Burke lamenting the loss of Patch Darcy:

> . . . and it's very lonesome I was after him a long while . . . and then I got happy again—if it's ever happy we are, stranger—for I got used to being lonesome (*Plays 1*, p. 39).

Through the use of such letters Synge forged the bilingual style which exploded upon the theatrical world in October of 1903.

In forging this style, Synge had fulfilled an aim outlined by Yeats as early as 1892 in the *United Irishman*. Yeats had politely questioned the realism of Hyde's ideal of a national literature in Irish and had gone on to ask: 'Can we not keep the continuity of the nation's life, not by trying to do what Dr Hyde has practically pronounced impossible, (i.e. saving Gaelic), but by translating and retelling in English, which shall have an indefinable Irish quality of rhythm and style, all that is best in the ancient literature? . . .'[40] Through his use of dialect, no less than his use of themes from native Irish literature, Synge succeeded in translating the elements of Gaelic life into a language which many regarded as being at odds with the native culture. He is one of those rare writers who forged a distinctive personal style on the translation from one language to another. His cautious, word-for-word translations of the poetry of Geoffrey Keating and other Irish writings had led, almost imperceptibly, to the evolution of his Anglo-Irish dialect. From the very outset Synge associated the development of this dialect with the systematic translation of literature and folklore in the Irish language. In a review of *Cuchulain of Muirthemne* on 7 June 1902, he wrote:

> Some time ago Dr Douglas Hyde used a very similar language in his translations of the 'Love Songs of Connacht', and more recently Mr Yeats himself has written some of his articles on folklore with this cadence in his mind, while a few other writers have been moving gradually towards it. The intellectual movement that has been taking place in Ireland for the last twenty years has been chiefly a movement towards a nearer appreciation of the country people, and their language, so that it is not too much to say that the translation of the old MSS. into this idiom is the result of an evolution rather than of a merely personal idea (*Prose*, p. 367).

In keeping with this perception, many crucial phrases and idioms in Synge's dialect have been shown to be simply literal renditions in English of poetry and prose in the Irish language. Indeed, the Irish scholar, Tomás Ó Máille has suggested that this dialect owes as much to the written Irish tradition—and even to the usage of Old Irish—as to the spoken idioms of the people:

> Tá leaganacha cainte de shórt 'fri deireadh aimsire', 'm'aon-bhuille', go han-choitcheann sa tsean-Ghaedhilg, ach níl a leithéid i n-úsáid i mBéarla ná i nGaedhilg i gcaint an lae indiu.

> (Constructions of speech such as 'in the end of time', 'my one blow' are very common in Old Irish, but are not in use in English or in Irish in contemporary speech.)[41]

If Synge's dialect represents a direct English version of phrases from the Irish, then he himself often made the actual translation. The notebooks which he kept on Aran are full of Irish idioms translated, not into standard English, but into a literal version of phrases from the Irish:

> go bhfághach sé a gh-dhóin aibh
> till he'd get his fill of it.[42]
> is dual dó é sin do dhéanamh
> it is natural to him to do that.[43]

It is a language that looks suspiciously like the dialect of his plays. Even in letters written in English by Synge from the Gaeltacht, one finds many phrases which seem to be unconscious echoes of Irish. For example, in a letter to Lady Gregory from Kerry in 1904, he wrote of his asthma: 'It is going away from me now'.[44] This is clearly an echo of the Irish construction: 'Tá sé ag imeacht uaim anois'. In a sense, the author was still writing Irish, but using English words; he was still thinking in Irish cadence, syntax, and idiom, but using an English vocabulary.[45] Nor was he alone in this. Because of the rapid changeover from Irish to English in the nineteenth century,[46] many peasants found themselves speaking English words, while still actually thinking in Irish syntax. Synge's deep study of Irish grammar and syntax can be attributed, in part, to the fact that they provided him with the basis for his own dramatic language.

Dáithí Ó hUaithne, in his study entitled *The Irish Language*, has remarked that Synge's dialect is an accurate reflection of the native language and that much can be learned from it about Irish syntax.[47] The ease with which Synge's plays have been translated into Irish affords telling proof of this point.[48] Indeed, some of the major speeches seem to gain rather than lose in richness, as they pass through the screen of translation back into the very language in which they may have been conceived. Synge was aware of this, for in a letter to his German translator he explained one of the idiosyncrasies of his dialect:

> There is another form which occurs often for instance 'I saw a man and he smoking his pipe' = I saw a man smoking his pipe. The idiom, of course, is a Gaelic one, and it has shades of meaning that cannot be rendered in ordinary English (*Plays 1*, p. 275).

The playwright was clearly aware of the evanescence of many phrases in the native language.

There are a number of phrases and words in the plays which do not seem to exist in the English of the folk, but which may 'have been translated from the Irish by Synge for his own special purposes'.[49] These words include 'ill-lucky', 'playboy', 'ridge of the world' and 'share of songs', from the Irish 'mí-ámhar', 'buachaill báire', 'imeall an domhain' and 'cuid amhrán'. Even more interesting is Synge's poetic use of conventional 'mistranslations'. These are words which do have a currency in the English of rural Ireland, but which are based on an original mis-translation of the source-word in Irish. As Alan Bliss explains:

> The connotations of an Irish word rarely coincide exactly with those of any individual English word, so that the correct rendering into English will depend on the context. It seems, however, that at some stage in their acquisition of the English language Irish speakers learned a 'standard' equivalent of each Irish word, which they used irrespective of the context; and this type of 'mistranslation' from Irish is a fruitful source of special Anglo-Irish usage.[50]

Synge was not slow to exploit the rich ambiguity of such words. For example, when the playboy woos Pegeen with promises to take her poaching fish by night, she replies 'That'll be right fun, Christy Mahon' (*Plays 2*, p. 147). 'Right' is here used in the Gaelic sense of 'great'—but the standard meaning of 'correct'—morally 'correct'—is also mockingly evoked as an ironic comment on their illicit enterprise. Similarly, when Sarah Casey, in *The Tinker's Wedding*, describes the priest as 'a big boast of a man' (*Plays 2*, p. 13), something permanent has been said not only about his gigantic girth but also about his personal vanity. In these ways, the ambiguity between the standard meaning of a word and its dialect meaning are often evoked for the purpose of moral exposure. When the ecstatic Christy tells Pegeen to wait 'till we're astray in Erris when Good Friday's by' (*Plays 2*, p. 149), the word 'astray' works on two very different levels. Christy intends it in the dialect sense of 'roaming freely'; but the illusory nature of his ambition is reinforced for the alert member of the audience by the ordinary English resonance of 'lost' or 'strayed'.

There are also some words in Synge's plays which are not translations, since they have been taken directly from the Irish language. There include 'banbh', 'boreen', 'cleeve', 'curagh', 'Dun', 'frish-frash', 'keen', 'loy', 'ohone', 'poteen', 'Samhain', 'shebeen', 'sluigs', 'sop', 'streeleen', 'streeler', and 'thraneen'. The present writer has heard all these words used in the English of the west of Ireland, with the sole exception of 'Samhain'. But even in using this word, Synge was simply developing an innate tendency of the language. P. L. Henry has noted that in areas where Irish was recently spoken, many Irish words are still used, though not always fully understood.[51] The meanings of these words are often very delicate in shade. One notes, for instance, the number of words in the list just given which end in the diminutive '-een': 'boreen', 'poteen', 'shebeen', 'streeleen', and 'thraneen'. This diminutive is normally applied to anything insignificant, small or of little consequence. As William Burke has written, 'the delicate flavour of contempt conveyed by this suffix cannot be adequately represented in English'.[52] However, the tone of contempt is reinforced by the surrounding context in *The Playboy*, when the suffix is applied by Pegeen to the very name of Shawn Keogh:

Wouldn't it be a bitter thing for a girl to go marrying the like of Shaneen, and he a middling kind of scarecrow with no savagery or fine words in him at all? (*Plays 2*, p. 153).

The suffix was used in similar fashion, at an earlier point in the play, when the Widow Quin parodied the priest's terrified reaction to the news that Christy would stay at the shebeen:

'It isn't fitting', says the priesteen, 'to have his likeness lodging with an orphaned girl' (*Plays 2*, p. 87).

Not all of the translations from Irish to the English dialect of his works were made by Synge himself. Sometimes, he left it to the Aran islanders themselves to make the 'translation'. It is undeniable that the author of *The Aran Islands* refers more frequently to the curious type of English spoken by the islanders than to their brand of Irish. Insofar as it is modelled on any spoken dialect, Synge's idiom is based on the English which he heard spoken by folk whose natural every-day language was Irish. This was 'the English idiom of the Irish-thinking people of the west',[53] as Yeats affectionately called Hyde's dialect. From the start of his first sojourn on Aran, Synge was fascinated by what he heard: 'The islanders speaking English with a slight foreign intonation that differs a good deal from the brogue of Galway . . .' (*Prose*, p. 50). He noticed that 'They spoke with a delicate exotic intonation that was full of charm . . . with a sort of chant . . .' (*Prose*. p. 52). It must have been this same chant which Synge demanded of the Abbey players at rehearsals of his plays, to judge by the account given by the actress, Máire Nic Shiubhlaigh:

> The speeches had a musical lilt, absolutely different to anything I heard before . . . I found I had to break the sentences—which were uncommonly long—into sections, chanting them, slowly at first, then quickly, as I became familiar with the words . . .[54]

The playwright regarded the English of Inishmore, the largest island which he first visited, to be a 'curiously simple yet dignified language' (*Prose*, p. 53). However, since he wished to learn Irish—the *substratum* of his dialect—he moved on to Inishmaan, 'where Gaelic is more widely used' (*Prose*, p. 53). On Inishmaan, Synge immediately was struck by the relation between the syntax of the Irish and English spoken by the islandmen. This was a relationship which he was subsequently to exploit in forging the language of his plays:

> Some of the men express themselves more correctly than the ordinary peasant, others use the Gaelic idioms continually and substitute 'he' or 'she' for 'it', as the neuter pronoun is not found in modern Irish. A few of the men have a curiously full vocabulary —others know only the commonest words in English, and are driven to strange devices to express their meaning . . . (*Prose*, p. 60)

Synge's study of Irish opened his mind to the possibility of new and striking combinations of words in English. In re-ordering the sentences of ordinary English in accord with Irish syntax, he was, in a sense, re-learning his daily language and discovering exciting new possibilities. He once told Yeats that 'style comes from the shock of new material'[55] and Aran afforded him that material. Like the islandmen, he came to use ingenious devices to express his meaning in dialect.

By the fourth book of *The Aran Islands*, which deals with his last visit, Synge was adept at spotting nuances in the speech of the island women. He noted of one:

> She plays continual tricks with her Gaelic in the ways girls are fond of, piling up diminutives and repeating adjectives with a humorous scorn of syntax . . . (*Prose*, p. 143)

Synge recreated these effects in English in his plays. Christy Mahon in *The Playboy* resorts to the device of repeated adjectives in order to evoke the lonely observations of his wanderings:

> . . . and I walking the world, looking over a *low* ditch or a *high* ditch on my north and south, into *stony scattered* fields, or scribes of bog, where you'd see *young, limber* girls, and *fine prancing* women making laughter with men . . . (*Plays 2*, p. 81)

In that sentence Synge wrote 'making laughter' rather than 'laughing', a direct translation from Irish which is a noun-centred language.[56] 'A humorous scorn of syntax' is also to be found just where we would expect it—in the lively speeches of the playboy himself: '. . . and I after toiling, moiling, digging, dodging from the dawn till dusk . . .' (*Plays 2*, p. 83). The same anarchic repetitions are the stock-in-trade of another poetic hero, Martin Doul: 'and they twisting and roaring out, and twisting and roaring again, one day and the next day, and each day always and ever . . .' (*Plays 1*, p. 123). Such tricks, as Synge noted, are often employed in Irish by native speakers. They are rarely if ever used in any Irish dialect of English. Yet here the dramatist resorts to them in his personal version of the dialect, which is an almost literal translation from the Irish of the islands.

It must now be obvious that St John Ervine's allegation that Synge faked peasant speech is true. It must also be obvious that the playwright's defence—that he used only one or two words not heard among the peasantry—is equally true. For the fact of the matter is that his dramatic dialect is an artefact. Synge, Yeats and Lady Gregory were fond of quoting to prospective playwrights of the Abbey Theatre the dictum of Goethe: 'Art is art because it is not nature'.[57] Synge's own private description of the attempt by the writer 'to produce an art more beautiful than nature' might be taken as a fair account of the process through which he forged his own dialect. He sought to heighten the natural genius of peasant English, by emphasising its peculiarly native constructions. When Maurice Bourgeois complained that Synge 'seems to exaggerate the co-efficient of Hibernicism',[58] he had made the false assumption that the dramatist was trying to reproduce accurately the everyday speech of country folk. But this was not so. If Synge called, in the privacy of a notebook, for an art more beautiful than nature, then a corollary of that call was the demand for a dialect more colourful than everyday speech.

That notebook also contains a draft for an unpublished essay 'On Literary and Popular Poetry'. In discussing the new school of poetry represented by Yeats, Synge writes with clear approval: 'The new poets did not copy the productions of the peasant but seized by instinct his inner mode of work'.[59] This is a perfect description of Synge's own transmutation of folk idiom. In the same notebook in an unpublished essay 'On Mallarmé', Synge quoted with deep interest the French poet's theory of language: ' "The language", he says, "of the streets, the common spoken language, has nothing to do with literature, it exists only as colours or sound exist for the painter or musician and the writer must use it in a free independent way to form the language of literature . . ." '[60] This theory had a lasting influence on Synge, long after 1896–7 when he wrote it down. It appears in another notebook, kept some years later, where the dramatist writes of two of his other models, Yeats and Maeterlinck: 'Their style is a direct idealisation of their own voices when at their fullest and best. They differ from the ordinary spoken language as the Venus de Milo differs from an average woman . . .'[61] The passages just quoted are all taken from articles which the author intended for publication. They never appeared in print and, now that they have failed to achieve inclusion in the *Collected Works* (1968), perhaps they never will. They represent, however, Synge's attempt to supply the critical theory by which his own use of peasant dialect was to be judged. His language represents not the talk of the folk, but a colourful intensification of the peculiarly Irish elements of their idiom. In particular, that dialect is based on the idiom of the Irish-thinking, English-speaking islanders of Aran. Synge said as much in a letter to Spencer Brodney in 1907:

> I look upon *The Aran Islands* as my first serious piece of work—it was written before any of my plays. In writing out the talk of the people and their stories in this book . . . I learned to write the peasant dialect which I use in my plays.[62]

In fact, his method could be even more complex, for it could involve 1) his own translation from Aran Irish; 2) his recreation in peasant English of linguistic devices normally peculiar to Irish; or 3) his immense reliance not so much on ordinary peasant English as on the distinctive type of English spoken on Aran by folk whose everyday language was Irish.

These discoveries represent a tentative attempt to answer the recent call by Synge's biographer for research which would explain 'what relationship Synge's idiom bears to Irish'.[63] The implications of these findings must be analysed in detail in a work entirely devoted to the nature of this dialect.

9 Synge, the Gaelic League, and the Irish Revival

SYNGE AND THE REVIVAL OF THE IRISH LANGUAGE

In the speech which led to the founding of the Gaelic League, Douglas Hyde outlined his aim. He hoped 'to keep the Irish language alive where it was still spoken', adding the significant words, 'which is the utmost at present we can aspire to'.[1] His most important collaborator in this work, Eoin MacNeill, told of how the League was founded on 31 July 1893 in a room at 9 Lower Sackville Street by a handful of men who 'resolved themselves into a society for the sole purpose of keeping the Irish language *spoken* in Ireland' and 'of preserving and spreading Irish as a means of social intercourse'.[2] The emphasis at the beginning was on 'preserving' the language in those Gaeltacht areas where it was yet spoken. Only later in the 1890s, when the movement had gained immense popularity, did the desire of 'spreading Irish as a means of social intercourse' supersede the aim of mere preservation.

By 1902, Synge's attitude to the revival of Irish had crystallised into clear support for its preservation in the Gaeltacht. However, he declared himself opposed to the re-imposition of the language on the rest of the country. This clear statement of policy was not reached without some preliminary confusion. When James Joyce met him in Paris early in 1902, Synge 'was inclined to take the Irish language revival seriously'.[3] Later in the year Synge's opinions seemed in flux, for they changed with each draft of the article which he was preparing on 'The Old and New in Ireland'. At no point in any draft did he express support for the League's object of a wholly Irish-speaking Ireland. In the rough initial notes which he sketched, his alarm at such a prospect is clear, as is his distrust of the rank-and-file nationalists who dominated the organisation:

> cruder forces hooded in the Gaelic League
> If Gaelic League could succeed   Catastrophy
> cannot . . .[4]

At this stage in his thinking, he was sure that the League would fail and glad of it.

In the first full-scale draft of the essay, Synge compared the work of contemporary writers in Irish and English, making his personal allegiance clear:

> In the last ten or fifteen years some national impulse has resulted in two distinct literary currents, which have nothing that is not antagonistic except a national feeling. On one side we have work like Mr. Yeats' *Shadowy Waters* full of sadness and refinement that is peculiar to so-called decadent literature and on the other side we have work in Irish that is full of crude vigour.[5]

Synge chose to oppose the modish notion that writers in Irish and English played complementary roles. He stated bluntly that they had nothing in common except 'a national feeling'. Speculating about the future of the two movements, he applied the adjective 'cultured' to writers in English, while authors in Irish were dubbed 'popular' in their appeal: 'One cannot but wonder what will be the ultimate destiny of these movements. Will the popular movement absorb the cultured movement or the cultured movement absorb the popular writers till they are cultured also? . . .'[6] This antagonism between 'cultured' writing in English and 'popular' work in Irish was the inevitable result of a plan of campaign initiated by Yeats in *The Secret Rose* in 1897. This book, the author had claimed, was 'an honest attempt towards that aristocratic, esoteric Irish literature, which has been my chief ambition. We have a literature for the people, but nothing yet for the few.'[7] Father Eugene O'Growney, the editor of the *Gaelic Journal*, was uncomfortably aware of this dichotomy. In a letter to Eoin MacNeill in 1899 he complained: 'what I find faulty in the method of our poets like Yeats is that they do not attempt to cater for the unsympathetic public'.[8] By 1900, Yeats had publicly separated himself from the writers of the Gaelic League, remarking in his preface to the revised edition of *A Book of Irish Verse*: 'We cannot move these leisured classes from their separation from the land they live in, by writing about Gaelic, but we may move them by becoming men of letters and expressing primary emotions and truths in ways appropriate to this country'.[9] Later still, Yeats was to provide an inspired definition of Synge's distinction between 'cultured' and 'popular' writing, when he asserted that the Gaelic League sought the peasant, but his movement sought something infinitely more precious—the peasant's imagination.[10]

Although MacNeill and O'Growney sought a folk audience, Synge held fast to the belief that 'Tolstoy is wrong in claiming that art should be intelligible to the peasant' (*Prose*, p. 351). He never tried to make his own plays comprehensible to country folk. On the contrary, his work consciously exploits the fact that it presents primitive material to a sophisticated urban audience. Many gifted writers in Irish, such as Patrick Pearse and Pádraic Ó Conaire, shared this belief. Pearse's poetry is written in the simple idiom of Gaeltacht folk, but many of his poems would be incomprehensible to the peasant.[11] He questioned the validity of folk convention as the basis for a national literature: 'The traditional style is not the *Irish* way of singing or declaiming, but the *peasant* way; it is not, and never has been, the possession of the nation at large'.[12] Pádraic Ó Conaire echoed Synge's warning on the dangers of a literature that sought to be 'popular', pointing out that writers of such work would be forced to satisfy the taste of the crudest members of their audience.[13]

Having made the crucial distinction between cultured and popular movements, Synge went on in his essay to speculate that the League's writers might absorb the more cultured artists: 'The Gaelic League is exercising a power so potent that to anyone who knows what it has done the supposition that it may gain the day will not seem preposterous. Suppose that it happens . . .'[14] This passage represents a definite deviation from the views expressed in the rough notes with which he had launched into writing the article. Then the word used to describe the League's chances of success was 'cannot'. Now we are told that such a supposition 'will not seem preposterous'. However, he did not entertain this possibility for any length of time. On the very next line of his draft, he proceeded immediately to make a more plausible suggestion: 'If on the other hand Gaelic remains powerful as it is likely to do for a considerable time but is in the end absorbed by Anglo-Irish work much may be hoped from the result . . .'[15] It was this hypothesis to which he finally gave support in the published essay.

Such a prediction must have made Synge most unpopular with the League. Nevertheless, it perfectly traced the future tensions between the rival traditions and the way in which the conflict was finally resolved. As his ideas formed through successive drafts of the 1902 essay, his attitude to writing in Irish hardened. He synchronised his attack on the poor quality of writing in Irish with yet another of his caustic references to the Gaelic League:

> The Gaelic enthusiasts when they write in Gaelic would certainly be attacked by Mr. Yeats if he could read them. Most of us have a certain satisfaction when we read the productions of the Gaelic League that their writers use a language that is not intelligible outside their clubroom doors. They have a vigour and often real talent but with it all a crudeness it would not be easy to qualify.[16]

It was at this point that Synge's thesis reached its climax. A general revival of Irish would lead to 'linguistic disorder', leaving the bewildered folk semi-literate in both languages, after many decades of confusion in which they had finally achieved the painful transition to English:

> These two currents are so different that it is not easy to suppose that they will ever be drawn together. If the hopes of the Gaelic Leaguers are fulfilled—an event that is it need hardly be said of the greatest possible unlikeliness though it is not impossible—and Ireland begin again to speak and write generally in Irish several centuries must pass before the country in general can have assimilated the language perfectly enough to produce anything that has real value as literature. Meanwhile we will lose the new feeling for English they have gained after three centuries of linguistic disorder.[17]

The linguistic disorder was at its most acute in the middle and end of the nineteenth century. Tomás Bán Ó Concheanainn described the confusion in one family of the period. The monoglot parents said the nightly Rosary in Irish and their children could make the responses only in English, 'which they themselves didn't know properly either'.[18] Even in Synge's own day the confusion in Irish-

speaking areas was considerable, giving us some idea of the disorder
which must have afflicted the whole country earlier in the century.
A good instance of this disorder is a letter written by an aged
Galwayman, living in the Breac-Ghaeltacht in the 1890s. The writer
had occasion to use both Irish and English, but he employed neither
with confidence. He misspelled such simple Irish words as 'dearg'
(dareg), 'Goll' (Gaul), 'Conn' (Cun), 'Laoi na mná móire' (Lee na
mna mora). Ending his letter in semi-literate English, he described
the confusion of folk caught between Irish and English in terms
which confirmed the worst suspicions of Synge:

> The people that is living now a days could not understand the
> old Irish which made me drop it altogether their parents is striving
> to learn their children English what themselves never learned so
> the boys and girls has neither good English or good Irish . . .[19]

By 1902, however, the disorder must have been at an end and English
used with relative ease in most areas outside the Gaeltacht.

The precepts of Synge had a demonstrable influence on other
writers. Many years later, Yeats echoed them to an Indian audience,
when asked why he did not write in Irish: '. . . no man can think
or write with music and vigour except in his mother tongue. I could
no more have written in Gaelic than can those Indians write in
English; Gaelic is my native tongue but it is not my mother
tongue.'[20]

In his essay Synge had expressed the hope that 'the Gaelic League
contrives to keep the cruder powers of the Irish mind occupied in
a national and healthy way'. He had no higher function for it than
that—the negative role of keeping the unsophisticated masses employed in the revival of the native language and lore. Lady Gregory
concurred in this view and assured Yeats that the task of engaging
the masses could be entrusted to the Gaelic League, while he got on
with the serious business of composing plays for finer minds. His
play, *The Countess Cathleen*, had been singularly unpopular with
devout Catholics in the national movement and Lady Gregory wrote
to him:

> Clearly, just now your work is not directly with the masses, which
> would be the most directly interesting work, but that matters less
> as the Gaelic movement has taken up their education, and any of
> the fine work you do, besides being an influence on the best

minds, is there ready for the time when your countrymen will dare to praise it'.[21]

Yeats seems to have come to a similar valuation of the League, for he wrote in his dairy: 'F— is learning Gaelic. I would sooner see her in the Gaelic movement than in any Irish movement I can think of. I fear some new absorption in political opinion'.[22] Furthermore, he never followed Hyde in advocating Irish as the primary literary language. Like Synge, he believed that he must put Irish emotion into the English language if he were to reach his generation.

On matters concerning literature in Irish, Yeats often turned to Synge for guidance and he exhorted his friend to write in newspapers for the general public on the subject. The poet knew no Irish, yet he wrote confidently in *Samhain* (1904) in denunciation of the tawdry journalese of the League's writers. Like Synge, he used populist imagery—'the feet of the mob'—to characterise its rank-and-file membership:

> When Dr. Hyde or Father Peter O'Leary is the writer, one's imagination goes straight to the century of Cervantes, and, having gone so far, one thinks at every moment that they will discover his energy. It is precisely because of this reason that one is indignant with those who would substitute for the ideas of folk-life the rhetoric of the newspapers, who would muddy what had begun to seem a fountain of life with the feet of the mob. Is it impossible to revive Irish and yet to leave the finer intellects a sufficient mastery over the gross, to prevent it from becoming, it may be, the language of a nation, and yet losing all that has made it worthy of a revival, all that has made it a new energy in the mind?[23]

This paragraph, in its distinction between popular and cultured traditions and in its denunciation of the Irish written by the journalists of the League, is astoundingly similar to the 1902 essay of Synge. One is entitled to ask how Yeats, with not even an elementary grounding in Irish, could know that all this was happening to the language. The answer is clear. He had read it all two years previously in Synge's article and especially in the following passage:

> Peasant Gaelic is full of rareness and unconscious beauty but if this language was padded out to suit modern use it would surely be misused by journalists and fools and translators, it would be

defiled in a little while and then the limits to which it owes the
great qualities in it at present would tend to keep it in degradation . . .[24]

This warning had a deep effect on Yeats. He explicitly recalled it in
a conversation with Thomas MacDonagh during the spring of 1904
and he reported the meeting in his memoirs:

> Met MacDonagh yesterday (5 March 1904) . . . He is very low-
> spirited about Ireland. He is managing a school on Irish and
> Gaelic League principles, but says he is losing his faith in the
> League. Its writers are infecting Irish not only with English idiom
> but with the habits of thought of Irish journalism, a most un-Celtic
> thing. 'The League', he said, 'is killing Celtic civilisation'. I told
> him that Synge about ten years ago foretold all this in an article
> in the *Academy*.[25]

Yeats has, characteristically, mistaken the date. In fact, the essay had
appeared in *The Academy and Literature* only two years earlier. But
he has unerringly recalled the substance of Synge's thesis, which
must have greatly impressed him.

Synge did not believe that Irish would become again the spoken
language of Ireland. His opposition to the Gaelic League can be
traced to his contempt for those who spread such a glib assumption.
In his vitriolic letter to the League, sub-titled 'Can We Go Back
into Our Mother's Womb?', he wrote:

> Much of the writing that has appeared recently in the papers
> takes it for granted that Irish is gaining the day in Ireland and
> that this country will soon speak Gaelic. No suppositions is more
> false. The Gaelic League is made up of a doctrine that is founded
> on ignorance, fraud and hypocrisy. *Irish as a living language is dying
> out year by year*—the day the last old man or woman who can
> speak Irish only dies in Connacht or Munster—a day that is
> coming near—will mark a station in the Irish decline that will be
> final a few years later . . .[26]

The important sentence is the one in italics, which seems to suggest
two things. It implies that fewer people are speaking Irish as the
natural language of daily life and that the quality of their spoken
Irish is itself being eroded. The language itself was dying and not

simply its speakers. Synge's grim predictions were fulfilled. The number of Irish speakers in the Gaeltacht declined drastically. In 1911, there were 313,508; in 1926, there were 246,811; and by 1946, the number was only 192,963.[27] The store of words in the language itself was reduced over subsequent decades. The Government Commission on the Restoration of the Irish language (1965) attributed this to the influence of English, rather than to numerical decline in speakers of Irish.[28] By 1969 Kevin Danaher could write that 'the ordinary Gaeltacht dweller of today does not speak Irish with the same fluency, the same precision and the same vigour as did his grandparents'.[29]

Synge regarded the hybrid brand of Irish, purveyed by the League in Dublin, as a contributory factor in this process. He characterised it as 'gibberish': 'I speak not of the old and magnificent language of our manuscripts, or of the two or three dialects still spoken, though with many barbarisms, in the west and south, but of the incoherent twaddle passed off as Irish by the Gaelic League' (*Prose*, p. 400). Synge's clear-eyed assessment of the real predicament of the Irish language was manifest again here. Even as he celebrated the 'magnificent' language spoken by the peasantry, he was not slow to admit that even these varieties of Irish were in decay, replete with 'many barbarisms'. He could make this appraisal, since his extensive studies had revealed to him the richness of the language in its earlier historical phases. Most Leaguers had not the leisure for such study and could not have known that the language they sought to revive was already half-dead. They would have attributed Synge's charge to Ascendancy prejudice rather than to his superior knowledge of the native tradition.

The accusation about 'twaddle' was no idle slur. Hyde had observed of the Gaelic Union, the predecessor of the League, that only six of its members could speak Irish correctly.[30] This situation did not greatly improve for quite some time. Daniel Corkery recalled the League's early classes: 'the teacher, hardly ever paid, in most cases was himself a student of the language, and often not much ahead, in knowledge of the language, of those he taught'.[31] Consequently, few learners ever became fluent speakers of Irish, although thousands were registered as members of the organisation.[32] The brand of 'twaddle' achieved by the remainder has been described by R. A. Breatnach, who explains how it first arose: 'Compelling large numbers of teachers and others, in a matter of months, to teach, use, adapt and develop it in accordance with the particular needs of a more advanced social milieu, had led to the development of a "hybrid speech", a travesty of Irish, pronounced as if it were English'.[33] It is only just to add that the long-term achievements of the League's campaign were far more noteworthy than its early failures—and that today thousands of students speak a better brand of Irish than did Douglas Hyde, the man whose work made their fluency possible. Nevertheless, the 'twaddle' also has been notoriously prevalent in Irish schools and it is not hard for the contemporary scholar of the language to understand Synge's initial irritation.

In opposing the restoration of Irish as the spoken language of the whole country, Synge parted with the mainstream of modern Irish thinking on the subject. Even the White Paper of 1965, noted for its enlightened realism, defined the revival as entailing 'the restoration of Irish as the normal means of communication and commerce employed by the people of Ireland'.[34] Nevertheless, if Synge blamed the League for seeking to impose a debased Irish 'twaddle' upon the English-speaking population of Ireland, he was at least consistent in his application of the underlying principle. For he also denounced the imposition of English on the children in Gaeltacht schools: 'The books they are compelled to use are often absurd. In one of their spelling-books I found "advice" explained as "counsel"; a few of the boys may know what advice means but not many people on the island are likely to have heard of counsel . . .' (*Prose*, p. 116) In opposing the imposition of English on the Gaeltacht and of Irish on the Galltacht, Synge displayed the practical and humane approach which he took to all contemporary social problems. He was motivated not by large political abstractions, but by practical concern for the difficulties of young children struggling to master a language. Knowing that few children would remain at school after the age of twelve, he knew just how vital it was for them to have attained competence in their mother tongue.

Synge was one of a host of Irish intellectuals who resolutely opposed the imposition of English as the language of instruction in Irish-speaking districts. In parliament in 1892, Tim Healy described the system as an absurdity, adding that 'if children are to be compulsorily educated let it be in their own language'.[35] Stephen Gwynn outlined the result of this policy: 'the scholars learned little, forgot quickly what they learned, and became the illiterate peasantry that they are to-day'.[36] Hyde insisted that Irish should be taught in Gaeltacht schools and that only fluent speakers of the language should be appointed as schoolmasters, petty-session clerks and magistrates.[37] He complained of 'schoolmasters who knew no Irish being appointed to teach pupils who knew no English'.[38] In the schools, no advantage was taken of the child's knowledge of Irish, with the result that the language of the home could not be exploited for educational purposes. In a pamphlet entitled 'The Case for Bilingual Education in Irish-Speaking Districts', Edward Martyn on behalf of the Gaelic League made a complaint similar to Synge's: 'The children are got to commit to memory the English of certain Irish words, but the knowledge which they possess of Irish, and which might be utilized to considerable profit as a means of training their intelligences, is wholly ignored'.[39] In 1900, George Moore joined Martyn in the call for 'National schools that are truly National . . . in which Irish shall be used as a vehicle of instruction in all Irish-speaking districts'.[40] In 1906, Patrick Pearse argued for bilingualism in Gaeltacht schools, with Irish as the first language of the classroom.[41] Synge added his voice to theirs in *The Aran Islands*. The agitation was crowned with success and bilingual education in the Gaeltacht was sanctioned in the winter of 1906–7. Ironically, this was some months after Synge had submitted his manuscript to Elkin Mathews and some months before its eventual publication in 1907. By the summer of that year, thirty-six schools had implemented bilingual education.[42]

Synge believed that the teaching afforded by the National Schools was killing the culture of the Gaeltacht. The area was rich in an 'unwritten literature which is still as full and as distinguished as that of any European people' but 'already the boys are indifferent to these things, degraded by the dull courses of national schools' (*Prose*, p. 116). Tim Healy complained that the result of these courses in 'English philistinism' was that folk around the fireside, who had once held conversations in Irish about knightly chivalry, were now reduced to talking in English about the price of a cow.[43] At their annual conference in 1874, the National School-Masters had unanimously passed a resolution pointing out just how degraded the dull courses attacked by Synge actually were:

The peasants in Irish-speaking districts have not English enough to convey their ideas, except such as relate to the mechanical business of their occupation. Hence, they are not able in any degree to cultivate or impress the minds of their children (though often very intelligent themselves), who consequently grow up dull and stupid if they have been suffered to lose the Irish language or to drop out of the constant practice of it.[44]

Nevertheless, Synge was not always so ready to endorse the policies of the League and his attitude to that organisation was often ambiguous. In 1905, he wrote a series of twelve articles for the *Manchester Guardian* on the poverty-stricken Congested Districts of the western seaboard. The final article, entitled 'Possible Remedies', reflects the ambiguity of his attitude. On the one hand, he praises the League for giving some hope to the west, 'probably doing more than any other movement to check emigration' (*Prose*, p. 341). On the other hand, he blames it for basing those hopes on a groundless assumption—that the native language will survive. This ambivalence is to be detected in other comments on the League. In an article in French in *L'Européen*, Synge wrote insultingly about Gaelic League girls using bad Irish to pale clerks at the Irish Literary Theatre; but on the same page he could movingly recall his feelings during the interval in the performance, when these same boys and girls sang in Irish: 'On venait de sentir flotter un instant dans la salle l'âme d'un peuple' (*Prose*, p. 382). (For one moment the spirit of a people had been felt to pass through the room.) He was never negative in his approach to such problems, but he refused also to lapse into a false optimism. The subtleties of his comments were often lost on Leaguers who noticed only the criticisms and not the creatively realistic approach which gave rise to them.

From all this, a pattern begins to emerge. When Synge is writing for a foreign audience, in *L'Européen* or in the *Manchester Guardian*, he comments kindly on the League and its work. The reason is simple. He fully endorsed the aim of saving the Irish of the Gaeltacht and of making folk proud of their native culture. He was always at pains to emphasise to foreign audiences the worthiness of that aspiration. Nonetheless, he was resolutely opposed to the methods employed by the movement in their various campaigns and, when writing for an Irish audience, did not scruple to say so. Colonel A. Lynch summed this up in a letter, written on behalf of the Gaelic League, to the *Irish Statesman* on 28 October 1928: 'Synge was critical rather in respect to our means of action than to our ultimate aim'.[45] An example of this was vividly recalled in the journal of Stephen MacKenna:

. . . he loathed the Gaelic League for ever on the score of one pamphlet in which someone, speaking really a half-truth, had urged the youth of Ireland to learn modern Irish because it would give them access to the grand old Saga literature; I have never forgotten the bale in his eyes when he read this and told me: 'That's a bloody lie, long after they know modern Irish, which they'll never know, they'll still be miles and years from any power over the Saga'. I have never known any man with so passionate, so pedantic a value for truth as Synge. He didn't so much judge the lie intellectually or morally as simply hate it—as one hates a bad smell or a filthy taste. This alone would put him off any public movement whatever.[46]

Nevertheless, Synge often agreed with the League on matters of practical national policy. When the language organisation joined forces with Arthur Griffith in a campaign to promote Irish goods under the Swiftian slogan 'Burn Everything British Except Her Coal', he proved himself no shirker. In November 1905, he wrote to his London publisher, Elkin Mathews, requesting that *The Aran Islands* be 'published and printed in Dublin on Irish paper—small matters that are nevertheless thought a good deal of over here'.[47] Furthermore, in reviewing de Jubainville's book on the Irish Mythological Cycle, he emphasised that it was 'printed and published in Dublin'. Such comments were not made for purely diplomatic reasons. They were deeply felt. Synge confided to Lady Gregory that he believed that every moment spent away from Ireland was wasted.[48] In a letter to his publisher introducing his articles on the Wicklow glens, he explained why he preferred to stay in Ireland, despite the financial rewards to be gained abroad by a writer of his repute: 'I greatly prefer . . . working here for people I know, and I have no wish at all to press for a big price'.[49] As MacKenna had so perceptively divined, Synge could never attach himself to any public movement or organisation. Nevertheless, in his practical patriotism, his commitment to economic self-reliance, and his crusade for the Gaeltacht areas, he was in total agreement with major policies of the League. The one great difference lay in his opposition to the restoration of Irish throughout the country, for, in so demurring, he set his face against the primary aim of that organisation.

THE LEAGUE AND THE WRITERS: SYNGE AS SATIRIST

The obsessive respectability of the Gaelic League did not recommend it to most contemporary writers. As late as 1912, Patrick Pearse was still vainly exhorting its members to go west and live among the Gaeltacht folk.[50] In an open letter to Douglas Hyde, Pearse remarked: 'When the Gaelic League was founded, its followers should have taken to the country. They should have mixed with those who had Irish and stayed with them'.[51] This was something which Synge and Pearse had done thirteen years earlier in the summer of 1899, when both men lived with the McDonough family on Inishmaan. If proof were needed that Synge did not have a condescending attitude to Gaeltacht folk, it lies in the fact that he went west to share their dangerous lives. Few Leaguers followed this example. Sean O'Casey noted how members in Dublin, far from living among the peasantry, were scared even to be seen with city labourers like himself. He recalled how members of his branch had winced at his working-man's muffler and complained that the movement had confused the 'fight for Irish' with a 'fight for collars and ties'.[52] Repeatedly, he charged that the Leaguers stayed in Dublin, 'lisping Irish wrongly'.[53] Nor was O'Casey the only sensitive soul to wince at the League's attitude to spoken Irish. David Comyn, the Celtic scholar, said that he could never forgive the movement for treating Irish 'as if it were an African jabber which people were endeavouring to write down from the mouths of the natives'.[54] Synge, for his part, loved to hear idiomatic Irish properly spoken and he wrote emotionally of the experience on his first visit to Aran: 'An old man who could not read has drawn tears to my eyes by reciting verse in Gaelic I did not fully understand' (*Plays 1*, p. xxix). For him, from the beginning, the qualities of the Irish language could be felt without being rationally understood. This account contrasts sharply with his description of an evening in Dublin, at a production by the Irish Literary Theatre, in 1902, of Hyde's *Casadh an tSúgáin*. Here, he sneered, uncharacteristically, at the Leaguers in the audience, 'les belles Irlandaises de la Gaelic League qui baragouinaient dans un fort mauvais irlandais avec de jeunes commis tout pâles d'enthousiasme' (*Prose*, p. 381). (The beautiful Irish girls of the Gaelic League who jabbered in extremely bad Irish with young clerks pale with enthusiasm.) It must have been difficult for an independent writer with a satiric cast of mind to avoid lampooning the League at the time. Even the gentle Lady Gregory could not avoid remarking, rather bitterly, that Irish had become the 'fashion'.[55] In *Dubliners*, James Joyce attacked this fashionableness and exposed the careerism of some of the League's members in his story, 'A Mother'.

For a time, Synge thought of satirising the League on stage, but the same discretion which prevented the publication of the open letter to the League must have restrained him also on this occasion. He did get as far as the scenario, *Deaf Mutes for Ireland*, which was written 'possibly during the attacks on his plays by the *United Irishman* in January and February 1905, or perhaps in December 1904'.[56] Had he developed his initial idea, it appears from the scenario that his play would have been as crudely propagandistic as the very people whom it sought to satirise. When Synge struck at the League in print, his tone was always strident; had he attempted to strike in his art, his touch would have been even less sure. Perhaps the scenario was merely composed as a piece of prose for his own amusement and was never seriously intended as a play, since in none of his papers is there evidence of an attempt to dramatise any of its situations. Nevertheless, he wrote to Stephen McKenna in 1905 concerning the League: 'I sometimes wish to God I hadn't a soul and then I could give myself up to putting those lads on the stage. God, wouldn't they hop!'[57] So we should not underestimate the violence of his feelings on the subject. *Deaf Mutes for Ireland* may not be the stuff of which great drama is made; but it does afford a unique insight into the private anger of a man who was singularly reticent amid the public turmoil unleashed by his plays.

SCENARIO

The Gaels have conquered. A Pan Celtic congress is being held in Dublin. A large prize is offered for any Irishman who can be proved to know no English. A committee is sitting to try them. They bring in each man in turn, throw a light on him and say 'God save Ireland' and 'To Hell with the Pope'. Men are detected again and again. One is found at last who baffles all tests. In delight the congress is called in in glorious robes; the victor is put up to make a speech in Irish, he begins talking on his fingers— he is deaf mute and advocates a deaf mute society as the only safeguard against encroaching Anglo-Saxon vulgarity.

POSSIBLE SCENARIO

Gaelic having proved useless to withstand English vulgarity Ireland does not know whether to choose to be deaf mute or blind.

An American Nerve Doctor is investigating epidemic of deaf-muteness in Ireland 2000 A.D. He reads out a tract which he has found:

'About the year 1920 it was discovered that the efforts of the

Gaelic League to withstand the inroads of Anglo–Saxon vulgarity, American commercialism, French morals and German free-thought had been unsuccessful, therefore the executive of the Gaelic League and the United Irish League decided that drastic measures must be taken without delay if the sacred entity of the Irish and Celtic soul was to be saved from corruption. At a crowded meeting it was resolved that as Ireland could not speak Irish rather than using the filthy accents of England she would be speechless. Young and intelligent organisers were at once secured, and before long they had touched the saintly and patriotic hearts of the sweet-minded Irish mother. From their cradles the future hopes of the Gaels—and indeed of Europe and the civilized world—heard no more dirty English stories, no more profane swearing, and their innocent hearts were delighted only by the inarticulation of those divine melodies which are the wonder and envy of all nations. A sympathetic conservative secretary was easily induced to force deaf-muteness on the Board of National Schools and in a few years the harsh voice of the National Schoolmaster was heard no more. In a little while the degrading tourist traffic ceased entering. A gang of cattle-maimers from Athenry broke into Trinity College on St Patrick's Day and cut out the tongues of all the professors, fellows and scholars, the students had become so engrossed with football that they were not regarded as human enough to require this mark of Nationality.'[58]

It is not difficult to see where Synge got the inspiration for this scenario. The source is Douglas Hyde's *Pléusgadh na Bulgóide* (or *The Bursting of the Bubble*), a bilingual playlet published in 1903 in Dublin.[59] This work is set in the Common Room of Trinity College, Dublin; and a 'translator's note' warns us at the outset that: 'The word "bulgóid" (bubble) bears a suspicious resemblance to "Tríonóid" (Trinity)'.[60] The action opens with MacEathfaidh (Provost Mahaffy) casually dropping the names of certain European kings with whom he was on intimate terms. He then proceeds to attack the Irish language and to boast of his evidence before the Board of Intermediate Education. An old woman who sells fruit on the university precincts enters with Gaelic question-papers which Mahaffy had contemptuously thrown out the window. He treats her roughly and bans her from the college. She exacts traditional Gaelic revenge with her curse that 'the thing which in this world ye most loathe and dread shall instantly come upon you'.[61] No sooner does she leave than Mahaffy, Traill (Mac Uí Triaill) and Dowden (Mac Uí Dúidín) find themselves turned into Irish-speaking mono-glots. Dowden pleads with Mahaffy to cast off this shame and speak English, but he evokes only this reply:

MAC EATHFAIDH: I'm tr' tr' tr' tr' Ó, a Thighearna, ní fhéadaim. Tá h-uile fhocal do bhí agam ariamh imthighthe glan as mo cheann.[62]

His shame is compounded when he learns of a sudden visitation to the College by the Lord Lieutenant. The visitor asks the stricken Fellows to 'be so good as to receive the representative of your Sovereign in your Sovereign's language'.[63] This they cannot do. The services of Dr Atkinson, Professor of Old Irish, are called upon and Hyde pokes wicked fun at Atkinson's notorious denial that modern Irish was a fully-fledged language:

DOCHTÚIR MAC HAITCINN: I am astounded. Sir, this must be the effect of the great heat, for it is no language at all. It is a kind of muttering only. It is not language.[64]

Atkinson's proven incompetence in Irish is satirised by Hyde who has him suggest that the utterances of Mahaffy may approximate to the sounds of Japanese.[65] But the most hilarious exposure of Atkinson's insecure grasp of Old Irish is to follow. Having finally identified Mahaffy's utterances as Modern Irish, he tries to speak to him in that language, but can only manage a stumbling, broken version of Old Irish:

MAC HAITCINN: Cad ro thárla—no, that brings in the sign of com-pleted action, the ro, twice—cad-rala-dib-a-fhoirend.*
*What has happened to ye, o troop. (This is an attempt at Old or Middle Irish—Translator.)[66]

Atkinson then proceeds to mis-translate everything he hears, the Lord Lieutenant suspects treason and the bubble is burst.

Synge took up this idea for the climax of *Deaf Mutes for Ireland*, but he gave the theme his own grotesquely violent twist. Instead of imposing the countryman's tongue on the Fellows of Trinity, he has their tongues cut out altogether by an invading peasantry. The allegory in *Deaf Mutes* is clear enough, as is the implication of the alteration to Hyde's basic plot. Synge is covertly suggesting what he had proclaimed openly in his essays, his belief that an Irish-speaking Ireland is tantamount to a vow of silence for all its people.

The author of the scenario hits impartially not just as the Gaelic League and Sinn Féin, but also at Yeats and the literary movement. In the opening lines he mocks the modishness of Pan-Celtic congresses, which took place in cities like Dublin rather than in their natural setting of the countryside. In particular, Synge makes wry fun of the idea of awarding prizes for the Irish spoken by peasants who have been dragged up to the Oireachtas in Dublin by the Gaelic League. O'Casey himself has commented caustically on the custom in his autobiographies.[67] The practice had been initiated by Hyde, who had proposed in his famous lecture on de-Anglicisation that medals be awarded to every family who would guarantee that they had spoken Irish during the previous year.[68] The dramatist, Edward Martyn, also had argued that the provision of prizes would stimulate a cultural revival among speakers of the language.[69] Such naked appeals to peasant materialism rather than Gaelic pride were to become a feature of later attempts to restore Irish in the west through subsidies and condescending state bribes. Synge heartily disapproved of such methods which characterised, he said, the land which lost the leprechaun but found the pot of gold.

Synge hits broadly at the League's fond notion that it was non-political and, therefore, in a position to appeal both to Nationalists and Unionists. 'God Save Ireland' and 'To Hell with the Pope' were characteristic slogans of the rival movements which Hyde had hoped to woo. The idea of any organisation in the country being in a position to use both slogans is clearly laughable. Synge was not the only commentator to marvel at the innocence of the League in this aspiration. Robert Kee has recently written: 'It is a measure of Hyde's political naïvety that he can seriously have supposed that in a lecture employing phrases like "this awful idea of complete Anglicisation" he could attract the Unionist gentry of his day'.[70] It is fair to point out that the League did win the support of a small number of Unionists, including the redoubtable Dr O'Kane of Belfast, who said that he might be an Orangeman but did not wish to forget that he was an O'Cahan.[71] In general, however, the League's members wished to translate their cultural into a more brazenly nationalist commitment. Non-aligned writers, other than Synge, were becoming doubtful of Hyde's capacity to steer his movement clear of political affiliation with the nationalists. In a letter to Hyde in April 1907, Canon James Hannay (the novelist 'George Birmingham') considered 'the Sinn Fein position to be the natural and inevitable development of the League principles. They couldn't lead to anything else.'[72] This warning was doubly significant in that it came from an Ulsterman.

The jibe against the fear of foreign influences was a leitmotif in Synge's writings on the national movement. His 'Open Letter to the Gaelic League' alleged that 'with their eyes glued on John Bull's navel, they dare not be Europeans for fear the huckster across the street might call them English' (*Prose*, p. 400). He had good reason for his anger on this occasion, for Arthur Griffith had written in the *United Irishman* that *The Shadow of the Glen* was inspired by 'the decadent cynicism that passes current in the Latin Quartier and the London salon'.[73] Synge was not the first writer of the dramatic movement to be accused of Parisian decadence. The *Freeman's Journal* had attacked the Irish Literary Theatre's production of *Diarmuid and Grania*, complaining that the depiction of the heroine contained 'an unmistakable echo of the Paris boulevards'.[74] Griffith, too, proved sensitive to Synge's portrayal of Irish womanhood in *The Shadow of the Glen*, where he accused the dramatist of 'treating woman's frailty as a subject for laughter'.[75] Hence Synge's jocular reference in his scenario to 'the sacred entity of the Irish and Celtic soul' and to the 'sweet-minded Irish mother'. This was doubtless a reply to Griffith who had accused him of treating adultery 'as a feature of rural Irish life'.

Synge was to attack Griffith even more directly in his playlet, *National Drama; A Farce*. But here in *Deaf Mutes* the humour is genial rather than acid, and is applied to men whom he respected, such as Yeats. The ironic reference to 'the future hopes of the Gaels—and indeed of Europe and the civilized world' may well be a parody of Yeats's famous speech to the Trinity College Historical Society on 1 May 1899. On that occasion Yeats had asserted that 'the work of Ireland was to lift up its voice for spirituality, for ideality, for simplicity in the English-speaking world'.[76] Synge's words may even be a mocking echo of Pearse's utterance that the destiny of the Gael was 'to become the saviour of idealism in modern intellectual and social life, the regenerator and rejuvenator of the literature of the world, the instructor of nations . . .'[77] It was a modish and sententious idea with a sinister underlying chauvinism and the realist in Synge disliked it whenever he encountered it. In a note scribbled in one of his notebooks, he chose to demur: 'WBY's idea of saving W(orld) by Ireland like decorating cabin when ship is sinking'.[78]

The sympathetic, conservative-minded secretary, who forces deaf-muteness onto the Board of National Schools, is a clear parody of Hyde. This affable traditionalist had convinced the Board of Education that they should recognise Irish as a legitimate school subject, despite the opposition from Mahaffy and Atkinson. The Trinity dons feared that the peasants would forget their ancient place and they regarded the Irish Revival as 'the resurrection of a myth for sinister political ends'.[79] In the opinion of at least one scholar, 'it was the battle with the Trinity dons in 1899 which massed public opinion throughout the country solidly behind the Gaelic League for the first time'.[80] Hence, in the scenario, Synge's lurid imagination sees an irate public invade Trinity. The mob attacks dons and scholars, leaving only the common students unscathed. The students, as players of foreign games like Rugby and Association Football, were already deemed by the League to be an irretrievable loss to Gaelic civilisation.

The next playlet, *National Drama; A Farce*, is a further application by Synge of the treatment employed by Hyde in *Pléusgadh na Bulgóide*. In both cases, the tactic is to dramatise the enemies of the writer on their home ground and to allow them to condemn themselves out of their own mouths. It was composed about the same period as the *Deaf Mutes* scenario, but here the attack on Arthur Griffith and the Gaelic League is a good deal more bitter. The farce opens with Fogarty, a patriotic Catholic, examining the green volumes on the bookshelf of a national club-room. Synge's sallies at his enemies in the Gaelic League crackle through the list of titles: 'The Five Parts of Father O'Growney, being the complete Irish course needed for a patriot' (*Plays 1*, p. 221)—a thrust at the *Simple Lessons* in Irish grammar by O'Growney, which sold so widely and taught so little.[81] A further title, 'How to be a Genius, by a Gaelic Leaguer', is the outcome of Synge's anger with the League for attempting to delude young people into the belief that an elementary knowledge of modern Irish would be sufficient for a reading of the ancient sagas.[82]

The stage is then set for a paper on the definition of Irish National Drama by a character named Murphy. He sees it as a drama which projects 'the manifold and fine qualities of the Irish race' (*Plays 1*, p. 222). He would not hold Molière as a model for Irish writers; but he argues that Molière is a national writer, because he describes evil and 'France is a decadent country' (*Plays 1*, p. 222). To his assertion that the Irish still live by their virtues, a scoffing member named Jameson replies that 'there are twenty-seven lunatics per thousand in Ireland, the highest figure on the earth' (*Plays 1*, p. 223). Murphy then asserts that Shakespeare was infected with the plague-spot of sex and Fogarty argues that the national drama of Ireland must have no sex. Jameson pours scorn on these ideas: 'With the help of God we'll make Ireland in this matter a glorious exception from the Catholic countries of the world' (*Plays 1*, p. 223). Jameson has here echoed a number of sentiments expressed by Synge himself in a letter to Stephen MacKenna, not only on the subject of sex, but also on the incidence of lunacy in the country:

> Heaven forbid that we should have a morbid sex-obsessed drama in Ireland, not because we have any peculiar sanctity which I utterly deny—blessed unripeness is sometimes akin to damned rottenness, see percentage of lunatics in Ireland & causes thereof,— but because it is bad as drama and is played out. On the French stage you get sex without its balancing elements: on the Irish stage you get the other elements without sex. I restored sex and people were so surprised they saw the sex only.[83]

In fact, with the introduction of Jameson, the play ceases to be a farce and becomes a serious monologue, almost a tract. In a long concluding speech, broken only by an exclamation of outrage from Fogarty, Jameson outlines his vision of a national drama. His views are clearly endorsed by Synge.

He opens with an attack on those in the Gaelic League who 'think that the Irish drama should hold up a mirror to the Irish nation and it going to Mass on a fine springdayish Sunday morning' (*Plays 1*, p. 224). This is exactly the point made by Synge in the letter to Stephen MacKenna, where he wrote: 'I do not believe in the possibility of a "purely fantastic unmodern ideal breezy spring-dayish Cuchulanoid National Theatre"'.[84] Jameson then proceeds to a broader definition of National Drama than that offered by the *United Irishman* or *An Claidheamh Soluis*. A drama written in Ireland about Irish people 'will and must be national in so far as it exists at all' (*Plays 1*, p. 224). It must project the beauty of the land, as Irish music has done, 'without knowing or thinking'. Unlike the propagandist plays of the Gaelic League, it must 'escape the foolishness that all wilful nationalism is so full of' (*Plays 1*, p. 224). Jameson asserts that art is sad or gay, religious or heretical, by 'accident' and 'causes we cannot account for'. In outrage, Fogarty asks if this means that all art is national. Jameson counters by pointing out that bad art is certainly not national. He cites as bad art those very genres most favoured by the writers of the League—Gaelic imitations of fourth-rate English poetry and nineteenth-century Irish novels. Real art, on the contrary, is the 'product of a few minds working together' and this work 'is and cannot help being national' (*Plays 1*, p. 225). So, he asserts that:

> . . . when two or three people use the infinite number of influences from the past and present of the country, *that* gives their work a local character which is all a nation can demand. If you do not like a work that is passing itself off as national art you had better show that it is not art. If it is good art it is vain for you to try to show that it is not national (*Plays 1*, p. 255).

Synge infused his own prose and plays with elements of the past literature of his country in the Irish language. It is scarcely too much to claim that the 'two or three people' cited by Jameson are Yeats, Synge and Lady Gregory, the three Directors of the Abbey, and that 'the product of a few minds working together' is the art of their theatre. Synge's challenge to the Gaelic League is that its members must attack the work of the theatre on artistic grounds or not at all. In such a fashion he replied to those critics who had denounced *The Shadow of the Glen* for its portrayal of a loveless marriage; and through the character of Jameson he presented his views on the nature of a national drama.

SYNGE, THE GAELIC LEAGUE AND THE NATIONAL THEATRE

From the foundation of the Irish Literary Theatre in 1899, Yeats had treated the Gaelic League with tact and caution. Hyde's movement had been involved in the work of the theatre from the outset, providing actors, producers and a large part of its audience. Yeats was aware of the extent of the theatre's debt to the language movement and he was at pains to convince the League of his goodwill. However, the advent of Synge, as the first dramatic genius of the new theatre, would sunder that friendship and cause violence inside and outside the playhouse. In 1902, nevertheless, all this was still in the future and even Synge seems to have echoed Yeats's attempt to assure the League of its key role. In 'Le Mouvement Intellectuel Irlandais', published in that year, Synge noted the close relations between the League, the Literary Theatre and the Agricultural Co-Operative Movement, 'trois mouvements de la plus grande importance': 'Ces trois mouvements sont intimement liés;—il est rare de trouver quelqu'un qui s'occupe d'un seul d'entre eux sans s'intéresser en même temps aux autres . . . (*Prose*, p. 378). (These three movements are closely allied; it is rare to find someone who is active in one of them without being interested at the same time in the others.)

In retrospect, it is clear that the sources of the rift between the League and the theatre were there from the very beginning. The Irish Literary Theatre (1899–1901) could have been more justly termed 'national' than 'literary', since it drew most of its actors and crew from nationalist societies in Dublin. These people saw their theatrical work as a logical but secondary extension of their political crusade; but to Yeats, Synge and Lady Gregory, the theatre was all-in-all. For every aesthete in the audience, there was a political dogmatist; for every dramatist behind the stage, there was a propagandist; for every actor who crossed the boards for art, there was another who crossed the boards for Ireland. At that time, each member of the society had an equal vote, so Yeats and his friends were forced to engage in much unpleasant lobbying in order to achieve their ends. It was into such an atmosphere of lobbying and counter-lobbying that the name of Synge was introduced to the Gaelic League.

One of the most popular dramatists, within the League and within the theatre, was Séamus Ó Cuisín (James Cousins). He had been one of the guiding spirits behind the literary theatre, for it was he who had introduced the Fay brothers to AE and had therefore paved the way for the production of *Deirdre* and of Yeat's *Cathleen Ní Houlihan*. In 1903, his drama entitled *Sold* had gone through four rehearsals and was popular with the players. Yeats chose this inopportune moment to introduce Synge's *The Shadow of the Glen* to the company.[85] Although some assented at once to its uniqueness and value, others considered it decadent. Nevertheless, by shrewd lobbying Yeats forced it upon the players and the rehearsals of *Sold* were abandoned. He told the Fays, who were still enthusiastic about Cousins's work, that *Sold* was 'rubbish and vulgar rubbish'.[86] The effect of this action was to poison forever the attitude of the Gaelic

League towards the Abbey Theatre's most Gaelic playwright, John Synge. With grim predictability, the attack on *The Shadow of the Glen* was joined by the patriotic press. Maud Gonne wrote in the *United Irishman* that it was 'a play which will please the men and women of Ireland who have sold their country for ease and wealth'.[87] Douglas Hyde, 'in the face of universal criticism',[88] did not immediately resign from his position as Vice-President of the National Theatre Society, hoping that the storm would soon be spent. But by March 1904, he too had left the society. In the meantime, the warm reception accorded the players in London's Royalty Theatre convinced many extreme nationalists that the theatre was pro-British. It is clear that the growing frustration among many Leaguers in the theatre suddenly burst forth and spent itself upon the luckless Synge. It was unfortunate for Synge that, from the beginning of his theatrical career, he should have been so closely allied to Yeats and Lady Gregory in the eyes of the public. In private his beliefs were often far closer to those of the Gaelic League than to the aristocratic attitudes of the Directors of the Abbey Theatre. Because of Yeats's high-handed lobbying, Synge's plays were foisted on the company as though they had no intrinsic merit, as though the dramatist could not stand on his own two feet. When the shy and retiring Synge subsequently became a target for the wrath of the League, its members may really have been vicariously attacking him in order to hit back at the more formidable and forbidding Yeats.

By 1904, Synge joined Yeats and Lady Gregory as a Director of the Abbey Theatre. In that year, the three leaders gave serious consideration to the foundation of an ancillary theatre group for the staging of Gaelic plays. As early as the autumn of 1901, Willie Fay had proposed to George Moore the formation of a bilingual touring theatre, which would perform throughout the country, both in Irish and English, under the aegis of the Gaelic League.[89] The suggestion came as a result of Fay's successful collaboration with Moore in the production of Hyde's *Casadh an tSúgáin*, but the project never materialised. In 1904, however, the idea was revived. A document by Yeats, entitled 'Reasons for and againt the Establishment of the Gaelic Company', may well have been produced in this period.[90] As the resident expert on Gaelic drama at the Abbey, Synge was brought onto the Board of Directors. It is likely that the possibility of employing him as the director of a subsidiary Gaelic theatre influenced this choice. The idea was revived to appease Leaguers within the theatre who were clamouring for plays in Irish and con-

stantly threatening to secede and form their own company. Yeats
received many warnings of impending disaster. He had been told
that 'an amalgamation of all the dissentients with a Gaelic dramatic
society would leave Synge, Lady Gregory and Boyle with yourself
and none of these have drawing power in Dublin'.[91] Nothing immediate came of the scheme, but Synge never allowed the ideal of
a Gaelic theatre, possessing strong links with the Gaeltacht, to be
forgotten. By December of 1904 a compromise seemed to be in the
offing with Synge as its primary architect. Yeats wrote to Lady
Gregory proposing Synge as the organiser of the projected Gaelic
theatre. This was a major consideration in his elevation of Synge to
a Directorship; as he explained to her: 'Synge is taking the reorganisa-
tion very much in earnest and will I think make a good director.
He has a plan for bringing a Gaelic company from the Blasket Islands,
we will have to consider it presently. Synge would stage manage it
himself'.[92] However, the emergence of Synge as the main target for
the League's wrath in the following years put an end to all this.
There could be no prospect of support in Dublin for a Gaelic theatre
under his control. The rapid deterioration in relations between the
theatre and the League made the enterprise impossible.

Despite the tensions surrounding *The Shadow of the Glen*, *An
Claidheamh Soluis* (the weekly journal of the League) greeted *Riders
to the Sea* with warmth, but added a note of warning about those
who tour Connemara and see . . . Scandinavia'.[93] The play is described as 'interesting', 'suggestive of Maeterlinck's *L'Intérieur*'. Its
psychology is deemed 'doubtful' and it is viewed as a sketch for a
play, rather than a play itself. Lest these judgements appear a trifle
hostile, it is fair to note that they are applied also to Hyde's successful
Casadh an tSúgáin. The concluding tone of the review is warm: 'There
will be sundry experiments for some time to come and they will
be welcome'. In private, however, the arguments over *Sold* and *The
Shadow of the Glen* had already divided the company; and that division
became public in the following year amid many resignations from
the theatre and attacks on Synge's play.

As editor of *An Claidheamh Soluis* in these years, Pearse tried to
cultivate good relations with the Abbey Theatre. As Lady Gregory
noted in her diary: 'Pearse I had seen in the little office of *An
Claidheamh Soluis*. He had asked me to write when I could for it,
and had written in 1905 in a kind letter: "I have been trying to
promote a closer comradeship between the Gaelic League and the
Irish National Theatre and Anglo-Irish writers. After all, we are

allies" . . .'[94] In his edition of 15 April 1905, however, Pearse showed that the closer comradeship he sought with Yeats and Lady Gregory did not apply to the work of Synge: 'Má leanann an Comhaltas so do dhrámannaibh de shaghas *Kincora* agus *On Baile's Strand*, níl aimhreas nach rachaidh a chuid saothair i dtairbhe do Ghaedhealaibh. Acht seachnaídís drabhfhuigheall de shaghas *The Well of the Saints* agus *In the Shadow of the Glen*'.[95] (If the Society proceeds with dramas such as *Kincora* and *On Baile's Strand*, there is no doubt that its labours will be of benefit to Irishmen. But let them avoid rubbish such as *The Well of the Saints* and *In the Shadow of the Glen*.) On 22 April in his column 'About Literature', Pearse repeated in English, for Yeats's benefit, what he had written the previous week in Irish: 'Except for the strange infatuation which makes him see a great dramatist in Mr Synge, Mr Yeats's views on the position and purpose of his theatre are entirely sane'.[96] In view of this mounting hostility, Synge had to tread carefully at times. In 1905, he wrote to Elkin Mathews, gently withholding permission to publish *The Tinker's Wedding*, because it might further injure his reputation with the Gaelic movement: 'As far as I am concerned I would rather have the two plays you have brought out now together, and hold over the third as a character in *The Tinker's Wedding* is likely to displease a good many of our Dublin friends and would perhaps hinder the sale of the book in Ireland'.[97] By 'our Dublin friends', he probably meant those Leaguers who were still patrons of the Abbey, but who might have been outraged by the violence to a priest in the play. The same phrase, 'our Dublin friends', would be used sardonically again in a similar context. By 9 September 1905, Yeats wrote to the author that 'we may find it too dangerous for the theatre at present'.[98] In fact, the play was not produced on Irish soil until 1971.

In 1906, as a Director of the Abbey, Synge found himself at the centre of the controversy surrounding the attempt by nationalist members to secede and form the Literary Theatre of Ireland. This group, led by Pádraic Colum, hoped to perform propaganda plays and work in the Irish language. On 11 January 1906, Synge wrote a detailed letter to Lady Gregory, outlining the legal position of the Abbey concerning their patent, their right to let the hall to other drama groups, and the problem of securing a majority in the voting against the nationalists. With great tact he ended: 'If the "others" have as strong a position as your copy of the patent seems to show it won't do to make them finally and firmly our enemies by rash legal proceedings such as making them stop their show'.[99] George Russell acted as a spokesman for the nationalist opposition in these delicate negotiations. He reported back to Synge with the good news that 'Colm (sic), Miss Laird, Starkey, Miss Walker, Roberts, and Ryan, have promised to resign if terms are come to that are satisfactory'.[100] These members undertook to resign from the rival enterprise, if the managers of the Abbey declared their willingness to allow the use of their hall for Theatre of Ireland productions. Miss Horniman (the Englishwoman who was lessee of the Abbey) would agree to such sub-letting only if the second company promised not to perform plays of nationalist propaganda; but she and the Abbey Directors considered it wiser not to make this stipulation before the deal had been sealed. Synge expressed his view of all this lobbying in a letter to Lady Gregory: 'I entirely agree with you that Russell had to know about Miss Horniman's move, and told him last night in confidence. He thinks that as they particularly want propagandist plays the move would simply be looked on as an under-hand way of refusing them the theatre altogether, and that any hint of such a thing would upset negotiations once and for all.'[101] Synge showed himself to be in some sympathy with the rights of the rival group: 'It is most provoking. I have written Yeats a long letter which he can show to Miss Horniman saying that, I, for my part, refuse to negotiate with the opposition if they are kept in the dark about this point, and that if they are told they will refuse to make terms. If you agree with me you had better write to him to that effect also to strengthen his hand in dealing with her.'[102] Much of this razor-edge diplomacy was carried out by Synge, since he was the only one of the three Directors permanently resident in Dublin.

Six days later, he reported with satisfaction to Yeats that 'Miss Horniman wrote practically saying that she would agree to anything we thought necessary. I have told Russell that she will let to them as to anyone else and that satisfies him'.[103] Three days later, after an attempt to sabotage the negotiations by the *United Irishman*, Synge remarked in a letter to Lady Gregory: 'I believe the *UI* attack must be got up by one of the "Irreconcilables" who wants to have a row and stop our negotiations. I agree with you that it is best to take no notice of it'.[104] Displaying his ability to seize control, even over Yeats, he went on: 'I wrote to Yeats as soon as I saw it advising him not to answer, and I have just heard from him to say that he agrees and will not. So all is safe for the moment. I think it is doubly important however to hurry on our arrangements . . . The *UI* may say something we shall have to answer and then no one knows what will be the end of it'.[105] There was, however, no further controversy in the *United Irishman* and the crucial meeting was held back for over a fortnight until 7 April, to give Synge and Russell time to work out an agenda. Events began to overtake Synge's skilled but slow diplomacy. Miss Horniman suddenly decided that on no account would she allow the nationalist group the use of her theatre. Wearily, Synge wrote to Lady Gregory on 12 July: 'I do not feel at all anxious to pin my career to her money. I feel inclined to fight it out here for ourselves and if we fail I'll go and live the rest of my natural life with the king of the Blasket Islands'.[106] Miss Horniman had been from the very outset an inveterate foe of the Gaelic League and now she spoke out strongly against the willingness of Synge and the Directors to accommodate the break-away group: 'I made the theatre for art, not to pander to the desire of the Gaelic League to encourage "patriotism"'.[107] She condemned the playing of Gaelic music during intermissions as a pandering to vulgar patriotism.[108] She even accused Yeats of retaining the services of Willie Fay in order to appease their 'friends in Dublin'.[109] This same euphemism, 'friends in Dublin', had been used already by Synge to describe those members of the League associated with the theatre.

In the clash with Miss Horniman, therefore, Synge showed a great deal of sympathy with those members of the Gaelic League who remained in the company. He always acted as an advocate for their point of view in discussions with other Directors. He insisted that the Abbey should neither employ foreign producers nor use foreign plays, while there was still native talent to be tapped. In particular, he vehemently opposed Miss Horniman's plan to 'dump' Willie Fay as a producer. He stated his views clearly in an ultimatum to Yeats:

So far our movement has been entirely creative—the only movement of the kind I think now existing—and it is for this reason that it has attracted so much attention. To turn this movement now—for what are to some extent extrinsic reasons—into an executive movement for the production of a great number of foreign plays of many types would be, I cannot but think, a disastrous policy . . . Our supply of native plays is very small and we should go on I think for a long time with a very small company so that the native work may go a long way towards keeping it occupied . . . I would rather go on trying our own people for ten years than bring in this ready-made style that is so likely to destroy the sort of distinction everyone recognises in our own company . . .[110]

The upshot of the controversy was that Synge agreed to accept the new producer with specific provisos: that Willie Fay be held on contract as a producer of dialect plays; that the emphasis on the 'national' character of the theatre be maintained; and that the incoming producer be 'a thorough business man, if possible an Irishman'.[111]

Most members of the Gaelic League knew nothing of Synge's silent struggle within the Abbey Theatre to maintain the national character of its productions. In public, he was known only by his unpopular plays, against which the antagonism of nationalists increased with every passing year. So extreme was D. P. Moran's aversion to Synge that he complained of 'a ghastly production' of *Riders to the Sea* in March 1904, which 'reminded me of a visit to a dissecting room'.[112] *The Well of the Saints*, with its apparent blasphemies, was even more poorly received when it opened on 4 February 1905. It 'lost sixty pounds and emptied the theatre'.[113] A kind of literary revisionism insinuated itself into the columns of *An Claidheamh Soluis* and a retrospective attack was made on *Riders to the Sea*, which had earlier won only praise. Now, on 3 February 1906 the paper thundered on its front page:

> Go bhfuil *Riders to the Sea* ró-bhrónach
> Nach dráma é i n-aon chor
> Agus, taobh amuigh de na brógaibh úr-leathair, nach raibh gaol
> ná cosmhalacht ag na daoinibh do bhí ar an árdán le muintir
> Inis Meadhoin thar mar bhí aca le muintir Hong-Cong.[114]

> (That *Riders to the Sea* is too gloomy
> That it is not a drama at all
> That, apart from their new leather shoes, the folk on the stage
> bore no closer relation to the people of Inis Meán than to the
> inhabitants of Hong Kong.)

Thus did the critic mock Synge's much-vaunted attention to the detail of props and costumes. It should be noted that the attack centred on Synge and that Pearse was still writing warmly about Lady Gregory's *Hyacinth Halvey* and Yeats's *The Hour Glass* as late as March 1906.[115]

On 31 March 1906, *An Claidheamh Soluis* announced on its front page the impending foundation of the Literary Theatre of Ireland by Pádraic Colum. Nevertheless, the paper continued to carry advertisements for productions at the Abbey Theatre. On 14 April, it advertised performances of the *The Shadow of the Glen*, *The Building Fund* and *Spreading the News*, with the information that 'Mr. Arthur Darley will play Irish Music'.[116] Yeats was clearly at pains to point out that Miss Horniman's attempt to suppress Darley's music had been without success. The issue of 28 April contains friendly references to the plays of Yeats and Lady Gregory, but there is no mention whatever of *The Shadow of the Glen*, over which a discreet curtain of silence had been drawn.[117] Although *The Well of the Saints* had been a financial disaster for the theatre, Yeats stood by his protégé. He insisted that Synge was a great writer and a great Irish writer at that. Irishmen, he said, had written well before Synge, but they had written well by casting off Ireland. Here, in Synge, was a man inspired by Ireland.[118]

Synge's relations with the Gaelic League were not irretrievably poisoned until the *Playboy* riots in 1907. While he was still known mainly as the author of *Riders to the Sea*, he could draw enthusiastic applause from members of the League who patronised the Abbey.[119] He received a flattering request from Tomás MacDomhnaill, a writer and teacher at St Enda's School, which was run by Pearse according to the principles of the Gaelic League. MacDomhnaill wrote:

Sgathamh roimh an Nodlag bhí Tomás MacDonnchadha ag cainnt liom faoí an dráma gearr sin a sgríobhais—*Riders to the Sea*. Léigheas é ina dhiaidh sin agus theathnaigh sé chomh mór sin liom gur chuir mé Gaedhilge air (Gaedhilge Chonnacht). Theasbánas do Phádraic Mac Piarais é, agus dubhairt sé go mbadh mhaith leis a chur Lá Fhéile Páraic den Claimhe Soluis. Má thabhrann tú cead dom leigint dó é sin a dhéanamh beidh mé an-bhuidheach díot . . .[120]

(Some time before Christmas, Thomas MacDonagh spoke to me about your short play, *Riders to the Sea*. I read it after that and enjoyed it so much that I have translated it into Irish [the Irish of Connacht]. I showed this translation to Patrick Pearse and he said that he would like to publish it in the St. Patrick's Day issue of *An Claidheamh Soluis*. I would be most grateful to you

if you would give me the permission which would allow him
to proceed . . .)

This request is couched in the most respectful language. It could
only have been made to a man with whom the League felt itself in
some sympathy or to a writer of such stature that it hoped to gain
by association with his work. The embarrassing lack of good plays
in Irish may have been another reason why the League was turning
to translations of the English masterpieces then being produced at the
Abbey. It is significant that the names of Pearse and MacDonagh
were invoked by MacDomhnaill in his request to Synge. Both of these
writers had repeatedly lamented the lack of good plays in Irish and
were too discerning to applaud the many poor plays then being
written in the language.[121] The letter may even have been written
in an attempt to woo Synge, then approaching the height of his
fame, to the League—just as Yeats had already wooed the League,
in the years of its greatest glory, to his idea of a national theatre.
Synge, an outspoken and internationally influential enemy, would
have made a powerful ally. A writer in *An Claidheamh Soluis* on 7
July 1906 made this very point: 'We may quarrel with Mr. Synge's
Well of the Saints on the grounds of morality, but the fact remains
that it was produced the other week in Berlin. Is it possible to
imagine any one of our Gaelic plays capable of presentation before
a foreign audience?'[122] Many a Gaelic Leaguer has since wondered
what might have been the effect on the Gaelic revival had Synge
chosen to write in Irish. Dr Micheál MacLiammóir, who wrote and
acted superbly in both languages, had no doubts on the matter: 'Had
he written the poetry and plays . . . in the language that has so
shaped his style that one might almost say that he has created in
one tongue and set down in another, it is indeed likely that the Irish
language would be nearer to rescue than it is today'.[123]

The frustration of these expectations by *The Playboy* may help to
explain the violence of the backlash against Synge on its first production. Pearse had extended many olive branches to the theatre
and his only thanks was *The Playboy* with its healthy refusal to
idealise the peasantry. In that play, Synge depicted Ireland as she was
after centuries of British domination, primitive and poor, yet colourful and poetic. The Irish nationalists were intent on changing all
this and on achieving respectability; so they denounced Synge for
his brutally frank portrait of the life produced by such oppression.
The clash was inevitable. To the Gaelic League, the Abbey Theatre

with its plays in English by ascendancy Directors seemed to have an anti-national ethos. John Eglinton isolated the cause of this distrust in his *Irish Literary Portraits*: 'All the great literatures have seemed in retrospect to have risen like emanations from the life of a whole people, which has served in a general exaltation: and this was not the case with Ireland. How could a literary movement be in any sense national when the interest of the whole nation lay in extirpating the conditions which produced it?'[124] In the *Playboy* riots, that clash erupted with spectacular violence.

THE GAELIC LEAGUE AND THE PLAYBOY RIOTS

On 29 January 1907, the *Freeman's Journal* reported that the cat-calls which greeted *The Playboy of the Western World* were accompanied by 'vociferations in Gaelic'.[125] Sean O'Casey recalled how he stood amid the hostile crowd outside the theatre and was pushed here and there by 'Gaelic Leaguers foaming at the mouth'.[126] Synge himself had no doubt that the League was the motive force behind the disturbances. In reply to a question from his nephew, Edward Stephens, he said 'it had been organised by Gaelic Leaguers and their friends, but that it did not matter, for *The Playboy* would live when they were all forgotten'.[127] Distaste for the play extended beyond the Gaelic League to such kindred movements as the Gaelic Athletic Association.[128] Even Lady Gregory privately admitted her dislike of the work and told Wilfred Scawen Blunt that 'it was a mistake to produce the play'.[129] We are told that, in fact, 'the whole Nationalist press was hostile'.[130]

Nobody is certain as to whether the rioters were regular Abbey patrons venting the frustration of their original expectations, or outsiders who came deliberately to suppress the production. Yeats inclined to the opinion that it was a deliberately planned attack by Irish nationalists.[131] He argued that 'the greater part of those who came to shout down the play were no regular part of our audience at all, but members of parties and societies whose main interests are political'.[132] Lady Gregory, on the other hand, seemed to feel that the disturbance was the outcome of an uncoordinated but simultaneous feeling of outrage on the part of individuals.[133] This view of the events was shared by many other witnesses, among them Frank Sheehy-Skeffington. He dramatised the debate in his 'Dialogues of the Day' column in *The Peasant*:

'And what', asked the Colonel, 'do you call the organised attempts to deny the play a hearing?' 'There weren't any organised attempts', replied the Curate. 'That was only the natural, healthy protest of decent and patriotic people. I should have thought but poorly of my countrymen if they had tolerated such an outrage.'[134]

A significant number of those involved in the protest were active members of the Gaelic League. The neutral reporter of the *Irish Independent* wrote on the morning of Wednesday 30 January 1907: 'Away at the back of the hall were crowds of young men whom one could have no hesitation in associating with the Gaelic movement'.[135] It is significant that the adjective used is not 'national', but the more precise 'Gaelic'. On this exceptional occasion, Miss Horniman praised Synge and reserved all her venom for the language movement: 'How little I expected that my hopes to annoy the Gaelic League into action would be so violently fulfilled'.[136] While a majority in the League appears to have supported the protests, there may well have been some members who were opposed to them. Piaras Béaslaoi, a prominent Leaguer respected by Yeats, testified at the subsequent trials that 'he was no member of any organised gang who went to the theatre for the purpose of objecting'. He cried out against those lines in the play which he deemed objectionable, but this cat-call was neither planned nor synchronised with others. He affirmed significantly that 'previous to this he had been an admirer of the Abbey Theatre and a regular supporter of it'.[137] In his study of the riots, James Kilroy notes that 'the accusations of the disturbances being organised were never proven'.[138] It is clear that a group of men went along to shout the play down, having been warned of its content by an editorial in the *Irish Independent* on that morning. Other men, who happened to be present and who disapproved of the play, joined in the protests. Among these were Piaras Béaslaoi and Patrick Columb (father of the writer, Pádraic Colum). These men were singled out from the protestors for prosecution, because they were recognised and named by Yeats in the melée. Patrick Columb was arrested in such a fashion, according to his son in a letter to the *Freeman's Journal*:

My father certainly went to the Abbey Theatre to hear Mr. Synge's play. He is not in sympathy with an organised opposition. As a matter of fact, he has friends in the present National Theatre Society. He disapproved of certain passages in Mr. Synge's play, and expressed his disapproval. When a policeman interfered he used a strong expression, the expression that a man in an excited crowd would be likely to use. For this he was brought before a magistrate this morning and treated as a member of a gang.[139]

However much they disliked it, many of the arrested Leaguers wanted to give the play a hearing and were clearly opposed to its suppression. It is clear, nonetheless, from motions passed by branches of the League throughout the country, that a majority of their members supported attempts to suppress the play. The precise origins of the rioters, and the extent of Gaelic League involvement in the violence, are not at all clear. For instance, at a meeting of the Athenry branch of the League, Mr Patrick Hynes seemed to imply that the agitators came specially from Galway for the protest. He praised the 'energy and National spirit of the people of Galway, who endeavoured, in the face of heavy fines and imprisonment, to suppress its production before an audience in Dublin'.[140] But the Gort District Council asserted that it was 'the good people of Dublin' who had opposed the play and therefore merited the praise.[141] The definitive article on the matter in *The Connaught Champion* (a significant title in this context) was published on 2 March 1907. It repeated the assertion that the agitators were from the West of Ireland, calling them a 'band of western peasants big and brave enough to make the continued production of such a disgusting travesty impossible'.[142]

The motion passed by the Athenry Branch of the Gaelic League was crucially worded. Its vice-president had said that it was their duty 'to condemn the conduct of Lady Gregory and Mr. Yeats',[143] but there was no mention of Synge in the report of the speech. Synge was not a name known generally in the west; but Yeats and Lady Gregory were known and admired in Galway, and much had been expected of them by Irish Irelanders. Speakers at this meeting repeatedly protested not at the content of the play, but at the fact that Yeats and Lady Gregory should have seen fit to produce such a work. The motion was carried unanimously, with no mention of Synge in a straightforward condemnation of 'the performance of *The Playboy of the Western World* under the superintendence of Lady Gregory and Mr. W. B. Yeates (sic)'.[144] Through all the motions condemning the play runs an undercurrent of disappointment with Lady Gregory, in the past so beloved of Galway folk. The Gort District Council added in its resolution that it would 'stop the children of this Union from partaking of the hospitality of Lady

Gregory in the future as a protest against her active participation and co-operation in the libelling of the Irish character'.[145] The St Colman's Branch of the Gaelic League in Gort recorded the frustration of its hopes for better things. Its unanimous resolution said that 'we are much surprised to find that Irish Irelanders like Lady Gregory and Mr. Yeats persisted in staging it throughout an entire week, notwithstanding the repeated protests of the Irish Irelanders of Dublin'.[146] After all the cooperation between the Abbey Theatre and the Gaelic League in the previous years, this surprise is understandable.

The official policy of the Gaelic League was outlined in the 'Irish Ireland' column of the *Irish Independent* on Wednesday 30 January 1907, under the heading 'A Leaguer's Point of View—An Mhéarthóg agus an Dráma'. The columnist describes how, after some consideration, he walked out in protest:

'Maiseadh, mo thruagh ghéar thú, a Mhéarthóg, mara bhfuil le feiceál agat i gcumha dráma náisiúnta acht an aisling fhallsa agus an bhrionglóidí bhaoiseach bhréagach so' . . .[147]

('You have my deep pity, Méarthóg, if you can witness only this false vision, this foolish and deceitful dream, under the guise of national drama'.)

The language here is simple and blunt, because the weekly column was written to give learners practice in reading elementary Irish. In the more advanced column on the same page, Eoghain Ó Neachtain supplied readers with some badly-needed information about the author of *The Playboy*:

An fear a scríobh an dráma úd nár thaithnigh leis an Méarthóg, deir siad gur fhoghlaim sé an Ghaedhilg agus go bhfuil eolas mór aige uirthi. Chaith sé seal fada i nÁrainn, agus Gaedhilgeoir maith atá anois ann. Deir sé féin nach bhfuil sa gcómhrádh atá sa dráma aige ach cainteanna a chualaidh sé ó na daoinibh san Iarthar. Má fuair sé a chuid Gaedhilge i nÁrainn agus a chuid comhráidh Béarla san Iarthar cá bhfuair sé bunúdhas an sgéil atá sa dráma so aige, ní fheadair mé?[148]

(They say that the man who wrote that play, which displeased An Méarthóg, has learned Irish and that he has a deep knowledge of the language. He spent a long period on Aran and is now a good Irish speaker. He himself says that the dialogue of his drama contains only those words which he heard from the folk of the West. If he learned his Irish on Aran and if he found his English dialogue in the West, one wonders where he found the basis of the plot of his drama?)

This more reasonable approach drew attention to Synge's knowledge of Irish and simply asked him to document his sources for the plot of the play. This seems to have been the official policy of the leadership of the League. Ten days later, Pearse came out in support of the 'walk out in protest' policy: '*The Playboy of the Western World* was not a play to be howled down by a little mob. It was a play to be left severely alone by all who did not care to listen to it'.[149] Pearse went on to denounce Yeats as a spoiled poet and Synge as his 'Evil Spirit'. Five years later, Pearse still saw the Abbey as a 'freak theatre', which 'should be treated as such; if you don't like it, stop away'.[150]

It is a curious quirk of Irish theatrical history that a similar disturbance occurred in Tuam, Co. Galway, at the same time as these violent scenes were being enacted in Dublin. On Sunday 27 January 1907, a travelling company of English players came to Tuam to present two 'stage-Irish' plays, *A Coastguard's Daughter* and *The Wild Irish Boy*. At a specially convened meeting in the Town Hall, a Mr Forde denounced their pernicious misrepresentation of the life of the peasantry and asked 'are we to allow them to pass without strenuously protesting?'[151] Citing the example of the Liverpool Irish, who had recently chased some 'stage-Irish' actors off the stage, he assured the public that the 'young men of the town are whole-heartedly with us in rendering impossible any insulting production which this itinerant company attempts to perform'. He urged his audience that they should 'take an active part in this praiseworthy movement'. He displayed a predictable sensitivity to one particular feature of the offending dramas, which 'did not even hesitate to revile our Irish women'. This was a common complaint in the attacks on Synge's own plays.

The parallels with the *Playboy* row are uncanny, though in Tuam the problem was resolved with a noteworthy final twist. The English management of the company was warned of 'hostile feeling' and sought the support of the police, as Yeats was to do in Dublin. After threats to the actors, a public meeting was held to debate the issue, as happened later in Dublin. The Tuam meeting was attended by 'Gaelic Leaguers, Sinn Feiners and Irish Irelanders generally' and 'much difficulty was experienced in keeping the crowd from storming the hall'. Then came the final twist. The English manager withdrew his plays. Unlike Yeats, he showed great sensitivity to the emotive effect on nationalist opinion of employing the hated Royal Irish Constabulary in defence of his performers. In a public statement to the people of Tuam, he emphasised that 'the police would take no further action in the matter and expressed his regret for ever applying to them'. The violent events in Dublin, a few days later, were to prove the wisdom of this approach. The introduction by Yeats of the British-controlled police force into the National Theatre was, if anything, even more inflammatory of nationalist opinion than anything contained in Synge's play.

AFTERMATH: PASSION, DEATH AND TRANSFIGURATION

Synge never made public his bitter 'Open Letter to the Gaelic League', written in fury after the *Playboy* protests. This reticence was futile, for the attendance figures at the Abbey declined at once to the lowest level in its history. Before the *Playboy* the average takings for a night at the Abbey were between forty and fifty pounds; whereas, after the play the takings for seven performances between 1 and 6 April amounted to only thirty pounds.[152] Joseph Hone commented that 'the company was playing to almost empty houses as a result of Yeats's championship of Synge'.[153] The boycott, ordered in *An Claidheamh Soluis* by an angry Pearse, was having its effect. Stephen MacKenna wrote despairingly in his journal some time later; 'They tell me, and I see many signs of it, that to value Synge's work is to be dreaded and disliked by the entire Gaelic League'.[154]

   The Playboy ended any chance of the closer comradeship between the theatre and the language movement formerly sought by Yeats and Pearse. On 9 February 1907 the crude predictability of the title of Pearse's leading article in *An Claidheamh Soluis* on 'The Passing of Anglo-Irish Drama' belied the critical intelligence of its insights. He opened shrewdly, not with an attack on the play, but with a revival of Colum's scheme of the previous year. The controversy should 'concentrate the attention of Gaels on the absolute necessity for the foundation of an Irish Theatre in the capital of Ireland'.[155]

In a tone of lofty austerity, unique among the editorials in the nationalist press, Pearse denounced the Abbey management, not so much for its production of the play as for its handling of the crisis— presumably the employment of the Royal Irish Constabulary. He also denounced the lack of humour among the protestors, in words reminiscent of Synge's language in the Preface to *The Tinker's Wedding*. Synge had praised 'country people, who have so much humour in themselves' (*Plays 2*, p. 3); and Pearse now wrote of 'the saving grace of humour which in his most tense and electric moments never deserts the genuine Gael'.[156] As he made the point, Pearse may well have recalled Synge's wry comment, printed four days earlier in the *Evening Telegraph*, about the need 'to found a Society for the Preservation of Irish humour'.[157] The Society for the Preservation of the Irish Language had, of course, been the precursor of the Gaelic League. Synge's jibe was clearly aimed at the fanatics of the language movement.

Pearse shrewdly seized the debate upon *The Playboy* as an occasion for self-criticism within the Gaelic movement. The agitators chose the wrong form of protest, he complained, and they failed to direct their attack at a fitting target. Of course, Synge's play was 'in-defensible', but it 'was defensible—and was ably defended—on almost every ground on which it was attacked'. The objections to the play's strong language were 'puerile' and the protests that the play libelled Irish character were 'almost as inept'. The riot was a disgrace, an unnecessary capitulation to the enemies of Ireland, who would find fresh justification for their claim that the Irish were a lawless and violent people. By their riot and disorder, the protestors had perpetuated the very myth which they professed to oppose. Instead of exposing the false image of the 'stage Irishman', the agitators had acted like so many Paddies before them, with drunkenness and rioting: 'Irish character does not need to be vindicated against Mr. J. M. Synge; and if it did, the audience went a passing strange way about vindicating it'. Pearse denied that Synge wrote his play as a caricature of rural Irish life. The charge which he levels against him is 'graver', the charge of a corrupt morality: 'Whether deliberately, or un-deliberately, he is using the stage for the propagation of a monstrous gospel of animalism, of revolt against sane and sweet ideals, of bitter contempt for all that is fine and worthy not merely in Christian morality, but in human nature itself'. He concluded this section of his attack on Synge with the allegation that 'it is not Ireland he blasphemes so much as mankind in general, it is not against a nation he blasphemes so much as against the moral order of the universe'.[158] This overall charge was instantly substantiated, said Pearse, by a play-by-play analysis of Synge's work. *The Shadow of the Glen* preaches contempt for moral conventions; *The Well of the Saints* throws 'sweetness' and 'charity' into question; the powerful dialogue of *The Playboy* has 'produced a brutal glorification of violence, and grossness, and the flesh'. *Riders to the Sea* is, admittedly, 'beautiful and wonderfully impressive', but it too sins in its view of mankind 'despairing in the hands of some strange and unpitying God'.

Having dealt with Synge, Pearse hastened to enforce discipline within his own ranks. He called for a return to the traditional weapon of Irish nationalism, the boycott. The disturbance was not only 'un-dignified' but also 'ineffective'. It left the agitators open to the charge of committing 'an infringement of the liberty both of the author and players and of the public'. This is a frank admission of the truth of Yeats's allegation that the riot 'being an annihilation of civil rights, was never anything but an increase of Irish disorder'.[159] But this is as much as Pearse will concede. Yeats's introduction of the police, with his vindictive attempt to secure convictions in court, was 'lamentable'. With a scarcely concealed jibe at Yeats's famous attempt to quell a hostile audience with the words 'The author of *Cathleen ni Houlihan* addresses you!', Pearse wickedly remonstrated: 'The author of *Cathleen ni Houlihan* at the head of a column of D.M.P. men was a sight which will long haunt the memory with the mixture of the odious and the ludicrous which clings to a recollection of the mean deeds of men made for fine things'. Pearse concluded the article by conceding victory to Yeats 'for the moment', but for Anglo-Irish drama it was, in his view, 'the beginning of the end'.

So much for Pearse. The author of an unsigned article in Irish in the same issue adopted a similar attitude, but with slight differences of detail. He opened with this report: 'Deir Rúnaidhe Craoibhe an Chéitinnigh gur árduigheadh glórtha gaoise ar an gceist seo thuas a nÁrus na gCéiteannach an Luan so ghabh tharainn'. (The Secretary of the Keating Branch says that wise voices were raised on this question last Monday at the Keating Building.) This is significant, for it was the Keating Branch of the League which had provided actors and audience for the production of the Irish Literary Theatre in October 1901. Apart from Hyde himself, the actors in *Casadh an tSúgáin* had all been drawn from the Keating Branch. Clearly, many of the protests against the *Playboy* expressed the frustration of ideals among those who had helped to found the theatre. Unlike Pearse, the author of this article commended those who voiced their objections to the strong language of the play; but he echoed Pearse in arguing 'Ba chóir go mbeadh cead cainnte ag gach éinne in Éirinn—ag Singe chomh maith le cách'. (Everybody in Ireland should have freedom of speech—and Synge as much as anyone else.) The article went on to suggest that these disturbances should have been treated by Yeats as an internal dispute among Irish Irelanders, to be settled by them alone. The protestors clearly regarded their agitation as something of a policy disagreement within the national movement. In that protest, which had all the fury of a fight between former friends, they were taken off-guard by the introduction of the police:

. . . ba náireach an bheart do rinne lucht stiúrtha na hAmharclainne & an t-arm do thabhairt isteach, & ba náirighe 'ná sin an mhaise don Yeatsach bleachtaire do dhéanamh de féin & fiadhnaise thabhairt i n-aghaidh Ghaedheal measamhail ós comhair cúirte Gallda. Nárbh fhéidir an cheist do phléidhe gan Gall thabhairt isteach san sgéal i n-aon chor?'

(It was a shameful deed by the managers of the theatre to call the police, and even more shameful of Yeats to have turned himself into a detective, giving evidence against reputable Gaels before a foreign court. Could not the question have been debated without the introduction of foreigners at all?)

The hostility of the League towards the Abbey after the *Playboy* row was not easily dissolved. An attempt was made by George Roberts, in an article in *The Shanachie* soon after the riots, to heal some of these wounds by emphasising Synge's debts to the native tradition. By a peculiarly Irish paradox, therefore, the first critic to draw public attention to Synge's affinity with Gaelic literature was this Englishman. Roberts had come to Ireland at the persuasion of James Cousins and had joined the publishing firm of Maunsel and Company. In 1905 he had corresponded with Synge concerning the projected publication of *The Aran Islands*, whose title was his suggestion. In his essay in *The Shanachie*, Roberts was concerned to defend Synge against the charge of foreign decadence and to present him as a truly national dramatist. His brilliant account of Synge's work has never been mentioned, nor equalled, by subsequent commentators. It might have marked the beginnings of a real rapprochement between writers in Irish and English, had petty-minded men not mocked it into obscurity. Had Corkery ever shared the perceptions of this essay, he might have read Synge's plays with the vision of a Gaelic artist and not the narrow theology of a Catholic dogmatist. Roberts wrote:

> *Another quality which marks Mr Synge's work as intensely national is its relation to Gaelic Literature. Just as the people he depicts still tell the stories of the Sagas, and consequently still feel the influence of their native literature, still shape some of their ideals from a delight in strong, courageous men, an appreciation of bodily perfection and of youth; so throughout these plays this influence is everywhere apparent. The feeling for youth, and horror of uncomely age, for instance, is surely a survival of that which prompted the imaginings of a Tír na nÓg—a paradise where there was no growing old. His method, too, of mingling the wildest incidents, the most exceptional occurrences, with incidents of everyday life reminds one of the extravagant realism of the folk-tale. And by his intense love and exquisitely sensitive rendering of natural appearances and effects; the marvellous way that by a few touches, a phrase here and there, he can re-create the feeling of a hillside, a country road at night, or still more subtle and undefinable effects, he accomplishes with a more perfect art what so many of the Gaelic poets attempted.*[160]

Roberts went on to remark on the blend of reality and fantasy in the idiom of *The Playboy*, observing astutely:

> so characteristically Gaelic is it in thought, feeling and expression that we must go to *The Love Songs of Connacht* for a parallel. The same intermingling of the wildest untrammelled fancy with homely details, the same passionate longing characterize equally this piece of purely Irish drama and the best example we know of Gaelic lyric poetry.

Roberts's comments are valuable, in that they come from a man who was a friend of Synge, an actor in the first production of *The Shadow of the Glen*, and a literary editor and publisher of the author's plays. It is very likely that this essay relays observations about Synge's work which are based on conversations and correspondence with the dramatist himself.

Militant nationalists, having invested so much energy in the assault on *The Playboy* in the previous weeks, could not afford to face and concede the devastating logic of Roberts's pithy analysis. No attempt was made to discuss the relationship with Gaelic literature outlined in his article. The truth of his thesis was never denied, merely deflected by the heavy sarcasm which characterised the patriotic press of the day. *The Peasant*, which numbered among its contributors such rustic luminaries as AE and Francis Sheehy-Skeffington, offered this response:

What so many of the Gaelic poets *attempted*—Mr Synge in a marvellous way accomplishes—in English prose! We are sorry Mr. Roberts wrote this. We had been thinking we were getting truth of the highest altitude about Drama, and now the grim suspicion begins to haunt us that Mr. Roberts has been trying a little fun all the time. We like fun but we do not quite care for it when disguised as literary criticism . . .[161]

After a year filled with recriminations between the Abbey Theatre and its critics, in November 1908 Pearse indicated that another attempt at détente was to be made:

In our sentiments and taste we are often too extreme. We worship our poets and politicians for a time as if they were gods and when we discover them to be human we stone them. Some writers and players of the Abbey may have sinned against our dearest sentiments, but the good they have done outweighs all their short-comings.'[162]

Nevertheless, the death of Synge was unmarked by any comment in *An Claidheamh Soluis*. Irish Ireland could not find anything good to say of the man and politely refused to speak ill of the dead. However, this silence was broken in 1909 in the columns of *Sinn Féin* by James Cousins, whose play had been suppressed by Yeats to make way for *The Shadow of the Glen*. Cousins had given a lecture in May entitled 'J. M. Synge: His Art and Message' and this was published on 17 July. Arguing that Synge was a 'non-didactic' artist, he presented his objections to such a method. Ireland was still attempting to forge a national literature, according to Cousins, and at this early stage didacticism was necessary. He also repeated the old nationalistic jibe at Synge as an ascendancy eavesdropper, the Turgenev of Ireland, snooping on the conversations of unsuspecting peasants and kitchen-maids.[163]

Within a year, however, the League's opposition to Synge softened, as stories of his hopeless love for Molly Allgood and gentle demeanour in the face of death circulated in Dublin's intellectual circles.[164] On 30 April 1910, *An Claidheamh Soluis* ran a short unsigned column entitled 'John M. Synge', placed innocuously on an inside page. All of a sudden, and for no apparent reason (other than the fact that it is demonstrably true), Synge was received into the central Gaelic literary tradition. His work was celebrated in the article as the equal of the epic *Táin* or the anonymous classic poem *Slán le Pádraig Sáirséal*. To crown it all, the play of Synge used to illustrate the point was none other than *The Well of the Saints*. This play, classed as rubbish in the same paper four years earlier, was now to supercede the work of Eoin Ruadh Ó Súilleabháin in the Gaelic canon. This change of heart may be connected with the change of editors in the previous year, when Pearse had been replaced by Seán MacGiollarnáth. Why the new editor of *An Claidheamh Soluis* chose to relegate this explosive article to the second column of the fifth page of an otherwise unexciting issue nobody will ever know. Perhaps he felt that front-page coverage would expose the paper to the charge of inconsistency and lead to demands for a public retraction of all past injuries to the dramatist:

John M. Synge
Cuir *Táin Bó Cuailgne* agus an t-abhrán adeir *Slán le Pádraig Sárséil* agus *The Well of the Saints* ar a chéile agus tá trí bharr ne nGaedheal agat. Gaedheal ar fearaibh iseadh Synge. Is Gaedheal-aighe go mór é ná Eoghan Ruadh Ó Súilleabháin. Duine des na daorchlanna iseadh Eoghan Ruadh, an dream a thug *The Fox Chase* agus a shórt eile dúinn. Dá dhéine dá ndeacha Yeats air an sgéil níor thug sé rún na nGaedheal leis, agus is daithnid dó é. Tamaillín eile agus ní bheidh aon oide múinte ann acht an Gaedheal.

Aon-fhuil do Cholum Cille agus do Synge, má's mar a chuid filidheachta féin do Cholum Cille. Má chuaidh éinne riamh i rún na gcnuc i bhfad uait sé Synge é. Ba mhaith leis an bhfear soin síneadh cois claidhe. Bhí an tsean-ithir ag tobhach i gcomhnaidhe air, agus is maith d'fhreagair sé í. Ba mhó aige Ára ná Páras na Fraingce. Féach an *Tinker's Wedding*. Coillte glasa agus balaithe na sgeach agus bóthar fada, aer agus aoibhneas. Is dán é do

chuirfeadh dalgas ort, an dalgas ná fuil a shásamh ar an saoghal
so.[165]

(Place *The Cattle-Raid of Cooley* and the song that says *A Farewell
to Patrick Sarsfield* and *The Well of the Saints* side by side and you
have the three crowning glories of the Gael. Synge is a Gael
among men. He is far more a Gael than Owen Roe O'Sullivan.
Owen Roe is one of the lower orders, the people who gave us
The Fox Chase and work of that sort. No matter how hard Yeats
tried, he never learned the secret of the Gael and regretted it. In
a short while, there will be no teacher but the Gael.

Colmcille and Synge are of the same blood, if indeed Colmcille
is the author of that poetry attributed to him. If anyone ever
came to know the secret of the faraway hills, that man is Synge.
He loved to stretch out by a hedge. The old land was always
calling to him and he answered her. Aran meant more to him
than Paris in France. Consider *The Tinker's Wedding*. Green woods,
the smells of the bushes and long roads, open air and light-
heartedness. It becomes a poem that would move you to desire,
the longing that cannot be satisfied in this life.)

It is astonishing to recall that, just five years earlier, Yeats had
described *The Tinker's Wedding* as 'too dangerous for the theatre at
present'.[166]

The foremost journal of literary criticism in Irish, *Irisleabhar
Muighe Nuadhad*, contributed further to this détente with an article
in its issue of Easter 1910 on 'The Anglo-Irish Dramatic Movement'.
This long analysis welcomed 'the ardent sincerity of the writers in
their efforts to create a native tradition'[167] and congratulated the
Anglo-Irish artists on having 'returned to the Gaelic tradition in
English'.[168] The easy concession of the existence of a Gaelic tradition in English was itself a significant retraction of the earlier doctrine
that a national literature could exist only in Irish. The author deemed
Synge's work too much a prey to melancholy and gloom but insisted,
nevertheless, that 'it is possible to trace a kinship of conception and
spirit between his work and Irish tradition'.[169]

With the passing of the years, as international acclaim for his work
increased, the melancholy strain in Synge's writing came to seem a
virtue. By 1913, Pearse had publicly repented of his part in the
attacks on *The Playboy*. With intimations of his own coming sacrifice,
he began to identify strongly with Synge in his martyr's role. He

praised the dramatist as a man who spoke what he believed the truth, suffered at the hands of an ignorant populace, and died young: 'When a man like Synge, in whose sad heart there glowed a true love of Ireland, one of the two or three men who have in our time made Ireland considerable in the eyes of the world, uses strange symbols which we do not understand, we cry out that he has blasphemed and we proceed to crucify him'.[170] Freed of the burden of editorship of *An Claidheamh Soluis*, Pearse was now able to write independently about literature and the image of Synge was never far from his mind. In November 1913, after the turmoil of the Dublin "Lock-Out', he saw in the events 'matter for a play by a Synge'.[171] Obviously, his reaction was not typical of the rank-and-file members of the League, who nursed an abiding distrust of Synge's work for decades after the riots. Like Synge, Pearse knew the Connacht peasantry and was a playwright himself. Furthermore, the passing years had brought home to Pearse that the one Irish dramatist who had conformed to his own rigorous criteria for artistic excellence was his erstwhile enemy, the author of *The Playboy*. The critical aphorisms by which Pearse is now remembered as a literary commentator read like a manifesto in defence of the methods of Synge. Pearse wrote that the Irish prose of the future 'will be found in the speech of the people, but it will not be the speech of the people; for the ordinary speech of the people is never literature, though it is the stuff of which literature is made'.[172] This declaration might well serve as an inspired account of Synge's dialect, which has now been proven to be a conscious artefact based nonetheless on a living speech. Nor are these unexpected agreements between the two former antagonists confined to matters of style and language—they were in harmony also on the more basic questions of inspiration and theme. Pearse's most celebrated critical pronouncement was that 'Irish literature, if it is to live and grow, must get into contact on the one hand with its own past and on the other with the mind of contemporary Europe'.[173] No words could more perfectly explain the themes of Synge's own plays, the works of a man whose bookshelf in Paris contained the *Love Songs of Connacht* next to the poems of Stephane Mallarmé. The playwright consciously aligned himself not only with the mind of contemporary Europe, but also with the past masterpieces of his native language. It was inevitable that the speeches of *The Playboy* would owe as much to 'Úna Bhán' and 'Bean Dubh an Ghleanna' as to the experiments of Mallarmé and Anatole France. Consequently, the artist in Pearse could not but admire the splendour of *The Playboy*, even while the propagandist went through the ritual public motions of denouncing it. His reaction was understandable. It was the reaction of a man divided against himself. But the Gaelic League's attack on the plays created a climate in which Synge's obvious debts to Gaelic literature could not be openly explored. That, although Pearse did not say so, was the greatest tragedy of all.

Notes

CHAPTER I

1 Quoted by Sean Lucy (ed.), *Irish Poets in English* (Cork, 1972) pp. 14–15.
2 Ibid., p. 15.
3 David H. Greene and Edward M. Stephens, *J. M. Synge: 1871–1909* (New York, 1959) p. 302.
4 David H. Greene, 'J. M. Synge—A Centenary Appraisal', *J. M. Synge: Centenary Papers 1971*, ed. Maurice Harmon (Dublin, 1972) p. 192.
5 Alan Price, *Synge and Anglo-Irish Drama* (London, 1961) p. 9.
6 Quoted by Alan Price, 'A Survey of Recent work on J. M. Synge', *Sunshine and the Moon's Delight*, ed. S. B. Bushrui (Gerrards Cross, 1972) p. 294.
7 P. A. Ó Síocháin, *Aran: Islands of Legend* (Dublin, 1962) p. 170.
8 Synge Manuscripts, Trinity College Dublin, MS 4384, f. 47.
9 Seán Mac Giollarnáth, *Conamara* (Cork, 1954) p. 47.
10 See, for example, Seán Ó Tuama, 'Synge and the Idea of a National Literature', *J. M. Synge: Centenary Papers 1971*, pp. 1–17.
11 T. R. Henn, *The Lonely Tower: Studies in the Poetry of W. B. Yeats* (London, 1950) p. 74.
12 David H. Greene, 'Synge and the Celtic Revival', *Modern Drama*, IV (December, 1961) p. 298.
13 Elizabeth Coxhead, *Lady Gregory: A Literary Portrait* (London, 1961) p. 52.
14 Nicholas Newlin, *The Language of Synge's Plays: The Irish Element*, unpublished Ph.D. dissertation, University of Pennsylvania (1949) Chapter 2.
15 P. H. Pearse, Letter to the Editor, *An Claidheamh Soluis*, 20 May 1899, p. 157.
16 J. M. Synge, *Collected Works: Prose*, p. 352. ✓
17 Ibid., p. 399.
18 Letter to Max Meyerfeld, 12 September 1905. National Library of Ireland, MS 778[10].
19 Despite this, a number of leading French and German magazines and

journals carried assessments of Máirtín Ó Cadhain's work on the occasion of his death in the autumn of 1970.

20 Thomas Kinsella, 'The Divided Mind', *Irish Poets in English*, pp. 208–9.

21 John Montague, 'A Lost Tradition', *The Rough Field* (Dublin, 1972) pp. 34–5.

22 Douglas Hyde, 'The Necessity for de-Anglicising Ireland', *The Revival of Irish Literature*: Addresses by Sir Charles Gavan Duffy, K.C.M.G., Dr George Sigerson and Dr Douglas Hyde (London, 1894) pp. 118–19.

23 D. P. Moran, 'The Battle of Two Civilizations', *Ideals in Ireland* ed. Lady Gregory (London, 1901) p. 29.

24 Ibid., p. 27.

25 Patrick Kavanagh, *Collected Poems* (London, 1964) p. 84.

26 Patrick Kavanagh, 'From Monaghan to the Grand Canal', *Studies*, XLVIII (1959) p. 33.

27 W. B. Yeats, Letter to the Editor, *The Leader*, September 1900.

28 W. B. Yeats, 'Ireland and the Arts', *Essays and Introductions* (London, 1961) p. 208.

29 W. B. Yeats, Preface to *A Book of Irish Verse* (London, 1895) p. xii.

30 W. B. Yeats, quoted by A. P. Graves, introduction to Samuel Ferguson, *Poems* (London, 1918) p. xxxiv.

31 James Joyce, *Finnegans Wake* (London, 1939) p. 171.

32 James Joyce, *Ulysses* (Harmondsworth, 1969) p. 20.

33 Ibid., p. 186.

34 James Joyce, *A Portrait of the Artist as a Young Man* (Harmondsworth, 1960) p. 203.

35 James Joyce, *Ulysses*, p. 296.

36 Pádraic Colum, '*Ulysses* in its Epoch', *Saturday Review of Literature*, 27 January 1934, p. 438.

37 James Joyce, *A Portrait of the Artist as a Young Man*, pp. 251–2.

38. Ibid., p. 252.

39. Quoted by Anne Clissmann, *Flann O'Brien: A Critical Introduction to His Writings* (Dublin, 1975) p. 238.

CHAPTER 2

1 Greene and Stephens, *J. M. Synge: 1871–1909*, p. 7.

2 J. M. Synge, *Collected Works: Prose*, p. 198.

3 Lady Gregory (ed.), *Ideals in Ireland* (London, 1901) p. 9.

4 Edward Stephens, *My Uncle John*, ed. Andrew Carpenter (Oxford, 1974) p. 65.

5 Synge Manuscripts, TCD, MS 4371, ff. 59–61.

6 Synge Manuscripts, TCD, MS 4413, f. 4.r. Entry for 21 March 1892.

7 J. M. Synge, *Letters to Molly*, ed. Ann Saddlemyer (Harvard, 1971) p. 210.

8 Synge Manuscripts, TCD, MS 4413. Entry for 24 May 1892. All references to entries in this diary of 1892 are taken from MS 4413.

9 Translated and quoted by Greene and Stephens, op. cit., p. 27.

10 Donal O'Sullivan, *Irish Folk Music, Song and Dance* (Cork, 1974) p. 24.

11 David H. Greene, 'Synge and the Celtic Revival', *Modern Drama*, IV, pp. 292–9.

12 O'Sullivan, op. cit., pp. 24–5.

13 Synge Manuscripts, TCD, MS 4374, f. 62.r.
14 Synge Manuscripts, TCD. See, for example, MS 4414 for June 1893; MS 4415 for October 1894; or MS 4418 for May 1897.
15 Dominic Daly, *The Young Douglas Hyde* (Dublin, 1974) p. 189.
16 Calendar for Trinity College, Dublin, 1893, pp. 125–7.
17 Edward Stephens, op. cit., p. 18.
18 Ibid., p. 66.
19 Daniel Corkery, *The Fortunes of the Irish Language* (Cork, 1954) p. 120.
20 Synge Manuscripts, TCD, MS 4414. All subsequent extracts from the diary for 1893 are taken from MS 4414.
21 Edward Stephens, op. cit., p. 39.
22 Maurice Bourgeois, *John Millington Synge and the Irish Theatre* (London, 1913) p. 30.
23 Douglas Hyde, *Mise agus an Conradh* (Dublin, 1937) pp. 21–2.
24 Dáithí Ó hUaithne, 'The Founding of the Gaelic League', *The Gaelic League Idea* ed. Seán Ó Tuama (Cork, 1972) p. 17.
25 Brian Ó Cuív, 'MacNeill and the Irish Language', *The Scholar Revolutionary: Eoin MacNeill 1867–1945*, ed. F. X. Martin and F. J. Byrne (Dublin, 1973) p. 4.
26 Douglas Hyde, *Leabhar Sgéulaigheachta* (Dublin, 1889) pp. 222–3.
27 Stephen Gwynn, *Today and Tomorrow in Ireland* (Dublin, 1903) p. 71.
28 William Larminie, *West Irish Folk-tales and Romances* (Dublin, 1893) p. 232.
29 *An Claidheamh Soluis*, 24 January 1903, p. 774.
30 Dáithí Ó hUaithne, 'Robert Atkinson and Irish Studies', *Hermathena*, CII (Spring 1966) p. 14.
31 Letter to the Editor from Fr Peter O'Leary, *An Claidheamh Soluis*, 18 November 1905.
32 Dominic Daly, 'The Young Douglas Hyde', *Studia Hibernica*, No. 10 (Dublin, 1970) p. 116.
33 Ibid., p. 123.
34 Ó Cuív, 'MacNeill and the Irish Language', p. 9.
35 Greene and Stephens, op. cit., p. 28.
36 Edward Stephens, op. cit., p. 48.
37 Synge Manuscripts, TCD, MS 4373, f. 15.v. According to R. A. S. Macalister, *Corpus Inscriptionum Insularum Celticarum*, Vol. 2 (Dublin, 1949), Item 569, p. 24, the Freshford inscription may be found 'on the Romanesque west doorway of the church in this village: surrounding the head of the inner-most order on the outside face'. Macalister inclines to ascribe the inscription to the twelfth century, 'the apparent date of the part of the church where the inscription exists'.
38 Ibid.
39 George Petrie, *Transactions of the Royal Irish Academy*, XX, (Dublin, 1845) p. 283.
40 Synge Manuscripts, TCD, MS 4373, f. 16.r.
41 Greene and Stephens, op. cit., p. 28.
42 Synge Manuscripts, TCD, MS 4375.
43 Edward Stephens, op. cit., p. 48.
44 Ibid.
45 Synge Manuscripts, TCD, Letter 696 (undated).

46   Synge Manuscripts, TCD, MS 4415, 22 January 1894.
47   Ibid., 31 December 1894.
48   Edward Stephens, op. cit., p. 105.
49   Greene and Stephens, op. cit., p. 45.
50   Passy was the great pioneer in the field of 'phonetic tendencies', the source of sound changes. See his *Étude sur les changements phonétiques et leurs caractères généraux* (Paris, 1890).
51   L. Marillier, Introduction to *La Légende de la Mort en Basse Bretagne* (Paris, 1892) pp. xi–xii.
52   Synge Manuscripts, TCD, MS 4417: '21 Dec 1896: Fait la connaissance de W. B. Yeats (sic)'.
53   Allan Wade (ed.), *Letters of W. B. Yeats* (London, 1954) p. 314.
54   David H. Greene, 'Synge and the Celtic Revival', p. 297.
55   W. B. Yeats, 'Preface to *The Well of the Saints*' (London, 1905) p. vi.
56   Synge Manuscripts, TCD, MS 4419. Entry for 18 February 1898.
57   Maud Gonne MacBride, *A Servant of the Queen* (Dublin, 1950) p. 158.
58   Quoted by Bourgeois, op. cit., pp. 34–5.
59   Ibid., pp. 35–6.
60   J. M. Synge, *Some Letters of John M. Synge to Lady Gregory and W. B. Yeats*, selected by Ann Saddlemyer (Dublin, 1971) p. 3.
61   *The Well of the Saints* was produced at the famous Deutsches Theater, Berlin, on 12 January 1906. A Bohemian version of *The Shadow of the Glen* was given at the Inchover Theatre, Prague, in February 1906.
62   H. d'Arbois de Jubainville, *Éléments de la Grammaire Celtique* (Paris, 1902), p. 103.
63   Synge Manuscripts, TCD, MS 4390, f. 2.r.
64   Ibid., f. 29.r.
65   Ibid., f. 17.v.
66   Ibid., f. 58.v.
67   Ibid., f. 6.r.
68   Ibid., f. 6.r.
69   This book was published in Paris in 1883. The English-language version, *The Irish Mythological Cycle and Celtic Mythology*, was published in Dublin in 1903, translated by Synge's friend, R. I. Best.
70   Synge Manuscripts, TCD, MS 4378, f. 65.r.–f. 65.v.
71   Greene and Stephens, op. cit., p. 125.
72   Synge Manuscripts, TCD, MS 4419, 25 January 1898: 'Paris—visited Best'.
73   W. B. Yeats, 'Preface to the First Edition of *The Well of the Saints*', *Essays and Introductions* (London, 1961) p. 299.
74   Greene and Stephens, op. cit., p. 74.
75   W. B. Yeats, *Essays and Introductions*, p. 298.
76   Ibid., p. 299.
77   A. Norman Jeffares, *W. B. Yeats: Man and Poet* (London, 1949) p. 107; also Joseph Hone, *W. B. Yeats 1865–1939* (London, 1942) p. 126 and pp. 128–9.
78   Quoted by Greene and Stephens, op. cit., p. 74.
79   David H. Greene, 'J. M. Synge—A Centenary Appraisal', *J. M. Synge: Centenary Papers* (Dublin, 1971) p. 188.
80   P. W. Joyce, *English as we Speak it in Ireland* (London, 1910) p. 6.
81   Corkery, *The Fortunes of the Irish Language*, pp. 13–14.

82 W. B. Yeats, Letter to the Editor, *The Leader*, September 1900.
83 J. M. Synge, *Collected Works: Plays 1*, ed. Ann Saddlemyer (London, 1968) p. xi.
84 Synge Manuscripts, TCD, Letter 92, 3 September 1900.
85 Edward Stephens, op. cit., p. 120.
86 Synge Manuscripts, TCD, MS 4349, f. 28.r.
87 Synge Manuscripts, TCD, MS 4378, f. 17.v.–f. 18.r.
88 Ibid., f. 59.v.
89 Synge, *Prose*, p. 59: 'our English conversation'.
90 Hyde, *Mise agus an Conradh*, p. 109.
91 Synge Manuscripts, TCD, MS 4420. 1 January 1899: 'Breton and Gaelic'.
93 Synge Manuscripts, TCD, MS 4384, f. 12.r, f. 25.r, f. 40.r, and f. 50.r.
93 Bourgeois, op. cit., p. 80.
94 Synge Manuscripts, TCD, MS 4384, f. 49.
95. Ibid., f. 47.
96 Edward Stephens, op. cit., p. 147.
97 Synge Manuscripts, TCD, Letter 85.
98 Greene and Stephens, op. cit., p. 101.
99 Synge Manuscripts, TCD, Letter 74.
100 Ibid., Literal translations in brackets all through the work are by the present author.
101 Synge Manuscripts, TCD, Letter 80.
102 Greene and Stephens, op. cit., p. 104.
103 Basic mistakes include; failure to aspirate *b* in *bhfuil*; use of *agam* instead of *chugam*; failure to aspirate initial letter of *Ghaedhilge* after feminine noun *litir*, also failure to aspirate medial *d* of same word; *moill* (delay) mis-spelled as *miol*; failure to aspirate initial *f* and *g* of words following *litir*; use of *agat* instead of *chugat* etc., etc.
104 Synge Manuscripts, TCD, Letter 76.
105 Synge Manuscripts, TCD, Letter 120.
106 Synge Manuscripts, TCD, Letter 80.
107 Gwynn, *Today and Tomorrow in Ireland*, p. 79.
108 *The Case for Bilingual Education in the Irish-Speaking Districts* (Dublin, n.d.). Gaelic League Pamphlet No. 2, p. 2.
109 Greene and Stephens, op. cit., p. 102.
110 Bourgeois, op. cit., p. 82.
111 Synge, *Some Letters of John M. Synge to Lady Gregory and W. B. Yeats*, p. 2.
112 Synge Manuscripts, TCD, Letter 92, 3 September 1900.
113 Synge Manuscripts, TCD, Letter 74, 23 July 1898.
114 Synge Manuscripts, TCD, Letter 718. Synge moved to this address on New Year's Day 1899. Internal evidence also links the letter with the period of Gaelic study noted in his diary in that month.
115 Synge Manuscripts, TCD, Letter 76.
116 Jack B. Yeats, *Evening Sun* (New York) 20 July 1909.
117 Synge Manuscripts, TCD, Letter 187, 27 July 1905.
118 Synge, *Some Letters of John M. Synge to Lady Gregory and W. B. Yeats*, pp. 12–13.
119 Ibid., p. 15.
120 Synge Manuscripts, TCD, MS 4404, f. 39.

121 Ibid., ff. 38–9.
122 Ibid., f. 37.
123 Ibid., f. 38.
124 Ibid., f. 39.
125 Ibid., f. 37.
126 Samuel Synge, *Letters to my Daughter* (Dublin, 1932) p. 137.

CHAPTER 3

1 Daniel Corkery, *Synge and Anglo-Irish Literature* (Cork, 1931) p. 56.
2 Douglas Hyde, *A Literary History of Ireland* (Dublin, 1899) p. 552.
3 Pádraic Colum, *The Road Round Ireland* (New York, 1927) p. 363.
4 Ibid., pp. 372–3.
5 Synge Manuscripts, TCD, MS 4413, 10 October 1892. Because of his keen interest in the progress and publications of the Irish Texts Society, Synge may also have studied Pádraig Ua Duinnín's edition of *Dánta Aodhagáin Uí Rathaile* (London, 1900); and the same scholar's edition of *Amhráin Eoghain Ruaidh Uí Shúilleabháin* (Dublin, 1902).
6 Hyde, *Literary History of Ireland*, p. 553.
7 Synge Manuscripts, TCD, MS 4384, f. 56.r.
8 Hyde, *Literary History of Ireland*, p. 553.
9 Ibid.
10 Synge Manuscripts, TCD, MS 4384, f. 55.v.
11 W. B. Yeats, *Explorations* (London, 1962) p. 401.
12 Hyde, *Literary History of Ireland*, p. 556.
13 W. B. Yeats, *Samhain*, October 1901, p. 7; also October 1904, p. 21.
14 E. R. Dodds (ed.), *The Journal and Letters of Stephen MacKenna* (London, 1936) pp. 217–18.
15 Arthur Griffith, editorial in *United Irishman*, 17 October 1903.
16 Hyde, *Literary History of Ireland*, p. 552.
17 Ibid.
18 J. C. MacErlean (ed.), *Dánta, Amhráin is Caointe Sheathrúin Céitinn* (Dublin, 1900), p. 60.
19 Ibid.; pages given with each reference.
20 Frank O'Connor, *The Backward Look: A Survey of Irish Literature* (London, 1967) p. 106.
21 MacErlean, op. cit., pp. 17–18.
22 Ibid.; pages as given with each reference.
23 Ibid., p. 86.
24 Synge Manuscripts, TCD, MS 4387, f. 5.r.
25 Seán O'Casey, 'The Gaelic Black-Headed Boy', *Blasts and Benedictions* (London, 1967) p. 218.
26 Charlotte Brooke, *Reliques of Irish Poetry*, 2nd ed. (Dublin, 1816) p. cxxxii.
27 Edward Walsh, *Irish Popular Songs* (Dublin, 1847) pp. 14–15.
28 See Chapter 5.
29 George Moore, *Vale* (London, 1914) p. 250.
30 MacErlean, op. cit., p. 19.
31 Synge Manuscripts, TCD, MS 4387, f. 54.v.
32 David Comyn (ed.), *Foras Feasa ar Éirinn*, Vol. 1 (Dublin, 1902) p. 76.

33 Ibid., p. 77.
34 Ronald Peacock, *The Poet in the Theatre* (London, 1946) p. 93.
35 Leonard Foster, *Aspects of Translation* (London, 1958) p. 50.
36 O'Connor, *The Backward Look*, p. 188.
37 Comyn, *Foras Feasa*, p. 76 and p. 78.
38 Ibid., p. 77.
39 Lady Gregory, *Cuchulain of Muirthemne* (Gerrards Cross, 1970) p. 5.
40 Douglas Hyde, *Sgéalta Thomáis Uí Chathasaigh* (Dublin, 1939) p. xxii.
41 See, for example, an attack on *The Academy* for inaccuracies in *An Claidheamh Soluis*, 23 December 1905.
42 Synge Manuscripts, TCD, MS 4387, f. 25.v. et seq.
43 T. S. Eliot, 'Reflections on "Vers Libre"' (1917), *Selected Prose*, ed. Frank Kermode (London, 1975) p. 33.
44 Synge Manuscripts, TCD, MS 4341. All quotations from this manuscript in this section are followed by the page reference, given in brackets in the text. This method is also employed in citing page references from O'Duffy's text and translation.
45 Máirtín Ó Cadhain always urged translators of Irish to opt for a concrete relative clause rather than a more abstract adjective, even though this manoeuvre inevitably lengthened the sentence.
46 Douglas Hyde, *Love Songs of Connacht* (Dublin, 1893) p. vi.
47 W. B. Yeats, Preface to *Love Songs of Connacht* (Dundrum, 1904) special edition, page not numbered.
48 Samuel Ferguson, 'Hardiman's Irish Minstrelsy', *Dublin University Magazine*, October 1834, p. 453n.
49 Samuel Ferguson, 'Hardiman's Irish Minstrelsy', *Dublin University Magazine*, November 1834, p. 529.
50 Quoted by Walter Benjamin, *Illuminations* (London, 1973) translated by Harry Zohn, p. 81.
51 George Steiner, *After Babel: Aspects of Language and Translation* (London, 1975) p. 321.
52 Renato Poggioli, 'The Added Artificer', *On Translation*, ed. Reuben A. Brower (Harvard, 1959) p. 142.
53 Quoted by Lady Gregory, *Seventy Years* (Gerrards Cross, 1974) p. 403.
54 Quoted in ibid.
55 Quoted in ibid.
56 Standish J. O'Grady, 'Current Events', *All Ireland Review*, III (9 August 1902) pp. 57–8.
57 W. B. Yeats, *Autobiographies* (London, 1955), p. 221.
58 Quoted by Lady Gregory, *Seventy Years*, p. 392.
59 Quoted in ibid., p. 394.
60 Ibid., p. 392.
61 Lady Gregory, *Cuchulain of Muirthemne*, p. 5.
62 Quoted by Lady Gregory, *Seventy Years*, p. 392.
63 Lady Gregory, *Cuchulain of Muirthemne*, p. 5.
64 Lady Gregory, *Seventy Years*, p. 400.
65 Synge Manuscripts, TCD, Letter 765.
66 Allan Wade (ed.), *Letters of W. B. Yeats* (London, 1954) p. 314.
67 Synge Manuscripts, TCD, Letter 236.

68 William Irwin Thompson, *The Imagination of an Insurrection* (Oxford, 1967) p. 67.
69 John P. Frayne (ed.), Introduction to *Uncollected Prose* of W. B. Yeats (London, 1970) p. 47. See also *Letters of W. B. Yeats*, p. 328 and p. 355; and *Autobiographies*, p. 218 and p. 361.
70 *Freeman's Journal*, 31 January 1907, p. 8. While testifying at the trial which resulted from the *Playboy* riots, Yeats remarked that 'I am sorry to say that I understand no Irish'.
71 Lady Gregory, *Seventy Years*, pp. 317–18.
72 Quoted in ibid., p. 329.
73 Ibid., p. 319.
74 John O'Leary, 'What Irishmen Should Know' (Dublin, 1886); pamphlet.
75 T. R. Henn, *The Lonely Tower* (London, 1950), p. 74.
76 David H. Greene, 'Synge and the Celtic Revival', *Modern Drama*, IV, p. 298.

CHAPTER 4

1   Harold Bloom, *Yeats* (New York, 1970) p. 87.
2   W. B. Yeats, 'Irish National Literature 1: From Callanan to Carleton', *Uncollected Prose 1*, ed. John P. Frayne (London, 1970), p. 361.
3   Alan Bruford, 'Gaelic Folk-Tales and Medieval Romances', *Béaloideas: The Journal of the Folklore of Ireland Society*, XXXIV (Dublin, 1969) p. 34.
4   Terence McCaughey, lecture given at Trinity College, Dublin, 24 November 1971.
5   Bruford, op. cit., p. 35.
6   Ibid.
7   Ibid.
8   Ibid., p. 34.
9   Ibid., p. 35.
10 Ibid., pp. 35–6.
11 Ibid., p. 36.
12 Ibid., p. 35.
13 Anatole Le Braz, *Essai sur l'histoire du Théâtre Celtique* (Paris, 1904) pp. 46–7.
14 Lady Gregory, *Poets and Dreamers* (Dublin, 1903) p. 196.
15 Ibid., pp. 196–7.
16 David Comyn (ed.), *Foras Feasa ar Éirinn*, Vol. 1 (Dublin, 1902) pp. 140–1.
17 *Evening Mail*, 29 January 1907, p. 2.
18 W. B. Yeats, *Autobiographies* (London, 1955) p. 220.
19 Synge Manuscripts, TCD, MS 4413, 29 July 1892.
20 W. B. Yeats, *Autobiographies*, p. 221.
21 Edward Stephens, *My Uncle John* ed. Andrew Carpenter (Oxford, 1974) p. 114.
22 Standish H. O'Grady, introduction to *Tóruigheacht Dhiarmuda agus Ghráinne* (Dublin, 1881) Vol. 2, p. xxvii.
23 Richard O'Duffy (ed.), *Oidhe Chloinne Uisnigh* (Dublin, 1898) p. 11.
24 Lady Gregory, *Cuchulain of Muirthemne* (Gerrards Cross, 1970) p. 35.
25 Osborn Bergin (ed.), 'Parlaimint Chloinne Tomáis', *Gadelica 1*, ed. T. F. O'Rahilly (Dublin, 1912–13) p. 43.

26 Standish H. O'Grady, introduction to *Tóruigheacht Dhiarmuda agus Ghráinne*, pp. xxviii–xxix.

27 Synge Manuscripts, TCD, MS 4378, f. 39.r.

28 Edward Stephens, *My Uncle John*, p. 114.

29 Lady Gregory, *Our Irish Theatre* (London, 1913) p. 124.

30 Greene and Stephens, *J. M. Synge: 1871–1909* (New York, 1959) p. 223.

31 Gerard Murphy (ed.), *Duanaire Finn 3* (Dublin, 1953) p. xcviii.

32 Ibid., p. xcix.

33 For O'Grady's attack on Russell's play, see *All Ireland Review*, 19 April 1902.

34 Quoted by Ann Saddlemyer, 'Synge to MacKenna: The Mature Years', *Irish Renaissance*, ed. Robin Skelton and David Clark (Dublin, 1965) p. 67.

35 Nicholas Grene, 'A Critical Study of the Comedies of J. M. Synge', Ph.D. dissertation, Cambridge University, 1972, p. 224.

36 P. L. Henry, 'The Playboy of the Western World', *Philologica Pragensia*, Rocnik VIII (Prague, 1965) pp. 189–204.

37 T. R. Henn, 'John Millington Synge: a reconsideration', *Hermathena*, CXII (London, Autumn 1971) p. 16.

38 See, for example, Alex Zwerdling, *Yeats and the Heroic Ideal* (New York, 1965).

39 Quoted by Dónal McCartney, 'Gaelic Ideological Origins of 1916', *1916: The Easter Rising*, ed. Owen Dudley Edwards and Fergus Pyle (London, 1968) p. 44. The remark was made by Desmond Ryan.

40 Nicholas Mansergh, *The Irish Question* (London, 1968) p. 235.

41 Quoted by Saddlemyer, 'Synge to MacKenna: The Mature Years', p. 68.

42 I am indebted for this formulation to Norman Podhoretz, 'Synge's Playboy: Morality and the Hero', *Twentieth Century Interpretations of 'The Playboy of the Western World'*, ed. Thomas R. Whitaker (New Jersey, 1969) p. 73.

43 Martin Lamm, *Modern Drama* (Oxford, 1952) p. 313. Translated by Karin Elliott.

44 W. B. Yeats, 'Notes and Opinions', *Samhain* (Dublin, 1905) p. 6.

45 Maxim Gorki, 'Observations on the Theatre', *English Review*, XXXVIII (April 1924) p. 495.

46 Lady Gregory, *Cuchulain of Muirthemne*, p. 34.

47 Ibid., p. 26.

48 Ibid., p. 28.

49 Ibid., p. 36.

50 Ibid.

51 Ibid.

52 Ibid., p. 46.

53 Gerard Murphy, *Saga and Myth in Ancient Ireland* (Cork, 1971) p. 21.

54 T. F. O'Rahilly, *Early Irish History and Mythology* (Dublin, 1946) p. 271.

55 Lady Gregory, *Cuchulain of Muirthemne*, p. 38.

56 Quoted by Saddlemyer, 'Synge to MacKenna: The Mature Years', pp. 73–4.

57 Lady Gregory, *Cuchulain of Muirthemne*, p. 38.

58 This has been demonstrated separately in an article appearing in *Long Room* (Dublin), Spring 1979.

59 H. M. and N. K. Chadwick, *The Growth of Literature*, Vol. 3 (Cambridge, 1940) pp. 153 and 158. See also Vol. 2, pp. 211–14.

60 Lady Gregory, *Cuchulain of Muirthemne*, p. 43.
61 Ibid., p. 44.
62 Ibid., p. 184.
63 Ibid., p. 49.
64 For an article by the present author on 'The Sweeney Legend in the Plays of J. M. Synge', see *Éire-Ireland*, XIV (Minnesota, 1979).
65 Quoted by John Scully, *Modern Poets on Modern Poetry* (London, 1966) p. 31.

CHAPTER 5

1 Peter Dronke, *Medieval Latin and the Rise of European Love Lyric* (Oxford, 1968), Vol. I, p. 2. See also Peter Dronke, *The Medieval Lyric* (London, 1968); and Cathal Ó Háinle, 'Na Dánta Grá', *Promhadh Pinn* (Dublin, 1978) pp. 10–36.
2 J. M. Cohen, *A History of Western Literature* (Harmondsworth, 1956) p. 12.
3 A. J. Denomy, *The Heresy of Courtly Love* (New York, 1947) pp. 29–33.
4 Ibid., pp. 40–8.
5 Synge, *Letters to Molly*, ed. Ann Saddlemyer (Harvard, 1971) p. 81.
6 Ibid.
7 Seán Ó Tuama, 'The New Love Poetry', *Seven Centuries of Irish Learning*, ed. Brian Ó Cuív, 2nd ed. (Dublin, 1971) p. 89.
8 Lady Gregory, *Poets and Dreamers* (Dublin, 1903) p. 65.
9 James Reeves, *The Idiom of the People* (London, 1958) p. 55.
10 John O'Daly (ed.), *Poets and Poetry of Munster* (Dublin, 1849) p. 264.
11 Christopher Dawson, *Medieval Religion and Other Essays* (London, 1934) p. 142.
12 Seán Ó Tuama, *An Grá in Amhráin na nDaoine* (Dublin, 1960) p. 286.
13 Cohen, *A History of Western Literature*, p. 25.
14 Ó Tuama, *An Grá in Amhráin na nDaoine*, p. 31.
15 Greene and Stephens, *J. M. Synge: 1871–1909* (New York, 1959) p. 153.
16 Ó Tuama, *An Grá in Amhráin na nDaoine*, p. 46.
17 Ibid., p. 36.
18 Ibid., p. 46.
19 Ibid., pp. 40–1.
20 Ibid., p. 42.
21 Ibid.
22 Ibid., p. 43.
23 Seán Ó Tuama, 'The New Love Poetry', p. 94.
24 W. B. Yeats, *Uncollected Prose*, ed. John P. Frayne (London, 1970) Vol. I, p. 295. The article is entitled 'Old Gaelic Love Songs'.
25 Douglas Hyde, *Love Songs of Connacht* (Dublin, 1893) pp. 60–1.
26 Ibid., pp. 8–9.
27 Ibid., p. 109.
28 Ibid., p. 113.
29 Synge Manuscripts, TCD, MS 4404, f. 29. This note is taken from Hyde, *Love Songs*, p. 113.
30 O'Daly, *Poets and Poetry of Munster*, pp. 222 and 224.

31 Synge Manuscripts, TCD, MS 4391, f. 35.
32 O'Daly, *Poets and Poetry of Munster*, pp. 223 and 225.
33 Synge Manuscripts, TCD, Letter 696.
34 Ó Tuama, *An Grá in Amhráin na nDaoine*, p. 277.
35 Synge Manuscripts, TCD, MS 4391, f. 34.v.
36 Hyde, *Love Songs of Connacht*, p. 103.
37 Ibid., pp. 102–3.
38 Ibid., p. 104.
39 Pádraig Ua Duinnín (ed.), *Amhráin Eoghain Ruaidh Uí Shúilleabháin* (Dublin, 1907) p. 32.
40 Hyde, *Love Songs of Connacht*, p. 104.
41 Ibid., pp. 42–3.
42 Ibid., p. 43.
43 Ibid., p. 91.
44 Nicholas Grene, *Synge: A Critical Study of the Plays* (London, 1975) p. 64.
45 Hyde, *Love Songs of Connacht*, pp. 142–3.
46 Arthur Griffith, editorial, *United Irishman*, 17 October 1903.
47 Quoted by Greene and Stephens, op. cit., p. 175.
48 Ibid., p. 176.
49 Ibid., p. 177.
50 *Freeman's Journal*, 30 January 1907, p. 7.
51 Synge Manuscripts, TCD, Letter 704, 13 July 1905.
52 Synge Manuscripts, TCD, Letter 143, February–March 1904.
53 Herbert Howarth, *The Irish Writers* (London, 1958) p. 93.
54 Hyde, *Songs Ascribed to Raftery* (Dublin, 1903) p. 43.
55 Ibid., pp. 25–6.
56 Ibid., p. 26.
57 Ibid., pp. 34–5.
58 Ibid., p. 39.
59 Ibid., p. 107.
60 Ibid., p. 225.
61 Charles F. McKinley, *John Millington Synge and the World Dimensional*, unpublished Ph.D. thesis, Trinity College, Dublin (1951) pp. 158–9.
62 G.-D. Zimmerman, *Songs of Irish Rebellion* (Dublin, 1967) p. 99.
63 Hyde, *Songs Ascribed to Raftery*, pp. 320–1.
64 'Fiona Macleod', *The Winged Destiny* (New York, 1910) p. 69.
65 Lady Gregory, *Poets and Dreamers*, p. 23.
66 Douglas Hyde, *Religious Songs of Connacht 2* (Dublin, 1906) p. 309.
67 Ibid., p. 311.
68 Bourgeois, *John Millington Synge and the Irish Theatre* (London, 1913) p. 179.
69 Hyde, *Religious Songs of Connacht 2*, p. 315.
70 Hyde, *Religious Songs of Connacht 1*, p. 191.
71 Synge Manuscripts, TCD, MS 4347, f. 1–f. 2.
72 Ibid., f. 2.
73 Synge Manuscripts, TCD, MS 4392, f. 2.v.
74 Ibid., f. 3.r.
75 Ibid., f. 4.r.
76 Translation by Lady Gregory, *Samhain*, No. 1 (October, 1901) p. 32.
77 Dominic Daly, *The Young Douglas Hyde* (Dublin, 1974) p. xiv.

CHAPTER 6

1 Synge Manuscripts, TCD, MS 4378, f. 39.v.
2 Synge Manuscripts, TCD, MS 4384, f. 36.v.
3 Synge Manuscripts, TCD, MS 4378, f. 71.v.
4 Ibid., f. 65.r.
5 J. M. Synge, 'A Story from Inishmaan', *New Ireland Review*, November 1898, p. 65.
6 Synge Manuscripts, TCD, MS 4378, f. 57.r.
7 Richard Dorson, Foreword to *Folktales of Ireland*, ed. Sean O'Sullivan (London, 1966) p. xxv.
8 Ibid., p. xix.
9 Lady Gregory, *Seventy Years* (Gerrards Cross, 1974) pp. 54, 321 and 343.
10 *Four Symposia on Folklore*, ed. Stith Thompson (Indiana, 1953) p. 158.
11 Synge Manuscripts, TCD, MS 4378, f. 40.v.
12 Ibid., f. 40.r.
13 Ibid., f. 39.v. E. S. Hartland's work was published in three volumes in 1894, 1895 and 1896 respectively.
14 Ibid., f. 56.r.
15 L. Marillier, Introduction to *La Légende de la mort en Basse Bretagne*, ed. Anatole Le Braz (Paris, 1892) p. xxi.
16 Ibid., p. xviii.
17 Ibid., p. x.
18 Ibid., pp. v, xiii, and xiv.
19 James Delargy, 'The Gaelic Storyteller', *Proceedings of the British Academy*, XXXI (1945) p. 6.
20 Quoted by Greene and Stephens, *J. M. Synge: 1871–1909* (New York, 1959) p. 181.
21 Delargy, 'The Gaelic Storyteller', p. 34.
22 Ibid., p. 32.
23 *Four Symposia on Folklore*, p. 293.
24 William Larminie, *West Irish Folk-Tales and Romances* (Dublin, 1893) p. 63.
25 Ibid., p. 84.
26 Quoted by Greene and Stephens, op. cit., p. 121.
27 Elizabeth Coxhead, Foreword to *Visions and Beliefs in the West of Ireland* (Gerrards Cross, 1970) p. 7.
28 Quoted by Greene and Stephens, op. cit., p. 84.
29 W. B. Yeats, 'The Message of the Folk-Lorist', *Uncollected Prose*, ed. John P. Frayne (London, 1970) Vol. 1, pp. 283 ff. This article was first published on 19 August 1893 in *The Speaker*.
30 Ibid., pp. 283–4.
31 Ibid., pp. 285–6.
32 Jon Stallworthy, 'The Poetry of Synge and Yeats', *J. M. Synge: Centenary Papers 1971*, ed. Maurice Harmon (Dublin, 1972) p. 149.
33 Synge Manuscripts, TCD, MS 4382, f. 50.v.
34 Ibid.
35 Ibid., f. 49.v.
36 Allan Wade (ed.), *Letters of W. B. Yeats* (London, 1954) p. 98.
37 Synge Manuscripts, TCD, MS 4382, f. 49.v.

Notes

38 John P. Frayne (ed.), Introduction to Yeats's *Uncollected Prose*, Vol. 1, p. 70.
39 Synge Manuscripts, TCD, MS 4382, f. 49.v.
40 Anatole Le Braz, *Essai sur l'Histoire du Théâtre Celtique* (Paris, 1904) pp. 46–7.
41 Delargy, 'The Gaelic Storyteller', p. 4.
42 Ibid., p. 30.
43 Joseph Wood Krutch, *'Modernism' in Modern Drama* (Cornell, 1966) p. 97.
44 Quoted by Máirtín Ó Cadhain, 'Conradh na Gaeilge agus an Litríocht', *The Gaelic League Idea*, ed. Seán Ó Tuama (Cork, 1972) p. 59.
45 Seán Ó Súilleabháin, *Irish Folk Custom and Belief* (Dublin, n.d.) p. 29.
46 Pat Mullen, *Man of Aran*, paperback ed. (Massachusetts, 1970) p. 134.
47 John Messenger, *Inis Beag* (New York, 1969) p. 102; also Lady Gregory, *Visions and Beliefs in the West of Ireland*, pp. 84–6.
48 William Shakespeare, *Macbeth*, ed. G. K. Hunter (Harmondsworth, 1967) p. 76.
49 Lady Gregory, *Visions and Beliefs in the West of Ireland*, p. 94
50 Ibid., p. 136.
51 Kevin Danaher, *Gentle Places and Simple Things* (Dublin, 1964) p. 95.
52 Lady Gregory, *Visions and Beliefs in the West of Ireland*, p. 175; Pat Mullen, *Man of Aran*, p. 43.
53 Lady Gregory, *Visions and Beliefs in the West of Ireland*, p. 298.
54 Ó Súilleabháin, *Irish Folk Custom and Belief*, p. 26.
55 Pat Mullen, *Man of Aran*, p. 189.
56 Ibid., p. 242.
57 Lady Gregory, *Visions and Beliefs in the West of Ireland*, p. 24.
58 Messenger, *Inis Beag*, p. 94.
59 Pat Mullen, *Man of Aran*, p. 53.
60 Lady Gregory, *Visions and Beliefs in the West of Ireland*, p. 99.
61 Seán Ó Súilleabháin, 'The Feast of St. Martin in Ireland', *Studies in Folklore in Honour of Professor Stith Thompson* ed. W. Edson Richmond (Indiana, 1957) pp. 252–8.
62 Robin Skelton, *The Writings of J. M. Synge* (London, 1971) p. 44.
63 Ó Súilleabháin, 'The Feast of St. Martin in Ireland', p. 256.
64 Ibid., p. 258.
65 Messenger, *Inis Beag*, p. 106.
66 Skelton, *The Writings of J. M. Synge*, p. 44.
67 Ó Súilleabháin, *Irish Folk Custom and Belief*, pp. 17–18.
68 Ibid., p. 18.
69 Reidar Th. Christiansen, 'The Dead and the Living', *Studia Norvegica*, No. 2 (Oslo, 1946) p. 15.
70 Ibid., pp. 4, 11 and 15.
71 Ibid., p. 22.
72 Ibid., p. 68.
73 Ó Súilleabháin, *Irish Folk Custom and Belief*, p. 40.
74 Lady Gregory, *Visions and Beliefs in the West of Ireland*, p. 125.
75 Quoted by Edward Stephens, *My Uncle John*, ed. Andrew Carpenter (Oxford, 1974) p. 164.
76 Pádraic Colum, *The Road Round Ireland* (New York, 1927) pp. 369–70.
77 Ó Súilleabháin, *Irish Folk Custom and Belief*, p. 8.
78 Quoted by Harold Orel, 'Synge's Last Play', *Modern Drama*, IV (December,

　　　1961) p. 309.
79　Seán Ó Súilleabháin, *Irish Wake Amusements* (Cork, 1967) p. 15.
80　Ibid., p. 14.
81　Ibid., p. 50.
82　Ibid., p. 15.
83　Ibid., p. 13.
84　Ibid., p. 15.
85　Ibid., p. 14.
86　Ibid.
87　Ibid., p. 15. See also Ó Súilleabháin, *Irish Folk Custom and Belief*, p. 50.
88　Christiansen, 'The Dead and the Living', p. 27.
89　Ibid., pp. 27–8.
90　Ó Súilleabháin, *Irish Wake Amusements*, p. 9.
91　Christiansen, 'The Dead and the Living', p. 32.
92　Crofton Croker, *Researches in the South of Ireland* (Dublin, 1824) pp. 170–1.
93　Christiansen, 'The Dead and the Living', p. 23.
94　Ó Súilleabháin, *Irish Wake Amusements*, p. 15.
95　Ibid., p. 16.
96　Ibid.
97　Ibid., pp. 56–7.
98　Ibid., pp. 41–2.
99　Ibid., pp. 85–6.
100　Ibid., p. 86.
101　Ibid., pp. 86–7.
102　Thomas Dineley, *Observations in a Tour through the Kingdom of Ireland* (Dublin, 1858) pp. 34–5.
103　Ibid., pp. 21–2.
104　Ó Súilleabháin, *Irish Wake Amusements*, p. 154.
105　Ibid., p. 92.
106　Ibid., p. 67.
107　Ibid., p. 22 and p. 153.
108　Christiansen, 'The Dead and the Living', p. 63.
109　Horatio Townsend, *Statistical Survey of the County Cork* (Dublin, 1810) p. 90.
110　Máire Nic Shiubhlaigh, 'Deirdre', *The Gael*, XXII (1904) pp. 85–6.

CHAPTER 7

　1　George Russell, *Deirdre: A Legend in Three Acts* (Chicago, 1970) is the most recent scholarly edition, with a detailed introduction by Herbert Fackler, pp. 1–7.
　2　W. B. Yeats, *Collected Plays* (London, 1952) p. 171.
　3　Quoted by Saddlemyer (ed.), *Plays 2*, p. xxvii.
　4　Quoted by Greene and Stephens, *J. M. Synge: 1871–1909* (New York, 1959) p. 227.
　5　Synge, *Letters to Molly*, ed. Ann Saddlemyer (Harvard, 1971) p. 231.
　6　Quoted by W. B. Yeats, *Autobiographies* (London, 1955) p. 435.
　7　Máire Nic Shiubhlaigh, 'Deirdre', *The Gael*, XXII (1904) pp. 85–6.
　8　Myles Dillon, *Early Irish Literature* (Chicago, 1948) pp. 61–2.

9 Walter Starkie, *Scholars and Gypsies: an Autobiography* (Berkeley, 1963) pp. 82–3.

10 R. I. Best and M. A. O'Brien, *The Book of Leinster*, Vol. 4 (Dublin, 1965) p. 836. See also Eugene O'Curry, *Lectures on the Manuscript Materials of Ancient Irish History* (Dublin, 1861) pp. 589–90.

11 E. G. Quin, 'Longas macc nUisnig', *Irish Sagas*, ed. Myles Dillon (Dublin, 1959) p. 56. This amplified form became the basis for the 1740 manuscript of MacCuirtin, treated in the fifth section of this chapter. The original version in the *Book of Leinster* served as the basis for A. H. Leahy's translation, treated later in this section.

12 Eleanor Hull, *A Textbook of Irish Literature*, Part 2 (Dublin, 1910) pp. 88–9.

13 Alwyn and Brinley Rees, *Celtic Heritage: Ancient Tradition in Ireland and Wales* (London, 1951) p. 291.

14 Eleanor Hull, 'The Story of Deirdre, in its Bearing on the Social Development of the Folk-Tale', *Folk-lore*, XV (1904) p. 25.

15 Rees and Rees, *Celtic Heritage*, p. 280.

16 Daniel Corkery, *Synge and Anglo-Irish Literature* (Cork, 1931) p. 211.

17 Ibid., p. 207.

18 Ibid., p. 223.

19 N. H. and H. W. Chadwick, *The Growth of Literature 1* (Cambridge, 1932) p. 551.

20 Alfred Nutt, 'Review of Deirdre and the Lay of the Children of Uisne', *The Celtic Review*, 11, 15 January 1906, p. 288.

21 Eleanor Hull, 'The Story of Deirdre, in its Bearing on the Social Development of the Folk Tale', p. 25.

22 Osborn Bergin (ed.), *Stories from Keating's History of Ireland* (Dublin, 1930) p. 3.

23 Douglas Hyde, *Beside the Fire* (London, 1890) for the first; and see *Celtic Magazine*, XIII (November, 1887) pp. 20–8, for the second.

24 Ibid., p. 236.

25 H. d'Arbois de Jubainville, *L'Epopée celtique en Irlande* (Paris, 1892) pp. xxvii–xxviii.

26 Anatole Le Braz, *Essai sur l'Histoire du Théâtre Celtique* (Paris, 1904) p. 7.

27 E. G. Quin, 'Longas macc nUisnig', p. 55.

28 Synge, *Letters to Molly*, p. 236.

29 Theophilius O'Flanagan, 'The Ancient Historic Tale of the Death of the Children of Usnach', *Transactions of the Gaelic Society of Dublin*, 1 (1808) pp. 146–76.

30 Whitley Stokes and Ernst Windisch (eds.), 'The Death of the Sons of Usnach', *Irische Texte 11*, ii (Leipzig, 1884) pp. 109–84.

31 Synge Manuscripts, TCD, MS 4341 — a note scribbled in the hand of Edward Stephens on the envelope containing Synge's translation.

32 Lady Gregory, *Seventy Years* (Gerrards Cross, 1974) p. 395.

33 Rudolf Thurneysen, *Die irische Helden—und Königsage bis zum siebzehnten Jahrhundert* (Halle, 1921) p. 327.

34 Quoted by Saddlemyer, introduction to *Plays 2*, p. xxix.

35 Herbert Howarth, *The Irish Writers* (London, 1958) pp. 213ff.

36 E. G. Quin, 'Longas macc nUisnig', p. 57.

37 Synge Manuscripts, TCD, MS 4341, f. 56.

38 Ibid., f. 13.
39 Georges Dottin, 'La mort des fils d'Usnech', *Revue Celtique* XVI (1895) pp. 421–29.
40 T. F. O'Rahilly, *Early Irish History and Mythology* (Dublin, 1946) p. 271.
41 Quoted by Saddlemyer, introduction to *Plays 2*, p. xxvi.
42 Quoted by Saddlemyer, ibid., p. xxviii.
43 Synge Manuscripts, TCD, MS 4378, f. 39.r.
44 Douglas Hyde, *Zeitschrifte für celtische Philologie* 2 (1899) p. 141.
45 Quoted by Saddlemyer, introduction to *Plays 2*, pp. xxvii–xxviii.
46 Quoted by David H. Greene, 'Synge's Unfinished Deirdre', *Proceedings of the Modern Language Association*, LXIII (4 December 1948) p. 1320.
47 Francis Bickley, 'Deirdre', *Irish Review*, 11 July 1912, p. 253.
48 Forrest Reid, *W. B. Yeats: A Critical Study* (London, 1915) p. 171.
49 Darrell Figgis, *Studies and Appreciations* (London, 1912) p. 56.
50 Ibid., pp. 56–7.

CHAPTER 8

1   Malcolm Brown, *The Politics of Irish Literature* (London, 1972) pp. 35–7.
2   Tomás Ó Fiaich, 'The Language and Political History', *A View of the Irish Language*, ed. Brian Ó Cuív (Dublin, 1969) pp. 109–10.
3   Frank J. Fay, 'An Irish National Theatre', *United Irishman*, No. 115, Vol. 5 (11 May 1901).
4   W. B. Yeats, *Samhain*, September 1903, pp. 6–7.
5   Frantz Fanon, *A Dying Colonialism* (Harmondsworth, 1970) p. 73.
6   Ibid.
7   Greene and Stephens, *J. M. Synge: 1871–1909* (New York, 1959) p. 75.
8   Synge Manuscripts, TCD, MS 4346, f. 10.
9   Ibid., f. 9.
10 Quoted by Brian Ó Cuív, 'MacNeill and the Irish Language', *The Scholar Revolutionary*, ed. F. X. Martin and F. J. Byrne (Shannon, 1973) p. 9.
11 Ibid., p. 10.
12 Synge Manuscripts, TCD, MS 4384, f. 54.
13 Ibid.
14 Synge Manuscripts, TCD, MS 4386, f. 6.
15 George Moore, 'The Irish Literary Renaissance and the Irish Language', *New Ireland Review*, April 1900, p. 66.
16 Robin Flower, *The Irish Tradition* (Oxford, 1948) pp. 1–23.
17 Synge Manuscripts, TCD, MS 4405, ff. 2–3.
18 Synge Manuscripts, TCD, MS 4383, f. 1.
19 G.-D. Zimmerman (ed.), *Songs of Irish Rebellion* (Dublin, 1967) p. 99. See also James Delargy, 'The Gaelic Storyteller', *Proceedings of the British Academy*, XXXI (1945) pp. 27–33.
20 Greene and Stephens, op. cit., p. 15.
21 Yeats, *Memoirs*, ed. Denis Donoghue (London, 1972) p. 177.
22 Thomas MacDonagh, *Literature in Ireland* (Dublin, 1916) pp. 47–8.
23 See Synge Manuscripts, TCD, MS 4382, for a number of unfinished novels begun by Synge in these pages.

24 Yeats, *Autobiographies* (London, 1955) p. 345.

25 Quoted by Saddlemyer, 'Synge to MacKenna: The Mature Years', *Irish Renaissance*, ed. Robin Skelton and David Clark (Dublin, 1965) p. 66.

26 'H. S. D.', 'A Dramatic Freak', *Evening Mail*, 28 January 1907, p. 2.

27 Edmund Wilson, *Axel's Castle* (London, 1961) p. 42.

28 St John Ervine, *Some Impressions of My Elders* (London, 1922) p. 201.

29 St John Ervine, *How to Write a Play* (London, 1928) p. 20.

30 W. B. Yeats, 'Preface to the First Edition of *The Well of the Saints*', *Essays and Introductions* (London, 1961) p. 300.

31 Synge Manuscripts, TCD, MS 4382, f. 69.v.

32 Alan Bliss, 'The Language of Synge', *J. M. Synge Centenary Papers 1971*, ed. Maurice Harmon (Dublin, 1972) p. 36.

33 Greene and Stephens, op. cit., p. 7.

34 For example, Donna Gerstenberger, *John Millington Synge* (New York, 1964) p. 46. She writes of the 'echo of the conclusion of Sophocles' *Oedipus* in Maurya's final words . . .'

35 Synge Manuscripts, TCD. Letter 109.

36 Greene and Stephens, op. cit., p. 105.

37 Nicholas Grene, *A Critical Study of the Comedies of J. M. Synge*. Ph.D. dissertation, Cambridge University, 1972, p. 119.

38 Synge Manuscripts, TCD, Letter 109.

39 Synge Manuscripts, TCD, Letter 120.

40 W. B. Yeats, Letter to the Editor of *United Ireland*, 17 December 1892; reproduced in *Uncollected Prose* (London, 1970) Vol. 1, p. 255.

41 Tomás Ó Máille, *An Ghaoth Aniar* (Dublin, 1926) p. 98.

42 Synge Manuscripts, TCD, MS 4384, f. 40.v.

43 Ibid., f. 50.v.

44 Ann Saddlemyer (ed.), *Some Letters of John M. Synge to Lady Gregory and W. B. Yeats* (Dublin, 1971) p. 8.

45 Samuel Synge, *Letters to My Daughter* (Dublin, 1932) p. 137.

46 Douglas Hyde, 'What Ireland is Asking For', *Ideals in Ireland*, ed. Lady Gregory (London, 1901) p. 55.

47 Dáithí Ó hUaithne, *The Irish Language* (Dublin, 1961) p. 6.

48 See, for example, Risteárd Ó Foghludha, *Uaigneas an Ghleanna* in *Naoi nGearra-Chluichí* (Dublin, 1930); Liam Ó Briain, *Deirdre an Bhróin* (Dublin, 1932); Tomás Ó Muircheartaigh & Séamus Ó Séaghdha, *Chun na Fairrge Síos* (Dublin, 1945); and Tomás Ó Flaithearta, *Uaigneas an Ghleanna* and *Chun na Farraige Síos* (Dublin, 1972).

49 Alan Bliss, 'A Synge Glossary', *Sunshine and the Moon's Delight*, ed. S. B. Bushrui (Gerrards Cross, 1972) p. 298.

50 Ibid.

51 P. L. Henry, *An Anglo-Irish Dialect of North Roscommon* (Dublin n.d.) pp. 15–16.

52 Rev. William Burke, 'The Anglo-Irish Dialect', *The Irish Ecclesiastical Record*, Vol. XVII, No. 8 (August 1896) p. 698.

53 W. B. Yeats, *Samhain*, October 1902, p. 8.

54 Máire Nic Shiubhlaigh, *The Splendid Years* (Dublin, 1955) p. 43.

55 Yeats, *Autobiographies*, p. 531.

56 Ó hUaithne, *The Irish Language*, p. 31.

57 Lady Gregory, *Our Irish Theatre* (London, 1914) p. 101.
58 Maurice Bourgeois, *John Millington Synge and the Irish Theatre* (London, 1913) p. 228.
59 Synge Manuscripts, TCD, MS 4382, f. 49.v.
60 Ibid., f. 46.v.
61 Synge Manuscripts, TCD, MS 4393, f. 17.r.
62 Synge Manuscripts, TCD, Letter 3460.
63 David H. Greene, 'J. M. Synge: A Centenary Appraisal', *J. M. Synge Centenary Papers 1971*, p. 192.

CHAPTER 9

1   Douglas Hyde, 'The Necessity for de-Anglicising Ireland', *The Revival of Irish Literature*: Addresses by Sir Charles Gavan Duffy, K.C.M.G., Dr George Sigerson and Dr Douglas Hyde (London, 1894) p. 138.
2   Eoin MacNeill, *Gaelic Journal*, No. 4 (November 1893) pp. 226–8.
3   Stanislaus Joyce, *My Brother's Keeper*, ed. Richard Ellmann (London, 1958) p. 213.
4   Synge Manuscripts, TCD, MS 4393, f. 2.
5   Ibid., f. 4.
6   Ibid., f. 12.
7   Allan Wade (ed.), *Letters of W. B. Yeats* (London, 1954) p. 286. Letter to John O'Leary, the veteran Fenian.
8   O'Growney to MacNeill, 29 September 1899. MacNeill Manuscript Collection, National Library of Ireland.
9   W. B. Yeats, Preface to *A Book of Irish Verse* (London, 1900) pp. xiii–xiv.
10 W. B. Yeats, *Explorations* (London, 1962) p. 401.
11 Frank O'Brien, *Filíocht Ghaeilge na Linne Seo* (Dublin, 1968) pp. 96–7.
12 P. H. Pearse, 'Traditionalism', *An Claidheamh Soluis*, 9 June 1906, pp. 6–7.
13 Pádraic Ó Conaire, 'An Fhírinne agus an Bhréag sa Litríocht', *An Claidheamh Soluis*, 12 May 1923, p. 1.
14 Synge Manuscripts, TCD, MS 4393, f. 12.
15 Ibid.
16 Ibid., f. 5.
17 Ibid., f. 6.
18 Quoted by Seán de Fréine, *The Great Silence* (Dublin, 1965) p. 161.
19 Quoted by Douglas Hyde, *A Literary History of Ireland* (Dublin, 1899) p. 636.
20 W. B. Yeats, *Essays and Introductions* (London, 1961) p. 515.
21 Lady Gregory Papers, Berg Collection, New York Public Library. T.S. acc. no. 65B, n.d. (c. 1899).
22 W. B. Yeats, *Autobiographies* (London, 1955) p. 504.
23 W. B. Yeats, *Samhain*, December 1904, p. 17.
24 Synge Manuscripts, TCD, MS 4393, ff. 9–10. Synge altered the wording of this passage in the published version, but the basic argument and most of the phrases are identical to those found in the draft; see *Prose*, p. 386.
25 W. B. Yeats, *Memoirs*, ed. Denis Donoghue (London, 1972) p. 177.
26 Synge Manuscripts, TCD, Notebook 49. See also *Prose*, p. 399.
27 M. W. Heslinga, *The Irish Border as a Cultural Divide* (Assen, 1971) p. 90.

28 An Coimisiún um Athbheochan na Gaeilge (Dublin, 1965) p. 69.

29 Kevin Danaher, 'The Gaeltacht', *A View of the Irish Language*, ed. Brian Ó Cuív (Dublin, 1969) p. 119.

30 Quoted by Desmond Ryan, *The Sword of Light* (London, 1939) p. 319.

31 Daniel Corkery, *The Fortunes of the Irish Language* (Cork, 1954) p. 136.

32 An Coimisiún um Athbheochan na Gaeilge, p. xiii.

33 R. A. Breatnach, 'Revival or Survival? An Examination of the Irish Language Policy of the State', *Studies*, XLV (1956) pp. 129–45.

34 An Coimisiún um Athbheochan na Gaeilge, p. xiii.

35 Tim Healy, *Gaelic Journal*, No. 4 (July, 1892) p. 156.

36 Stephen Gwynn, *Today and Tomorrow in Ireland* (Dublin, 1903) p. 79.

37 Douglas Hyde, 'The Necessity for de-Anglicising Ireland', p. 138.

38 Douglas Hyde, *A Literary History of Ireland*, p. 631.

39 Edward Martyn, 'The Case for Bilingual Education in Irish-Speaking Districts', Gaelic League Pamphlet 2, p. 2.

40 George Moore, 'The Irish Literary Renaissance and the Irish Language', *New Ireland Review*, Vol. XIII, No. 2 (April, 1900) p. 72.

41 P. H. Pearse, 'The Case for Bilingualism', *An Claidheamh Soluis*, 7 April 1906, p. 6.

42 By 1909, 168 schools used Irish as the language of instruction. See 'Gleo na gCath', *An Claidheamh Soluis*, 25 September 1909, p. 9.

43 Tim Healy, *Gaelic Journal*, No. 4, July 1892, p. 156.

44 Quoted by Hyde, *A Literary History of Ireland*, p. 631.

45 Quoted by Corkery, *Synge and Anglo-Irish Literature* (Cork, 1931) p. 44.

46 E. R. Dodds (ed.), *The Journal and Letters of Stephen MacKenna* (London, 1936) p. 39.

47 Synge Manuscripts, TCD, Letter 208.

48 Lady Gregory, *Our Irish Theatre* (London, 1913) p. 124.

49 Synge Manuscripts, TCD, Wilson Collection, Letter to Joseph Hone, 17 January 1907.

50 Críostóir MacAonghusa, 'Mar a chuaigh an Conradh i bhfeidhm ar an nGaeltacht', *The Gaelic League Idea* ed. Seán Ó Tuama (Cork, 1972) p. 79.

51 P. H. Pearse, 'To Douglas Hyde', *Scríbhinní* (Dublin, 1924) p. 253.

52 Sean O'Casey, *Drums Under the Windows* (London, 1945), p. 73.

53 Ibid.

54 Quoted by Dáithí Ó hUaithne, 'The Foundation of the Gaelic League', *The Gaelic League Idea*, p. 15.

55 Lady Gregory, *Seventy Years* (Gerrards Cross, 1974) p. 318.

56 Ann Saddlemyer (ed.), *Plays 1*, p. 218.

57 Quoted by Robin Skelton, *John Synge* (Bucknell, 1972) p. 58.

58 Synge Manuscripts, TCD, MS 4391, ff. 15–16.

59 The play was published by Gill and Company in 1903, with a translation and notes by Lady Gregory. It had already been published in that year in *New Ireland Review*, Vol. 19. So Dr Saddlemyer's belief that Synge's scenario was written between December 1904 and February 1905 seems highly plausible.

60 Douglas Hyde, *Pléusgadh na Bulgóide* (Dublin, 1903) p. 1.

61 Ibid., pp. 8–9.

62 Ibid., p. 9.

63   Ibid., p. 17.
64   Ibid., p. 19.
65   Ibid., p. 20.
66   Ibid., p. 21.
67   O'Casey, *Drums Under the Windows*, pp. 7–8.
68   Douglas Hyde, 'The Necessity for de-Anglicising Ireland', pp. 138–9.
69   Denis Gwynn, *Edward Martyn and the Irish Revival* (London, 1930) pp. 27–8.
70   Robert Kee, *The Green Flag* (London, 1972) p. 429.
71   Quoted by Stephen Gwynn, *Today and Tomorrow in Ireland*, p. 68.
72   Hannay to Hyde, letter of 15 April 1907, MacGlinchey collection.
73   Arthur Griffith, editorial, *United Irishman*, 17 October 1903.
74   *Freeman's Journal*, 24 October 1901, p. 5.
75   Arthur Griffith, editorial, *United Irishman*, 31 October 1903.
76   Quoted in a report entitled 'Trinity College and the Literary Theatre', *Daily Express*, 1 June 1899, p. 5.
77   P. H. Pearse, *Three Lectures on Gaelic Topics* (Dublin, 1898). Address to the New Irish Literary Society, 1897.
78   Synge Manuscripts, TCD, MS 4396, f. 62.
79   Terence de Vere White, *The Anglo-Irish* (London, 1972) p. 185.
80   Tomás Ó Fiaich, 'The Great Controversy', *The Gaelic League Idea*, p. 69.
81   Desmond Ryan, *The Sword of Light*, p. 233.
82   E. R. Dodds (ed.), *The Journal and Letters of Stephen MacKenna*, p. 39.
83   Quoted by Ann Saddlemyer, 'Synge to MacKenna: The Mature Years', *Irish Renaissance*, ed. Robin Skelton and David Clark (Dublin, 1965) p. 66.
84   Ibid.
85   Robert Hogan and James Kilroy, introduction, *Lost Plays of the Irish Renaissance* (Prescenium, 1970) pp. 11–12.
86   Ibid., p. 12.
87   Maud Gonne, *United Irishman*, 24 October 1903.
88   Peter Kavanagh, *The Story of the Abbey Theatre* (New York, 1950) p. 36.
89   George Moore, *Salve* (London, 1937) p. 81.
90   In possession of Senator Michael Yeats. Undated.
91   Quoted by Lady Gregory, *Our Irish Theatre* (London, 1913) p. 104.
92   Quoted by Lady Gregory, *Seventy Years*, p. 431.
93   'I mBaile 's i gCéin', *An Claidheamh Soluis*, 24 October 1903, p. 5.
94   Lady Gregory, *Seventy Years*, p. 548.
95   *An Claidheamh Soluis*, 16 April 1905, p. 1.
96   P. H. Pearse, 'Gleo na gCath', *An Claidheamh Soluis*, 22 April 1905, p. 7.
97   Quoted by Saddlemyer, *Plays 2*, p. xii.
98   Synge Manuscripts, TCD, Letter 195, 9 September 1905.
99   Ann Saddlemyer (ed.), *Some Letters of John M. Synge to Lady Gregory and W. B. Yeats* (Dublin, 1971) p. 21.
100   Ibid., p. 22.
101   Ibid.
102   Ibid., pp. 22–3.
103   Ibid., p. 23.
104   Ibid., p. 24.
105   Ibid., pp. 24–5.
106   Ibid., p. 32.

107 Quoted by James W. Flannery, *Miss Annie F. Horniman and the Abbey Theatre* (Dublin, 1970) p. 27.

108 Ibid., p. 25.

109 Ibid., p. 27.

110 Synge Manuscripts, TCD, Letter 282, 15 December 1906.

111 Synge Manuscripts, TCD, Letter to Yeats. Not yet catalogued.

112 D. P. Moran, *The Leader*, 5 March 1904.

113 Peter Kavanagh, *The Story of the Abbey Theatre* (New York, 1950) p. 50.

114 *An Claidheamh Soluis*, 3 February 1906, p. 1.

115 Ibid., 3 March 1906, p. 1.

116 Ibid., 14 April 1906, p. 1.

117 Ibid., 28 April 1906, p. 1.

118 Quoted by George Moore, *Vale* (London, 1937) pp. 135–7.

119 *Freeman's Journal*, 29 January 1907, p. 7, reported that *Riders to the Sea*, the curtain-raiser on the night of the *Playboy* riots, was 'most favourably received'.

120 Synge Manuscripts, TCD, Letter 652. MacDomhnaill was the only Gaelic playwright of talent at the time; see *An Claidheamh Soluis*, 5 November 1910, for a review of his *Áine agus Caoimhghin*, where he is chided for not producing more work.

121 See *An Claidheamh Soluis*, 29 April 1905, p. 1. where Pearse complains about the lack of Gaelic plays; and the issue of 16 June 1906, where he attacks the poor quality of those that are written, p. 6. For MacDonagh's despairing comments on Gaelic drama, see Thomas Mac Donagh, *Literature in Ireland* (Dublin, 1916) pp. 157–61.

122 'An Irish Pressman', *An Claidheamh Soluis*, 7 July 1906, p. 8.

123 Micheál MacLiammóir, introduction to J. M. Synge, *Plays, Poems and Prose* (London, 1972) p. viii.

124 John Eglinton, *Irish Literary Portraits* (London, 1935) p. 5.

125 *Freeman's Journal*, 29 January 1907, p. 17.

126 O'Casey, *Drums Under the Windows*, p. 136.

127 Quoted by Edward Stephens, *My Uncle John*, ed. Andrew Carpenter (Oxford, 1974) p. 190.

128 Robert Farren, *The Course of Irish Verse in English* (London, 1948) p. 125.

129 Wilfred Scawen Blunt, *My Diaries*, Vol. 2 (London, 1922) p. 172.

130 Joseph Hone, *W. B. Yeats 1865–1939* (London, 1942) pp. 219–21.

131 W. B. Yeats, *Essays and Introductions*, p. 312.

132 Quoted by S. B. Bushrui, *Yeats's Verse Plays: The Revisions 1900–1910* (Oxford, 1965) p. 171.

133 Lady Gregory, *Our Irish Theatre*, p. 117.

134 Francis Sheehy-Skeffington, 'Dialogues of the Day', *The Peasant*, 9 February 1907, p. 4.

135 *Irish Independent*, 30 January 1907, p. 5.

136 Quoted by Flannery, *Miss Annie F. Horniman and the Abbey Theatre*, p. 27.

137 *Freeman's Journal*, 31 January 1907, p. 8.

138 James Kilroy, *The 'Playboy' Riots* (Dublin, 1971) p. 51.

139 Pádraic Colum, Letter to the Editor, *Freeman's Journal*, 31 January 1907, p. 8.

140 *Connaught Champion*, 16 February 1907, p. 2.

141 Ibid., 9 February 1907, p. 3.

142 Ibid., 2 March 1907, p. 4.

143   Ibid., 16 February 1907, p. 2.

144   Ibid.

145   Ibid., 9 February 1907, p. 3.

146   Ibid.

147   *Irish Independent*, 30 January 1907, p. 4.

148   Ibid.

149   P. H. Pearse, *An Claidheamh Soluis*, 9 February 1907, p. 7.

150   Robert Hogan and Michael J. O'Neill (eds.), *Joseph Holloway's Abbey Theatre: a selection from his unpublished journal, 'Impressions of a Dublin Playgoer'* (London, 1967) p. 151.

151   *Connaught Champion*, 2 February 1907, p. 4.

152   Gerard Fay, *The Abbey Theatre: Cradle of Genius* (Dublin, 1958) p. 125.

153   Joseph Hone, *W. B. Yeats*, p. 221.

154   E. R. Dodds (ed.), *The Journal and Letters of Stephen MacKenna*, p. 122.

155   P. H. Pearse, 'The Passing of Anglo-Irish Drama', *An Claidheamh Soluis*, 9 February 1907, p. 7.

156   Ibid.

157   *Evening Telegraph*, 4 February 1907, p. 7.

158   P. H. Pearse, 'The Passing of Anglo-Irish Drama', *An Claidheamh Soluis*, 9 February 1907, p. 7.

159   W. B. Yeats, *Plays and Controversies* (London, 1935) p. 194.

160   George Roberts, 'A National Dramatist', *The Shanachie*, 2, (1907), p. 160.

161   *The Peasant*, 13 April 1907, p. 2.

162   P. H. Pearse, *An Claidheamh Soluis*, 21 November 1908, p. 10.

163   Séamus Ó Cuisín, 'J. M. Synge: His Art and Message', *Sinn Féin*, Vol. 4, No. 100 (17 July 1909) p. 1.

164   Hogan and O'Neill (eds.), *Joseph Holloway's Abbey Theatre*, pp. 125–9.

165   *An Claidheamh Soluis*, 30 April 1910, p. 5.

166   Synge Manuscripts, TCD, Letter 195, 9 September 1905.

167   'The Anglo-Irish Dramatic Movement', *Irisleabhar Muighe Nuadhad*, Vol. 1, No. 3 (Easter 1910) p. 7.

168   Ibid., p. 6.

169   Ibid., p. 16.

170   P. H. Pearse, 'From a Hermitage—June 1913', *Political Writings and Speeches* (Dublin, 1924) p. 145.

171   Ibid., p. 183.

172   P. H. Pearse, '*Séadna* and the Future of Irish Prose', *An Claidheamh Soluis*, 24 September 1904, p. 8.

173   P. H. Pearse, 'About Literature', *An Claidheamh Soluis*, 26 May 1906, p. 6.

Select Bibliography

The comprehensive bibliography for this study comprises the various books and journals listed in the foregoing footnotes. The following list gives details of all primary and the major secondary sources.

PRIMARY SOURCES

Manuscripts

Synge Manuscript Collection, Trinity College Dublin; MS 3460, MS 3554 and MSS 4328–4429. This collection includes all the material from notebooks, diaries and letters referred to in the text. For further information on the collection, see Grene, Nicholas, *The Synge Manuscripts in the Library of Trinity College, Dublin* (Dublin, 1971).

Eoin MacNeill Manuscript Collection, National Library of Ireland, Dublin. Letter from Father Eugene O'Growney to MacNeill, 29 September 1899.

Works by Synge

J. M. Synge: *Collected Works*. General ed. Robin Skelton (London: Oxford University Press, 1962–8)
    i. *Poems*, ed. Robin Skelton (London, 1962)
    ii. *Prose*, ed. Alan Price (London, 1966)

iii. *Plays 1*, ed. Ann Saddlemyer (London, 1968)
iv. *Plays 2*, ed. Ann Saddlemyer (London, 1968)
Letters to Molly: John M. Synge to Maire O'Neill, ed. Ann Saddlemyer (Harvard, 1971)
Some Letters of John M. Synge to Lady Gregory and W. B. Yeats, selected by Ann Saddlemyer (Dublin, 1971)
'Synge to MacKenna: The Mature Years', ed. Ann Saddlemyer, in *Irish Renaissance*: A Gathering of Essays, Memoirs, Letters and Dramatic Poetry from the Massachusetts Review, ed. Robin Skelton and David R. Clark (Dublin, 1965) pp. 65–79.
'A Story from Inishmaan', *New Ireland Review*, X (November 1898) pp. 153–6.

Bibliography

Levitt, Paul, *J. M. Synge: A Bibliography of Published Criticism* (Dublin, 1974)

SECONDARY SOURCES

Books Wholly Devoted to Synge:

Bickley, Francis L., *J. M. Synge and the Irish Dramatic Movement* (London, 1912)
Bourgeois, Maurice, *John Millington Synge and the Irish Theatre* (London, 1913)
Bushrui, S. B. (ed.), *Sunshine and the Moon's Delight: A Centenary Tribute to John Millington Synge, 1871–1909* (Gerrards Cross, 1972)
Corkery, Daniel, *Synge and Anglo-Irish Literature* (Cork, 1931)
Frenzel, Herbert, *J. M. Synge's Work as a Contribution to Irish Folklore and to the Psychology of Primitive Tribes* (Duren-Rhld, 1932)
Gerstenberger, Donna, *John Millington Synge* (Twayne's English Authors Series, 12) (New York, 1964)
Grene, Nicholas, *Synge: A Critical Study of the Plays* (London, 1975)
Greene, David H. and Stephens, Edward M., *J. M. Synge, 1871–1909* (Collier Books edn., New York, 1961)
Harmon, Maurice (ed.), *J. M. Synge: Centenary Papers 1971* (Dublin, 1972)
Henn, T. R., *The Plays and Poems of J. M. Synge* (London, 1963)
Howe, P. P., *J. M. Synge: A Critical Study* (London, 1912)

Johnston, Denis, *John Millington Synge* (Columbia Essays on Modern Writers, 12) (New York, 1965)

Kilroy, James, *The 'Playboy' Riots* (Dublin, 1970)

MacLiammoir, Michael, *Synge; Plays, Poems and Prose* (introduction) (London, 1972)

Masefield, John, *John M. Synge: A Few Personal Recollections with Biographical Notes* (Dublin, 1915)

Price, Alan, *Synge and Anglo-Irish Drama* (London, 1961)

—— *'Riders to the Sea' and 'The Playboy of the Western World'* (Notes on English Literature Series, 31) (Oxford, 1969)

Saddlemyer, Ann, *J. M. Synge and Modern Comedy* (Dublin, 1968)

Setterquist, Jan, *Ibsen and the Beginnings of Anglo-Irish Drama: 1. John Millington Synge* (Upsala Irish Studies, 2) (Upsala, 1951)

Skelton, Robin, *The Writings of J. M. Synge* (London, 1971)

—— *J. M. Synge* (Bucknell University Press: Irish Writers Series, Lewisburg, 1971)

Solomont, Susan, *The Comic Effect of 'The Playboy of the Western World'* (Bangor, Maine, 1972)

Stephens, Edward, *My Uncle John*, ed. Andrew Carpenter (Oxford, 1974)

Strong, L. A. G., *John Millington Synge* (London, 1941)

Synge, Rev. Samuel, *Letters to my Daughter: Memories of John Millington Synge* (Dublin, 1931)

Casebooks

Clark, David R. (ed.), *John Millington Synge: 'Riders to the Sea'* (Columbus, Ohio, 1970)

Whitaker, Thomas R. (ed.), *Twentieth Century Interpretations of 'The Playboy of the Western World'* (New Jersey, 1969)

Index